# A Shepherd Tends His Flock

*Letters from a priest to his beloved parishioners
and
all others interested in the Faith*

## Fr. John Girotti

# A Shepherd Tends His Flock

Fr. John Girotti
Copyright © 2010, Catholic Diocese of Green Bay, Inc.

Cover Image: Katie Jagiello
Cover and book design: Tau Publishing Design Department

Nihil Obstat:
*Reverend Alfred McBride, O. Praem.*

Imprimatur:
*The Most Reverend David L. Ricken DD, JCL,*
Bishop of the Diocese of Green Bay, Wisconsin
September 21, 2010

"Scripture taken from the NEW AMERICAN STANDARD BIBLE®, Copyright ©
1960,1962,1963,
1968,1971,1972,1973,1975,1977,1995 by The Lockman Foundation. Used by permission."

No part of this publication may be reproduced, stored in a retrieval system or transmitted in any form or by any means, electronic, mechanical, photocopying, recording, or otherwise, without written permission of the publisher.

For information regarding permission, write to:
Tau Publishing,
Attention: Permissions Dept.
1422 East Edgemont Avenue
Phoenix, AZ 85006

First Edition, 2011
10 9 8 7 6 5 4 3 2 1

Published by Tau Publishing, Phoenix, AZ
For reorders and other inspirational materials visit our website:
Tau-Publishing.com

Tau-publishing.com
*Words and Works of Inspiration*

# Dedication

*I* dedicate this book to the parishioners of St. Anthony Parish in Tigerton, St. Mary Parish in Marion, Holy Family-St. William Parish in Wittenberg, and St. Mary Parish in Leopolis. Here, in Central Wisconsin, you have taught me how to be a priest. You have shaped me into the pastor and shepherd that I now am. No matter where God leads me and no matter what office or responsibility I will have in the life of the Church, for the rest of my days, these four parishes will remain my first love. For this, I thank God. To those of you whom I have yet to meet, I offer my loving encouragement and prayers on your journey of Faith.

✠ Fr. John Girotti

# Acknowledgment

So many have assisted me in bringing this book to fruition. First and foremost, I would like to thank Almighty God for the gift of Life, the gift of Faith, and the gift of my Priesthood. "Lord, with your grace, I promise to follow you!" I thank my parents for their love and for their wonderful example of a lived Faith which has greatly inspired me. I must also thank Julianne Donlon-Stanz for her vision, direction and coordination of this project. She, along with Dr. Joseph Bound of the Department of Education for the Diocese of Green Bay, urged me to bring these simple letters from a country pastor to a wider audience. Additional thanks go to Christine Conklin for her excellent job editing this large book and for providing such helpful suggestions. I am most grateful to Bishop Robert Banks for welcoming me to the Diocese of Green Bay as a seminarian and for ordaining me a priest. I offer my thanks to Bishop David Zubik for the trust he placed in me by assigning me to the four country parishes where I learned so much and where my priesthood blossomed. Finally, I would like to express my appreciation to Bishop David Ricken for his kind endorsement of this book, for the trust he has placed in me, and for his fatherly support.

Fr. John Girotti

# Foreword

"Seeing the crowds, he went up on the mountain, and when he sat down his disciples came to him. And he opened his mouth and taught them." These words from the beginning of the Sermon on the Mount in the Gospel according to Matthew paint for us a portrait of Christ the teacher.

This book paints for us a portrait of how Christ still teaches through the shepherds he has chosen to act in his person. Father Girotti, a priest of the Diocese of Green Bay, is ever dedicated to teaching his parishioners what they need to know for salvation. As you read these pages, you will learn of the Catholic Faith, and also experience the heart of the Good Shepherd. Father Girotti wrote these pages without the intention that they would ever be bound in a book. Rather, through the weekly parish bulletin, he simply sought to teach his parishioners as Christ did, because he loved them.

This book meets an important need to explain the Catholic Faith in a simple, down-to-earth manner. These pages are encouraging, and sometimes challenging, as they point out to us the road by which to follow Christ with the help of His love, grace and mercy.

It is my hope and prayer that your reading of this book draws you ever closer to the heart of Jesus, the Good Shepherd.

✠ **Most Reverend David L. Ricken, DD, JCL**
*Bishop of Green Bay*

# Index

Dedication – Fr. John Girotti
Acknowledgement – Fr. John Girotti
Foreword – Bishop David L. Ricken
1   Introduction – Jesus said, *"Feed my lambs."*
3   It's a Beautiful Faith!: So, get out there and nourish it!
4   Speaking The Truth: If I must, I will ruffle feathers!

## Section I – The Creed – The Faith Professed

8   The Catholic Church as Universal and One: From many lands, many cultures, we share one Faith.
9   Precepts of The Church: How many of the five "ground rules" can YOU name?
10  Rules of The Faith: (OR, you shouldn't stop for burgers on the way to Mass. Remember fasting?)
12  "Man-Made Rules" – Part I: These rules actually come from Jesus!
13  "Man-Made Rules" – Part II: The sin of pride often causes dissent.
15  The Catechism of The Catholic Church: Here's a great new tool to help you know your Faith.
16  The Holy Trinity: We can try to explain, but it's still a MYSTERY!
18  The Crucifix: Do you know the difference between a cross and a crucifix?
19  The Tabernacle: It's the "dwelling place" of God.
21  Angels: Could I become an angel after I die?
22  The Problem of Evil: Look to the Cross – and Resurrection – for consolation.
24  Death and The Last Judgment: Start planning now for your final destination!
26  Reincarnation: Are you suggesting that God didn't get it right, the first time?
28  Do Animals Go To Heaven?: (OR, I want my dog, but the mosquitoes can just stay here!)

## Section II – The Sacraments – The Faith Celebrated

32  Baptism: You wouldn't deny a child food or love. Don't forget Baptism!
33  The Importance of Choosing Christian Names: Why you really shouldn't name your child "Hitler."
35  Confession/Sacrament of Reconciliation: Shhh! Want to hear about a secret gift that will bring great joy?
36  How To Celebrate The Sacrament of Confession – Part I: Here's everything you wanted to know – but were afraid to ask!
38  How To Celebrate The Sacrament of Confession – Part II: Be prepared. Don't eavesdrop! Be concise.
39  How To Celebrate The Sacrament of Confession – Part III: How long has it been? What did you do?
40  How To Celebrate The Sacrament of Confession – Part IV: Express sorrow. Do penance. (Omit details about annoying relatives!)
41  How To Celebrate The Sacrament of Confession – Part V: Just follow this outline – for Confession made easy.
43  Examination of Conscience: How well do you know your vices – AND virtues?
44  General Absolution: No lines, no embarrassment – but, in most cases, it doesn't work!

| | |
|---|---|
| 46 | **The Liturgy as The Source and Summit of Christian Life:** Is a "Communion service" the same as a Mass? |
| 47 | **The Reception of Holy Communion – Part I:** Show respect! The Eucharist is not a "door prize." |
| 49 | **The Reception of Holy Communion – Part II:** Everyone cannot receive communion everywhere! |
| 50 | **Bread and Wine:** This ancient formula is still the best! |
| 52 | **Reception of Holy Communion Under Both Forms – Bread and Wine:** It's one Lord, one Eucharist - in two forms. |
| 54 | **How Many Times A Day May I Receive Communion?:** What if there's a wedding or funeral before Saturday evening Mass? |
| 55 | **The Eucharistic Prayer:** How many saints can YOU name from this prayer? |
| 57 | **The Homily:** Maybe Someone is trying to tell you something! |
| 58 | **Intentionally Missing Mass:** (Hint: vacation, sporting events and laziness are NOT good excuses!) |
| 60 | **Liturgical Colors:** Why do the colors change at Mass? (OR, why is that priest wearing PINK?) |
| 61 | **Ringing of The Sanctus Bell:** Now, you can again hear bells in many Catholic churches. |
| 62 | **The Use of Incense:** It symbolizes our prayers rising to God. |
| 63 | **The Latin Mass – Part I:** Pope Benedict XVI has allowed more widespread celebration of this rite. |
| 64 | **The Latin Mass – Part II:** Requests were increasing for the return of this rite. |
| 66 | **The Latin Mass – Part III:** It may bring more young Catholics back to the Faith. |
| 67 | **Mass Intentions:** (OR, *"No, Virginia, we don't BUY Masses!"*) |
| 69 | **Confirmation–The "Forgotten Sacrament":** Do you REALLY know its purpose? |
| 70 | **Marrying Outside of the Catholic Church:** Forget Vegas. Skip the gazebo. Don't even think about the zoo! |
| 72 | **Marriage Preparation:** It's an investment in forever together. |
| 74 | **The Blessing of Marriage:** Focus on the best parts of this "cross-country trip." |
| 75 | **The Three Ranks of Holy Orders:** (OR, just what IS a "Monsignor," anyway?) |
| 76 | **Religious Celibacy – Part I:** You have an opinion about it? Do you even know what it is? |
| 78 | **Religious Celibacy – Part II:** A priest ALREADY is married – to the Church! |
| 79 | **Religious Celibacy – Part III:** Arguments against it are flawed. It's a "powerful" witness. |
| 81 | **The Ordination of Women – Part I:** Men and women are not "interchangeable." |
| 82 | **The Ordination of Women – Part II:** A priest acts in the place of Christ, the Bridegroom. |
| 84 | **The Ordination of Women – Part III:** Pope John Paul II made it clear. The matter is closed. |
| 85 | **The Ordination of A Bishop:** He becomes a successor to the Apostles. |
| 87 | **The Selection of A Pope:** Here's what happens in the secret conclave ... |
| 89 | **The "Great" Popes – St. Leo and St. Gregory:** Will John Paul II receive this title, too? |
| 90 | **Anointing of The Sick:** Do you know when to call a priest? (Hint: not for that stubbed toe!) |
| 92 | **Stipends for The Celebration of The Sacraments:** This isn't wrong. It's a matter of charity! |

## Section III – Christian Morality – The Faith Lived

| | |
|---|---|
| 96 | **Creation as The Foundation of Human Sexuality:** Love people for WHO they are, not WHAT they are! |
| 97 | **Sexuality as A Gift From God – Introduction to Human Morality:** Should the Church "get out of my bedroom?" |

98 **Chastity:** It's not just for priests and nuns!
100 **Tempting or Impure Thoughts:** Pray – or even "laugh" – about them!
102 **Modesty:** Refuse to unveil what should be hidden!
104 **Dressing Appropriately for Church:** Forget the flip flops. Skip the Speedos.
105 **Christian Dating:** Too early and too exclusive can equal one broken heart.
107 **Cohabitation:** It's NOT okay to "test drive" a person before marriage.
109 **The Use of Contraceptives – Part I:** In reality, there is no "birth" and no "control."
111 **The Use of Contraceptives – Part II:** "Pills" are for disease, not for unity and commitment!
112 **The Use of Contraceptives – Part III:** *"Let the little children come to me, and do not hinder them."*
114 **Abortion:** In ALL circumstances, it's wrong. This is why ...
116 **Artificial Reproduction Technologies:** A child should not be "made to order" in a laboratory!
118 **Stem Cell Research:** Human life must be respected from the moment of conception!
119 **Homosexuality:** The sin lies in the action, NOT in being tempted.
121 **An Introduction to Same-Sex Marriage:** Let's review basics.
123 **Same-Sex Marriage – Part I:** No way. Nohow. God has spoken.
124 **Same-Sex Marriage – Part II:** Don't let the pressure to be "nice" lead to acceptance!
126 **Divorce:** There are no winners; all are left wounded.
128 **The Annulment Process:** It can heal wounds, help one return to spiritual health.
130 **The "Just War" Theory:** Here are five criteria to consider ...
132 **Death and Dying:** You'll never be an angel – but, consider one for your gravestone!
134 **End-of-Life Decisions – Part I:** There's no "mercy" in "mercy killing."
135 **End-of-Life Decisions – Part II:** Don't let the Culture of Death invade your home!
136 **Euthanasia:** This is thinly disguised murder!
138 **Suicide:** Is it still possible to go to Heaven?
140 **Cremation:** Is it okay to do this? Could my ashes be sprinkled in the lake?
142 **Capital Punishment – The Death Penalty:** We must not short-circuit the process of repentance.
144 **Morality in Elections:** Truth is not measured by a majority vote.
145 **The Internet:** Beware – it can lead to sinful choices!
147 **Gambling:** Don't let the "bright lights" blind you to the risks!

## Section IV – Remember The Golden Rule
152 **Racism:** God doesn't care about skin color – and neither should we!
153 **Reaching Out To Your Struggling Neighbor:** Even a small gesture can mean so much!
154 **Miscarriage:** The death of a child is an occasion of sadness – yet hope.
156 **Disagreements Between Friends or Family Members:** When all else fails, apologize!
158 **When a Loved One Leaves The Church:** Use love – not a stick – to coax him back!
159 **On Answering The Difficult Questions of Children:** (OR, where is THIS in the parenting manual?)

## Section V – The Commandments and Seven Virtues (plus one!)
164 **The Ten Commandments:** They're more than a list of what NOT to do! They're a "road map."
165 **The First Commandment:** Are there other "gods" in your life?

166 **The Second Commandment:** What do YOU say when you're upset?
168 **The Third Commandment:** You must go to Mass – AND take some time for relaxation.
170 **The Fourth Commandment:** As the song says, we're talking about r-e-s-p-e-c-t.
172 **The Fifth Commandment:** It covers abortion, euthanasia, stem cell research, and more!
173 **The Sixth Commandment:** There's nothing very "adult" about "adultery."
175 **The Seventh Commandment:** It also applies to human dignity, animals – and the environment!
176 **The Eighth Commandment:** You don't lie? What about boasting, rash judgment or gossip?
178 **The Ninth Commandment:** If it might involve lust, just don't do it!
180 **The Tenth Commandment:** Don't be left with "emptiness, junk and debt."
181 **Introduction to The Seven Virtues (plus one!):** Does this sound a little dry? They can change your life!
183 **The Seven Virtues – Faith:** It's a gift – which someone must CHOOSE to accept.
184 **The Seven Virtues – Hope:** It's something needed by our modern world!
186 **The Seven Virtues – Charity:** We use the word "love" a lot – but, do we live it?
187 **The Seven Virtues – Prudence:** With the choices in today's world, this really comes in handy!
189 **The Seven Virtues – Justice:** Listen to the inner voice which tells you, "That's not fair!"
190 **The Seven Virtues – Fortitude:** You don't need to be a superhero to live your Faith.
191 **The Seven Virtues – Temperance:** Remember moderation?
193 **Living in Humility:** Our role model is a Baby born in a manger.

## Section VI – Prayer – The Faith Prayed

196 **The Sign of The Cross:** It's a gesture that goes to the heart of Catholicism ...
197 **The Rosary:** It won't be boring, if your heart is in the right place!
199 **Praying for Others:** Do this if someone asks – or even if he DOESN'T ask.
200 **The Bible – Where Do I Begin to Read?:** (Start with the New Testament. It's about Jesus.)
201 **Adoration of The Blessed Sacrament:** Who could say "no" to being in the presence of Jesus?
203 **Fasting:** It benefits more than the waistline. It has soul!
204 **Sacramentals and Devotionals:** These sacred signs and prayers help us prepare for Easter.
206 **Images of Mary and The Saints:** We DON'T worship them! They remind us of our "heroes."
207 **Making a Retreat:** Try getting away from it all – to find God.

## Section VII – A Year of Faith

210 **The Liturgical Year:** (OR, there's nothing "ordinary" about Ordinary Time.)
211 **New Year's Resolutions:** It's time to tackle that issue – you know the one!
212 **The Feast of Mary, Mother of God:** She is our heroine – a role model for the ages!
213 **Mary as "Theotokos":** A day to celebrate the wonder of God's birth to a human being.
214 **The Feast of the Epiphany:** (OR, the secret meaning of a "partridge in a pear tree.")
216 **The Feast of St. Joseph:** What if he had been a vindictive man?
217 **Lent – Prayer, Fasting and Almsgiving:** Start planning how you can do something extra.
219 **The Season of Easter:** It's actually 50 days of rejoicing!
220 **The Celebration of Easter:** Here are the answers to the three most important questions of life!
221 **The Hope of The Resurrection:** Easter gives us the happiest of happy endings.
222 **Divine Mercy Devotion:** Remember that no sin is too great to be forgiven by God.

224 **Corpus Christi – The Feast of the Eucharist:** We celebrate the greatest gift we have been given ...
225 **The Assumption of Mary:** It's as beautiful as a fairy tale – but REAL!
227 **Halloween/All Saints' Day:** Whatever happened to the "hallow?"
228 **Advent – Preparation for Christmas:** As nature waits for Spring, we wait for Christ's coming.
229 **Advent – Season of Hope:** The "rose" reminds us that the Lord is right beside us.
230 **Advent:** Are YOU ready for the Lord to come?
232 **The Feast of the Immaculate Conception:** Honoring Mary, the most perfect of all human beings.
233 **Have A Merry Christmas:** (Notice, I didn't say, *"Happy Holidays!"*)

## Section VIII – The Similarities – and Differences – Between Catholicism and Other Religious Denominations

236 **Divisions Within the Christian Faith:** This is NOT what Jesus intended!
237 **The Eastern Orthodox Church:** We share most of the same beliefs!
239 **Old Catholics and Polish National Catholics:** Their main objection is to authority within the Church.
241 **Protestant Communities – Part I:** They have key differences with Catholics – yet, much in common!
243 **Protestant Communities – Part II:** Varying scripture interpretations led to various denominations.
245 **The Lutherans:** Among Protestants, they have the most in common with Catholics.
247 **The Episcopalians:** They are really two churches in one.
249 **The Methodists:** They've been called the most "American" church.
251 **The Presbyterians:** Their name comes from "presbyters" – or church leaders.
252 **The Baptists:** A "Born Again" experience is required for salvation.
255 **The United Church of Christ:** Ever wonder who started Harvard and Yale?
256 **The Quakers:** Final religious authority rests in the individual.
258 **The Mennonites/The Amish:** Traditional dress, behavior and family life are the norm.
260 **Seventh Day Adventists:** They believe that Saturday is the Lord's Day.
262 **Pentecostals and Evangelicals:** Once called "holy rollers," now they're more mainstream.
264 **Nazarenes, Moravians and Salvationists:** They're smaller – yet very devoted – groups.

### On The Edge Of Christianity:

268 **Unitarian Universalists:** They're best described as "humanists."
269 **Christian Scientists:** Sickness and death are "illusions."
271 **Mormons – Part I:** All of us are "potential gods."
273 **Mormons – Part II:** They believe that angels told Joseph Smith he was to rebuild the true church.
274 **Jehovah's Witnesses – Part I:** "Only 144,000 people – born before 1935" will enter Heaven.
275 **Jehovah's Witnesses – Part II:** They have success recruiting those ignorant of Christianity.
277 **Christian Unity:** All Christians do NOT believe the same thing – yet.

### Religious Movements:

280 **"Moonies" and Scientologists:** They differ in their beliefs – but both are non-Christian.
281 **The New Age Movement – Part I:** Shamans? Witchcraft? Magic? Beware!
283 **The New Age Movement – Part II:** Christianity is ending? The "Age of Aquarius" is coming?

284 **The New Age Movement – Part III:** It's helping to popularize "Wicca" – a revival of medieval witchcraft.
285 **The New Age Movement – Part IV:** Be wary of practices disguised as our Faith that just don't feel right.
287 **Atheism – Part I:** *"God doesn't exist"* – or, people just live as though that's the case.
288 **Atheism – Part II:** Other philosophies have promoted its rise.
290 **Atheism – Part III:** Since Atheism's roots were in Europe, Christianity was challenged.
291 **Atheism – Part IV:** Try this approach to prove God's existence to them!
292 **Agnosticism:** They may "hedge their bets" about God.

## Other Religions:

296 **Introduction to World Religions:** Most have some elements of truth.
297 **Judaism – Part I:** Despite positive contributions, they've endured discrimination.
299 **Judaism – Part II:** We believe the Messiah is Jesus. Jews still await the Messiah.
301 **Islam – Part I:** Soon, there may be more Muslims than Christians.
302 **Islam – Part II:** Both Sunnis and Shiites worship Allah.
304 **The Bahai Religious Tradition:** Their goal is unity for all humanity.
306 **Buddhism – Part I:** They neither accept nor reject the existence of God.
307 **Buddhism – Part II:** This religious tradition is not "interchangeable" with Christianity!
308 **Taoism and Confucianism:** They profoundly influence the Asian way of life.
310 **Hinduism – Part I:** They believe in a supreme god who created other gods.
311 **Hinduism – Part II:** All the world's a stage?
313 **Conclusion – World Religions:** We all believe "there must be something more."

## Section IX: Other Information You Need To Know

316 **The Mystery of Priestly Activities/A Day In The Life of A Priest:** (Hint: I don't just sit there, with my hands folded!)
318 **On Being Busy:** Busy priests still want to help you!
319 **What Do People Want in a Catholic Parish? – Part I:** (Hint: It's not rambling homilies, a "warehouse" building and off-key music.)
320 **What Do People Want in a Catholic Parish? – Part II:** It's a basic formula of strong teaching, love and caring.
322 **Becoming a Member of a Parish:** There are several good reasons. (Money isn't one!)
323 **Financially Supporting Your Parish:** Tough times call for creative measures.
325 **Visiting Other Catholic Churches:** See the sights. Smell the smells. Pray well.
326 **Religious Education Challenges – Part I:** Where are the parents?
327 **Religious Education Challenges – Part II:** Have the courage to do what is right for your child.
328 **Religious Education – Attending Mass:** "Walking the walk" is the best example for children.
330 **Catholic Colleges and Universities:** Beware, some are "Catholic" in name only!

*333 A Special Thank You To My Parishioners ...*

335 Conclusion

# Introduction:
## *Jesus said, "Feed my lambs." (John 21:15)*

Praised be Jesus Christ! I am pleased and honored that you have chosen to read this book. It is my hope that you will find these many articles to be of assistance to you in your life of faith.

Where did this book originate? It is comprised of 200 bulletin articles, which I wrote over a period of five years, while serving as pastor of four rural parishes in Central Wisconsin. I wrote them early in my priesthood, acting on a deep desire I had to teach and preach Jesus Christ and the Catholic Faith. I limited myself, more or less, to a single page of single-spaced writing. This way, the given article fit in our weekly parish bulletin and it didn't become too drawn out, technical, or overwhelming. I must confess that it was difficult to condense many of these subjects into such a short space! The reader must remember that my intention for these articles was not an in-depth theological investigation of a given topic, but an introduction and overview of the subject. I do not pretend to have said everything there is to say about a given issue! Also, I remind the reader that these articles were intended for rural communities with men and women who work hard for a living, and value family, tradition, the land, and their Catholic Faith. That was the intended audience – and not a bad one at that!

My reason for writing these articles was to teach and guide the people of my four parishes. I chose various topics that I believed to be relevant to their daily lives as well as issues that were in the news and/or perhaps controversial. I saw these articles as an extension of the Sunday homily and as an opportunity to address issues of greater complexity that are better addressed in print than by the spoken word. Many times, I wrote about an important issue first, and then preached on it sometime later when the people were better prepared to hear it. I have found that in the preaching of homilies, one slip of the tongue on the part of the priest or a single misinterpretation on the part of the people, can lead to a complete misunderstanding! In first writing on these difficult and sometimes controversial issues, I found that I could be more precise in my delivery of the teachings of our Catholic Faith. Certainly, there are many other topics that might have been addressed. Perhaps these might be the basis for future articles! We have published these articles now because of a widespread demand for their use throughout the Diocese of Green Bay and beyond.

My deepest desire in writing these articles was to lead God's people into a greater love for Jesus Christ and a deeper love for His Catholic Church. I willingly and joyfully submit everything I have written here to the final judgment of the Magisterium of the Catholic Church. It is my prayer that this collection of articles, written lovingly by a young pastor to his parishioners, will be of assistance to you on your journey with Our Lord Jesus Christ. Let us pray for each other on the Way!

☩ Fr. John Girotti

# It's A Beautiful Faith:
*So, get out there and nourish it!*

As a priest, I really enjoy writing a weekly bulletin article that teaches about our Faith. I'm not usually able to say everything that needs to be said in the Sunday homily I give. There's so much to be said! So, I've been writing such articles now, for several years. In this book, I've selected a number of my favorite articles that cover a wide variety of topics. I hope that you will find these articles to be helpful.

I would like to encourage Catholics, especially adults, and those interested in the Catholic Church, to learn more about our Faith - through this and other means. For many of us, our religious education seemed to end after our senior year of high school - or even before that. So, many know little about our Faith beyond that level. This is a great shame because our Faith is so beautiful and so rich. There's always something new to learn!

Our culture, especially today, is starving for knowledge of Jesus Christ. We need to bring His message to all we meet, but how can we do this if we don't know what we believe and why? Added to this is the confusion today among some Catholics as to what we believe and what we don't. It's no wonder many of us are confused!

What can we do? My suggestion is that we surround ourselves with good Catholic resources for learning about our Faith. For example, the EWTN cable television network is an excellent source for learning more about the Catholic Faith. You may not like every show, but there is bound to be one that you will enjoy. In addition, there is Relevant Radio, the national Catholic radio network based here in the Diocese of Green Bay, where I live! Listen and learn! Perhaps you might enjoy a good Catholic newspaper - the "National Catholic Register" and "Our Sunday Visitor" are fine sources of knowledge about our Faith. There are also many faithful Catholic websites that can help to nourish our Faith.

I urge you to purchase the <u>Catechism of the Catholic Church.</u> This is the first official catechism published in more than 500 years and it's an excellent source of information about our Faith. Also, of course, buy a Bible. Make sure it's a Catholic edition. <u>The New American Bible</u> (NAB) and the <u>Revised Standard Version</u> (RSV) are faithful translations. Remember, too, when you read the Bible, be sure to "pray the Bible!" - stop and reflect on the words, offering your own spontaneous prayers to Our Lord.

Whatever you do, continue to learn and nourish your Faith. It is the most precious gift we have. For my part, I will do my best to explain the Catholic Faith to you with the mind and heart of Christ and His Church. May God bless you.

*Reflection Questions:*
1. What are the really big questions I have about the Catholic Faith?
2. What resources do I have at my fingertips to learn more about the Faith?
3. How can I share my Faith with others?

---

# Speaking the Truth:
## *If I must, I will ruffle feathers!*

The one big lesson I have learned these past years as a priest is that ministry is an art, not a science. When you go to seminary for five years, and learn from all of those books, you begin to think it's a science. What a rude awakening I had when I discovered that this wasn't the case! No, being a shepherd is an art, not a science – and I'm still learning.

> **"My vocation is to be a shepherd – and that includes guiding you and warning you about dangerous and sinful things."**

With this in mind, let me speak from the heart. It seems that many of my brother priests, for whatever reason, have shied away from preaching and writing about issues that are controversial. For example, most homilies during the past few decades have focused on love and understanding – or perhaps explained the scriptures from a particular standpoint. This is all very fine and good.

However, when was the last time you heard a homily about what we believe as Catholics? When did you hear a homily that addresses the hard issues such as sin, damnation, or even sexual morality? This is very rare, I'm afraid. I think that all of us, including myself, want to be popular – we want to be liked! So, sometimes, we priests shy away from controversial subjects because we just don't want to deal with the negative reaction some people might have to what we're saying. It's sad but true.

Unfortunately, I don't have that luxury. My vocation is to be a shepherd – and that includes guiding you and warning you about dangerous and sinful things. If I simply sugar-coated everything I said, I would be able to live a comfortable life here in the country and none of you would have your feathers ruffled or your consciences bothered. However, when I died, I would need to answer to God for why I didn't feed my flock and protect them from danger. Put another way, a pastor who tells his people what they **need** to hear, initially might lose some parishioners. Yet, a pastor who tells his people what they **want** to hear eventually will lose his soul. My friends, this is not a difficult decision for me to make!

If you went to a doctor, and the doctor noticed something wrong during the course of the exam, you would expect him to tell you. If the doctor decided not to trouble you with the problem he found for fear of upsetting you, you would rightly be upset and ready to sue for malpractice. The same can be said for my role - if I don't shepherd you and warn you of dangers to your soul, we'll both be in trouble!

So, on the following pages, I will sometimes be addressing difficult and controversial subjects. These are issues such as divorce and remarriage outside the church, abortion, homosexual marriage, birth control, dissent from Church teaching, women's ordination, priestly celibacy, the death penalty, etc. These are topics that impact our Faith directly and we need to understand them from the standpoint of the teachings of Christ and His Church. I will make every attempt to preach the Truth with love, for without love, the Truth is lost. I ask for your prayers that I might be a good shepherd for all of you.

*Reflection Questions:*

*1. Do I speak up about controversial issues or do I remain quiet? Why?*

*2. How was Christ treated when He taught the Truth?*

*3. Have I prayed for courage in living and professing my Faith?*

# Section I
## The Creed – The Faith Professed

# The Catholic Church as Universal and One:
*From many lands, many cultures, we share one Faith.*

As many of you know, I recently returned from a pilgrimage to some of the holy shrines of the Virgin Mary in Europe. A pilgrimage is basically a trip undertaken for the purpose of prayer. We 50 pilgrims visited the sites of Mary's appearances at Lourdes, France, and Fatima, Portugal. We also visited many shrines and holy places throughout the beautiful country of Spain. It was a very spiritually enriching trip for all of us.

> **"It is inspiring to catch a glimpse of the larger Body of Christ – and this is very much the experience of pilgrimage to another land."**

The word "Catholic" means universal and it has been used since the first century to describe the Church founded by Our Lord Jesus. The "universality" of our Catholic Faith means that ours is the Faith in its totality – and in keeping with the whole of God's Revelation. The Catholic Church was the first and has remained by far the largest of all Christian groups in the world.

Sometimes, when we practice our Faith on the local level of a parish community, we can lose sight of the larger nature of the Church. However, it's important to remember that our Church is made up of many small Christian communities, much like many cells make up our bodies. It is inspiring to catch a glimpse of the larger Body of Christ – and this is very much the experience of pilgrimage to another land.

When we were traveling in Europe, we saw and heard people from many different parts of the world – all speaking their own language and bringing with them their own customs and culture. Yet, in terms of our Faith, we all were one! In the Mass, we were praying in unison. In our love and worship of Jesus Christ and our devotion to His Blessed Mother, we were in union. We were – and remain – one: the Body of Christ. Somehow, the peoples of the world seem closer together when one travels. Wars and hatred between peoples appear even more tragic when we see how similar we really are.

The Church is alive. It is a living, breathing entity – and we are members of this Body of Christ. It includes all those in Heaven, all those being purified for Heaven in Purgatory, and all of us here in this world striving to live out our Faith in obedience and love for Our Lord. When we go on pilgrimage – whether it is across our Diocese or around the world – we are presented with the immense beauty of our Catholic Faith. Indeed, we are reminded that we all are One.

Reflection Questions:
1. Have you ever been on a pilgrimage? If not, could you plan one soon?
2. What does it mean when we say that the Church is the "Body of Christ?"
3. Jesus prayed that we "might all be one." What did He mean by this?

# Precepts of the Church:
*How many of the five "ground rules" can YOU name?*

The Church is a living thing – the living Body of Christ in the world. The Church is a visible entity – instituted by Jesus Christ Himself to bring His Word, sacraments and salvation to all. As Catholics, we are blessed to be part of the Church that Christ founded in its fullness.

Now, in any organization, whether it be large or small, a certain order must be maintained. There must be ground rules or everything would be in chaos! So it is in the life of the Church – there are many teachings that help to guide us in our life of Faith. Some of these teachings that are meant to guide us are called the *Precepts of the Church*.

> **"You shall attend Mass...confess your serious sins...receive Communion...observe the days of fasting and abstinence... provide for the needs of the Church... This is pretty basic stuff..."**

Perhaps you might remember these precepts from your childhood. Like so many things over the past 40 years, they didn't really change, they just faded from view. Today, they are re-emerging and being explained once again to the faithful. Let us now review the five precepts of the Church ...

**First Precept:** *You shall attend Mass on Sundays and on Holy Days of Obligation.*

**Second Precept:** *You shall confess your serious sins at least once a year.*

**Third Precept:** *You shall receive Communion at least once a year. (Easter Season)*

**Fourth Precept:** *You shall observe the days of fasting and abstinence during Lent.*

**Fifth Precept:** *You shall provide for the needs of the Church.*

This is pretty basic stuff, really. Most of these precepts are fulfilled just by living our Catholic Faith. Going to Mass every weekend and on all Holy Days is one of the main ways in which we, as Catholics, worship God. Going to

Confession when we have committed a serious sin is clearly part of our Faith. Receiving Holy Communion in a worthy manner, and as often as possible, is vitally important in nourishing our Faith. The season of Lent, with its fasting and abstinence, reminds us of the cost of our redemption. Assisting the Church by donations, volunteering and prayer, is standard fare for all believers.

Some may say that these are just a bunch of man-made rules. I would not be so quick to judge. Yes, these are precepts, guidelines and rules. However, we can trace each of them back to the teachings of Jesus Christ and God's Word, as found in both the Old Testament and the New Testament.

The Precepts of the Church are yet another means by which we are aided in our life of Faith. Let us strive to live these teachings so that we can grow in love for Christ and His Church.

*Reflection Questions:*

1. What are the five precepts of the Church?
2. "Sometimes we need guidelines to help us on the way." Reflect on this.
3. Do I fulfill these five precepts of the Church? How could I do better?

# Rules of The Faith:
## *(OR, you shouldn't stop for burgers on the way to Mass. Remember fasting?)*

So many times as a priest, I have heard the following: *"I don't want to be Catholic anymore. There are just too many RULES."* Similarly, I have heard, *"I just don't understand all of those RULES we have to follow – especially since Jesus didn't make them ..."* I always cringe a bit, because the person generally means, *"I want to make up my own rules to follow and you'd better not tell me what to do!"* Christ Himself was obedient to His Father. Why should we think that we don't need to be obedient to His Church?

> "I think that the key to understanding and embracing any rule or law is to understand the spirit behind it."

Regarding all of those rules, think about the laws of the road. What would driving be like if we had none? Chaos! Yet, it's difficult to imagine a young person today saying, "I don't want to drive any more; there are just too many rules!" I think that the key to understanding and embracing any rule or law is to understand the spirit behind it. If we just stare at the letter of the law, it will seem pointless. However, when we look behind the rule to search for its meaning, the rule will begin to make more sense. This is especially true when it comes to the teachings of our Faith.

One of the laws or rules of our Faith that is very much misunderstood today is the "Eucharistic fast." In short, any Catholic receiving Communion should ordinarily fast from all food for one full hour beforehand. (Yes, the Church still teaches this. Yes, we still believe this!)

Those of you a bit more seasoned by life might remember when the fast was from midnight. That must have been interesting! However, for the past 40 years, the Church has asked each Catholic to fast for just one hour before receiving Communion. So, what is the purpose of this? What's the point? I think that the spirit behind this discipline is to have each of us do something special, something tangible before receiving the Lord of the Universe in Communion. You know, we humans sometimes take things for granted. One prime example is the miracle of the Holy Eucharist. However, if we do something like abstaining from food for one hour before Communion, we remind ourselves that we are about to receive something very special. Believe me, nothing makes us stop and take notice like not eating!

Another way of looking at this, is that we are doing penance - fasting from food is a penance; it is doing without something in order to say we are sorry for our sins. Fasting one hour before Communion is another way of saying, *"Lord I am not worthy to receive You, but only say the word and I shall be healed."*

Now, if a person is ill, or in need of nourishment, by all means he or she should eat. Also, medicine and water never break the fast. If you forget during the hour fast and accidentally drink a cup of coffee, do another penance or activity to prepare yourself to receive the Eucharist. However, to knowingly and intentionally break the hour fast is a sin. Why? Because by our actions, we are saying, *"The Eucharist is nothing special for which I need to prepare."*

The Church knows what it's talking about, my friends! Try fasting, and you will see how it puts your mind and your body in the proper place for Mass.

Look, this is not that difficult. Basically, it means to stop eating one half hour before coming to Mass. I think that all of us can do this for Our Lord - a small sacrifice in thanksgiving for all that He has done for us.

*Reflection Questions:*
   1. *What are some of the "rules" of the Catholic Faith that I do not understand?*
   2. *Have I ever looked into why we believe what we believe as Catholics?*

3. Do rules become easier to follow when we find the love behind them?

---

# "Man-made Rules" – Part I:
## These rules actually come from Jesus!

Recently, I have heard a number of people criticize our Catholic Church because it makes and upholds *"all of those man-made rules."* The person complaining about the Church typically doesn't cite the particular teaching with which he or she disagrees. However, whenever this statement is made, there is usually something else behind it.

Why do people say this? Often, what they really mean to say is: *"I am angry because the Church won't let me do what I want. I don't understand why the Church teaches what it does and I am not interested in taking the time to find out. I feel guilty and I'm looking for someone to blame."* Although this assessment might seem rather harsh, in my experience, this is usually what is happening.

> **"Christ gave the Church authority…the authority of binding and loosing. The Church rightly uses this authority to proclaim Jesus Christ to the world."**

How can we, as Catholics, understand why our Church teaches the things that it does? First of all, where does the Catholic Church get its teachings about Faith and morals in the first place? They're from Jesus Christ, of course! Remember, the Church is the Body of Christ; Christ is its head. The two have become one body. (Ephesians 5) Thus, we cannot separate the two. If we honor Christ, we also honor His Body: the Church. If we hate and disagree with the Church, however, we also hate and disagree with Our Lord.

As Catholics, we believe that our Church is the Church founded by Jesus Christ, and thus, we subsist in this fullness of the Body of Christ. What does all of this mean? Basically, we believe that when the Catholic Church teaches something having to do with Faith and morals, this teaching is trustworthy because it comes from the Body of Christ: Jesus Himself.

The Church receives its teachings from two sources: Sacred Scripture and Sacred Tradition. Sacred Scripture is the Bible, the Word of God written down in 73 books. Sacred Tradition is the Word of God passed down orally through the centuries and written on the hearts of believers. Both of these sources of Divine Revelation are taught and preserved by the "Magisterium." The Magisterium is the teaching authority of the Church comprised of the world's bishops in union with the Pope. Thus, the teachings of the Catholic Church have a firm foundation based on the teachings of Jesus Christ which have been passed down and preserved through the centuries.

Christ gave us a Church to "unpack" and distribute all of His teachings to a waiting world. For example, what exactly does *"Love God above all things and love your neighbor as yourself"* mean? In all of life's intricacies – from marriage to war, from medicine to the environment – how exactly should we love our neighbor? How exactly should we love God? The teachings of the Catholic Church aim to explain and make relevant for our waiting world these – and many other – words of Our Lord.

The Church is a living thing and we all are a part of it. The Catholic Church has a sacred duty and a right to teach in the name of Jesus Christ the truths which He taught and which He entrusted to His Body to preach to the ends of the earth. Christ gave the Church its authority (Matthew 16 and 18) – the authority of binding and loosing. The Church rightly uses this authority to proclaim Jesus Christ to the world.

# "Man-made Rules" – Part II:
*The sin of pride often causes dissent.*

A few examples of the most common "man-made" rules might help, here ...

Why does the Catholic Church teach that marriage is permanent? Quite simply, this is because Jesus Christ taught that marriage is permanent! Many times, we read in the New Testament, *"He who divorces his wife and marries another, commits adultery ..."* (Matthew 19:9) Now, what is the Church to do? This teaching is from the mouth of Christ Himself!

Other Christian communities allow remarriage. It is only the Catholic Church that demands that the previous marriage first be investigated and (potentially) annulled before a second marriage may proceed. Is this simply a man-made law or are we trying to uphold the teaching of Christ?

> "Being a Catholic is not about doing my own thing, but rather about doing God's Will and coming to great peace and joy in doing so."

What about celibacy for the clergy? Certainly, this is a discipline of the Church which could change; however, it has great merit. It is not merely a man-made law, but rather an attempt to live as Christ and many of his apostles did.

What about fasting before receiving the Eucharist? Is this a pointless man-made law? No! This is an attempt to reflect and prepare ourselves to receive the Lord Of The Universe. Nothing makes us pay attention like going without food for a while!

The list could go on and on ...

I do realize that many reject the Catholic Church out of ignorance, stubbornness, or sin. Others might have seemingly well-thought-out arguments against the Church.

Some might even have been scandalized by the sinfulness of some members of the Church.

However, I am amazed at the audacity of those who have never been Catholic, perhaps not even Christian, who attack the Church for what it teaches and believes. Why should they care and what gives them the right to comment on something in which they have little or no part? Others who attack the Church might be fellow Christians who have been misinformed. They, too, complain about "man-made rules" – yet, I wonder if they ever took the time to study why we believe what we believe?

Sadly, still others who malign the Church come from within. Perhaps these Catholics have fallen away from the practice of their Faith. Feeling guilty and lost, they look to blame the very Church which will always welcome them back. In the heart of the "man-made laws" statement often resides the sin of pride. What did Satan say when He fell? "I will not serve!" In other words, "I want to do my own thing!" Being a Christian is not about doing my own thing, but rather about doing God's Will and coming to great peace and joy in doing so.

For those who have rejected the Catholic Church, either from within or from without, I challenge you to look behind those so-called man-made rules and laws. Be intellectually honest with yourself and with God. Learn from a reliable source exactly why we, as Catholics, believe what we do. You might be surprised! As Catholics, we have a great gift in the teachings of the Church. May we all strive to follow Christ more closely. He is the Way, the Truth, and the Life!

*Reflection Questions:*

   *1. When a person complains about "man-made rules," what is he or she really saying?*

   *2. How can we better explain our Catholic beliefs and practices to the world?*

   *3. "Humility is key to following Jesus Christ." Explain what this means.*

# The Catechism of the Catholic Church:
*Here's a great new tool to help you know your Faith!*

In another article of this book, I spoke about reading the Bible and how important this is for Christians. I also spoke, in passing, about using the Catechism of the Catholic Church as a guide. I'd like you to know more about this new catechism which is a great gift to our Church!

A catechism is a summary of Catholic doctrine about Faith and morals, designed for use in teaching and learning about the Faith. There have been many catechisms in the history of our Church, all designed to summarize and pass on our Catholic Faith. In short, a catechism summarizes, "What does a Catholic believe?"

> "This new work is the first universal catechism in 500 years. It is an official summary of the teachings of our Church."

Many of you remember the Baltimore Catechism - an American catechism that was used successfully in our country for many years. After the Second Vatican Council ended in 1965, and with the many changes in our culture, there grew a need for a new catechism that would present and teach the Faith to a new generation.

Several attempts were made with varying results. The most successful of these was Father John Hardon's Catechism. The least satisfying was the Dutch New Catechism, written in the Netherlands.

It became clear to the whole Church that a new and universal catechism was badly needed. So, in 1985, Pope John Paul II along with the bishops of the world began the task of writing and compiling a new and official catechism for the Catholic Church. This great task was completed in 1992, when the Catechism of the Catholic Church was published.

This new work is the first universal catechism in 500 years. It is an official summary of the teachings of our Church, along with ample footnotes and Biblical quotations. It is a reference work, not necessarily a book to be read cover to cover. However, its presentation is logical and complete.

Having this book is important because it will help you to grow in your Faith. We all have questions about what we believe and why, and this book will help you to answer some of these questions. It should be readily available during Bible study, because it will assist us in interpreting the Holy Scriptures as Christ's Church has done through the ages. I highly recommend that you find a copy of the new catechism. The standard edition comes with a green binding, and is available in hard- or soft-cover. The price is around $15 to $25. With this great new tool, along with the Word of God, you will come to know and love your Faith more fully!

*Reflection Questions:*

1. Do I have a copy of the new <u>Catechism of the Catholic Church</u>?

2. Why is having a catechism important?

3. How do the Bible and a catechism work together?

# The Holy Trinity:
*We can try to explain, but it's still a MYSTERY!*

I always will remember when I was in grade school religious education classes and it came time to learn about the Holy Trinity. The good religious sister who taught the class said, *"Now, children, the Holy Trinity is ... a mystery!"* She went on to try to explain it - which made no sense at all! Then, she ended by saying, *"Remember, children – it's a mystery!"* That seemed to work much better.

> **"This love between Father and Son is so strong that it takes on a life of its own – the Holy Spirit!"**

So, as the world turns, it is now my time to try to explain the Holy Trinity. I will follow the same path as this holy nun did many years ago. First of all, I must say, *"IT'S A MYSTERY!"* Alas, now it's time for more details ...

The existence of the Holy Trinity is one of the core teachings of Christianity. One cannot deny the existence of the Holy Trinity and be a Christian - it is simply impossible. We believe that God is one in three and three in one. Put another way, we believe that God is three Persons, yet one God. So, what does this mean?

Let's think of God as a relationship within Himself - a family or community of Persons, if you will. We use the word "Person" not in a biological way, but to denote a relationship. One must first be a person before one can be in a relationship with another. So, God the Father loves His Son Jesus with a divine, powerful, fatherly love. Jesus loves His Father with a divine, powerful love of a son. This love between Father and Son is so strong that it takes on a life of its own – the Holy Spirit! The Holy Spirit, thus, is the love of God within Himself which is then poured out upon all of us. So, God IS love – not just loving, but He IS love within Himself. This love is the Holy Trinity – a relationship of love between Persons.

God is never alone. Where the Father is, you'll find the Son and the Holy Spirit. The same is true for the Son and for the Holy Spirit. Although the three Persons cannot be separated, they remain distinct from each other. The Holy Trinity then becomes a model for the life of the Church which, after all, is a community of persons. The Holy Trinity also is the model for family life. So, we believe in one God who is a relationship of love within Himself – a community of Persons.

Although the word "Trinity" is not written explicitly in the Bible, there are numerous references in both the Old Testament and the New Testament that refer to this reality. For example, at the end of Matthew's Gospel, Jesus tells His followers to baptize *"In the Name of the Father, and of the Son, and of the Holy Spirit."* The early Church believed in the existence of the Holy Trinity, although the Trinity was spoken of in more informal terms.

By the 300s, however, there was a need to formally define exactly what we believe regarding the Holy Trinity. After all, it is a difficult concept to understand and is easily open to misinterpretation. Thus, in 325 A.D. at the Council of Nicea, the Church developed the Nicene Creed which delineates in a precise manner what we believe regarding the Holy Trinity. This is the same Nicene Creed which we pray at Mass!

Sadly, there were (and still are) many false teachings or heresies regarding the Holy Trinity. Some have mistakenly stated that we actually believe in three gods. (This is the heresy of "tri-theism.") Others believed that God appeared throughout history in various ways or modes – sometimes as the Father, sometimes as the Son, and sometimes as the Holy Spirit. (This is the heresy of "modalism.") Others believed that Jesus was not God but only perfectly human. (This heresy is known as "Arianism.") All of these false teachings were condemned by the Church.

So, we have an explanation of the Holy Trinity. God is a relationship of love within Himself which He then pours out upon all of His creation. God is one in three and three in one. He is not alone, but rather a community of Persons. If this explanation is not helpful, might I suggest we return to the old stand-by? THE HOLY TRINITY IS A MYSTERY! Thus it remains.

*Reflection Questions:*

1. *What do we mean by the word "person?"*

2. Do we believe that God takes on different forms throughout human history?

3. We often say that "God is love." How is this true?

---

# The Crucifix:
*Do you know the difference between a cross and a crucifix?*

Perhaps one of the most distinctive and recognizable symbols of our Catholic Faith is the crucifix. A crucifix is distinguished from a simple cross in that a crucifix is a cross with a "corpus" or figure of Christ's body attached to it. The word crucifix means very literally "the one having been fixed to the cross."

An understanding of the word itself helps us to recognize why we as Catholics use a crucifix instead of a simple cross as one of our primary symbols. By using a crucifix, our attention is drawn not to the cross itself - as an instrument of torture or death - but rather to the Lord Himself and to what He did for us. By directing our attention to the Lord's very real suffering and death, we recall that it was this offering of Himself as a sacrifice on our behalf which makes our salvation possible.

> "We need to see how much God loves us, how He suffered and died for us...and the crucifix is a powerful reminder to us."

Sometimes, it is suggested that an empty cross best symbolizes the fact that, although Christ suffered and died for us on the cross, He also rose from the dead. Thus, the empty cross may be taken as a symbol of His Resurrection and His triumph over death. Christ is indeed risen! Certainly, Easter - the Resurrection - is the culmination of Christ's redemptive act and the cornerstone of our Faith. We never simply stop at Good Friday! Sometimes, however, we need to see, perhaps even graphically, what sin does. We need to see how much God loves us, how He suffered and died for us. Sadly, we can be so quick to forget - and the crucifix is a powerful reminder to us.

You might have noticed that every Catholic Church has an image of Christ crucified prominently displayed near the altar: in short, a crucifix. The reason for this is that the Mass is no mere commemoration of the death or Resurrection of Christ. It is more! The Mass is rather the *continuation* and the *participation within* the one and infinite sacrifice of Christ on the Cross at Calvary. Therefore, it is most fitting to see this image near the altar where Mass is celebrated.

We must not see the crucifix as a negative or dark image. If it troubles us, this may be because we are focusing on the effect of sin. Sin is not pleasant. Rather, we should see the image of Christ crucified as a sign of His complete love for us. Let us see His arms outstretched, gathering all the world to Himself!

Reflection Questions:
1. Have I ever prayed while looking at a crucifix?
2. Do I have a crucifix in my home?
3. How does the depiction of Christ's suffering help me with my own struggles?

# The Tabernacle:
*It's the "dwelling place" of God.*

What is a "tabernacle?" The word comes from the Latin *"Tabernaculum"* which literally means a tent or dwelling place. For Catholics, the tabernacle is the place where we put the Blessed Sacrament – the consecrated Hosts from Mass. Thus, Christ who is present, Body, Blood, Soul and Divinity in the Eucharist, also is present in every Catholic Church in a special way in the tabernacle. That is why it is called a tabernacle – the dwelling place for God!

In Old Testament times, a tabernacle was built by Moses to house the Ark of the Covenant. God was present with His chosen people in a special and powerful way wherever the Ark of the Covenant was carried. The Temple in Jerusalem was built to hold this Ark – a kind of tabernacle to hold God's presence among His people.

> "For Catholics, the tabernacle is the place where we put the Blessed Sacrament – the consecrated Hosts from Mass."

In New Testament times and beyond, Jesus is God's presence among us. He has given us His Body and Blood in the Eucharist to nourish us and unite us with Him. Thus, in a very real way, the tabernacle in each of our parishes is a kind of dwelling place of God among us, His people. Certainly, God is present everywhere and we can never build something that "contains" God. However, in keeping with Biblical practice and tradition, God always has chosen to be present in a special way among His people. The tabernacle in our churches is such a special place.

In the early Church, the tabernacle had a practical use as well. After Mass, the consecrated Hosts were placed there in case there was a need for Communion to be brought to a sick or dying person. Even today, this function remains. Although the Precious Blood is rarely kept in the tabernacle because of practical reasons, consecrated Hosts are reserved there in case of need. Also, a large consecrated Host often is kept in the tabernacle and used for Eucharistic Adoration. Near every tabernacle is placed a candle, typically red, which continually burns in order to symbolize Christ's presence among His people.

The location of the tabernacle has been a point of some confusion over the past 40 years. Some in the Church have advocated placing the tabernacle to the side of the main altar or in another location inside the main Church. They reasoned that a tabernacle in the front and center of a Church was a distraction from the altar, which rightly should be the focal point at Mass. Others have argued that the priest should be front and center in the Church as the leader of the congregation at prayer. Still others have said that, in cathedral churches and shrines with many visitors, the tabernacle should be placed in a side chapel where people could pray undisturbed.

Today, however, there is a movement away from such thinking. We naturally place the most importance front and center – why would we not want Jesus to be there? With the loss of reverence for and understanding of the Eucharist today, it seems that once again we need to place Our Lord front and center so that we don't forget about Who really matters! Jesus is at the center of our Faith – the same Jesus Whom we receive in the Eucharist at Mass. This same Jesus in the Eucharist waits for us in the tabernacle – God's "dwelling place among us."

*Reflection Questions:*

1. *What does the word "tabernacle" mean?*

2. *Why is it important to have the tabernacle in a prominent place in our churches?*

3. *How does the tabernacle in your Church reflect the Ark of the Covenant from Old Testament times?*

# Angels:
*Could I become an angel after I die?*

I'd like to speak to you a bit about angels. Yes, I said "angels," those spiritual creatures who watch over us and serve God, their Creator.

There's been much ado about angels recently. Images of angels are appearing everywhere and books are being written claiming to "know" all about them. However, I'd like to tell you what we, as Catholics, believe about angels, so that you will not be confused by what our popular culture says.

> "....angels exist. They are pure spirits...created by God to serve Him..."

First and foremost, angels exist. They are pure spirits - they have been created by God to serve Him and to do His bidding. There are numerous references to angels in the Bible. We know that, in the Old Testament as well as in the New Testament, angels served as messengers. Angels waited on Christ when He was tempted in the desert, and angels set St. Paul free from prison. It was the Angel Gabriel who came to the Blessed Virgin Mary to announce the Good News of our salvation.

Because they are pure spirits, angels have no bodies. (Yes, that means they have no wings ... sorry.) Occasionally, they may assume human form so that their messages can be received by us, but, otherwise, they have no physical form. Because they are pure spirits, they have very powerful intellects and, thus, are very intelligent. However, despite their intelligence, they cannot read hearts and minds. Like us, they have free will which they may use to obey God - or not to obey Him.

The great majority of angels are good and holy; they have remained obedient to God. However, there are fallen angels - those who have refused to obey God. The chief among them is the Devil: Satan, or Lucifer. The Devil is a fallen angel - first and foremost - with all the powers and limitations that go with this state of being. The Devil is not nearly as powerful as God. Because he and his followers are angels, however, they possess a very keen intelligence which they use to tempt and lure us away from God.

Reasons for Satan's fall from grace are many and open to conjecture. It is generally believed that when God the Father revealed to all the angels His plan to send Jesus to save us, Satan couldn't accept that God would suffer so much for us lowly humans.

Today, after a loved one dies (especially a child), some people say that he or she now is "an angel in Heaven." This is rather sweet and nice, but really not correct. When we die, we remain children of God. We don't turn into anything. Let me remind you that Jesus Christ suffered and died to save us, not the angels! The dignity we possess by our baptism is enough. We will not turn into angels when we die. Although angels possess a greater intellect than ours, we have a greater dignity because of what Jesus did for us.

So, now you know a bit about angels. I would advise each of you to ask the angels to pray for you. Especially ask St. Michael, the Prince of the Angels, to keep your family and our Church from all harm.

*Reflection Questions:*

    1. Do I pray to my guardian angel every day? Have I named my guardian angel?

    2. How does our Catholic Faith's explanation of angels differ from the culture's?

    3. Have I ever met an angel or experienced an angelic visitor?

# The Problem of Evil:
*Look to the Cross - and Resurrection - for consolation.*

We've all followed news coverage of various natural disasters which have caused thousands of deaths and much destruction around the world. An earthquake in Haiti, a cyclone in Burma, multiple tornadoes in our own country - and no doubt many more examples could be listed. Often, we wonder, "Why does this happen?" Such suffering, such loss of life, seems so pointless and impossible to comprehend.

> **"Why does God allow evil, whether moral or natural? Our Christian faith teaches that the Lord is all good and all loving... God does not directly cause cancer, a murder, or an earthquake."**

What we are speaking about here is what philosophers and theologians call Natural Evil. A natural evil is different from a moral evil in that it doesn't directly involve a human person. Examples of moral evils are stealing, murder, slander, assault. These all involve a person choosing in some way to do wrong and harm another.

Natural evils, however, are much more difficult to understand. A cold air mass collides with a warm air mass over the Great Plains, which causes rotation in the atmosphere, which forms a tornado, which wipes out a town that took 150 years to build. Plates hundreds or thousands of feet below the earth's surface shift, cause friction, then buckle, causing a tremor which levels cities and towns and kills thousands. Lightning from a thunderstorm hits dry ground in a forest, igniting trees and brush, causing a forest fire that destroys hundreds of homes and other property.

Why do these things happen? More to the point, people may question how a loving God can allow such things to happen. Some individuals have tragically concluded throughout history that either God does not care about such suffering or is seemingly powerless to prevent it. Some have abandoned their faith because of this. However, as Christians, we look to our faith for answers.

Why does God allow evil, whether moral or natural? Our Christian faith teaches that the Lord is all good and all loving. We know that God does not directly cause cancer, a murder, or an earthquake. However, He does sometimes permit evil to occur - but only when a greater good can result. The greatest proof of this is the Cross - that most vital and important of all Christian symbols. God the Father permitted the evil of the suffering and death of His only Son, Jesus, in order to bring about a greater good - the greatest of all goods, which is our salvation! That's what Easter is all about - the Resurrection, our hope. As Christians, we believe that, for every Good Friday in our lives, there always will be an Easter Sunday. We always look to our own resurrection.

Well, this is all fine and good for those of us sitting comfortably at home in our easy chairs, reading this article. It is much less pleasant for someone digging through fallen concrete to find the lifeless body of a beloved child crushed in an earthquake. So, we return to natural evil - why does it exist?

A possible answer might be that these natural disasters are another manifestation of original sin and the brokenness of our world caused by the fall of man. That initial act of disobedience by Adam and Eve sent shockwaves of disorder throughout the spiritual and physical universe. The broken physical world in which we live sometimes manifests its brokenness in these disasters. In other words, natural evil is a result of moral evil.

Another possible answer to the question of natural evil might be that this is just how the natural world works. This is how the machine functions and we just happen to get in the way. This is not a very satisfying answer, but one way of looking at it.

Another perspective might be that the so-called evil of a forest fire always brings with it a stronger, healthier forest with new trees. The earth eventually settles after an earthquake, and new nutrients are brought to the surface. A tornado brings with it rain which waters the earth and brings forth life, etc. It seems that, even in natural evils, there is a resurrection of sorts after the evil has passed.

In the big picture, this is a mysterious subject which prompts many questions. I have only scratched the surface and in a very simple manner at that! In the end, we cry out to God for mercy and we know that in His great love, He will hear us. As always, His ways are for the best - even if we do not fully comprehend them at the time. In the midst of such suffering today, may the Lord Jesus strengthen our faith!

*Reflection Questions:*
1. Why are there natural evils in the world? How would you explain this mystery?
2. How do we find an answer to the mystery of human suffering in the Cross of Jesus Christ?
3. Have I ever experienced a natural evil? What happened?

# Death and The Last Judgment:
*Start planning now for your final destination!*

What happens when we die? Are we judged by God? How does this happen and why? Do we go straight to Heaven? What about Purgatory? What about the reality of Hell? So many questions and misconceptions surround this subject of the "Last Things." Let's learn more ...

First of all, I must say that this will be a simple overview of the subject. Much more could be and has been written about it. This is just a beginning. Also, we are talking about something that we have never experienced! We rely on what God has told us, in the Bible and in the teachings of His Church. However, the "Last Things" remain a mysterious part of our Faith.

> " ....we live our lives of faith with one eye focused on this world to make it a better place and with the other eye focused on the world to come."

All of us will die some day. When we are young, we rarely think about this fact. As we age, it becomes a reality that we all must face. As Christians, we prepare for the day of our death without fear - but, rather, with great hope. We want to be with the Lord! So, what happens at the end of our lives?

**Death:** When we die, our souls separate from our bodies. Our bodies typically are buried and decay, but our souls live on. Because the soul is a spiritual entity, it cannot experience the corruption of death.

**Particular Judgment:** Immediately after we die, God will judge the worthiness of our souls. Did we love God above all things? Did we love our neighbor as ourselves? After the particular judgment, we may enter directly into Heaven or be found unworthy of Heaven and go off to the infinite pains of Hell. If we die in friendship with God, but with some lingering attachment to sin on our souls and without having made up for the damage our sins have caused, we go to a place called Purgatory. There, we are purified and made ready for Heaven.

**Heaven:** This is our goal! It is a place of perfect happiness and joy. In Heaven, we will see God face to face and finally know peace. We will be with the angels, the canonized saints – and ideally, with our family and friends. Together, we will give glory to God. Heaven will be so wonderful that it defies our imagination!

**Purgatory:** Purgatory is a place of purification and preparation for Heaven. We know from the Scriptures that nothing impure will enter into Heaven, so Purgatory is a place where God's mercy will make us ready. Purgatory is where the attachments we have to sin and the damage our sins have caused while on earth are made right with God. Purgatory fulfills God's justice while demonstrating His mercy. After our purification is completed, we enter directly into Heaven. As Catholics, we pray for those who have died, asking the Lord to make their purification quick and complete.

**Hell:** Eternal separation from God is what Hell is all about. The pain will be excruciating and it will last for all eternity. Jesus speaks often of Hell in the Gospels and He warns us that our sins have consequences. God does not damn us to Hell; we may choose to go there. The good Lord will give us every opportunity to repent, but if we refuse His mercy, He will allow us to get what we want – an eternity of separation from Him. We must fear Hell. It is real, and we can go there.

**Last Judgment:** At the end of the world, when Christ comes again, the bodies of the dead will rise from their graves and all those still living will be brought to this judgment. The bodies of the dead will rejoin their souls and we will be judged in the sight of all. God's justice will be fulfilled. Those in Heaven will go off to the Kingdom of God glorified in body and soul. Those in Purgatory will have their purification fulfilled and they, too, will enter into the fullness of the Kingdom. Those souls in Hell will rejoin their bodies and go off to an eternity of punishment and fire.

If we stay close to Our Lord Jesus Christ, all will be well! As Christians, we live our lives of faith with one eye focused on this world to make it a better place and with the other eye focused on the world to come. Heaven is our goal – let's be there!

Reflection Questions:
1. What is the difference between the particular judgment and the last judgment?
2. What is Purgatory?
3. How is God both merciful and just?

---

# Reincarnation:
## Are you suggesting that God didn't get it right, the first time?

There seems to be an innate human desire to live forever. It goes against our human nature to want to die; death to us seems totally absurd. Yet we do die, and human beings are troubled by this. Why do we die?

Until recently, our Western culture dealt with such questions by turning to its Christian roots. Now that many have drifted away from faith in Christ, there is a desperate grasp for an answer to this troubling question. Sadly, some people are turning towards paganism in order to find a solution. To this end, I would like to address an issue about which I have been hearing a lot in our community these days: reincarnation.

> **"Jesus Christ...came...to save human beings from sin. We do not save ourselves by being reincarnated until we finally make it!"**

Modern-day paganism comes to us under the guise of the "New Age" Movement. Needless to say, the New Age Movement is not compatible with Christianity. The former includes everything from feminist goddess worship to environmentalist earth religion, from the supposed power of crystals to ancient Asian mysticism. Also, within this ever-expanding movement, lies the common belief in reincarnation. The New Age Movement takes the view that only the spirit is real. Time, space and matter all are illusions. All is God, and death is merely an illusion. The spirit lives on in other living creatures - hence, reincarnation.

Reincarnation is the belief that the soul or character of a person who dies is reborn into another living being. This belief states that the soul is the true self and that the body actually is a prison. Those individuals who are most detached from worldly things will eventually reach a state of bliss after they die, but those souls who are weighed down by attachments to this world will return to earth after death and inhabit another creature's body until they reach a state of eternal bliss. In this way, the modern-day belief in reincarnation is similar to the non-Christian religion of Buddhism.

Although the belief in reincarnation seems to appreciate the dignity and beauty of the human soul, it departs very quickly from our Christian faith. Jesus Christ, Our Lord and Savior, came to this world to save human beings from sin. We do not save ourselves by being reincarnated until we finally make it! Jesus did not suffer and die on the Cross for animals or other created things. He suffered and died for all people - this should show us the greatness of our human dignity.

We cannot and will not inhabit another body after we die - our own bodies are the perfect reflection of our individual souls. Our individual soul simply cannot express itself in any other way. To say otherwise would imply that God didn't get it right the first time! Furthermore, the belief in reincarnation is simply not Christian because it makes a mockery of Jesus' passion, death AND Resurrection. Christ rose again after His death in His own body, not in someone else's! We, too, shall rise again at the end of the world.

I do realize that, for most of us, this is a non-issue. Of course, we don't believe in reincarnation! However, I have a great concern that, among some of our teens and young adults, this belief has taken hold. I have heard it expressed many times. Sadly, our culture has slowly drifted away from Christianity.

Please know that God suffered and died for YOU - not for someone else inhabiting your body. As Christians, we have Easter - Christ's Resurrection - which is something much more beautiful and powerful than reincarnation. Please stay close to Jesus and His Church!

*Reflection Questions:*

1. *Why is the belief in reincarnation becoming more popular today?*

2. *What does the Resurrection of Jesus Christ tell us about our bodies?*

3. *How can we respond to a person who believes in reincarnation?*

# Do Animals Go to Heaven?:
## (OR, I want my dog, but the mosquitoes can just stay here!)

Believe it or not, one of the most common questions I'm asked deals with animals. People of all ages ask me, *"Do animals go to Heaven?"* It's a good question! I often wonder about it myself. I love animals and take great joy in watching them. Like many of you, I see God reflected in nature.

To answer this question, we need to be clear. When we say "animals," do we mean our pet dogs or do we mean those pesky mosquitoes? Hmmm. They're both "animals" - aren't they? How about the deer that jumps in front of my car? Does it go straight to Heaven as I go straight to the repair shop? We must be specific, here. Perhaps a better way of asking the question is, *"Do all furry, cute animals that I love and that do me no harm go to Heaven?"*

> "I'm inclined to believe that we will see our animal friends again...How, I do not know..."

The Book of Genesis tells us that God created man and the animals from the earth. However, only to human beings did He impart the breath of life: an immortal soul. Human beings were given dominion over nature and the animals - to use them responsibly, as needed. A crucial point here is that the earth has been created for us - we have not been created for the earth! This is an important distinction often forgotten today. Only human beings are created in the image and likeness of God. No other living thing shares in this dignity.

The great joy of Heaven will be seeing God face to face. Sacred Scripture also tells us that, at the end of the world, there will be *"a new heaven and a new earth."* (Revelation 21:1) St. Paul speaks of *"the whole of creation awaiting redemption."* With these thoughts in mind, there are two different ways of answering our question about animals.

One way involves arguing that, since all created things - including all animals - have been made to help human beings towards Heaven, they are tools and nothing more. Since animals do not have immortal souls, and since we will not need animals or any other worldly things to help us once we are in Heaven, it does not seem that animals will be in Heaven.

A second approach is to cite Scripture, noting that, at the end of the world, there will be *"a new heaven and a new earth."* (Revelation 21:1) Thus, it does not seem far-fetched to believe that, in a way known only to God, our animal friends might have a place in the world to come. Because they do not have immortal souls as we have, they would not be able to enjoy Heaven in the way we would. However, because of the power of Christ's Resurrection, we can hope that all things will come to life again, even animals.

An interesting topic. I'm inclined to believe that we will see our animal friends again. How, I do not know – but at the end of the world, we know that death will be destroyed forever. So, we have hope. The question remains, though, where WILL God put all of the mosquitoes?

*Reflection Questions:*
　1. *Do I see the presence of God in the created world of nature?*
　2. *Do I show respect for animals and other created things?*
　3. *Do some people respect animals more than human beings?*

# Section II

## The Sacraments - The Faith Celebrated

# Baptism:
*You wouldn't deny a child food or love. Don't forget Baptism!*

What is Baptism? Sure, we all know what it is. Perhaps we've even witnessed many baptisms in our lives. We know what it's all about – or do we? What is its purpose – why does it matter, anyway? Let's learn more about it!

The simplest way that I can explain Baptism is to say that it is the primary way by which we connect to what Jesus Christ did for us some 2,000 years ago. After all, that's a lot of time and territory to cover – how can we get plugged into what Our Lord Jesus did for us? Put another way, Baptism is the only ordinary way that the gift of salvation can be offered to us – it's that important! Salvation flows through the Sacrament of Baptism because it is the gateway to all of the other sacraments.

> "Put another way, Baptism is the only ordinary way that the gift of salvation can be offered to us – it's that important!"

At the end of Matthew's Gospel (Matthew 28:19), Jesus says, *"Baptize all nations in the name of the Father, and of the Son, and of the Holy Spirit."* He then ascends into Heaven! Thus, these last instructions are very important, and we, as Catholics, have followed them closely. When a person is baptized, he or she becomes part of the Body of Christ, the Church. He or she becomes a Christian and the consequences of any original sin or "actual" (committed) sins are washed away.

In Baptism, the person becomes a new creation and is born again in Jesus Christ! We, as Catholics, believe that the Sacrament of Baptism completely transforms and renews a person. It is not simply a covering over of sins by God but a complete transformation, a rebirth and a spiritual cleansing.

In the very early Church, most of the recipients of Baptism were adult converts to the Faith. As time passed and the Faith quickly grew, more and more children and even infants were baptized. In the book of Acts of the Apostles in the New Testament, we hear about entire households being baptized. This most certainly included children. Also, as the early Church developed a fuller understanding of original sin and the consequences of such sin, the baptism of children grew in importance. As more and more adults came to faith in Christ, infant baptism eventually became the norm.

Today, Catholics, along with many other Christian communities, regularly baptize infants. These infants presumably do not have the use of reason and hence cannot make an act of faith themselves. So, the parents, the godparents and the entire Church profess the faith for them and then bring them up in its practice. This, after all, is part of being the Body of Christ - the Church! Although some Protestant Christians disagree, the Catholic Church believes that, just as we provide children with nutrition, shelter and love, we would not want to keep from them the most precious thing of all: salvation.

Those who desire to be baptized and who die before they are able to receive the Sacrament are considered to have been baptized by their desire. Those who die for the Faith before they are able to be baptized are believed to have been baptized by their blood. Those infants who are stillborn or who die before being baptized we entrust to the mercy of God Who loves us all and Whom we trust will bring them to Himself. Those adults who, through no fault of their own, do not know Christ and yet still seek Him with a sincere heart, can be saved. However, Our Lord Jesus has tied salvation to Baptism, and the Church knows of no other ordinary way by which this gift of salvation can be imparted. Thus, Baptism remains vitally important and must never be postponed or taken for granted.

Quite simply, the date of our Baptism was the most important day of our life! Most of us simply do not remember it, although the graces God gave us on that happy day are active still. May we share the gift of salvation with all we meet, and bring others to faith in the Lord Jesus!

*Reflection Questions:*

1. *What is Baptism? Why is Baptism important?*

2. *Why do we baptize infants?*

3. *Can those who die without Baptism be saved?*

---

# The Importance of Choosing Christian Names:
*Why you really shouldn't name your child "Hitler."*

Perhaps you've heard it asked, "What's in a name?" Names are identifiers; they always tell us something. For example, those who have a business spend a long time thinking of a name for their enterprise - something that is both memorable and identifiable. When a baby is given a name, the choice always means something to the parents - something they find to be important. In short, a name says something about a given person, place, or thing.

> "....parents should name their children after saints or after Christian virtues because of the powerful witness this gives..."

For Christians, a person's name always has held great importance. In the early Church, adult converts to the Faith took new names of saints or virtues in order to show how they had been born again in Baptism. Even today, many people change their names when they enter into religious life or convert to Christianity.

The name one receives at Baptism is one's name for all eternity. This name can be the name of a saint, that is, of a Christian man or woman who has lived a life of exemplary fidelity to the Lord. Examples would be John, Joseph, Mary and Anne. This patron saint then provides an example of faith for the person with the same name. A baptismal name also can express a Christian mystery or a Christian virtue, such as Trinity, Grace, Charity or Hope.

Parents, godparents, and pastors should make sure that the name given at Baptism is not contrary to our Christian beliefs. For example, first names such as Satan, Lucifer, Judas, and Hitler would not be appropriate Christian names. I don't think we have had many problems with this ... yet. However, my concern is that recent trends have turned away from Christian names for children. Often, today, children's names are chosen because they are novel and unique, but sadly reflect little of the Christian faith of their parents. What might sound cute or trendy at the time will become outdated very quickly. On the other hand, the name of a saint or of a virtue will mark the person as a Christian and will bring with it many graces from God.

Certainly, there are many of us who have not been named after "patron saints." Indeed, this is often a factor in choosing a Confirmation name - so that each of us will have a saint to emulate, one to intercede for us.

It is very possible that some of us will be the first saints to bear our names. Now that's a challenge! However, all things being equal, parents should name their children after saints or after Christian virtues because of the powerful witness this gives - to the world and to their children. Please consider this for your children and grandchildren. One day, they will thank you for it!

*Reflection Questions:*

1. *Am I named after a saint or after a Christian virtue? If so, what is the significance?*

2. *If my name is not explicitly Christian in origin, do I have a favorite saint or virtue that I can take as my own?*

3. *Why is it important to choose a name carefully? What does it say to others?*

# Confession/Sacrament of Reconciliation:
*Shhh! Want to hear about a secret gift that will bring great joy?*

What is the best kept secret of our Catholic Faith? I believe it is the incredible Sacrament of Confession! This beautiful sacrament is offered weekly in most parishes, but very few people make use of it. How sad! This sacrament literally changes lives.

All of us yearn (consciously or unconsciously) for the real and tangible forgiveness of Jesus Christ! We receive this forgiveness every time we make a good Confession.

> "All of us have a need to talk about what we have done – and what we regret."

When we sin, we distance ourselves from God. Sin says "No" to God - it's like turning our back on Him. Today, some people claim that they do not go to Confession because they have no sin. This is very often an unrealistic and prideful assessment of one's own spiritual life. A simple reflection on our lives will most certainly help us realize that we are far from perfect.

Still others today have the mistaken notion that we only need to confess our sins to God alone, without a priest being present. This seems to make some sense at first, but it is not in keeping with the mind of Jesus Christ. He gave priests the power to forgive sins in His Name. In Matthew, chapters 16 and 18, as well as in John, chapter 20, we read about the apostles receiving the power to bind and loose sins as well as to forgive them. This action would have been pointless if the Lord had not intended to forgive us through the sacramental absolution of a priest.

It is crucial to remember that God alone forgives sins. Through the manner in which He accomplishes this, He truly shows His love for us. Throughout history, God has used human beings to mediate His presence and His love - to do His Will. He doesn't do it alone. For example, He inspired people to write down His Word - which the Catholic Church assembled into the Bible. God uses a man and a woman to create new life in a child. So, why can't we accept, after acknowledging all of this, that God can use a human being (a priest) to be His instrument to forgive sins? He uses us for everything else, why not to forgive sins? This IS exactly what He does!

All of us have a need to talk about what we have done – and what we regret. Sound advice says not to "keep it inside," but to talk about it and get help from others. Isn't that what the Sacrament of Reconciliation is all about? True, it is humbling to go to Confession – nobody likes to admit that he or she is not perfect. Isn't it interesting that in the very action of this sacrament and the humility that it requires, our pride is conquered? This pride is the base root of every sin.

So, just how does the Sacrament of Confession work? As you kneel or sit by the priest, he will greet you. Say how long it has been since your last confession. Add a bit about your state in life: married, single, etc. Then, proceed to confess all of your sins, as best you can recall, being sure to include any serious sins.

The priest will offer some advice and encouragement that is meant to support you in living a holy life. Then, he'll give you a penance – prayers to say or a deed to do – something that shows your sorrow for sin. You'll make an act of contrition, which can be quite simple. (All that you need to say is that you're sorry for your sins and that you want to do better.) After this, the priest will pronounce the words of absolution – the prayer by which God sacramentally forgives our sins.

Once the sacrament is completed, your soul is clean and your sins are gone forever. I guarantee that you will feel differently: relieved, lighter and more joyful.

Please take advantage of this great gift of forgiveness in the Sacrament of Reconciliation. You won't regret it. I promise.

*Reflection Questions:*

1. When did I last go to Confession?
2. How did I feel when I went? Before? Afterwards?
3. Fewer people make use of this sacrament today. Why?

---

# How to Celebrate the Sacrament of Confession – Part I:
*Here's everything you wanted to know – but were afraid to ask!*

From time to time, I receive requests from some of you to write about certain topics pertaining to our Faith. Recently, many of you have suggested that I write about going to Confession. You haven't been asking about the sacrament itself – or about what we, as Catholics, believe. You'd like me to outline exactly HOW you should celebrate the sacrament and the procedures for doing so. I think it is a great suggestion!

Sometimes, we all need to be reminded about how to do something. I wonder if an unfamiliarity with the Sacrament of Confession keeps people away ... ? Hmmmm. Let's review how to do it properly!

**When should a person go to Confession?** The <u>Catechism of the Catholic Church</u> teaches that a person should confess his or her (grave) sins at least once a year (CCC#1457). This is the second of the Five Precepts of the Church. However, this teaching is based on common sense, and in no way limits the frequency of Confession. If a person has a grave (mortal) sin on his or her soul, the individual needs to approach the Sacrament of Confession immediately! You shouldn't take a year to get around to it. From the moment of sin, the soul is in real jeopardy; it has turned away from God.

> **"I recommend that you should receive this sacrament at least once each year, whether or not you have committed a serious sin. More frequent Confession is highly recommended..."**

Of course, it sometimes can be difficult for an individual to discern whether a given sin was so serious as to be a mortal sin. This is precisely why we need to make use of this sacrament with the graces and spiritual counsel it provides.

Strictly speaking, if a person has not committed a mortal sin, he or she does not need to go to Confession. The sacrament is primarily for the restoration of sanctifying grace lost through mortal sin. However, the Sacrament of Confession also is very beneficial for receiving graces needed to avoid sin in the first place. As such, it is vitally important for the Catholic life.

I recommend that you should receive this sacrament at least once each year, whether or not you have committed a serious sin. More frequent Confession is highly recommended for those who want to grow in holiness. Either way, let's take advantage of God's gift of forgiveness!

**Where should a person go to Confession?** The answer to this question varies. For example, in my parishes, confessions are heard at a regularly scheduled time every Saturday morning. In other parishes, confessions are held before the weekend Masses. Certainly, an individual might call or e-mail a priest to set up an appointment to celebrate the Sacrament of Confession. Also, if there is a reluctance to celebrate the sacrament with a particular priest, there are numerous other priests who could assist you.

# How to Celebrate the Sacrament of Confession - Part II:
*Be prepared. Don't eavesdrop! Be concise.*

**How should a person prepare to celebrate the sacrament?** An excellent way to do this is to examine your conscience. An examination of conscience is recommended daily for each of us, but certainly is required before a person approaches the sacrament. Take a moment to collect yourself and listen to God's movements in your soul. Perhaps you might ask yourself the following questions, "How have I not loved God? How have I not loved my neighbor?"

> "....you need to properly prepare yourself to receive this sacrament. Don't rush into it! Take a moment to listen to your conscience."

I recommend going through the Ten Commandments and reflecting on the Seven Virtues and the Seven Vices as well. Perhaps you might need to write down on a sheet of paper what you wish to confess. There's nothing wrong with that! Just remember to burn the paper (or, I suppose you could shred it or eat it - a good source of fiber) when you're done! Either way, you need to properly prepare yourself to receive this sacrament. Don't rush into it! Take a moment to listen to your conscience.

**What should I do when I arrive at the Church?** First of all, kneel or sit in a pew and place yourself before the Lord. You are about to experience the loving mercy of God - prepare yourself. After a few minutes, you may approach the place where confessions are being heard.

It helps to keep in mind a few practical suggestions: When you come into the Church, be aware that other confessions might be taking place. Stay far enough away from the confessional so that you don't hear! Remember, if you hear another person's sins, you are morally bound to keep them a secret! Please be considerate and give the person ahead of you plenty of room. Also, when you arrive for the sacrament, please wait patiently. The priest is ministering as quickly as he can - sometimes, the situation is very difficult; sometimes, the sins are very serious; and sometimes, which is usually the case, the person ahead of you is very talkative! Be patient and don't sin by criticizing or judging another person while waiting! Also, please be as concise as possible when confessing your sins. Keep in mind that, often, there are people after you and we don't want them to leave in frustration.

**Once in the confessional, what should I do?** Typically, when you enter the confessional itself, you have a choice. The current practice of the Church in our country is to provide the choice of face-to-face Confession, or anonymous Confession behind a screen. The universal practice of the Church remains anonymous Confession, but, in our country, it has been seen as pastorally beneficial to provide for the option of a face-to-face conversation. The choice is yours. Traditionally, Confession behind the screen is done while kneeling. However, a chair can quickly be provided if requested. Face-to-face Confession usually is done while sitting.

# How to Celebrate the Sacrament of Confession – Part III:
*How long has it been? What did you do?*

**How do I begin and what do I say?** Typically, the priest will greet you and begin by making the Sign of the Cross. You then will say in these or similar words, *"Bless me Father for I have sinned, it has been 'X' weeks/months/years since my last Confession."* The bottom line here is that the priest needs to know how long it has been. A 40-year confession is typically a bit different than one that happens every week! Try to remember the best you can – estimate the amount of time if you must.

> **"Make your Confession as complete as possible! Remember, Confession is like cancer surgery. You want the doctor of souls to take out all of the cancer of sin – not just part of it!"**

Then, you proceed to tell your sins. First, you should list all of the serious – or mortal – sins in number and kind. In other words, what were the sins and how many times were they committed? The priest does NOT need intimate details here. What he does need is for the sin to be named. For example, if it is adultery, you must call it what it is – adultery. Don't simply say, "I was mean to my spouse … " Name the sin, and if the priest needs any more information, he'll ask.

After naming all of the mortal sins, if any, list the lesser or venial sins that were committed. Make your Confession as complete as possible! Remember, Confession is like cancer surgery. You want the doctor of souls to take out all of the cancer of sin – not just part of it! Certainly, sometimes we forget a sin or we remember it later. This is fine; God accepts our good will. Simply confess the sin next time you go to Confession. However, to intentionally withhold a <u>serious</u> sin during Confession is a tragedy. Not only is the Confession invalid because you truly are not contrite and/or you are withholding information, the additional sin of sacrilege could be committed. When going to Confession, you must endeavor to do a complete job. Be brave - it is our loving Lord and Savior, Christ Himself, who is present!

# How to Celebrate the Sacrament of Confession - Part IV:
*Express sorrow. Do penance. (Omit details about annoying relatives!)*

**What happens after I name my sins in Confession?** After you have confessed all of your serious sins and any lesser sins that you can remember, you might end by saying, *"For these and all of my sins, I am truly sorry."* When you have concluded, the priest will counsel you. Listen to his advice. Sometimes, this can be difficult, but pay attention! Remember, Christ is present in this sacrament!

> "....the priest will say the words of 'absolution' by which your sins will be forgiven...Immediately after these words are uttered, your sins are forgiven by the power of Jesus Christ."

Then, the priest will give you a penance - usually, some prayers to say. The purpose of your penance is to earnestly demonstrate your sorrow for sin and to contribute spiritually towards repairing the damage caused by your sins.

Think of it like repairing a broken window caused by a carelessly thrown baseball. We are sorry we did it, we apologize to the owner of the house, and he or she forgives us. However, the window still is broken! The penance we perform after Confession "fixes the broken window," if you will. Make sure that you do your penance and don't forget! If you would like another penance, you may ask the priest for a different one.

Next, the priest will ask you to make an "Act of Contrition." There are literally hundreds of acts of contrition, and almost every time I hear a Confession, I listen to a different version! The bottom line is this: the priest needs to hear that you are sorry for your sins and that you want to do better. If you have trouble memorizing a specific Act of Contrition, don't worry about it! Make up one, from your heart, and say that. Many times, these are very beautiful. If you don't know which words to say, it's fine to ask the priest to help you. After your Act of Contrition, the priest will say the words of "absolution" by which your sins will be forgiven. They are:

"God, the Father of mercies, through the death and resurrection of His Son has reconciled the world to Himself and sent the Holy Spirit among us for the forgiveness of sins; through the ministry of the Church may God give you pardon and peace, and I absolve you from your sins,+ in the name of the Father, + and of the Son, and + of the Holy Spirit."

Immediately after these words are uttered, your sins are forgiven by the power of Jesus Christ. The priest will end the Confession by saying these or similar words, *"The Lord has freed you from your sins, go in peace ... "* The penitent might say, *"Thank you"* or *"Thanks be to God,"* and then departs. Immediately, he or she does the penance, if applicable, and leaves Church, giving thanks to God.

**What are some common misconceptions people have about Confession?**
A few suggestions might help here. When going to Confession, it is wrong to confess ONLY one sin if you have others to confess. Do a complete job! Also, in Confession, the priest needs to know the number of times a sin has been committed only when the sin is mortal - not venial. Next, please remember that Confession is not spiritual direction! Many times, people like to list their faults, their relatives' faults, and all of what's wrong with the world in Confession. Just name your sins! If you need to set up an appointment to talk about the broader struggles in your life, do this at another time. Confession is not the appropriate place. Finally, remember that a penance service including general absolution usually is not a legitimate form of the Sacrament of Confession. One-on-one Confession remains the norm.

# How to Celebrate the Sacrament of Confession - Part V:
*Just follow this outline - for Confession made easy.*

To summarize, here is a brief outline you can follow when you come to the Sacrament of Confession:

1. When you arrive at the Church, pray for a while. Collect your thoughts, ask the Holy Spirit to guide you as you confess your sins.
2. Go to where the priest is hearing confessions and either kneel behind the screen or sit in the chair facing the priest. You always should have the option of being anonymous when you go to Confession. Some people prefer face-to-face, others prefer being behind a screen. The choice is yours.

"There's nothing to fear – and, if you need help, the priest will assist you. Come and receive this beautiful Sacrament of God's mercy and forgiveness."

3. After you are situated, the priest will greet you. The two of you will make the Sign Of The Cross together, and then you say: *"Bless me, Father, I have sinned..."* You can use a similar phrase, if you'd like.

4. At the beginning, it is important that you tell the priest how long it has been since your last Confession. You don't need to be precise down to the day; weeks, months or years will be just fine. Also, if you are behind the screen, or if you're face-to-face and the priest doesn't know you, briefly telling him your state in life will help. Ex: Married, single, divorced, etc.

5. Next, you proceed to confess your sins as completely as you can. First, name every serious – or "mortal" – sin that you can remember. This is important. You must never keep anything back because of fear or embarrassment. You must be as complete as you can in naming your serious sins. If you intentionally leave a serious or mortal sin out, it prevents the sacrament from occurring. Think of it like an operation to remove a cancer. The doctor must remove all of it or it will grow back. Serious or mortal sin is the same as cancer – it is cancer of the soul. In confessing your sins, you don't need to go into intimate detail. Simply state the facts, and, if the priest needs more information, he will ask for it. After naming all of your serious sins (if any), you may confess any lesser or "venial" sins. If, for any reason, you should remember a sin later that you had forgotten during the Sacrament, there is no reason to be concerned. God always takes our good faith into account during the Sacrament.

6. After you have finished confessing your sins, the priest will give you some counsel. Sometimes, he will address everything you mentioned, but often, he will just comment on one or two subjects. He will give you concrete advice on how to improve your spiritual life and to avoid sin. Listen to what he has to say.

7. Next, the priest will assign a penance. There is no way we could possibly "pay back" God for his great forgiveness. The purpose of the penance is rather for us to demonstrate that we are sorry and to begin to make reparation. If the penance is difficult or impossible for you to complete, you may ask the priest for another.

8. The priest then will ask you to recite an Act of Contrition. If you do not remember the Act of Contrition, there is no need to worry! Make up a brief prayer from your heart, saying that you are truly sorry for what you have done and that you want to do better.

9. The priest will say the prayer of absolution, by which God forgives our sins.
10. The priest will bless you with the Sign Of The Cross and kindly send you on your way. After thanking God and doing your penance, you go forth to sin no more!

Okay, now you know how to do it. There's nothing to fear - and, if you need help, the priest will assist you. Come and receive this sacrament of God's mercy and forgiveness. You'll be glad you did! I hope that this information has been of some assistance to you, in understanding how to go to Confession. It truly is a beautiful Sacrament of healing and peace!

*Reflection Questions:*
1. How soon should we go to Confession if we have committed a serious sin?
2. What is the purpose of the penance that is given during Confession?
3. Why do so many people avoid going to Confession?

---

# Examination of Conscience:
*How well do you know your vices - AND virtues?*

All of us are called to holiness. We all are called to be saints. We can grow in holiness by acknowledging that we are not perfect and that we need God's grace, mercy and forgiveness each and every day. One powerful means of growing in holiness is to make a frequent examination of conscience. This can be done in the evening before we go to sleep, by reflecting on our day.

> "One powerful means of growing in holiness is to make a frequent examination of conscience."

First of all, we might ask ourselves, "How have I followed the Lord Jesus this day? How have I turned away from Him?" After this, we might briefly go through the Ten Commandments and ask ourselves if we have followed them. In addition to this, I have found that reflecting on the Seven Virtues and the Seven Vices has greatly assisted me in examining my conscience. What are they? Here's a list:

Seven Virtues: 1. Faith - Do I put God first in my life?
2. Hope - Do I believe that with God, all things will work out?
3. Charity - Do I treat others as I would like to be treated?
4. Justice - Do I treat others fairly?

5. Prudence – Do I think before I act, in order to avoid sin?
6. Temperance – Do I practice moderation in my behavior?
7. Fortitude – Do I stand up for my Faith and for what is right?

Seven Vices:
1. Pride – Do I put others down to make myself feel better?
2. Lust – Am I chaste or do I give in to sexual temptation?
3. Anger – Am I harsh and cruel to others?
4. Envy – Am I never satisfied with what I have?
5. Greed – Do I worship money and wealth?
6. Sloth – Am I lazy and do I waste time?
7. Gluttony – Do I give in to excesses that harm myself and others?

Review these Seven Virtues and Seven Vices as you make your examination of conscience. It will help you to grow in holiness! By the way, they make a great tool to prepare for the Sacrament of Confession. (Hint, hint ... )

*Reflection Questions:*

1. Do I make an examination of conscience every day? If not, why?
2. Which of the Seven Virtues do I desire the most?
3. Which of the Seven Vices is the most tempting for me?

# General Absolution:
*No lines, no embarrassment – but, in most cases, it doesn't work!*

Recently, several people have asked me about having "general absolution." I have said – and will continue to say – NO, we will not be doing this. It seems that various parishes have been offering penance services with general absolution, in place of penance services with individual reconciliation. In other words, a general sacramental absolution of sins is given instead of an individual celebration of the sacrament with the priest.

> "....(general absolution) is a legitimate form of the Sacrament of Confession which may be used ONLY in extraordinary circumstances."

The appeal of this practice is obvious – it is easier for the priest and it's easier for the person going to Confession. There are no long waiting lines and there is no embarrassment about confessing sins! However, like so many quick fixes in life, it simply doesn't work in most cases.

The question may be asked, "What is general absolution?" Basically, it is a legitimate form of the Sacrament of Confession which may be used ONLY in extraordinary circumstances. For example, general absolution may be used if there is a danger of death and not enough time for the priest to hear individual confessions. It also may be used, with the permission of the diocesan bishop, if there is an extraordinarily large number of people going to Confession and not enough priests to hear all of these confessions.

However, general absolution is best suited for a situation in which the danger of death is near. For example, during the sinking of the Titanic, if an airplane is captured by a terrorist, or when soldiers are preparing for battle, a priest could legitimately give general absolution to a large group of people. There simply isn't enough time to hear the confessions individually and the situation is very dire. However, a normal parish penance service is certainly not a danger-of-death situation! Even though the number of people may be large, an hour of waiting does not constitute a denial of the sacrament! Thus, penance services in which general absolution is given are most often grave abuses of the sacrament.

To make matters worse, the true requirements of general absolution often are withheld from the people. In order for the sacrament to be VALID, the penitent must be properly disposed (have sorrow for sin and intention to not sin again) AND also be resolved to confess, if possible, all mortal (serious) sins in an individual confession with a priest at the earliest possible date. Thus, if these requirements are not met, the person who goes to a parish penance service with general absolution receives no sacrament at all. Such a tragedy!

In conclusion, the priests who give general absolution in normal parish penance services may be doing so in opposition to their bishops and contrary to the teaching of our Catholic Church. I strongly advise you to stay away from any parish where this abuse still takes place.

*Reflection Questions:*

1. *When may general absolution be used?*
2. *When did I last receive the Sacrament of Confession?*
3. *Do I encourage my children or other family members to receive this sacrament, too?*

# The Liturgy as the Source and Summit of Christian Life:
*Is a "Communion service" the same as a Mass?*

Perhaps the most quoted passage from the documents of the Second Vatican Council (1962-1965) is the following: *"The liturgy (the Mass) is the summit toward which the activity of the Church is directed, and at the same time it is the fount from which all the Church's power flows."*

From this, we can see that the Mass is the greatest, most important religious event for us as Catholics. The Eucharist is everything to us, for we believe that we receive Jesus! When Our Lord said at the Last Supper, *"Do this in memory of me,"* (Luke 22:19) what He intended was for the Eucharistic Sacrifice - the Mass - to be repeated and continued in His Name.

> "....the action of 'doing this in memory of me' does not occur at a Communion service."

In many parishes across our country, there has been an increase in "Communion services," due to the shortage of priests. As you know, there cannot be a Mass without a priest. So, when a priest is unavailable on a weekday or even on a Sunday, a "liturgy of the word" is celebrated. It includes the readings of the day, followed by the Lord's Prayer and then Communion. The hosts that are distributed in Communion were consecrated by a priest at a previous Mass. Many parishes are well acquainted with this practice of Communion services and find it to be beneficial.

However, some people seem to be confused about the difference between a Mass and a Communion service. Some think that they are the same. Some even prefer a Communion service because it is shorter, etc. This is a fundamental error.

We all must realize that a Communion service is not a Mass! The Mass is a continuation and participation in the one and infinite sacrifice of Jesus Christ on the Cross. Participation in the Eucharistic Sacrifice of the Mass is the highest act of worship for us as Catholics. In no way can a Communion service be seen as an equivalent, or comparable, to a Mass. Certainly, the same Sacrament of the Eucharist is received at both. However, the action of "doing this in memory of me" does not occur at a Communion service. Therein lies the key difference between the two.

In conclusion, we can be thankful for the many people who assist at prayer in the absence of a priest. We can be very thankful for the gift of the Eucharist, which binds us together as Catholics and gives us the strength to live our Faith every day. However, we must be most thankful for the Mass which gives us the gift of the Eucharist!

*Reflection Questions:*

1. *How far would I travel to go to Mass? Ten miles? Fifty miles? One hundred miles?*
2. *How is a Communion service different from a Mass?*
3. *Do I pray every day for more vocations to the priesthood?*

# The Reception of Holy Communion - Part I:
*Show respect! The Eucharist is not a "door prize."*

Sometimes, we forget things. Life is busy, our schedules are full, and even important details can be lost over time. For example, it is necessary from time to time to review the guidelines for receiving Holy Communion.

I fear that many people today believe that the reception of Communion is an automatic action – something one does when one goes to Mass. This is not true. As I often say, the Eucharist is not a door prize. Its reception is not to be taken lightly. Reception of the Body and Blood of Christ should be an expression of our unity with Christ and with His Catholic Church.

> **"If an individual is in a seriously sinful situation, he or she may not receive Communion until...Confession is received or an 'Act of perfect Contrition' is made."**

Following the guidelines of our bishops, united with the Pope, we see that our Church's teaching on this issue is quite clear. Catholics are encouraged to receive Holy Communion devoutly and frequently. Those who receive Communion should be properly prepared to receive the sacrament. The individual should normally have fasted for an hour beforehand and should not be conscious of grave sin.

The purpose of the Eucharistic Fast is to call to mind what we are about to receive – nothing seems to make us humans sit up and take notice like not eating! The hour fast before Communion is a way in which we prepare to receive this most awesome of gifts. Certainly, if one is ill or elderly and cannot fast from food for that amount of time, he is not required to do so. Another act of preparation can take its place. However, ordinarily, we must fast before we receive Communion.

The bishops also speak about not receiving Communion if one is in a state of "grave sin." What exactly is grave sin? Grave sin is serious sin; it is the doing of evil. Most commonly, it is called mortal sin. For a sin to be mortal, it must involve a seriously sinful act, the person must have full knowledge of its seriousness, and the person must fully consent to doing it.

Such mortal sin destroys our relationship with God. We cut ourselves off from the sanctifying grace that we received at Baptism, and we set ourselves adrift. Sadly, mortal sin is quite common today. Many of us think that the only really serious sin is murder! Not true! While murder would certainly be a grave sin, so would intentional drunkenness; slander of another's reputation; physical violence or abuse; abortion; adultery; the viewing of pornography; and robbery. Other grave sins include not practicing one's Faith because of laziness, or marrying outside of the Church without permission. In addition, remember that divorce followed by remarriage without a declaration of nullity is a serious sin.

The appropriate action after falling into any of these serious situations is to immediately turn towards God and ask for His forgiveness. The Lord is so merciful! This great mercy is made sacramentally available through Confession. Unrepentant and unforgiven mortal sin at the end of our lives will send us to Hell. Thus, it is of utmost importance for us to turn towards the Lord and receive His forgiveness.

If an individual is in a seriously sinful situation, he or she may NOT receive Holy Communion until the Sacrament of Confession is received or an "Act of perfect Contrition" is made. (In an Act of perfect Contrition, one expresses sorrow not for the punishment he might receive, but rather because he has hurt God.) To receive Communion anyway would be to commit the additional mortal sin of sacrilege. The relationship with Our Lord would be broken by the individual's actions. Our Lord wouldn't have abandoned the person – the person would have abandoned Him!

St. Paul states, *"Whoever eats the bread or drinks the cup of the Lord unworthily will have to answer for the body and blood of the Lord. A person should examine himself, and so eat the bread and drink the cup. For anyone who eats and drinks without discerning the body, eats and drinks judgment upon himself."* (I Corinthians 11:27)

It is important for us to be well prepared spiritually before we receive Communion. If one is in a seriously sinful situation, he or she may not receive Communion but always may come forward in the line and ask for a blessing, instead. There are individuals with integrity who abstain from receiving Communion because they realize that they are not properly disposed. These individuals, although objectively in sinful situations, often have a very strong Faith and are examples of holiness.

The Lord is kind and merciful. We all rely on His forgiveness. Let us all strive to receive the Eucharist worthily.

# The Reception of Holy Communion-Part II:
*Everyone cannot receive communion everywhere!*

Today, there also is confusion about the issue of "intercommunion" with other Christians – whether they can receive in our Church and whether we can receive in theirs.

It must be clearly stated, from the start, that intercommunion with those who do not share our Faith in the Eucharist is not permitted in the Catholic Church. In extraordinary circumstances, with expressed permission from the diocesan bishop or in danger of death, Holy Communion may be offered to a non-Catholic Christian – if certain additional qualifications are met. It is important to note, too, that we as Catholics are not permitted to receive communion in another Christian community that we happen to be visiting. To do so would indicate that we are in agreement with what they believe, which, sadly, we are not.

> "How can we share communion with others if we are not in communion with what we believe communion to be?"

This teaching can be difficult for many to accept. To some, it appears to be uncharitable or even egotistic. The fact remains that Christians believe different things about what the Eucharist really is. How can we share communion with others if we are not in communion with what we believe communion to be? The word "communion" means unity – oneness. Regrettably, there is no such unity among Christian denominations.

When we receive Holy Communion as Catholics, we are saying that we are in union with Christ and with the teachings of the Church He founded. When we receive the Body of Christ into ourselves, we become more fully united with what we already are by our Baptism: the Body of Christ.

A body cannot be disjointed and still remain healthy. Thus, we work and strive towards unity. Our separateness is a great tragedy and a disunity that Jesus certainly did not intend. However, it suggests a false sense of charity to think that allowing everyone to receive communion everywhere will somehow heal old wounds. Rather, by honestly addressing and understanding the differences between us, we might be better able to move forward together.

These are difficult and sensitive issues. If you have questions about whether you should be receiving Communion or not, you do need to speak with a priest. We will do anything and everything in our power to allow you to receive the Body and Blood of Our Lord. If you have been away from the Sacrament of Confession, you truly must go. If you are divorced and remarried outside of the Church, you must petition for an annulment before you may receive Communion. You must. If you have a health issue that prevents you from receiving Communion, please let a priest know about it. If you are a non-Catholic and have been receiving Communion all along, I ask you to stop. Have you ever considered becoming Catholic? Perhaps you might speak to a priest about this.

The Eucharist is the greatest gift that we, as Catholics, have. The Eucharist is the Body and Blood of Jesus Christ. It is vitally important for all of us to approach the altar in a state of grace so that we can receive the Lord worthily in Holy Communion. Let us examine ourselves anew lest we take this greatest of gifts for granted.

*Reflection Questions:*

  *1. Why do we ordinarily fast for one hour before receiving Holy Communion?*

  *2. What does "receiving Holy Communion in a state of grace" mean?*

  *3. Why is intercommunion not allowed for Catholics?*

# Bread and Wine:
## *This ancient formula is still the best!*

Why do we always use bread and wine for Mass? Doesn't this become rather boring? Why don't we use something more interesting - how about cookies and coke - preferably chocolate chip and diet? Why not pita bread and mineral water - healthy, you know! How about rice cakes and spring water - for those of us on a diet? Why do we, as Catholics, keep using unleavened bread and pure grape wine?

The reason for this is quite simple - this is what Our Lord Jesus Christ used at the Last Supper! Furthermore, this is what the Sacred Tradition of His Church has maintained through the centuries. After all, Jesus did not say, *"I am the cookie of life"* – good heavens! He said, *"I am the Bread of Life."* (John 6:51)

> **"....this is what Our Lord Jesus Christ used at the Last Supper... He said, *'I am the Bread of Life.'*"**

I realize that many of us have never questioned this tradition. However, today, there are numerous individuals, some well-meaning and some not, who are challenging this teaching of our Faith.

First of all, let's be clear about a few basic things. The bread used for the Eucharist must be wheat-based and recently made. Nothing may be added that could alter its makeup. Sugar, salt, honey, milk, eggs, or raisins would invalidate the Eucharist – the sacrament would not take place. The wine must be natural wine, made from grapes of the vine. Grape juice would not be valid matter for Mass.

This is all pretty straightforward. However, we all know of individuals who suffer from certain illnesses that involve a reaction to alcohol or wheat.

For those laity or priests who suffer from alcoholism, there is a substance called "mustum" which is an early stage of wine with its fermentation suspended – thus lowering the alcohol content. This is permissible and often used by priests.

Today, there is an increasing knowledge of an illness called Celiac Disease. In this digestive disorder, ingestion of something called gluten which is found in various grains and cereals – including the wheat found in Communion Hosts – could trigger complications such as weight loss or abdominal pain. In a few cases, any exposure to gluten could place one's life at risk. There are now low-gluten Hosts that are available to assist those with this illness.

What should a person do if he or she struggles with these illnesses? First of all, if a person has an illness that involves either the element of bread or wine, then he or she should simply receive Communion under the form that can best be tolerated. As Catholics, we believe that the whole of Christ - Body, Blood, Soul and Divinity - is contained completely under the forms of bread and wine. This means that when receiving Communion, one may receive either the consecrated Host or the Precious Blood and still be receiving Communion. It is not necessary to receive both the consecrated Host and the Precious Blood to receive the Eucharist. Receiving one is sufficient.

The bottom line is that those who suffer from either Celiac Disease or the disease of alcoholism still may receive Communion. In the rare case when one suffers from both illnesses, other provisions can be made. If you suffer from Celiac Disease or have another medical condition that keeps you from receiving

Communion, please speak with a priest and try to work out a solution together.

*Reflection Questions:*
1. Do I receive Communion under both forms – the consecrated Host and the Precious Blood? Why or why not?
2. Have I ever made a Spiritual Communion when I was unable to receive Communion at Mass?
3. Bread and wine are truly universal foods – they are found in every culture. What does this tell us about our Catholic Faith?

---

# Reception of Holy Communion Under Both Forms - Bread and Wine:
*It's one Lord, one Eucharist - in two forms.*

Each time you go to Mass, you have the opportunity to receive Holy Communion. If you are properly disposed (i.e., a Catholic, free from serious sin who has fasted), you are able to receive the Body and Blood of Christ. You might notice that Communion is offered under two forms - the consecrated Body and the chalice or "cup" containing the Precious Blood. You may wonder why this is the case. Also, you might be unsure whether it is necessary to receive from both in order to "completely" receive Communion.

> "....we do not need to receive under both forms in order to receive the Eucharist completely."

In the Biblical accounts of the Last Supper, we hear about Jesus taking bread and wine, blessing them, and sharing them with His apostles. The Last Supper was the beginning of the institution of the Eucharist. It rightly can be called the first Mass. The early Christians did likewise when they gathered together every Sunday - the bishops or priests took bread and wine, repeated the words of Christ, and offered the Eucharist to the people. This practice of offering Communion to the laity under both forms, that is under the forms of bread and wine (the consecrated Body and the Precious Blood), continued until the late 1100s.

By the early 1200s, however, the Western Church began to offer Communion to the laity under the form of bread alone. The priest, of course, received both, but the laity only received the consecrated Host. Historically, there were many reasons for this change. Perhaps the cost of wine was too great for the number of communicants. Perhaps there was a genuine concern about spilling the Precious Blood or of intentional sacrilege.

During the 16th century, the Protestants took issue with many Catholic practices, including the offering of Holy Communion under the form of bread alone. They often asserted that Communion was "incompletely" received by the laity if they received only the consecrated Host. In order to truly receive the Eucharist, it was necessary to receive both the consecrated Host and the Precious Blood, they contended. This ran contrary to the Catholic teaching which held that the Eucharist was completely received even if under only one form.

Because of this confusion, the Church postponed any change back to Communion under both forms. By the middle of the 20th century, during the Second Vatican Council (1962-1965), it was felt that the danger of confusion had passed and that Communion once again could be offered to the laity under both forms.

Holy Communion is more completely represented when it is received under both forms. The understanding of the Eucharist as both a sacrifice and a sacred banquet also is underscored by both elements of the Eucharist being offered to all. When there are excessive numbers of people, or if the priest believes there is a danger of profanation of the Precious Blood, Communion still is offered under one form only. However, today, it is quickly becoming common practice to offer Holy Communion under both forms to all.

It is important to realize that Christ is really and truly present - Body, Blood, Soul and Divinity - in the Eucharist. Although we call it the Body and Blood of Christ, Christ is not divided, as if to say His Body is here in the consecrated Host, and His Blood is over there in the cup. No. Logic AND the doctrine of "concomitance" affirm that Christ is present under both forms and that He cannot be physically divided in His Glorified and Mystical Body. Thus, we do not need to receive under both forms in order to receive the Eucharist completely. However, if we desire to receive both the consecrated Host and the cup, we are taking advantage of an option the Church allows us so that we can visualize what we are doing and receive more fully.

The Eucharist is a great gift which the Church has fostered and protected for more than 2,000 years. Let us make use of this tremendous privilege by worthily receiving Our Lord as often as we are able.

*Reflection Questions:*
1. Why did the reception of Holy Communion under the forms of bread and wine fall out of practice?
2. Why has it returned to prominence in the Church today?
3. Do I receive the Eucharist totally and completely if I receive only the consecrated Host or only the Precious Blood? Why or why not?

# How Many Times a Day May I Receive Communion?:
## What if there's a wedding or funeral before Saturday evening Mass?

As a priest, I'm often asked questions about our Catholic Faith. The questions vary, but lately, the most common question has been: *"How many times in a day may I receive Communion?"*

The short answer is that one may receive Communion TWICE in a given day - as long as the second time is in the context of a Mass. Implicit in this teaching is that the person **participates** in both Masses. For example, it would be an abuse of the sacrament to simply show up at Communion time, receive the sacrament, and then go to another Church and do the same thing. (Don't laugh - this happens more often than you think!) So, you may receive Communion twice in a given day.

> "....one may receive Communion: TWICE in a given day...as long as...the person participates in both Masses."

The issue arises most often on Saturdays. For example, a person attends a funeral or wedding Mass on Saturday morning or afternoon, then attends the "anticipated Mass" for Sunday on Saturday evening. One may receive Communion twice in this case - once for the wedding or funeral and once more for the anticipated Sunday Mass.

Because it is in keeping with the very meaning of the Eucharist, ordinarily, we should receive Holy Communion every time we participate at Mass. (This presumes, of course, that we are able to receive Communion, being free from mortal sin.)

Now, we should look at the spirit behind this law. The purpose behind this precept is for us to receive the Eucharist as often as possible. For example, if a person innocently receives Communion more than twice in a day, it is not a sin - my goodness! However, there have been - and continue to be - certain superstitious practices that involve running from Church to Church just to receive Communion. This, of course, would be a sinful abuse of the sacrament and represent a total misunderstanding of the Sacrifice of the Mass. So, the Church, in its wisdom, has said that Communion may be received twice in a given day.

There is another frequent question, related to this. Quite simply, people ask: *"Does a wedding or funeral Mass celebrated on a Saturday before 4 p.m. 'count' for a Sunday Mass?"* It does not. The Sunday Mass of anticipation typically takes place at 4 p.m. or later on a Saturday. A number of years ago, the Church first allowed Masses of anticipation to take place on Saturday evenings. This follows the ancient Jewish and early Christian practice of beginning celebration of a feast day at sundown the previous evening.

I hope that this information answers some of your questions. We should not be looking for the minimum just to get by, but for the maximum we can give to God. The bottom line is that the Eucharist is the most precious gift which we, as Catholics, have - it is truly Jesus. Let's not take Him for granted!

*Reflection Questions:*

1. *Have I ever been to Mass twice in a given day? What was it like?*
2. *Have I ever gone to a weekday Mass?*
3. *Why do we sometimes give God the minimum and not the maximum?*

# The Eucharistic Prayer:
*How many saints can YOU name from this prayer?*

The holiest and most sacred part of the Mass is the Eucharistic Prayer. During this prayer, the miracle takes place - Jesus Christ becomes present on the altar in order to feed us with His Body and Blood. At this time, we all kneel, to humble ourselves before this great miracle.

Actually, there are SEVERAL versions of the Eucharistic prayer used within the Catholic Church. At their core, however, they are all the same - they all include the words of the institution of the Eucharist from the Last Supper, *"Take this all of you and eat it ... .do this in memory of me."* (Luke 22:19).

> **"During this prayer, the miracle takes place – Jesus Christ becomes present on the altar in order to feed us with His Body and Blood."**

The First Eucharistic Prayer, often called the Roman Canon, has been in use for the longest period of time. I prefer it because of its beautiful Eucharistic theology. Some of you have asked about the many names which are mentioned during the course of this special prayer. Let's discuss them ...

In the First Eucharistic Prayer, there are two lists of saints whose memory we honor in union with the whole Church. At the head of the first group is Mary, the Mother of God. St. Joseph comes next, followed by two groups of 12 saints in each.

The first 12 are the apostles. There are Peter (the first Pope) and Paul, both apostles to the Gentiles. Then, there are: Andrew; James; John; Thomas; James; Philip; Bartholomew; Matthew; Simon; and Jude. (Paul replaces Judas Iscariot, the betrayer.)

The next group of 12 mirrors the 12 apostles – the number 12 being the biblical number of fullness. This group includes: Linus; Cletus; Clement; Sixtus; Cornelius; and Cyprian, all six of whom were bishops, five of them Popes. These are followed by: Lawrence (a deacon); Chrysogonus (a priest); then John; Paul; Cosmas; and Damian, all lay members of the Church.

The second list of saints is made up entirely of Roman martyrs – those who have sacrificed their lives for their faith in Christ. First is named John the Baptist. Then they are listed in two groups of seven – seven being a biblical number of perfection. First, there are seven men listed: Stephen (a deacon and the first martyr of the Church); Matthias; Barnabas; Ignatius; Alexander; Marcellinus; and Peter. The next seven are women. They are: Felicity; Perpetua; Agatha; Lucy; Agnes; Cecilia; and Anastasia.

So, these are the saints' names you hear in the First Eucharistic Prayer. I hope that this explanation helps you to understand who they were and why they are placed in this holiest of prayers!

*Reflection Questions:*

1. Which Eucharistic Prayer do I hear most often in my parish?
2. Have I ever slowly read through the four main Eucharistic prayers and reflected on them?

3. Choose a saint who is mentioned in the First Eucharistic Prayer and read about his or her life.

---

# The Homily:
*Maybe Someone is trying to tell you something!*

After Mass, it's fairly typical for one of my parishioners to come up to me and ask a question about the homily I gave. No matter which Sunday, and no matter who asks the question, it basically goes like this: *"I felt like your homily was aimed right at me! Were you talking to me?"* I always chuckle when I hear this and I very much appreciate the question - and the compliment! However, my answer is always the same. I have never intentionally directed a homily at any particular person. That would be very embarrassing and pastorally inappropriate.

> **"....please know that every priest's homily is meant for everyone in the congregation. If you feel that one was meant just for you, that's probably the Holy Spirit knocking. Please let Him in!"**

To be honest, if I'm ever intentionally directing the homily at anyone, it would be me! However, if my homilies do strike a chord and parishioners think that this is helpful for their life in Christ, I am most pleased. That is my intention every weekend, when I speak.

Preaching homilies is one of my favorite things to do as a priest. I enjoy preaching and consider it an enormous privilege - as well as a great responsibility. When I was in seminary, my teachers and mentors told me that I should start preparing a homily the Monday before the coming weekend. Well, that doesn't always happen - especially with multiple parishes! I typically glance at the readings for the coming weekend on Tuesday or Wednesday. By Thursday or Friday, I construct the homily. On Saturday afternoon, I practice it. Sometimes, an idea or a theme for the homily comes quickly to me. At other times, it's like pulling teeth! I always try to say a prayer to the Holy Spirit before I begin preparing.

As many of you know, I always like to start with a story, either from my life or from some other source. I do this to ground the homily in everyday life and to catch the congregation's attention. (I hope that people don't think that I'm always talking about myself!) Typically, I use stories from outside of my parishes so that I don't betray any confidences. (Trust me, my current parishes have given me lots of material for any future assignments in other areas!)

After the opening story, I typically move to a reflection on the Scriptures that we have just heard and then on to various Church teachings that are connected to these Scriptures. I try to vary the homily subjects from weekend to weekend. Some are about the Bible readings themselves, while others have to do with the basics of our Catholic Faith. Sometimes, I preach on a moral subject. At other times, I touch upon a topic that is in the current news. Regardless of the subject, I try to make the homily relevant to life today.

On most weekends, I preach four times - one time each for four Masses. Typically, the homily does change a bit each time. Sometimes, after I deliver a homily a few times, I get tired of it and write another. Some homilies work better than others. I have my favorites, but I also have some that I don't particularly like. The blessing is that when one bombs, I get to start from scratch the next week! I do memorize the key points of the homilies because I find that it makes for a smoother delivery and more earnest conversation. Typically, I have six points that I make. I memorize these six points and construct the homily around them. I usually preach for 10 to 12 minutes, or more if I get excited ... !

The bottom line is that I thank God for giving me this opportunity to talk about Him. I also thank all of the people who are willing to listen! Finally, please know that every priest's homily is meant for everyone in the congregation. If you feel that one was meant just for you, that's probably the Holy Spirit knocking. Please let Him in!

*Reflection Questions:*

1. *What makes for an excellent and relevant homily?*
2. *Preaching relies heavily upon the Holy Spirit. Why?*
3. *Preaching is a great responsibility. Why?*

# Intentionally Missing Mass:
*(Hint: vacation, sporting events and laziness are NOT good excuses!)*

Teachers have difficult jobs. As they try to impart knowledge to their students, the students often try to find excuses not to learn. Teachers are particularly troubled by the incessant question, *"Will this be on the test?"* This question reflects a tragic lack of understanding of the purpose of education! Interestingly, a similar question is often asked of me. The question is formulated somewhat differently. In a nutshell, people ask: *"Is it a sin to miss Mass?"*

> "....if we intentionally miss Mass...we commit a serious sin, because we are putting something in place of worshipping God."

The answer is YES! Yes, it's still a sin to INTENTIONALLY miss Mass on a weekend or Holy Day. This is not because of some arbitrary Church law - or because of some rogue priest who wants more money for his collection! We can discover why it's sinful not to go to Mass, by asking ourselves the following question: "What am I putting in its place?"

If we truly believe that Jesus is present - Body, Blood, Soul and Divinity - in the Eucharist, why would we not want to go to Mass every week? What could be more important than worshipping the Lord and giving thanks for all He has done for us? By missing Mass intentionally, we are basically saying, *"I have something more important to do than to worship God."* This is always a sin.

Now, certainly, there are reasons which may excuse someone from attending Mass on a given weekend or Holy Day. An illness, frailty due to old age, the care of a sick loved one, or severe weather is a serious reason that excuses one from this obligation. Also, if there is no Catholic Church in the area or if the Church is closed when you get there for Mass - this is a legitimate excuse.

However, there are many bad excuses. Going on vacation does NOT excuse one from attending Mass unless you are in the middle of an ocean or on a mountain top. Going to a sporting event does NOT excuse one from going to Mass. Being lazy or tired from a hangover does NOT excuse one from going to Mass. Also, except in the most dire circumstances where personal and family survival is at stake, working on Sunday does NOT excuse one from attending Mass. We need to ask ourselves the following question: What can be more important than worshipping God and receiving Him in the Eucharist? A sporting event? Money? A vacation? I think not. Without God, we wouldn't have any of these.

What is "number one" in our lives? What do we put first? If it is our faith in God, then we must show this by our actions. Attending Mass every weekend can be a sacrifice, but it's a small sacrifice to make for all that God has given us. So, yes, if we intentionally miss Mass on a weekend or Holy Day, we commit a serious sin, because we are putting something in place of worshipping God. He deserves better. Let's try to work on this!

*Reflection Questions:*

*1. Do I go to Mass every weekend? Why or why not?*

*2. How many hours are in a week? How many of these hours do I dedicate to God?*

*3. Is going to Mass an obligation for me or do I go to Mass out of love?*

# Liturgical Colors:
*Why do the colors change at Mass? (OR, why is that priest wearing PINK?)*

In downtown Milwaukee, there is an old building which once housed the Wisconsin Gas Company. On top of this building is an enormous glass greenhouse-like structure that is shaped like a flame. Depending upon the weather, a light inside this flame turns various colors. Red is for hot. Blue is for cold. Yellow means the weather is changing. (This is usually the case!) This "flame" can be seen throughout the city. It has become a landmark for those from Milwaukee, and of particular interest for those who want to see what the weather is like outside.

> "The liturgical color of a given day is ...(a) means by which we are drawn into the mystery of our Faith."

In our Church, too, we have various colors which are symbolic. We're not talking about the weather, in this case, but rather about which liturgical season we are in or which feast we are celebrating. Just in case you've ever wondered why the priest is wearing a certain color at a certain time, here's a list that might explain more fully:

**Green:** Symbolizes hope and spiritual growth. Worn during Ordinary Time.

**Red:** Symbolizes the blood of martyrs who died for Christ. Also symbolizes the Holy Spirit. Worn on the feast days of martyrs and also on Pentecost.

**Violet:** Symbolizes penance. Worn during Advent or Lent. May be worn for a funeral Mass.

**White:** Symbolizes joy or celebration. Worn on a feast day of Christ or the feast day of a saint. May be worn any day, for any celebration, as well as for funerals.

**White with Blue:** Symbolizes the Blessed Virgin Mary. Worn on feast days of Mary.

**Gold:** Symbolizes the richness of a grand celebration. Worn on high feast days: Christmas, Easter, Corpus Christi, Trinity Sunday, etc.

**Rose:** (It's not really called "pink!") Symbolizes hope. Worn two Sundays of the year: the 4$^{th}$ Sunday of Lent, the 3$^{rd}$ Sunday of Advent.

**Black:** Symbolizes mourning. Traditionally worn for funerals or for All Souls' Day.

Symbols are such an important part of our Catholic Faith. They lead us by our senses towards God. The liturgical color of a given day is yet another means by which we are drawn into the mystery of our Faith. Look for the color of the day!

*Reflection Questions:*

1. What is the liturgical color at Mass today?
2. How many of the eight colors or color combinations have I seen?
3. Do we see similar colors being used during everyday life?

# Ringing of the Sanctus Bell:
### Now, you can again hear bells in many Catholic churches.

We Catholics have many signs and symbols that make up our worship at Mass. We have many traditions and rituals. Certainly, some external parts of the Mass have come and gone. However, one tradition has been maintained in various parishes. This is the action of ringing a bell at the Consecration.

> **"....the bell calls our attention to the very moment when the Eucharistic miracle occurs."**

In your travels, I'm sure that you've been to parishes that no longer use the bell. This, I think, is a great shame, because the bell calls our attention to the holiest part of the Mass: the very moment when the Eucharistic miracle occurs.

The history behind the "Sanctus" bell is a little murky. Most likely, the tradition came about for several reasons. One reason was that the Mass, for most of our history, was in Latin. Since it was sometimes difficult to follow the words, a bell was rung to remind the people when the Consecration occurred. Perhaps another reason was that the priest was facing the altar, and so it was not always easy to see what was going on. The ringing of a bell was another way of telling people what was happening.

After the Second Vatican Council (1962-1965), Mass could be said in the vernacular - or native language of the people. At the time, many priests thought that the bell was no longer necessary, because the people now could follow along. However, over the past 40 years, something most troubling has occurred. Today, a large number of Catholics have lost an understanding of what the Eucharist actually is - of the miracle that occurs at each and every Mass. The bread and wine become the Body, Blood, Soul and Divinity of Jesus Christ! So, today, many priests are returning to use of the bell, to remind people that something special is happening.

The bell is rung at the following times: once at the Elevation of the Host, once again at the Elevation of the chalice. Also, the bell may be rung at the Epiclesis (the calling down of the Holy Spirit) at the beginning of the Eucharistic Prayer. By the way, a good prayer to say as you gaze upon the Host and chalice is the prayer of St. Thomas the Apostle: *"My Lord and My God!"* ( If my lips are moving, that's what I'm saying!)

So, now you know all about the bell at Mass. If you're really nice to me, I might even let you ring it some time ... !

*Reflection Questions:*

1. *Is the bell rung in my parish?*
2. *Do I pay attention at Mass or does my mind wander?*
3. *Do I realize that a miracle takes place at every Mass?*

---

# The Use of Incense:
*It symbolizes our prayers rising to God.*

From time to time, incense is used at Mass. Actually, it is a very ancient form of worship, representing God's presence among His people. Symbolically, as the incense rises to the heavens, so our prayers rise up to God.

Even before the coming of Christ, incense was used by the Jewish people as they worshipped God. Our Jewish ancestors used incense during their temple worship as they offered sacrifices to the Lord. Remember, frankincense was one of the gifts of the Magi to the infant Jesus! This type of incense symbolized how Christ would be offered as a sacrifice to God for our sins. As incense is offered to God, so the Magi offered this gift to Christ, the Son of God. Even today, five grains of incense are placed in the wax of the Easter candle at the Easter vigil to represent the five wounds of Christ.

> **"It has a lovely fragrance and assists with making our Masses more prayerful and reverent."**

At Mass, incense is normally used at specific times. These include: the entrance procession; the beginning of Mass, with the blessing of the altar and the cross; the Gospel procession; the proclamation of the Gospel; the Offertory, for the blessing of the bread and the wine; and the Elevation of the Host and the chalice at the Consecration. Also, the priest and the people may be incensed at various times during the Mass. Incense also is used for blessing the body of the deceased during a funeral Mass. Outside of Mass, incense is often used during exposition, adoration and benediction of the Blessed Sacrament.

The incense that we use, locally, is of a very high quality. It is produced by monks and is made up of various fruits and spices. It is apparently hypo-allergenic which should cut down on coughing. It has a lovely fragrance and assists with making our Masses more prayerful and reverent. I hope you like it!

*Reflection Questions:*
   1. *How does the use of incense symbolize our prayers?*
   2. *Is the use of incense a new invention or is it ancient in origin?*
   3. *Have I seen (and smelled!) incense being used at Mass? What were my impressions?*

# The Latin Mass - Part I:
*Pope Benedict XVI has allowed more widespread celebration of this rite.*

On July 7, 2007, Pope Benedict XVI issued a document called *Summorum Pontificum*. In this letter, our Holy Father addressed the issue of the Mass and the manner in which it is to be celebrated. In short, the Pope allowed, under certain conditions, for any priest to celebrate the Mass using the form that is commonly known as the Tridentine or Traditional Latin Mass.

> "Over time, the language of the Mass became fixed in Latin, because Latin was the language...universally used."

To Catholics, the Mass is the source and summit of our Church's life - it is the highest and most perfect form of worship. The Mass is the celebration of the Holy Eucharist - the Body and Blood of Christ become really and truly present on the altar. If we are properly prepared and disposed, we may receive the Eucharist. Catholics have been celebrating the Mass since the very beginning of Christianity, because we have taken seriously Our Lord's words at the Last Supper, *"Do this in memory of me."* (Luke 22:19)

Throughout the history of the Church, the Mass has been celebrated in various languages and in various forms. The essence has remained the same:

readings from the Bible, a sermon, the Eucharistic Prayer from the Last Supper, Holy Communion, etc. However, the form or ordering of these common themes has changed over time.

In the early Church, the Mass was said in the language of the people. Over time, the language of the Mass became fixed in Latin, because Latin was the language of the Roman Empire and universally used. Gradually, the Latin language fell out of daily use among the people; however, it remained in use by the Church. Latin was seen as a universal (common) language for the universal Church. Indeed, even today, all official Church documents are first published in Latin and then translated into the particular language of a given people.

The form - or way that the Mass was said - became highly structured during the late 1500s. This was in response to the Protestant Revolution, as well as to curb errant priests from changing the way Mass was said. Thus, from the late 1500s until around 1970, the Catholic Mass was highly ritualized, strictly ordered, and said in the Latin language.

Between 1962 and 1965, the Second Vatican Council took place. During this major event in the life of the Church, all of the world's bishops gathered in Rome to discuss ways in which our Faith could be proclaimed anew to the modern world.

The first of 16 official documents that came from Vatican II dealt with the Mass. In this document, permission was given for the Mass to be said in a language other than Latin. Although it took some seven years to prepare, the new form of the Mass was presented in published form and began to be implemented in 1970. This is the most common ritual and form of the Mass used today.

# The Latin Mass - Part II:
*Requests were increasing for the return of this rite.*

Those of you who are a bit more seasoned by life might remember the changes that took place in Catholic worship in the late 1960s.

During that troubled and tumultuous time in our history, many people were overjoyed by the changes. Mass was now in English or in another language understandable to the people. The priest now faced the people and invited them into greater involvement in the Mass. Many felt that they were actively involved in worship - not just silent spectators.

> "Many Catholics had their Faith shaken when the silent, ritualized and mystical Mass they had known all of their lives gave way to a Mass which was...very different."

However, a significant number of Catholics felt greatly hurt by the abruptness and the substance of these changes. Many Catholics had their Faith shaken when the silent, ritualized and mystical Mass they had known all of their lives gave way to a Mass which was externally very, very different. Of course, the Mass in its essence remained the same. The prayers were the same, the order was mostly the same, the theology was the same. Yet, the external form had changed. There were as many people who were alarmed and hurt by this change, as there were people who were pleased to accept it.

Tragically, what followed the Holy Spirit-filled moment of the Second Vatican Council were several decades of unfaithful experimentation within the Church. Some in positions of authority in the Church tried out different forms of theology, alternate methods of catechesis, and "innovative" ways to celebrate Mass. It was the time, in some parishes, in which novelties such as cookies and Coca-Cola were being used instead of bread and wine for the Eucharist. Some Catholics became so angry with the Church during this period that they either stopped practicing their Faith altogether or formed break-away churches or sects that only celebrated the Mass in Latin. The Catholic Faith was cast into turmoil by all of this.

During the 1980s and 1990s, Pope John Paul II permitted, on a limited basis, the celebration of the Mass according to the 1962 Missal. (This was the last form of the Latin Tridentine Mass in use before the new Missal was issued in 1970.) With approval from bishops, rapidly growing communities of people who wanted the Tridentine Mass began to form parishes. The initial purpose of allowing these new parishes was to help heal divisions within the Church. As these communities grew, however, more and more requests were made for a widened permission for the Mass to be again celebrated according to the old form of the rite.

Now, Pope Benedict has granted this permission, formally declaring that there are two forms of the Mass in the Roman Rite. The "ordinary" form is the way in which we have been celebrating Mass these past few decades – the Mass of the 1970 Roman Missal in the vernacular language. The "extraordinary" form of the Mass is now the form of the Mass many of you remember from your childhood – the Mass of the 1962 Roman Missal in Latin.

# The Latin Mass - Part III:
*It may bring more young Catholics back to the Faith.*

Recently, I have heard from many people regarding Pope Benedict XVI's permission for any priest, under certain conditions, to celebrate the Traditional Latin Mass. Some people are elated. Others are angry.

I think that it is important to realize that the purpose of the Pope's teaching is to foster greater unity and peace within the Church. Indeed, there is a rich and diverse tradition of worship in the Church and one form is not better or worse than the other, as long as the Mass is said reverently.

> **"They (young families) love the Latin Mass because they say that it is more transcendent, more 'other-worldly' and better suited to prayer and contemplation than other forms."**

What was held in highest esteem for centuries could never be rejected by the Church! It is inaccurate to say that the Church is "going backwards." This is impossible! It also is inaccurate to say that the Church has finally rejected the Second Vatican Council. This also is impossible. What is happening is a rediscovery of our roots as we strive to worship God more perfectly.

As I mentioned at Mass recently, I do not know the Latin language well enough to celebrate the Mass according to the 1962 Missal. This form of Mass is more complicated and precise - it requires altar servers trained in Latin, music in Latin, and a congregation prepared and catechized to understand and accept this ritual. Finally, there must be a stable group from a parish that formally requests this Mass. I do hope to learn Latin soon so that I might prepare to say the Tridentine Mass. However, this is an involved process which will take time.

Finally, a personal note. I was born in 1975, some 10 years after the end of the Second Vatican Council and about five years after the new form of the Mass was introduced. I have no memory whatsoever of the way "things used to be" when Mass was in Latin. However, I do have a fresh memory of how my generation of Catholics was subjected to experimentation in theology, religious education and worship. Because of this, many in my generation no longer practice the Faith.

On the other hand, I have numerous friends who worship at Latin Masses around the country. Most are young families, blessed with many children, and they take their Catholic Faith very seriously. They love the Latin Mass because they say that it is more transcendent, more "other-worldly," and better suited to prayer and contemplation than other forms. This remains their opinion. However, if by Our Holy Father's permission, more and more young Catholics are brought back into the practice of the Faith and grow in love for the Eucharist, this will be a most wonderful thing.

It seems we must avoid two extremes in the life of our Church. The first is the notion that everything was better in the past – a kind of nostalgia which often is misguided. The second is the pride-filled rejection of everything that is old or different. Oftentimes, what is older has passed the test of time and has been shown to be of greater substance. Time will tell.

I am certain that you already have or soon will come in contact with a person who worships at a Latin Mass. I personally have experienced Mass in Latin numerous times and have found it to be quite beautiful. At the same time, I also believe that our "ordinary" rite of Mass, said in English, can be just as beautiful if done reverently.

There is a legitimate diversity of approved worship within the Church. Mass can legitimately be said in either the language of the people, or in the ancient and universal language of Latin. However, what must be avoided is elitism on either side or rejection of any approved rite. If you have the opportunity to go to a Latin Mass, take advantage of it. It's part of being Catholic! I invite you to rejoice with me about the richness and diversity of our Faith which has Jesus at its center and the Eucharist at its heart.

*Reflection Questions:*

1. *Why did the Pope officially declare the Latin Mass to be the extraordinary form of the Roman Rite?*
2. *Have you ever been to a Latin Mass? Why or why not?*
3. *Speak with a Catholic who attended the Latin Mass prior to Vatican II. What are his or her memories?*

# Mass Intentions:
## (OR, "No, Virginia, we don't BUY Masses!")

In many Catholic parishes, it is customary to read a name to the congregation before Mass, indicating that this is the person for whom the Mass is being offered. During the intercessions (before the Offertory of the Mass), the individual's name may be mentioned again. In the bulletin, the name may appear yet again, listed as "The Mass Intention." What is this all about and why is it important?

> "Having a Mass said for a given intention remains popular today. It is primarily an act of mercy towards the subject of the prayers."

The Mass is a participation within the one and infinite sacrifice of Christ on the Cross. The Mass is Holy Thursday, Good Friday and Easter Sunday all wrapped up into one! In the Mass, we are connected in the most powerful way possible with what Jesus did for us 2,000 years ago. The Mass is indeed the most powerful prayer on earth, for it is the very prayer of our salvation.

Early on, Christians who were aware of the significance of the Mass, began to offer the Mass for a given prayer intention. This intention certainly did not take the place of what the Mass represented. However, when added to what Christ did for us, it took on even greater meaning and power.

Having a Mass said for a given intention remains popular today. It is primarily an act of mercy towards the subject of the prayers. If the person is alive, the Mass intention is for his or her protection and growth in holiness. If the person has died, the Mass intention is for his or her completion of purification in Purgatory and speedy entrance into Heaven.

Reflecting this act of mercy, people in the early Church often gave alms when they asked for a Mass to be said. This money was for the support of the priest, as well as for the charitable works of the Church. The custom does not mean that someone is "buying a Mass" or being a corporate sponsor – *"This Mass is being brought to you by ... "* Rather, the giving of alms or money in connection with having a Mass said is a way of praying and sacrificing for the good of the subject of those prayers.

Today, the Church tightly regulates the suggested donation for a Mass intention, as well as how many Masses may be offered for a given donation. The bishops in our area have set the suggested donation for one Mass at $10. Again, this is a suggested donation – the giving of alms. Certainly, a Mass may be requested without money being offered. The prayer is much more important than the money! However, any money offered for the saying of Masses goes towards supporting the parish and the priests assigned to it.

Please consider having Masses said for your relatives who have died or for any other intention you might have. Wedding anniversaries, birthdays and private needs all are beautiful intentions for Masses. Let us join our prayers with the most perfect prayer of the Mass, and ask God's blessing upon those we love.

*Reflection Questions:*

1. *What is the purpose of a Mass intention?*

2. How is having a Mass said for the dead a merciful and kind act?

3. Is money required for a Mass to be said for a particular intention?

---

# Confirmation – The "Forgotten Sacrament":
*Do you REALLY know its purpose?*

Often, Confirmation has been called "the forgotten sacrament." It certainly is misunderstood today by many people. Some have a confused idea that Confirmation is about becoming an adult in the Faith. Others think that it is just another version of Baptism. Still others believe it to be a graduation from practicing the Faith! Let's see if we can clear up some of these misunderstandings surrounding this beautiful sacrament ...

> **"....Confirmation unites us more firmly with Christ, increases the gifts of the Holy Spirit within us, unites us more closely with the Church, and gives us the grace to share and defend our Faith..."**

The sacraments of Confirmation, Baptism and the Eucharist are known as the three sacraments of initiation. Traditionally, in the Roman Rite of the Church, Baptism was received first, followed by Confirmation, and finally by the Eucharist. With the Sacrament of Confirmation, the recipient receives a spiritual strengthening and bond of unity with the Holy Spirit. The fullness of the gifts of the Holy Spirit are poured out upon the person and he or she is prepared to live the Faith in a mature way. Confirmation often has been called the Sacrament of the Holy Spirit and it remains a powerful aid in the living out of our Christian lives.

In the early Church, the sacraments of Baptism and Confirmation were so closely tied that they were known as a "double sacrament." Typically, both sacraments were received at the same time and administered by the bishop. As the Church quickly grew, it became more difficult for the bishop to attend to all of the baptisms and confirmations. In the Western part of the Roman Empire, bishops soon gave priests the authority to baptize but retained the right to confirm at a later date. This emphasized the importance of early Baptism, while underlining the importance of unity with the bishop. In the Eastern part of the Roman Empire, bishops permitted priests to baptize and confirm, and they taught that both sacraments were to be received at the same time. This emphasized the importance of the unity of these two sacraments.

Even today, in Catholicism, the Sacrament of Confirmation is received at various times. In the West, Roman Catholics typically are confirmed by their bishop after reaching the age of reason. In the East, Eastern Rite Catholics are baptized, confirmed and receive the Sacrament of the Eucharist at the same time, in infancy.

Confirmation is not about graduating from the Church and it certainly is not about becoming an adult in the Church. Rather, Confirmation unites us more firmly with Christ, increases the gifts of the Holy Spirit within us, unites us more closely with the Church, and gives us the grace to share and defend our Faith in the world. Confirmation, like Baptism, is a permanent sacrament and imparts an indelible mark of Christ's presence on a person's soul. The age of Confirmation in the Western - or Roman Catholic - Church varies. In our country, it typically takes place between the ages of seven and 16. While some believe that its reception is better left to the later high school years, others believe that the graces of the sacrament are needed much earlier in life. The bishop of a given diocese decides when the sacrament may be properly received.

Confirmation is vitally important - and this is especially true today. In the time in which we live, the Faith is mocked and immorality and unbelief have become rampant. Thus, the graces of the Holy Spirit which are received at Confirmation are all the more important. If you already have been confirmed, ask God to re-inflame the graces and gifts that you were given at that important moment. If you have not yet been confirmed, strive to prepare well to receive this beautiful sacrament!

*Reflection Questions:*

1. What is the Sacrament of Confirmation?
2. Why is it important to receive this sacrament?
3. How does the reception of this sacrament vary throughout the universal Church?

# Marrying Outside of the Catholic Church:
*Forget Vegas. Skip the gazebo. Don't even think about the zoo!*

A sacrament is a sign, instituted by Christ and entrusted to His Church, to confer grace. In other words, the seven sacraments are seven special gifts by which and through which our Lord Jesus comes to us and blesses our lives.

The seven sacraments are: Baptism, Confirmation, Eucharist, Confession

Anointing of the Sick, Holy Orders and Marriage. As Catholics, we celebrate these seven sacraments in the Church – the community of believers gathered together in God's presence.

> "Sacraments are...celebrated in the context of the Catholic community – in the presence of the Blessed Sacrament, Jesus Himself."

Now, since Marriage is one of these sacraments, Catholics should celebrate it in the context of the parish community with a priest, deacon or bishop officiating. However, it seems today that many Catholics mistakenly believe that they can celebrate the Sacrament of Marriage outside of their parish community. Although a marriage on the beach in the Bahamas, at a wedding chapel in Las Vegas, underneath a gazebo, or in another Christian community without prior permission seems quite romantic, it is not a valid sacrament for Catholics.

Why is this? It seems rather harsh at first. After all, the couple is in love and they want to pledge their lives to each other. Does it really matter where such a wedding takes place? Isn't love enough? Does it matter who the minister of the wedding is?

To review, Catholic weddings normally take place within the setting of a parish community. The reason for this is that Marriage, as with all the sacraments, involves the Christian community. So, sacraments, including Marriage, are celebrated where the community can gather and support the individuals involved.

Ordinarily, you would not be baptized in your upstairs bathtub! Normally, you would not receive your First Communion at the zoo! Confirmation does not ordinarily take place on an airplane and Holy Orders does not usually take place at the beach! Marriage, like all of the sacraments, ordinarily takes place where the faithful can gather – at the parish church. The priest, deacon or bishop who witnesses the marriage acts as the official representative of the Church and ensures that those to be married are prepared to enter into such a sacramental union. Once again, Catholics believe that Marriage is a sacrament. Most other Christians do not.

Alas, love is blind – often, very blind! Our emotions can get carried away and sometimes lead us away from our Faith. This, although very common today, is always tragic. Catholics decide to marry outside the Church for all sorts of reasons. One person desires a more exotic location. Another was married before and his or her previous marriage was not annulled. Still another wants to keep peace with the non-Catholic party in the marriage and thus abandons the Faith.

The sad fact remains that such marriages entered into outside of the Church are sacramentally invalid for the Catholic. Objectively, this means that the couple is not married and thus, is living in sin. Such an invalid marriage prohibits a person from receiving Communion and closes his or her soul to much grace. Tragic spiritual consequences follow. Parents and grandparents, please urge your children to receive the Sacrament of Matrimony. This Catholic sacrament is not to be found at a wedding chapel in Las Vegas. It is not to be found on the windswept rocks of Door County, nor beneath a gazebo on a country estate. Sacraments are ordinarily celebrated in the context of the Catholic community – in the presence of the Blessed Sacrament, Jesus Himself.

For those of you in an invalid marriage, there is always hope. If you were married outside of the Catholic Church without permission, I urge you to contact a priest and he can arrange to have your marriage "convalidated," or blessed. For most couples, this is an easy process that might take a month or less to complete. The priest will assist you.

Marriage is tough; today more than ever, it is a most challenging vocation. As Catholics, don't we owe it to ourselves to begin married life on the right footing – in the presence of God and with the Christian community gathered together? Let us celebrate the sacraments and receive God's grace! Spiritually, we cannot live without it.

*Reflection Questions:*

1. *Why must Catholics marry in the Catholic Church?*
2. *Why does it matter?*
3. *Catholics (uniquely) believe marriage to be a sacrament. What does this mean?*

# Marriage Preparation:
*It's an investment in forever together.*

When I finally discerned that God was calling me to become a priest, I knew that the next step was for me to enter seminary. Seminary is a place of study and discernment for men who are called to the priesthood. I went to seminary for five years, studying, praying and preparing for the priesthood. Then, on a happy day in May of 2002, I was ordained a priest. I often tell this story to young couples during our first meeting for marriage preparation. In explaining the purpose behind marriage preparation, I tell them that I had to study and prepare for "my sacrament" for five years! How could I possibly prepare them for marriage in just a few meetings?

> **"In today's world, especially, marriage is difficult. This is all the more reason for a series of classes to prepare a couple for this lifetime of commitment."**

Marriage preparation sessions – or "pre-Cana" classes – are a necessary part of our sacramental life as Catholics. This is because Marriage is a sacrament! Like all of the sacraments, including First Holy Communion, we need to understand what we are receiving and prepare ourselves well to receive God's gift of grace. In today's world, especially, marriage is difficult. This is all the more reason for a series of classes to prepare a couple for this lifetime of commitment.

What happens during marriage preparation? The style of the program varies from parish to parish, but basically, marriage preparation begins with a meeting between the engaged couple and their priest. After getting to know each other, the priest formally interviews the two individuals separately and asks them a number of questions under oath. One example is, *"Are you entering into this marriage freely and without reservation?"* Another example might be, *"Are you hiding anything from your future spouse?"* Obviously, the answers to these questions have an impact on the future marriage. Perhaps the most important question that is asked is whether either one has been married before. The answer to this often dictates the direction of marriage preparation.

After that initial meeting, more meetings are held. The religious aspects of marriage are pointed out, children and child-raising are discussed, and family background and potential difficulties are explored. Often, the couple will go on a marriage retreat weekend with other engaged couples. The engaged couple also will take an assessment called the FOCCUS. This multi-question assessment raises issues such as, *"How many children do you desire to have?"* If their answers vary widely, more discussion is needed! Finally, the engaged couple usually meets with a married couple who will instruct them in Natural Family Planning (NFP). NFP is a beautiful and life-giving way to space childbirth, in cooperation with God's gift of life through married love.

All in all, marriage preparation typically involves between five and 10 meetings, depending upon the situation and the couple.

The benefits of marriage preparation should be obvious. It readies the couple for their life together, and potential problems are raised and investigated before the couple approach the altar. This is why a couple should speak with their priest a year before their wedding date, so that appropriate preparations can take place. This is far from being a series of hoops through which a couple must jump! Rather, marriage preparation is a way in which the Catholic Church reverences the Sacrament of Marriage and assists couples in making a lifelong commitment of love to each other.

Reflection Questions:
1. Having a successful and loving marriage is a real challenge today. Why do you think this is true?
2. Why is marriage preparation important?
3. "Marriage preparation begins in grade school." Reflect on this statement. What does it mean?

# The Blessing of Marriage:
*Focus on the best parts of this "cross-country trip."*

All too often, it seems, we must address the challenges and threats to marriage. Now, however, I would like to focus on the positive – and address how marvelous marriage is and what a blessing it has been for so many of you.

In its essence, marriage is beautiful because it is the union of two people who will help each other get to Heaven. Yes, Heaven! Perhaps through example, perhaps through patience, perhaps through trial – if someone is honest, his spouse is probably the most influential person in his life. If the spouse loves God, then she will bring him closer to God. Often, this is very subtle, but it is very real and very beautiful.

> "It seems that the secret to marriage is to be flexible enough to hold on to each other during the ups and downs of this trip called life."

I once heard marriage described as a cross-country trip on a train. When you look out the window, there is always different scenery. Sometimes, it is very beautiful, sometimes plain. Sometimes, you are on mountain tops; other times, you're crossing deserts. It seems that the secret to marriage is to be flexible enough to hold on to each other during the ups and downs of this trip called life. Those who have been married for many years will tell you that even though their wedding day was 50, 60, or even 70 years ago, they are more in love today than ever. Love grew and matured into a work of art.

Those of you who have had struggles in marriage – I urge you to persevere. Try to hold on – carry the cross the best you can. Those of you who have divorced or been abandoned by your spouse, try to pray for him or her and for your own healing. Those of you who have lost a spouse through death, thank God for the gift of your spouse! Ask for his or her prayers that together you might rejoice forever in Heaven. For those of you who are happily married, make sure that the routine of married life and the assumptions that come with it do not dull your love for each other. Remember to intentionally love your spouse every day.

As a Catholic priest who is not sacramentally married and who never will marry, I have a unique view of marriage. Although I have no experiential knowledge of it, I can say with all of my heart that those of you who are married have been given a unique blessing. Do not take it for granted! Thank God for this gift.

*Reflection Questions:*

1. *Think of a couple who have been married for many years. What is unique or special about their love?*
2. *"Marriage is a series of daily gifts of yourself to your spouse." What does this mean?*
3. *Marriage is the " primordial" or first sacrament. Reflect on what this means.*

# The Three Ranks of Holy Orders:
*(OR, just what IS a "Monsignor," anyway?)*

Many people have asked me recently what the difference is among deacons, priests and bishops. They also wonder, what are monsignors, archbishops and cardinals? So, I thought I would take a moment to explain the ranks of Holy Orders and their various roles within the Church.

Fundamentally, there are three ranks of the Sacrament of Holy Orders: deacon, priest and bishop. Even the Pope is a bishop - the Bishop of Rome. However, each of these ranks has a different role to play in the Church.

> "....there are three ranks of the Sacrament of Holy Orders: deacon, priest and bishop."

Deacons are ordained to serve. Deacons assist the parish community in its needs and they assist the priest at the altar. To understand the diaconate is to understand what it means to serve others. Deacons may celebrate the sacraments of Baptism and Marriage. Today, there are two kinds of deacons: permanent deacons and transitional deacons. Permanent deacons are ordained with the intention of remaining deacons for a life of service. Permanent deacons can be married and often serve in parish ministry. Transitional deacons are those who eventually are to be ordained as priests, but first must be ordained as deacons. I was a transitional deacon for six months before I became a priest in 2002.

Priests are ordained to offer the Sacrifice of the Mass and to shepherd the parish community. Priests are co-workers with the diocesan bishop, meaning that they work closely with the bishop in his ministry. Priests may administer the sacraments of Anointing of the Sick, Penance, Eucharist, Baptism, Marriage, and, with permission, Confirmation.

Bishops possess the fullness of the priesthood of Jesus Christ. They are the spiritual successors of the apostles and have the responsibility of governance over geographical areas of the Church called dioceses. Archbishops are bishops of older and larger dioceses in a given area. Bishops may celebrate all of the sacraments.

Now, in addition to these three categories, there are honorary "titles" that are granted to certain priests and bishops. I call them titles for lack of a better word, but they are not in any way insignificant. The title of "Monsignor" is granted to a priest who has served the Church well for many years. The title of "Cardinal" is granted to those priests or bishops who are given the privilege of taking part in the election of a future pope. Typically, cardinals are bishops of major archdioceses. The title of "Pope" is given to the bishop of Rome who has been chosen to lead the entire Church under the guidance of the Holy Spirit.

So, now you can impress your friends with your knowledge of ecclesiastical rank. Fundamentally, no matter the title, Holy Orders is all about serving Christ and His Church.

*Reflection Questions:*

1. *Have I ever met a deacon, priest, or bishop?*

2. *Why is service to the Church so important?*

3. *Is ministry about service or about power?*

# Religious Celibacy - Part I:
*You have an opinion about it? Do you even know what it is?*

One of the most misunderstood practices of the Catholic Faith today is that of religious celibacy. It seems that everyone has an opinion about it, yet very few people actually understand its purpose and meaning. In the next three articles, I will speak with you about celibacy – and explain why the Church still embraces this practice.

> "Celibacy...involves an individual freely giving up all of the goods of marriage in order to follow a specific vocation."

First of all, we need to be clear about what "celibacy" means. Celibacy should not be confused with "chastity." All Christians are called to remain chaste – integrating their own sexuality with their given vocation in life. Married people are to be chaste. Priests and sisters are to be chaste, as well. Celibacy, on the other hand, involves an individual freely giving up all of the goods of marriage in order to follow a specific vocation. In most cases, the life of celibacy involves not marrying.

To be sure, living the celibate lifestyle is a specific calling. Those who are called to it are in no way better or holier than those who are called to be married. Rather, it is another way to serve Our Lord and to build up His Church.

Since most of today's controversy surrounding celibacy involves priests not marrying, I will focus on this issue. Clerical celibacy is an ancient custom of the Church; indeed it can be traced back to Jesus and his 12 apostles. It is worth noting that Our Lord Jesus was not married and that a priest is called to act in His person – to be His representative to the people.

Some of the 12 apostles were indeed married, at one time. We read about St. Peter having a mother-in-law (Mark 1:29-31) and other passages speak about bishops being married only once (1 Timothy 3:2-7). So, there were married clergy in the early Church.

However, we also see quite clearly that there was a general preference that the clergy be unmarried. Some scriptural passages that reflect this are Matthew 19:10-12, Luke 18:28-30, and 1 Corinthians 7:32-34. Many Church historians believe that, although several of the apostles and early deacons, priests, and other bishops of the Church were married, they freely and consensually separated from their wives and children so that they could focus more completely on their ministry.

As early as 305 A.D., at the Spanish Church Council of Elvira, celibacy was spoken of as mandatory for those to be ordained. Despite this and various other Church pronouncements, celibacy still was incompletely practiced by the clergy. From time to time, abuses set in, with great scandal to the faithful. It was Pope Gregory VII (c. 1080) who strongly advocated clerical celibacy. From that time until today, the practice of priestly celibacy has been more consistently practiced.

# Religious Celibacy - Part II:
## *A priest ALREADY is married - to the Church!*

The question remains, WHY don't Catholic priests marry - why are they celibate? First of all, speaking as one who has recently taken this vow, I can honestly tell you that I have freely chosen this life. Nobody forced me to be celibate! The Church, in her wisdom, has required celibacy for those ordained as priests or bishops, for several compelling reasons.

> "If, at the same time, (a priest) were married to a woman, the many important duties and responsibilities that he would have would be conflicted."

First and foremost, the priest is spiritually married to the Church. I cannot stress this point enough! So, in a very real way, the priest already is married - his spouse, his bride, is the Church. As we often read in the Bible, Jesus speaks about Himself as bridegroom and the Church as His bride. Think about all of those parables that He used that spoke about brides and bridegrooms. St. Paul builds upon this, by also speaking about Christ as bridegroom and the Church as His beloved bride (Ephesians 5:21-33).

So, just as a husband and wife become one in marriage, so Christ and His Church are one. The two have become one body! Now, a priest acts in the person of Christ; a priest is Christ's representative on earth. So, a priest who acts in Christ's place and who represents Christ in the sacraments is in fact the bridegroom to Christ's bride, the Church. Thus, a priest is married to the Church! If, at the same time, he were married to a woman, the many important duties and responsibilities that he would have would be conflicted. Whom should he serve, his bride the Church or his bride from the Sacrament of Marriage? A terrible tension would occur, often with tragic results. It is worth noting that there is a very high divorce rate among ministers of other Christian communities. Why? It is very difficult to be committed to two marriages at the same time!

Another good reason for priestly celibacy is its witness to the world. What is the god that is most worshipped today? By watching television or visiting many stores, we see quite clearly that lust or unbridled sexuality is what is most worshipped. Is it any wonder, then, why celibacy is so ridiculed? Indeed, celibacy flies in the face of everything that our secular culture holds to be good and true. However, herein lies a powerful witness to our world!

The celibate person reflects Jesus' words from Matthew 28:23-33, noting that people do not marry in Heaven nor at the Resurrection of the Dead at the end of the world. In other words, the life of celibacy does not point simply to this world, but rather it points beyond - to Heaven and to the fulfillment of the Kingdom of God.

---

# Religious Celibacy - Part III:
## Arguments against it are flawed. It's a "powerful" witness.

People give many reasons why priests should NOT be celibate. These reasons tend to fall into three categories. The first is a presumed shortage of priests. The second is a presumed ignorance among priests of the experiences of the married life. The third is a belief that having a small pool of candidates for the priesthood is unhealthy.

> "....among the various Christian churches and communities around the world who allow clergy to marry, there also is an increasing shortage..."

Taking these concerns in order, we first turn to the notion that celibacy keeps potential young men away from choosing the priesthood as a way of life. Thus, some contend, a shortage occurs in priestly vocations. Herein lies the problem with this opinion: we do not truly choose our vocation in life. In the end, God calls us! While it is true that many find celibacy to be a terrible burden and are not interested in the priesthood because of it, this reaction often stems from immaturity or a lack of openness to God's Will.

However, God still calls us to a specific vocation in life. Are we listening? It must be said that among the various Christian churches and communities around the world who allow clergy to marry, there also is an increasing shortage of clergy.

The second concern about celibacy is that priests are generally ignorant of the married life. The objection is worded as follows: *"How can Father help me with my marriage if he isn't married himself and knows nothing about it?"* Experience is an excellent teacher, to be sure. However, I presume that a person with heart disease would not specifically search out a heart surgeon who has had a heart attack because of his or her "experience." This is faulty reasoning. It is true that most priests do not experientially know the inner workings of marriage. However, perhaps this actually helps them to be more objective.

The third concern is that celibacy reduces the potential pool of priesthood candidates to an unhealthy level. This topic usually revolves around the recent tragedy involving sexual abuse of children by some clergy. However, it is significant to note that the largest number of abuse perpetrators are, in fact, married persons. Typically, they are parents. It is important to remember, also, that God does the choosing of candidates and presumably he is not affected by "small pools" of people. In the end, this concern is unwarranted.

By the way, did you know that there are married priests? In the many Orthodox churches, priests are married. Eastern Rite Catholic priests also may be married. Indeed, in our own Roman Catholic Church, there are a few married priests. These are mostly converts from the Lutheran or Episcopalian churches who had served as ministers in those communities before becoming Catholic. By special permission from the Pope, they were later ordained as Catholic priests. However, these individuals are typically placed in ministry outside of parishes, so that they can care for their families.

I have met several of these men and they are remarkable not only in their love for Christ and His Church, but also in their complete support for clerical celibacy. They agree wholeheartedly with the Church's discipline and they see the wisdom in it! In all of the above cases, if a priest's wife should die, he must then remain celibate for life. He cannot remarry. In this, we see the universal and ancient preference for celibacy for priests.

Celibacy remains a discipline of our Church. Although it has deep roots and great spiritual meaning, it is not a doctrine or a dogma of the Faith. It could be changed or relaxed in the future. However, I do not see it changing in any way in the future. The value of its witness today is too powerful to lose.

It is my hope that this article will assist many of you in understanding why celibacy exists in our Church and why many have chosen to live it. Whereas married people give themselves as gifts to each other, a priest gives himself completely as a gift to Christ's people - the Church. The more I see the Church as my spouse and all of you as my spiritual children, the greater joy I have in living out my vocation as a priest.

*Reflection Questions:*

1. *What is celibacy and what does it mean for Catholic priests?*

2. *How do we respond to common objections to celibacy?*

3. *How are the priesthood and married life similar?*

# The Ordination of Women – Part I:
*Men and women are not "interchangeable."*

The Church is the Body of Christ. Christ is the Head of His Church and all of its members make up this one Body. As a body cannot be separated from its head, so Christ and His Church are one - they cannot be separated. So, in a very real way, we all are united with Christ, and, from our Baptism, we become members of His Body, the Church.

> "Even though each of us has a different role to play, we all have equal dignity and importance under Christ our Head."

Now, just as our human bodies have different organs and parts that function differently, so do we as members of the Body of Christ have different roles to play in the Church. No one part of the human body is more important than the others - all have a role to play. So, too, it is in the Church. Even though each of us has a different role to play, we all have equal dignity and importance under Christ our Head.

With this in mind, in the next few articles I will be discussing with you a most important issue. It is an issue which divides many people and has brought disunity to our Church. It is, furthermore, an issue which must be understood properly and explained sensitively. I would like to address the issue of women's ordination.

It must be said from the outset that women and men are equal in dignity. Christ came to this earth, suffered, died and rose again, for both men and women. He is the Savior of all! Men are in no way better than women, and women are in no way better than men. There are very real differences between the sexes to be sure - this is obvious to even the most casual of observers. Furthermore, it is true that men and women fulfill different roles in society. Some of these roles are culturally conditioned while others are deeply rooted in biology. However, it must be maintained that there is a complementarity between the sexes.

One of the errors of today's culture is the presumption that men and women are the same in all ways and hence, interchangeable; that there is no distinction between them. Sadly, this has led to great confusion over the roles of men and women in society and especially in family life. For example, there is the plain biological fact that a man cannot be a mother. Its corollary is that a woman can never be a father.

It is unfortunate that the sin of sexism has long plagued our society, often perpetrated by men against women. Any such discrimination against women should be rejected by Christians. Men and women are equal in dignity before

God.

However, the roles of men and women remain different. This is especially obvious within the family, and it is manifested within the family of the Church. There are different roles within the Church - the Body of Christ. Within the Church, there are vocations to the married life, the single life and the religious life. We all are called to a particular state in life.

The accusation has been made that the Catholic Church discriminates against women because it will not ordain them as priests. This accusation is quite troubling, for, if it is true, such discrimination would be a serious sin. If the Church has indeed been in error on this issue for almost 2,000 years, is it not possible that the Church is wrong about other things? What about the Divinity of Christ, the existence of the Holy Trinity, or the composition of the Bible? We need to better understand the issue of women's ordination, to understand the very nature and authority of the Church.

# The Ordination of Women - Part II:
*A priest acts in the place of Christ, the Bridegroom.*

Holy Orders is one of the seven sacraments. This sacrament is divided into three parts or roles. The first role is that of a deacon, the second is that of a priest, the third is that of a bishop.

Since all of the sacraments are gifts from God, the Church has a right and duty to administer these sacraments. Now, our Church teaches that the ordination to the ministerial priesthood is reserved to men alone. There are several reasons that might help us to understand this teaching more clearly.

> "Jesus was anything but a conformist – and yet he still chose 12 men to be His apostles...the Catholic Church has followed His example."

First of all, the Church is bound to follow the example of Jesus Christ who chose 12 men as his first apostles. These apostles were the first bishops and they, in turn, ordained other men to serve as bishops, priests and deacons. These men ordained still more men to serve in ministry, etc. From the very beginning of the Church until the present time, only men have been ordained.

Some may say that Christ's decision to choose only men as his 12 apostles was conditioned by the culture of the time. However, this is unsound reasoning. Yes, it is true that Our Lord came to this earth in a particular time and place and in a culture that was unique. However, being Divine, He was incapable of being negatively influenced by such a culture - especially if it would lead to the sin of discrimination. To say that Jesus discriminated or was influenced by a sexist culture would raise the logical question - *"How else was He influenced? Perhaps all of His teachings are culturally conditioned and we need not follow any of them?"*

It must be noted that Christ was in fact quite counter-cultural. He spoke with women, he affirmed their dignity, and many women were His followers. A great appeal of early Christianity was its respect for the dignity of women. Jesus was anything but a conformist - and yet, He chose 12 men to be His apostles. The Church Christ founded, the Catholic Church, has followed His example.

Another way of looking at this issue is to reflect on how Christ speaks of Himself as the Bridegroom and His Church as His bride. There are numerous references in parables and in Paul's letters (Ephesians 5), in which Christ is portrayed in this manner. You see, the theology of the priesthood is that a priest acts "in persona Christi" - or in the person of Christ. In other words, an ordained Catholic priest acts in Christ's place - takes His place if you will.

Notice that when a priest says Mass, he does not say, *"Take this all of you and eat it, this is **Christ's** Body."* No, he says *"This is **MY** Body."* The priest does not say in Confession, *"**Christ** absolves you from your sins,"* but rather, *"**I** absolve you from your sins."* In other words, Christ is acting through the priest at that very moment.

You'll notice that Christ clearly refers to Himself as the Bridegroom and His Church as His bride. As we've discussed, priests act in the person of Christ the Head. Hence, by this logic, priests must be male, because a bridegroom must be male. Also, the Church, as bride, is seen as female. Just as Christ gave His life for the Church, so, too, a priest gives his life for his bride, Christ's bride, the Church. (Another reason why priests do not marry ... )

If a woman were ordained a priest, we would have an unacceptable situation of a bride giving herself to a bride. In order to maintain the sacred distinction of the roles, only a man can be a priest because only a man can fulfill the role of bridegroom to the Church.

# The Ordination of Women – Part III:
*Pope John Paul II made it clear. The matter is closed.*

In Baptism, we all were baptized into what is called a *universal* priesthood – a priesthood of all believers. As men and women who follow Christ, we all are rightly called priest, prophet and king. We are priestly because of our prayers of intercession and the sacrifices we make for others. We are called prophets because of our sharing of the Word of God with the world around us. We also are called kings because of our cooperation in the ministry of the life of the Church.

> "While the teaching of the Church is clear, every effort must be made to reverence the contribution of women in the life of the Church."

However, there also is another priesthood called the *ministerial* priesthood. This is the priesthood of the Sacrament of Holy Orders. As the Second Vatican Council clearly taught, *"Although the ministerial priesthood and the universal priesthood are ordered to one another they differ essentially and not solely in degree."* (Lumen Gentium 10) So, there is a difference. The universal priesthood is exercised in the living of the Christian life. The ministerial priesthood is exercised by a special sacrament in service to the universal priesthood. One is not better than the other, and both are needed to make up the Body of Christ.

The teaching that priestly ordination is to be reserved to men alone has been preserved by the constant and universal Sacred Tradition of the Church. It has been firmly taught by the Church for the past 2,000 years. Only in recent times, has there arisen large-scale dissent from this teaching. In order to settle this question and restore unity to the Church, Pope John Paul II, in 1994, wrote the Apostolic Letter, "Ordinatio Sacerdotalis" (Reserving Priestly Ordination to Men Alone). The language that the Pope used was very important and I will repeat it here:

*"Wherefore, in order that all doubt may be removed regarding a matter of great importance, a matter which pertains to the Church's divine constitution itself, in virtue of my ministry of confirming the brethren I declare that the Church has no authority whatsoever to confer priestly ordination on women and that this judgment is to be definitively held by all the Church's Faithful."*

The language used by the Pope in this teaching was very formal and very serious. The Pope, as the successor of St. Peter and the chief shepherd of the Church on Earth, has now settled this issue. In fact, further reflection leads many to see this as an exercise of infallibility according to the Ordinary Magisterium of the Church (Lumen Gentium 25). In other words, the matter is closed.

It is very important that we now strive towards unity in the Church. It is true that certain women feel in some way called to the priesthood. Many others feel that they are unjustly persecuted by not being ordained. While the teaching of the Church is clear, every effort must be made to reverence the contribution of women in the life of the Church. I can honestly say that I could not shepherd my parishes without the able assistance of numerous women who love Our Lord deeply.

It seems that, as a Church, we must move beyond seeing ministry as power to seeing ministry as service. We look to Mary, the Mother of God. She who had no sin, she who was blessed and chosen above all women to be Christ's Mother, she who was most present and who knew the apostles personally, was not chosen to be a priest!

The Church remains the Body of Christ. Each of us has a different role to play in the Church, and each of these roles has a different purpose, with an equal dignity. Let us pray that we might fulfill our own role well and thus grow in holiness.

*Reflection Questions:*

1. *Why can only men be ordained as Catholic priests?*
2. *Is this unjust discrimination against women? Why not?*
3. *Why is the role of the Pope so important for our unity as Catholics?*

---

# The Ordination of a Bishop:
*He becomes a successor to the Apostles.*

Recently, I had the opportunity to witness the ordination of a bishop. The pastor of my home parish in Milwaukee, Father William Callahan, was named by Pope Benedict XVI to be the auxiliary bishop of the Archdiocese of Milwaukee. Bishop Callahan is a kind and holy man, and able administrator, and he has served God and the Church well in his new responsibilities.

Bishops are the spiritual successors to the Apostles. Their role in the Church includes teaching, sanctifying and governing. Bishops are the authentic teachers of the Faith in their given dioceses or jurisdictions. They have the right and mandate to teach in the name of the Church, while at the same time maintaining unity with the Pope. Bishops also can celebrate all seven of the sacraments for the good and sanctity of the faithful. Finally, bishops are assigned the responsibility of leading and shepherding the flock of Christ. Like Jesus, they are called not to be served, but to serve.

> "The ring symbolizes his commitment to a particular diocese. The miter (hat) and crosier (staff) symbolize the bishop's role as chief shepherd of the flock."

Men who are ordained bishops receive the fullness of the Sacrament of Holy Orders. Within the sacrament, as you may recall, there are three degrees: deacon, priest and bishop. Those who are ordained to the episcopate (who become bishops) sometimes are assigned by the Pope as "Ordinaries" - or chief bishops - of a given diocese. Other men are appointed as "Auxiliary" bishops and become assistant bishops to the Ordinary Bishop of a given diocese. Finally, some bishops are appointed as "Coadjutor" bishops with the right of succession to a particular diocese when the current bishop retires. My friend was ordained an Auxiliary bishop to assist the Archbishop of Milwaukee in the administration of the Archdiocese.

What qualities does the Church seek in a candidate to be bishop? First of all, the man must be outstanding in holiness, that is, he must have a strong Faith, good morals, piety, and zeal for souls. He also must be wise, prudent, virtuous and possess the natural gifts necessary to allow him to succeed in the office. The candidate must be held in good esteem by both the laity and the clergy and be at least 35 years of age. He must be ordained a priest and have at least five years of experience. He must hold a doctorate or another similar degree in theology - or at least be truly knowledgeable in theology.

Practically speaking, men who have been priests for 25 years and have had great and varied experience in teaching and administration are good candidates for the office of bishop. In the end, it is the Holy Spirit working through the Church who chooses those to be ordained bishops.

The ordination of a bishop takes place in the context of a Mass, typically in the cathedral church of a given diocese. Most importantly, three bishops must be on hand to perform the ordination. This ensures obedience to the Pope and prevents illegitimate ordinations. An official letter from the Pope is read aloud by the Papal Ambassador. The ordaining bishops then ask the candidate a number of questions and he states that he is willing to undertake the office of bishop.

After this, the candidate prostrates himself while the Litany of Saints is sung. Then, the three bishops lay hands on the candidate's head, representing the imparting of the gifts of the Holy Spirit. The Book of the Gospels is held over the kneeling candidate like a roof, while the Prayer of Consecration is read. The head of the newly ordained bishop is anointed with the Oil of Chrism. The Book of the Gospels is presented to the new bishop and he is invested with a ring, a miter and a crosier. The ring symbolizes his commitment to a particular diocese. The miter (hat) and crosier (staff) symbolize the bishop's role as chief shepherd of the flock. Lastly, the newly ordained bishop is led to his cathedra (chair) and is seated.

Let us pray for Bishop William Callahan and all of the bishops of the world that they will be faithful shepherds.

*Reflection Questions:*

   1. *What are some of the qualities that a man must have to become a bishop?*

   2. *Explain the ordination of a bishop and what takes place at the ceremony.*

   3. *"Being a bishop is a very lonely position." Reflect on what this means.*

# The Selection of a Pope:
*Here's what happens in the secret conclave ...*

In 2005, Joseph Cardinal Ratzinger was chosen by God to be our pope. He selected the name of Benedict XVI. The effect that he is having on our Church today is incalculable. Indeed, we are living in the time of a giant - a man who loves the Lord Jesus and His Church most intensely.

Pope Benedict was selected by a vote of his fellow cardinals to fill the shoes of Pope John Paul II - another holy and venerable man whom many believe should be called, "The Great." The succession followed an orderly and time-tested protocol, after the death of John Paul II.

> **"We must remember that the election of a pope is a divine – and human – event."**

It is important for us to understand how a new pope is chosen to lead our Church. We must remember that the election of a pope is a divine – and human – event.

As is the custom, when John Paul II died, the Church mourned for a period of 15 days. During this time, preparations were made for a funeral as well as for the election of the new pope. After the days of mourning, the cardinals of the Church gathered at the Vatican and entered into a secret locked meeting called a "conclave." The reason for the secrecy is to prevent outside influences or intrigues.

Pope Benedict XVI was chosen by the cardinals of the Church acting as a council of electors. (There are about 120 cardinals who are eligible to vote.) During the conclave, the cardinals were bound by a solemn oath of secrecy. They could not give or receive information through contact with the outside world. No television, radio, magazines, telephones or computers were allowed.

Voting began with one ballot on the first day. More ballots were cast the next day. Cardinals were asked to write the name of the candidate they choose on the ballot under the words, "I Elect as Supreme Pontiff ... ". (Usually, candidates for the next pope are chosen from among the cardinals of the Church, but, in reality, any Catholic man in good standing could be elected.)

Joseph Cardinal Ratzinger was elected in the fourth ballot on the second day, by a two-thirds majority. After the ballots were cast and counted, they were burned. After the first three ballots, the smoke that arose from the Sistine Chapel chimney was black, indicating that no pope had been chosen. After the fourth ballot, however, the smoke that rose from the chimney was white, and the world rejoiced because the Church had a new pope.

Once a two-thirds majority was reached, Cardinal Ratzinger was approached and asked if he accepted the decision. As soon as he said, "I accept," he became the new pope. Immediately upon accepting, the Pope was asked what name he had chosen for himself. Usually this is a saint's name, such as Benedict. All of the cardinals in attendance pledged their obedience to him and he was vested in new, white papal vestments. Then, Pope Benedict XVI went to the balcony overlooking St. Peter's Square and greeted the many people present - as well as the millions watching TV from around the world.

Remember that Christ is the Good Shepherd who never leaves His flock untended. We always will have a Holy Father - on this earth AND in Heaven to watch over the Catholic Church!

*Reflection Questions:*

1. *What do I know about our current Pope?*
2. *Do I pray for the Pope and his intentions?*
3. *The Pope is a visible sign of our unity as Catholics. Why is this important?*

# The "Great" Popes – St. Leo and St. Gregory:
*Will Pope John Paul II receive this title, too?*

Recently, we have begun hearing Pope John Paul II referred to with the added title of, "The Great." Indeed, this is a title which first gains ground popularly and only then is ratified by the Church. Only two other popes in history have been given the title of, "The Great." They are Pope St. Leo and Pope St. Gregory.

Let's learn a bit more about these two great men (sorry, I couldn't resist saying that) who have had such an impact on our Church, as well as on Western culture:

> "....in their holiness of life, in their teaching and in their steadfastness in faith, they remind us very much of our deceased Holy Father."

Pope Leo the Great guided the Church from 440 until 461. From early on in his life, he was a strong supporter of the Catholic Faith. He was born in Rome and was serving there as a deacon when he was elected pope. During his 21 years as pope, his primary goal was to assist all dioceses and bishops to recognize the universal authority of the pope as the successor of St. Peter.

Leo's strength and steadfastness, along with his outgoing personality, prompted the Roman Emperor, Valentinian, to give him full jurisdiction over the Western part of Europe. In addition to Church matters, Leo also aided and protected Western culture. When Attila the Hun was poised to sack Italy, the Pope bravely met him face to face and convinced him to retreat. (No small feat!)

Leo the Great's surviving writings include 143 letters and 96 homilies. Because of his steadfastness in assisting the Church and the world, soon after his death he was given the title, "The Great."

Pope Gregory the Great shepherded the Church from 590 until 604. He was the son of a Roman senator and a member of a noble family. His early adult life was filled with a very promising secular career. However, after a spiritual conversion, he used his large inheritance to establish monasteries all over Europe.

Eventually, Gregory became a monk and was ordained a deacon in 578. Such was his reputation, that he was unanimously elected pope in 590. He protested vigorously, even begging the Emperor to intercede. He became pope under protest and referred to himself ever afterwards as the "servant of the servants of God." This very same title is used by the Pope today.

When Gregory became pope, much of Italy was in ruins. He stepped into the political vacuum and aided the citizens of Italy with civil and charitable activities. He is credited with introducing various prayer forms in the Church. In addition, he introduced a new form of liturgical music that came to be known as Gregorian chant. He wrote more than 850 letters and numerous theological books, many of which survive today. Because of his accomplishments and his many physical sufferings, he was known for his great holiness of life. At his death, he was immediately declared a saint and soon received the title, "The Great."

We see in the lives of these two great shepherds a certain similarity to John Paul II. Indeed, in their holiness of life, in their teaching and in their steadfastness in faith, they remind us very much of our deceased Holy Father.

As we look to the future, we can be certain that the Holy Spirit will guide our Church. We always will be thankful for the gift of the Spirit that was John Paul The Great.

*Reflection Questions:*

1. What made Pope Gregory and Pope Leo "great"?
2. What is your fondest memory of Pope John Paul II?
3. God never abandons His Church. Give examples of this.

# Anointing of the Sick:
*Do you know when to call a priest? (Hint: not for that stubbed toe!)*

I would like to take this opportunity to speak about a powerful, but often-forgotten sacrament. This is Anointing of the Sick. This sacrament is so very beautiful and life-changing, but sadly, it is frequently overlooked.

First of all, let's get the name of the sacrament straight. It is called, "Anointing of the Sick." It was formerly called, "Extreme Unction," but this title is no longer officially used. Many times, it is incorrectly called the "Last Rites" – but the last rites are actually three sacraments given in quick succession to a dying person: Confession, then Eucharist, and finally Anointing of the Sick. I hope this clears things up a bit!

> "This sacrament...help(s) us to carry the cross of any serious illness, or infirmity due to old age, so that we won't give up on God or on our Faith."

What is the purpose of Anointing of the Sick? The purpose of this sacrament is spiritual healing - spiritual strengthening. Physical healing from disease is NOT the primary purpose of the sacrament. True, many times the sacrament brings about an improvement in health; but this is primarily a sacrament for the soul, not the body. During any serious illness, we might be tempted to despair – to give up on God. This would be a great tragedy and a sin. This sacrament is intended to help us to carry the cross of any serious illness, or infirmity due to old age, so that we won't give up on God or on our Faith.

When is Anointing of the Sick to be received? Who may receive it? It is to be received when a person is seriously ill to the point where death becomes a possibility, and also when a person is frail due to old age. There are two extremes to be avoided here. One extreme is to receive the sacrament only when death is imminent. This is very often too late! The other extreme is to receive the sacrament when we have a minor problem such as a hangnail or a stubbed toe. This would be an abuse of the sacrament. However, when a person is seriously ill or a serious operation is needed, or when a person becomes frail due to old age, the sacrament should be received.

I cannot stress this enough! Family members must call a priest when a loved one becomes seriously ill. We need to know! Sadly, we are not (yet) able to read your minds! We don't know about your sick loved ones unless someone tells us. Often, there are priests working in hospitals who will be able to administer the sacrament if a parish priest is unable to come right away. However, you must ask! Don't wait until it's too late. You'll be glad you didn't. What a powerful sacrament!

*Reflection Questions:*

1. *Have I ever been anointed?*
2. *Do I know someone who has been healed by this sacrament?*
3. *Read James 5:13-15. Does this sound familiar?*

# Stipends for The Celebration of The Sacraments:
*This isn't wrong. It's a matter of charity!*

From time to time, I receive inquiries about "buying a Mass" or "paying for" a baptism or marriage ceremony. Most of the time, these questions are innocent. However, they remind me that we need to understand the custom of paying stipends or "stole fees" - and why the Church makes such recommendations.

The Catholic Church is the only truly universal church in that it encompasses the entire world, with its 1.2 billion members. The Church also is ancient, founded by Our Lord Jesus Christ Himself and first led by St. Peter, the first pope. Because the Church is so large - in size, scope and history - there are customs and activities that might make sense in one culture, time and place, and not in another. An example of this could be stipends and stole fees paid for Masses or sacraments.

> **"....in many parts of the world, these are the ONLY sources of support for a priest...In our country ... (any fee) that is paid usually goes directly to the parish and not to the priest."**

The universal law of the Church states that a stipend for the priest is recommended when he celebrates Mass for a given intention, and a stole fee for the priest is recommended when he celebrates another sacrament such as Baptism, Marriage, or a funeral Mass.

As Americans, this might strike us as rather odd. Doesn't a priest receive a salary already? Why is the Church "charging" for sacraments? Isn't this rather unseemly? The reason for stole fees and Mass stipends is this: in many parts of the world, these are the ONLY sources of support for a priest. He does not receive a salary, but lives only from these sources of income. In our country, priests do receive salaries and thus, any stipend or stole fee that is paid usually goes directly to the parish and not to the priest.

This is in contrast to "simony," the sinful and despicable practice of charging for a sacrament. The request for Mass stipends and stole fees to be paid is not simony, but rather a recommendation for the support of the Church. It is charity. If someone is unable to give the requested amount, the sacrament still will be celebrated. The donation always is optional and never required. In our country, the bishops of a given region set the suggested amount for stipends and stole fees. The current, suggested donation amount should be somewhere around:

$10 for a Mass intention

$10 for a Baptism

$50 for a Funeral

$75 for a Wedding

This amount, when given, usually goes to the parish for its support. If an individual wishes to give more than the suggested donation, the difference may go to the priest as a gift.

I realize that the subjects of money and sacraments don't mix very well. I rarely speak about this. However, many people have asked, so I must address this matter. In the end, we support the Church as it carries out the work of God in the world. Ultimately, what matters most is our relationship with God and the grace which He gives us. This is a blessing that no money can buy!

*Reflection Questions:*

1. *Why does the Church recommend that stipends and stole fees be given for the celebration of sacraments?*
2. *Will the Church deny a sacrament if someone cannot pay the recommended amount?*
3. *How does the practice of Church support for priests in our country differ from the practice of Church support for priests in other countries?*

# Section III
## Christian Morality – The Faith Lived

# Creation as The Foundation of Human Sexuality:
*Love people for WHO they are, not WHAT they are!*

I hope that, by now, you know that I take my role as a priest and spiritual father very seriously. Part of the role of being a spiritual father, like the role of any parent, is to speak with the family about pitfalls that lie ahead and to give firm guidance on how to avoid these dangers. Sometimes, difficult issues must be addressed. Sometimes, correction and discipline must lovingly be given.

> "The body is created by God and hence, is good. Our sexuality, be it male or female, is a gift from God."

On the following pages, I will address various controversial issues that impact our Catholic Faith. For the most part, the issues addressed will deal with human sexuality and morality. These will be issues on which there is a great deal of confusion among Christians today. The topics covered would not always be appropriate for a general Sunday homily.

*"God created man in His own image; in the divine image He created him; male and female He created them."* (Genesis 1:27) This passage from Genesis contains a powerful message: God created us! Thus, God must have created us to accomplish some great task. He does not do things without a reason. Furthermore, because we were created, we must indeed be good. God does not create junk!

Then, the passage goes further - in His own divine image we were created. This means that we are mirrors, although imperfect, of what God must be like. Imagine - we were created by God and reflect His Divinity. What an honor and blessing we possess as human beings! Male and female He created us. God didn't just create some generic human form. He created us in two specific, complementary and beautiful forms of male and female.

I think that if we keep this scriptural passage in mind when we study the Church's views on morality - especially sexual morality - we will understand its teachings more clearly.

What then is the Church's view on human sexuality? Above all, it is positive! The body is created by God and hence, is good. Our sexuality, be it male or female, is a gift from God.

Sometimes, however, we can abuse this gift. Instead of treating each other with respect, we use each other as objects. So often, we fail to see each other as brothers or sisters. This, my friends, is at the core of every sexual sin - it is treating the other person as a thing. Put another way, when we truly love people, we love them for *who* they are, not for *what* they are. This is an important distinction to make. Please remember it!

*Reflection Questions:*

1. *Is it difficult to be a faithful Catholic today? What are the challenges?*

2. *Why is sexual morality so often controversial?*

3. *Do I treat other people as objects? Do I love them for who they are, not for what they are?*

# Sexuality as A Gift From God - Introduction to Human Morality:
*Should the Church "get out of my bedroom?"*

Most of the controversial moral subjects in our culture today have something to do with human sexuality. This may be surprising to some; indeed it is surprising to me. Certainly, there is MORE to human morality than just this one topic! However, the amount of confusion surrounding sexual morality today – especially among Catholics – leads me to focus my articles around these issues.

> "....the Church has an obligation, as the Body of Christ, to step in and to object to the destruction and perversion of this creative act."

First of all, our Catholic Faith has something important to say about each of these sexual moral issues in light of the teachings of Jesus Christ. However, people are not always anxious to be enlightened by the Church! In fact, some may unfairly label the Church as anti-sex or even obsessed with human sexuality.

Negative reaction to the teachings of our Church usually takes the form of, "The Church should get out of my bedroom!" or "No celibate bachelor is going to tell me how to live my life!"

In response to these objections, I would first say that God is everywhere – even in your bedroom. Secondly, I would dare say that Jesus Christ Himself was a "celibate bachelor." Sadly, objections to Church teaching on sexual morality are almost always objections to Christ Himself.

The gift of human sexuality is the means by which God brings about the miracle of new human life. When human beings start abusing this gift, or perverting it, the Church has an obligation, as the Body of Christ, to step in and to object to the destruction and perversion of this creative act. The bottom line is that the Church has every right to speak about human sexuality.

Looking at this subject from another side, we must understand one thing about the Devil. The Devil hates human souls and he will do anything to pervert them, destroy them or prevent them from coming into existence. It is no surprise, then, that the Devil tempts us by perversions in sexuality. It is precisely in this - whether through the evils of abortion, embryonic stem cell research, birth control or pornography - that human lives are lost. The Devil hates souls - your soul and mine. Why? Because he doesn't want us to get to Heaven! We must never forget this.

I realize that, for some of you, what I will say on the following pages will be challenging. However, I will tell you up front that what is written in these articles is not my personal opinion. I will simply be repeating the teachings of Our Lord and of His Church. Please also know that I condemn no one. Not one of us is without sin! However, if we want to get to Heaven some day, we must be willing to admit that fact and humbly repent and reform our lives. God's mercy and forgiveness are so great; all that we need to do is turn toward Him.

So, prayerfully, I will shepherd you through these challenging - but beautiful - aspects of our Faith.

*Reflection Questions:*

　1. *Why does the Devil hate souls?*

　2. *How does sexual immorality destroy human life? Give examples.*

　3. *Do I realize that I am in a spiritual battle? How am I doing?*

# Chastity:
*It's not just for priests and nuns!*

What comes to mind when we hear the word "chastity?" Some might think it means avoiding all sexual behavior. Others might think of a medieval code of conduct. Still others might think it applies only to certain people - like priests and nuns.

> "....this is a virtue to be practiced by all Christians – no matter who they are or what their particular vocation might be."

In fact, chastity or "being chaste" is quite different from the above three misconceptions. Chastity is the faith-filled integration of one's own sexuality into his or her vocation in life. Priests and nuns are called to be chaste. Single people are called to be chaste. Married people are called to be chaste! So, this is a virtue to be practiced by all Christians – no matter who they are or what their particular vocation might be.

Sins against chastity are many, today. Sadly, the most common remains the sin of fornication. As a priest, I fear that people don't realize the seriousness or the consequences of this sin. So, let's be clear about this: fornication is the act of sexual intercourse outside of marriage. It may be only once, or in a perpetual situation of living together. Either way, it is always morally wrong and a serious sin.

The question that is often asked is, "Why?" Why is fornication a sin, why is having sex with someone you really love, but to whom you are not married, a sin? First of all, we must understand what is meant by love. Love is something sacred and enduring – a total gift of oneself to another. Fornication is anything but that – it is not directed towards the good of the other person, but rather towards one's own personal pleasure. Fornication is, in reality, a lie – the individuals claim to love each other, but in effect they are using each other. This is not love.

The beautiful gift of human sexuality which God uses to create new life is naturally ordered towards the good of the spouses and the procreation and education of children. The proper setting for such a gift must be a committed and stable relationship recognized by all – in short, a marriage. Sexual intercourse outside of marriage abuses this gift, and the persons involved often are left emotionally and spiritually wounded.

Let's look at this in another way. The precious gift of sexuality, received from God, is a gift that we all are called to give away- according to our vocation in life. However, if we give this gift to another in an uncommitted, unstable and selfish relationship – then this becomes a tragic waste of a gift. The gift is liable to be damaged, or perhaps even lost. It is a sin to waste a gift that God has given us!

There is yet another way of looking at this same issue. Sex is a beautiful and valuable thing – it's like a diamond. However, diamonds need to be put in a proper setting, such as a ring. If not, they can scratch, be stolen, or be lost. Just as the proper setting for a diamond is a ring, the proper setting for the gift of sex is marriage.

I would be remiss if I did not relate to you what the Bible has to say about this issue. The Word of God, Jesus Christ, is very firm and very clear about fornication. In 1 Corinthians 6:9, we read that, *"No fornicator, idolater, adulterer, sodomite, thief, miser, drunkard ... . will inherit the kingdom of God."* In Ephesians 5:5, we read, *"Make no mistake about this: no fornicator, no unclean or lustful person – in effect an idolater – has any inheritance in the kingdom of Christ and of God."* There are many more such passages in the Scriptures. We would do well to heed God's Word!

Fornication is a serious sin; if one knowingly commits it and refuses to repent before death, one cannot be saved. Any Catholic, young or old, who is guilty of this sin **must** abstain from receiving Communion until he or she has repented and, ordinarily, received the sacrament of Confession.

As always, every one of us relies on the love and mercy of God – God who can forgive any sin. If you have sinned in this area of your life, you must never despair of God's great mercy. Rather you should return to the Lord and ask for His forgiveness – and it will surely be given.

Let us pray for a greater respect for each other and for the gift of our sexuality. As Christians, let us live holy and chaste lives.

*Reflection Questions:*

1. *Why is chastity important?*
2. *Living a chaste life is a real challenge today. Why is this true?*
3. *Fornication is an offense against God and one's future spouse. Why?*

# Tempting or Impure Thoughts:
*Pray - or even "laugh" - about them!*

From time to time, a person pulls me aside saying, *"Father, I need to speak with you."* After getting my attention, the person confides in me that he or she struggles with something *"so terribly embarrassing."* When I ask what it is, the answer comes back, *"I'm so ashamed – I struggle with impure thoughts."*

Impure thoughts – dirty images – violent or ugly ideas. Most people have struggled with these temptations at one time or another. We don't always know where the thought, image, or idea comes from, but it is troubling. Why me?

That's not what I want – that's not the kind of person I am! Yet, these thoughts do creep up from time to time and they can become a heavy cross.

> **"Such thoughts are NOT sinful if we dismiss them right away. They can become a sinful offense against God when we dwell on them or entertain them again."**

First of all, what are these images? Most of the time, "dirty thoughts" are thoughts having to do with some kind of sexual activity. We might be single, married, or in the religious life. Nevertheless, the thought comes and we are shocked by it. Other times, ugly ideas come into our minds about revolting things or practices. Sometimes, these thoughts or ideas have to do with violence to ourselves or others. Sometimes, these impure thoughts even have to do with God Himself.

Where do these thoughts originate? Many times, images that come into our minds are based on things we have recently seen. Perhaps it was a lust-filled or violent image on a television program or in a movie. Maybe it was a scene from a book. Perhaps we recently saw someone who was inappropriately dressed. Then, suddenly, the image pops into our heads. Other times, such images are from our distant past and have remained with us for many years. Sometimes, impure thoughts can come simply because of our fallen human nature and our inclination to sin. Many times, such impure thoughts can be temptations from Satan intended to cause us to fall into sin. Such demonic temptation often comes when we least expect it and when we are most vulnerable.

What can we do? First of all, we need to realize that most people struggle with these things! You are not the only person to have these thoughts! Next, we need to clearly understand that such thoughts are not reality and not what we want or intend. When impure thoughts arise, we need to meet them head on and dismiss them quickly. Such thoughts are NOT sinful if we dismiss them right away. They can become a sinful offense against God when we dwell on them or entertain them again. This is an important distinction: HAVING AN IMPURE THOUGHT IS NOT A SIN! Yes, it is troubling, ugly and contrary to everything we believe. However, it is not sinful unless we take it in and make it our own.

When impure thoughts arise, a quick, *"Get behind me, Satan,"* will do a good job in dispelling the images. Making the Sign of the Cross, saying the Our Father or some other prayer, or asking God for help at the moment will do much to banish the ugly thought. Sometimes, impure thoughts can be dispelled by laughing at them. Yes, laughing! It's possible that we can become so ashamed and afraid of such thoughts that the Devil has us right where he wants us. Laugh at his temptation! He hates that and will leave quickly. Another technique when we are tempted with an impure thought of a sexual nature is to immediately thank God for making such a beautiful person and ask the good Lord to bless the person! Nothing throws more cold water on lustful thoughts than prayer! The Lord knows our hearts! He knows that we do not want to do these things.

Impure thoughts are a mysterious aspect of our humanity. All of us remain clay pots. We all are easily broken – we all are weak. Yet, what matters most is the treasure inside! So, when impure thoughts come our way, let us remember the words of Jesus, *"Be not afraid"* (Deuteronomy 20:1), and let us stay close to Him.

*Reflection Questions:*

1. Where do impure thoughts originate?
2. What can we do to dismiss them when they come?
3. Are impure thoughts sinful? Why or why not?

---

# Modesty:
*Refuse to unveil what should be hidden!*

We ARE our brother's keeper. We ARE our sister's keeper, too. We are responsible not only for ourselves. In charity, we also are responsible for our neighbor. We don't want to be alone in Heaven! We want others to be there with us – so how we live and how we act is very important.

As Christians, we must never act, speak or live in such a way that leads another person into sin. We've all heard the word "scandal," in recent years. However, many people don't know what the word actually means. For Christians, the word means, "to lead another person into sin by one's own actions." To live or act in such a way that leads another person to sin is itself morally wrong.

> **"Leading another person into sin by our actions or clothing is looked upon very harshly by our Lord Jesus."**

In Spring, the grass is green and the birds are singing. The weather is getting warmer. Our heavy set of clothing is becoming less of a necessity. So, each year, we come to the issue of modesty in clothing. Modesty, in this sense, means refusing to unveil what should remain hidden. Fashions in our country – especially women's fashions – are not particularly modest. In fact, they are harming as many men as women.

I realize that, in writing this, some will object - saying that my comments appear to be one-sided. Some might say: *"After all, what about immodesty in dress for men? Why pick on the women? You're just writing it from a male perspective."* Indeed, I am writing this from a male perspective. Yet, in truth, I have not heard much of an outcry from women or men about immodesty in men's fashions. On the other hand, I have heard and read volumes decrying the immodesty of some women's fashions. Many of you have spoken to me personally about this issue.

Some people might declare, *"It's my right to wear whatever I want!"* I would respond that the Christian answer is simply, *"No!"* No one has a right to hurt another person or to lead another person into sin. Some of popular fashion today has had an enormously harmful effect on men, as well as on women.

Men can be harmed because alluring fashions that openly and intentionally display a women's sexuality often lead them into the sin of lust. Men are led to see a woman as an object - "a piece of meat" - rather than as a person with dignity. Obviously, the man bears some responsibility for his own actions; the issue is not simply one-sided. However, women who call themselves Christians must be aware that they are to act and dress in such a way that does not lead men into sin. They are their brothers' keepers.

Women also are hurt by the immodest fashions of today. Parents of teenage girls, who are either inept or worn down by their daughters' nagging, seem to cave in and allow these young women to dress immodestly. The young women then fall into a culture that treats them as objects. Rather than being respected for who they are, they are lusted after for what they are. This is quite wrong and very dangerous for women.

Parents have a serious moral responsibility to make sure that their children and teens live and dress appropriately. It really makes no difference whether their children or teens complain - or whether the young people are seen as "popular" or not. Their souls and the souls of others are far more important! Parents must be aware that they are morally responsible for this before the Lord and will need to give an accounting of it someday.

I realize that some of you may think that I'm a bit of a prude. So be it. However, this is a very serious moral issue. **We are our brother's and sister's keeper.** Leading another person into sin by our actions is looked upon very harshly by our Lord Jesus. *"It would be better for him if a millstone were tied around his neck and thrown into the sea, than if he should lead one of my little ones astray."* (Luke 17:2)

There are fashionable and attractive clothing styles for women AND men to wear, that respect their dignity and the dignity of others. I ask you to join with me in praying that all people may embrace the Christian way of life, and reflect this in the clothing they wear.

*Reflection Questions:*

1. *Would someone recognize you as a follower of Jesus Christ by the kind of clothes you wear? Why or why not?*
2. *Do men's or women's clothing items that have immodest or ugly words or slogans lead others into sin?*
3. *Why are young women seemingly targeted by manufacturers of immodest clothing?*

---

# Dressing Appropriately for Church:
*Forget the flip flops. Skip the Speedos.*

Every morning, I glance inside my closet and need to make a difficult decision. Do I wear black ... or black? Some days, it can be quite overwhelming!

The clothes that a priest wears are called "clerics." Traditionally, they are black in color. They are formal clothes: dress shoes, dress socks, pants and a shirt with a collar. Priests wear formal attire because of the public role and responsibility we have.

However, when I go home to visit my family, I usually do not wear clerics. I wear shorts and a tee shirt or a sweatshirt and jeans. Although these clothes are easier to relax in, I sometimes find that I miss the formal clerical attire. Somehow, in wearing the stiff and often-hot dress shirt and pants, I am reminded of my vocation and the vows that I have taken. It's a vocation that I love so much!

> **"A rule of thumb for choosing what we wear to Church is to think of how we might dress if someone very important were coming to our home to visit."**

Clothing is, of course, a necessary thing; for protection certainly, but also for propriety and for all sorts of other cultural reasons. For most of us, the clothing we choose to wear in some way reflects what we want others to think about us. We wear different clothes for different times and occasions. A swimsuit probably would not be seen as appropriate attire for work (unless you are a lifeguard). A formal dress or suit would not be appropriate to sleep in at night. Obviously, clothing has to be appropriate for a given situation. Often, by our choices, we make a statement.

When we come to Mass, we must make an effort to dress appropriately. After all, we are going to worship God and, ideally, to receive Him in Holy Communion. How we dress can be an outward sign of the importance we place on this event. Does it matter to us? I certainly hope so. Then, let us dress in a manner that shows how much we value the Mass! A rule of thumb for choosing what we wear to Church is to think of how we might dress if someone very important were coming to our home to visit. In other words, we should wear clothing that is our best - and not our worst.

Certainly, God will welcome us no matter what we wear. However, the way we dress can greatly assist us in focusing on the event at hand. If we take the time to wear our special clothes, chances are the Mass will become something more than routine. This is essential. Also, we would not want our clothing to be a distraction to other people as they come to worship God. Clothing should not be too tight or too revealing, but rather, reserved and more formal. Why? Because when we come to Mass, it's not about us, it's about worshipping God. The clothing we wear should help us and others to focus solely on the Lord.

In the warm months of the year, especially, please reflect on the choices of clothing that you make before coming to Mass. Please help your children and teenagers to make appropriate choices. By making the extra effort to dress nicely for God, we are offering Him praise and thanksgiving for the many gifts He has given us.

*Reflection Questions:*

1. *Why should we wear our best clothing when we go to Mass?*
2. *How can the clothing we choose to wear be a distraction to others?*
3. *Who are we going to visit at Mass?*

# Christian Dating:
*Too early and too exclusive can equal one broken heart.*

Who can forget his or her first date? For many years, we remember our nervousness and awkwardness, plus the giddiness that came with all of the preparations.

I remember my first date, when I was in high school. It was a classic dinner and movie deal that included one other couple. We saw the movie *Groundhog Day* (1993, for those who are interested) and had pie at Bakers Square afterwards. It was great fun.

> **"You should court or date a member of the opposite sex because you want to find out whether this is the person you are to marry!"**

Of course, dating has changed over the years – and usually not for the best. As Christians, how should you bring the light of faith to the issue of dating and courtship?

First, you must remember that dating has a purpose. That purpose is marriage. You should court or date a member of the opposite sex because you want to find out whether this is the person you are to marry! If your intentions in dating are other than this, you are using the other person and allowing yourself to be used. Many people have learned this the hard way.

Today, people date for all sorts of reasons – some of them noble, some of them not. Indeed, dating is a social activity – and it can be lots of fun! However, most of you know that, since intentions in dating can vary, people often get hurt. These hurt feelings may result from being emotionally and even physically used by the other person and then tossed aside as a piece of human garbage. This is not what God intended.

This is why many writers on this subject today advocate the return of "courtship" to the dating process. Rather than a couple immediately pairing off and being exclusive, there are large group activities such as wholesome parties. Then, if two people have an interest in each other, their families are introduced. This can lead to further discussions about things in common or differences to be worked out – all under the watchful eye of the family.

After this, the couple begins to actively court each other with an eye towards spending the rest of their lives together in marriage. If things do not work out between the two people, they at least have courted each other honestly and have not been as emotionally intertwined as a couple who started immediate, exclusive dating. There is something to be said for laying a proper foundation for the rest of our lives and for guarding our emotions.

There are many dangers of immediate, exclusive dating without courtship. As I mentioned, this can include both emotional and physical abuse, as well as a broken heart. We all know that love can be blind, but lust is always so. When that blindness is coupled with the hormonal rages of the teenage years, dating usually brings sadness and confusion.

It is reprehensible that some parents allow their young children, some still in middle school or even grade school, to date exclusively. Because of a lack of family oversight and immaturity – on the part of both the children and their parents – dating at such an early age violates a child's innocence and gives him or her a warped view of human sexuality. Parents who think this is "cute" are, in fact, endangering their children's souls. Sexual activity too often is seen in this setting as a way to have fun and not as something that brings with it great responsibility. This has long-lasting repercussions for a person's life.

When is it appropriate for young people to start dating? Because of the objective delayed maturity of young people today, an older age is recommended. It would seem that late teens or early 20s would be an appropriate age for people to begin courting and dating. Dating should start at an age when people are ready to be married. Only when people have reached this point of maturity in their lives, can they rightfully engage in planning to spend the rest of their lives together.

*Reflection Questions:*
1. What is the main reason why a couple should date?
2. Why is early, exclusive dating morally dangerous?
3. Love is blind. What does this mean?

# Cohabitation:
*It's NOT okay to "test drive" a person before marriage.*

Preparing couples for marriage is one of the most crucial and challenging things I do as a priest. The Sacrament of Marriage is so beautiful and powerful, yet so misunderstood, today. For example, most couples who come to see me are cohabitating – by this, I mean that they are living together under one roof in a sexual relationship before marriage.

> **"Perhaps they never were taught that the sin of fornication (premarital sex) could separate them from God for all eternity."**

When I challenge a couple on this, they often look at me with a blank stare. Perhaps they are unaware of the sinfulness of their situation. Perhaps they never were taught that the sin of fornication (premarital sex) could separate them from God for all eternity!

Being part of the same generation of people who now are marrying, I know quite well the extent of religious ignorance among my peers. I remember one fellow who responded to my objection about his cohabitation by saying, "Well,

*Father, before I buy a car, I always take it for a test drive."* As he said this, his fiancée was sitting right next to him! How tragic.

Cohabitation is a serious issue. It has many causes. One major factor is that the breakdown in marriage in our culture – with more than 50 percent of marriages ending in divorce – has frightened many young people. Cohabitation appears to be the only way they can "be sure" that marriage is right for them.

Unfortunately, studies have shown that those who cohabitate before marriage are 50 percent *more* likely to divorce if they marry than non-cohabitating couples who marry. It seems that attitudes and behavior common to cohabitation — namely a lack of commitment and flagrant immorality — usually are destructive to a future marriage.

Those who indulge in cohabitation rarely are happy, although on the surface they may appear so. Frequently, one (or both) of the partners feels used. The couple usually avoids tackling the tough issues that must be ironed out between them, fearing that an argument would break up their rather tentative living arrangement. Often, sexual gratification is used in place of honest dialogue between the couple. Then, this behavior may be carried into marriage.

Marriage is permanent. Cohabitation is not. However, couples rarely see the difference. A couple who avoid cohabitation and wait for marriage experience the joys of sexual intimacy within the graces and strong walls of marriage. Cohabitating couples, however, desire to "have their cake and eat it too," and this impatience really is selfish indulgence.

Intrinsic to any cohabitating relationship is the unspoken message that, "I can leave you at any time I wish. I don't respect you or love you enough to make a formal promise to you in marriage." This mentality almost always carries into marriage – often with disastrous results. Put another way, indulging in a sexual relationship which is dissoluble, uncommitted to lifelong fidelity and closed to life, cannot possibly prepare a couple for marriage.

One thing is known for sure about a cohabitating couple – both parties are willing to have sexual relations with someone to whom they're not married. Again, this is the wrong way to prepare for the Sacrament of Marriage!

Yes, cohabitation is a critical problem, today. It is a grave sin and places the souls of those involved in jeopardy. However, as I said, a majority of the couples who come to see me for marriage preparation are cohabitating. Even more frightening, many seem to see no problem with their situation. Often, their own parents – and perhaps grandparents – are divorced and cohabitating with others. Families may assist them in moving in together, and thus share in the sin. The scandal that comes from cohabitation affects all of us by lowering standards of morality and tempting others to sin.

In our culture of death, where sexual intercourse is seen as merely recreational, where marriage is disposable, and where children are seen not as a gift but as a choice, it should come as no surprise that cohabitation is on the rise. I realize that there are tremendous pressures brought upon people today to cohabitate. These could take the form of peer pressure, media hype, or even financial strains. The fact remains, however, that, as Christians, we must be counter-cultural, especially if what the culture advocates is sinful. Cohabitation is the wrong way to prepare for the Sacrament of Marriage. As the well-known slogan advises, "Just say no!"

Reflection Questions:
1. Why do couples cohabitate? Why is it wrong?
2. What message does cohabitation send to young people who witness it?
3. Have I spoken up when I witnessed cohabitation in my family? Have I defended my Faith or was I a coward?

# The Use of Contraceptives – Part I:
*In reality, there is no "birth" and no "control."*

In the next few articles, I will speak with you about a most important issue. Like most critical issues, it is controversial and arouses very strong opinions. However, it is an issue which must be discussed in the light of our Catholic Faith. It is an issue which I believe is at the heart of the disintegration of our culture, today. It has brought much division and sadness to families and to the Church. I believe it to be one of the most significant evils in our world today. Although some of you might disagree, I ask you to prayerfully read the entire article before reacting to it. The issue now at hand is birth control.

> **"....the truth remains that birth control prevents the creation of human life and, as such, is contrary to the Will of God."**

The term, "birth control," is a curious one. In reality, there is no "birth" and no "control." For the sake of this article, I will use the words contraception and birth control interchangeably – they mean the same thing and accomplish the same thing. They involve human beings actively preventing God from creating new life. This alone should give us pause, but, in reality, the issue is even more troublesome.

To understand this issue, we first must look to history. If you were to go back just 100 years and ask the average Christian what he or she thought about this topic, you might be surprised by the answer. Until 1930, every Christian church or community, whether it was Catholic, Lutheran, Baptist or Methodist, believed and taught that the use of birth control was a serious sin and always morally wrong. This opinion was held even by the early Church, which believed and taught that contraception was an immoral and pagan practice.

It was only in our own time, in 1930, when the Anglicans (Episcopalians) changed their stance and stated that the use of birth control now was acceptable for serious reasons within marriage. Soon, almost all Christian churches or communities followed suit, teaching that birth control now was acceptable. Only one Church remained true to the anciently held belief in the immorality of birth control. Only one Church stayed true to the Sacred Tradition passed on from Jesus Christ. That Church was and remains our own Catholic Church.

In the early 1960s, however, the invention of the contraceptive pill caused the issue to be reexamined. Barrier methods of contraception were more easily seen as selfish and contrary to new life. The birth control pill, with its hormonal regulation, was much more difficult to evaluate, morally. There even was some debate inside and outside the Catholic Church as to whether this form of contraception could be permissible. The issue was studied at the Second Vatican Council, but the conclusion was postponed.

With the invention of the "pill," many people hoped that all birth control now would be permitted by the Church in order to assist troubled marriages or to prevent "unwanted" births. A reversal in Church teaching was expected. Then, on July 25, 1968, Pope Paul VI released a teaching letter called, "Humanae Vitae" (On Human Life). In this letter, the Pope strongly reiterated the Catholic Church's teaching *against* the use of contraception. Many lay people and even some priests bitterly disagreed with this teaching, and the disunity they caused still plagues our Church today.

What many failed to realize was that the Catholic Church is the Church Christ founded, and as such could not teach what popular opinion wanted. The Church could only teach the Truth; and the truth remains that birth control prevents the creation of human life and, as such, is contrary to the Will of God.

# The Use of Contraceptives - Part II:
*"Pills" are for disease, not for unity and commitment!*

Now we know the history of what the Catholic Church teaches about birth control. So, we turn to the more important question, *"Why?"* To quote Pope Paul VI, *"The Church teaches ... that it is necessary that each and every conjugal act remain open to the procreation of life ... There is an unbreakable connection between the unitive and procreative meaning of the sexual act ... This connection was established by God and cannot be broken by man."*

"The Church insists that the sexual act involves a great commitment, and that accepting children is part of this commitment."

To put it another way, as Catholics, we believe that sexual intercourse has two purposes: the good of the spouses coming together as one (unity) and the procreation of children. Morally, we cannot separate these two purposes. Using contraception during intercourse closes the act to new life (which prevents procreation), and also places a barrier of selfishness between the couple (which harms unity). Sexual intercourse is for coming together as a couple in love and unity as well as for potentially bringing new life into the world. If a couple is not ready for either one of these two parts, they ought not to be having sex!

The Catholic Church believes that sexual intercourse and being open to having children are intimately connected. Biology agrees. Also, the unity of the couple is affected by the use of birth control. When a couple comes together in the beauty of sexual intercourse, they should be saying by their actions, *"I love you completely – I give myself totally to you."*

However, with the use of contraception, couples really say by their actions, *"I love everything about you, except your fertility. That part I do not love about you, or, I am keeping that part of me intentionally for myself."* This is selfishness! As we well know, selfishness destroys marriage. So, we see that the unitive and procreative ends of sexual intercourse must never be separated. Yet, we know that contraception does just that.

Looking at this another way, we take pills when we are sick – for a headache, for high cholesterol, or for the heart. Is having a child a disease? Is fertility something bad? Do we need to take a pill to cure a disease – or rather to prevent new life? Is life an evil to be avoided? Is it a disease? Our culture today often says, *"yes."* Our Catholic Faith says, *"no!"*

The Church insists that the sexual act involves a great commitment, and that accepting children is part of this commitment. A child is the most wonderful of gifts! At the moment of conception, God creates a new human life, infusing an immortal soul in the individual. It is the greatest of privileges to take part with God in His creation. However, contraception says *"no"* to God. It clearly says that one desires the wonderful physical pleasure of sex, but does not want any part of sharing in God's creation. Birth control is anti-God, for it says, *"I don't want to take part with You in creation."*

In addition, birth control is anti-marriage, for it says, *"I love you, but not enough to have a child with you. I just want to use you for pleasure, but I'm holding something back."* Birth control is anti-child, for it says, *"Children are a burden, and if I choose to have one, it will be when I want."* Birth control is anti-woman, for it says, *"As the man, I can control the woman; I can use her for my own pleasure."* Birth control is dangerous, for cancer, strokes and other diseases have been linked to its use. Birth control allows for increased promiscuity, for it gives rise to the feeling of, *"I won't be caught."* Birth control leads to adultery in marriage because of similar feelings of *"not getting caught."*

With the use of birth control, sex is seen as something recreational, rather than as something sacred and beautiful. There is nothing good about contraception – it is completely destructive to marriage and to society!

# The Use of Contraceptives - Part III:
*"Let the little children come to me, and do not hinder them."*
*(Matthew 19:14)*

When Pope Paul VI wrote his encyclical, "Humanae Vitae," in 1968, he made a number of predictions as to what would happen if birth control were widely accepted and used in our culture.

He stated that, *"Widespread use of contraceptives would lead to conjugal infidelity and to the general lowering of morality. Couples would lose respect for each other, coming to see each other as only instruments for selfish enjoyment. Widespread use of contraception would place a dangerous weapon in the hands of authorities who take no heed of moral exigencies. It would lead people to think they have limitless dominion over their bodies. It would lead to a breakdown in marriages."* Have these predictions come true in our own time? Tragically, we know the answer.

> **"When we take a chance and are generous with God, he always will reward us beyond our imagining!"**

It is a sad truth that many couples today use artificial contraception. Various forms are used: the Pill, condoms, IUDs and others. Sterilizations - vasectomies and tubal ligations - also are tragically common. Each of these choices is a serious offense against God and seriously sinful.

However, it gets even worse! Certain forms of contraception, such as the Pill, can cause abortions if there is a break-through ovulation and a child is conceived. With the use of the Pill, there is no place in the womb for the child to survive.

The contraceptive attitude also can lead to (scheduled) abortion. Abortion is sometimes regarded as just another form of birth control! Since contraceptives are being used, a child is not wanted. If a child is conceived, even after birth control is used, the attitude of not wanting the child often remains. A scheduled abortion may be the next step.

I do realize that many of you who are reading this article have used or are now using contraception. Perhaps you didn't know all of the facts, or perhaps you were misled. Whatever the reason or the situation, God is the God of second chances. He always will forgive us as long as we repent and turn towards His great mercy.

Reflect on your own lives and, if necessary, bring this sin to the Sacrament of Confession. I do realize that it is a difficult and complex issue. If you still have the opportunity, be open to life. Say "yes" to life. Be generous!

It also is important to remember that married couples are called to be responsible parents. Sometimes a situation arises when having another child would present a serious or dangerous burden on the couple. If there is a serious reason to postpone a pregnancy at this time, Natural Family Planning (NFP) is a wonderful and life-giving method to use to space pregnancies.

NFP is not the old "rhythm method," but rather a more scientific and natural manner by which to space births. First, it is accurately determined when a woman is fertile in her monthly cycle. Then, a couple abstains from sexual relations during that time if they have a serious reason to do so. In this way, a child is not actively prevented from coming into existence, for the couple is simply cooperating with God and with the natural cycles He has given them. NFP draws a husband and wife closer together and husbands very often grow in respect for their wives. NFP is almost cost-free and is up to 99 percent effective. Because no chemicals are used, it is much safer than the birth control Pill or other contraceptives.

I have journeyed with many couples who have attempted to be open to new life. I have found them to be some of the most joyful, peaceful and faithful people I ever have known. They are an inspiration to us all! When we take a chance and are generous with God, He always will reward us beyond our imagining!

A story is told of a reporter visiting Mother Teresa of Calcutta and posing this question, "Why do you and your Sisters work and slave all day over these people who are dying of cancer and AIDS? Why don't you become angry with God for allowing such suffering to occur in the world?" Mother Teresa replied, "God did send someone to cure cancer, but she was aborted. God did send someone to cure AIDS, but his parents used contraception."

What did our Lord Jesus Christ say about contraception? He simply said, "Let the little children come to me, and do not hinder them." (Matthew 19:14) May we all more fully embrace God's gift of new life!

*Reflection Questions:*

1. Why is the use of artificial birth control immoral?
2. Why do couples use it? What lies does our culture teach about contraception?
3. If our parents had successfully used birth control, we would not exist. Reflect on this!

# Abortion:
*In ALL circumstances, it's wrong. This is why ...*

Abortion is murder. Human life must be protected and respected absolutely from the moment of conception. From the first moment of existence in the womb of his mother, the child must be recognized as having the rights of a person.

Since the First Century, the Church has affirmed the moral evil of every procured abortion. This teaching has not changed and is unchangeable! Each of us was in our mother's womb at one time. Hopefully, the safety that was provided and the nourishing love that was given helped us to be formed. Whether she knew it or not, or cared or not, she was cooperating with God in His creation.

> "From the first moment of existence in the womb of his mother, the child must be recognized as having the rights of a person."

The mere thought that nations and individuals take it upon themselves to destroy the life within them is beyond comprehension. If murder is terrible, and murder of the innocent even worse, then murder of an unborn innocent child is beyond description. Yet, this happens 3,500 times a day in our country.

Many people today say that abortion is a woman's right. Curiously, 150 years ago, our Supreme Court said that slavery was a right, too. No person has a right to kill another person!

An unborn child may be unwanted, but he already exists. He moves in his mother's womb; within weeks of conception, he can feel pain. If anyone says that the child is not alive or is not a human being, he is deluded. Any expectant mother will tell you that she is carrying a baby – not a bunch of anonymously dividing cells.

Yes, the Church is aware that women may be forced into circumstances in which abortion seems to be the only alternative. Poverty, abuse by her family, and/or pressure from the father of the child can lead a woman into abortion. However, this is precisely why we must educate women and men today – to prevent the horror of abortion.

It seems that, every week, I meet another couple who desperately want children but are unable to have them. There is a great suffering here. Adoption can be a "win-win" situation for both an expectant woman in an unwanted pregnancy and the couple, especially today with the many excellent programs available.

What about cases of incest or rape? These terrible abuses of women continue today, even though we supposedly are more "educated." However, let's be clear, here. The child conceived under these trying circumstances is no less alive or human than a child conceived in a loving marriage. Why punish the child for the "sins of the father?"

Also, abortion to save the life of the mother is wrong. Such circumstances are rare. However, when a health crisis occurs during a pregnancy, there are certain actions which the Church always permits to save the woman's life. An example of this might be the legitimate removal of a cancerous uterus which indirectly would result in the death of the child. The mother's life matters, too! Direct abortion, however, never is an option.

Those who support abortion never seem to discuss the horrible toll it takes on women and men. The popular pro-life slogan, "Abortion: one killed, one wounded" (or perhaps even "several wounded") is an apt description. Most women, and many men, suffer terribly for years after a child is aborted. This suffering may be both emotional and physical. The Church provides excellent programs for people in such situations. "Project Rachel," for example, is designed to help women and men through the consequences of their decision, and to reconcile with God.

As with any other grave sin, the appropriate action after abortion is to confess one's sin and to receive God's sure and promised forgiveness. No sin is too great for God's loving forgiveness. You can be healed - you can be forgiven.

Let us continuously pray that the scourge of abortion will be lifted from our nation and from our world. As the popular saying goes, "A nation that kills its children is a nation without hope."

Reflection Questions:

1. If you were born after January 22, 1973, it would have been legal for your parents to have murdered you through abortion. How does that make you feel?
2. One out of three people in the previous two generations has been murdered through abortion. What effects has this had on our country?
3. How can I work to stop abortion?

# Artificial Reproduction Technologies:
*A child should not be "made to order" in a laboratory!*

One of the most common struggles for young married couples today is infertility. The desire for a child is a natural one, and couples who are unable to have a baby of their own carry a heavy cross. We know from scripture that Rachel cries to her husband Jacob saying, "Give me children, or I shall die!" (Genesis 30:1) Reasons for infertility are many, but its increase may be connected to the use of birth control, pollution, lifestyle and nutrition.

> "As Christians, we must remember that God is the Creator of human life and we cooperate with Him in creating this life."

Recently, a number of technologies have been invented which offer infertile couples the chance to have children. However, some of these technologies are used to manufacture a child rather than to help a couple to conceive naturally. As Christians, we must remember that God is the Creator of human life and that we cooperate with Him in creating this life. A child is not an object to be manufactured, but rather a gift that comes forth from a couple giving themselves to each other in love.

Now, there is nothing wrong with techniques or medicines that assist a couple in conceiving a child. These have been a great blessing to many people over the years. However, moral problems arise when fertility assistance turns into replacing the husband and the wife with doctors and technicians in a laboratory.

One such example is artificial insemination (or "AI"). Many of us immediately think of cattle, when we hear of AI. This technique of manually impregnating the female with sperm is used on cattle, to produce the best offspring. This is a legitimate business practice, used to boost milk production. However, human beings are not cattle! We don't make a child to our own specifications. The human person has an immortal soul which gives him a dignity infinitely greater than that of any animal. I trust you see the distinction.

Another immoral fertility technique is called in-vitro fertilization. In this practice, the male's semen is collected, often involving self-gratification. Then, the semen is placed among several of the woman's eggs in a laboratory dish, to "conceive" a child. The new human embryos are kept frozen until needed. Eventually, they are placed in the woman's womb, in the hope that a pregnancy will occur.

Often, these tiny human beings are spontaneously aborted once in the womb. If pregnancy does occur, it is common for multiple children to be implanted. Tragically, doctors often advocate the "selective reduction" of one or more of the children in the womb so that the remaining embryo(s) has/have a better chance of surviving and the woman is more "comfortable." This is abortion.

Procedures to "make a child" can cost thousands and thousands of dollars and are rarely successful. Add to this the moral dilemma that "unused" human embryos are keep frozen in a laboratory, indefinitely, or are harvested for use in embryonic stem cell research.

The supreme gift of marriage is a new human person. However, a child must never be considered as a piece of property - an object to be planned, constructed and sold. Artificial insemination and in-vitro fertilization show a lack of respect for the children conceived because the children are treated as objects, not as people. Still, we must realize that any child conceived in such a manner has a dignity equal to any other person. Even though we so often force God's hand, this does not affect the dignity of the newly created human person.

Children are an enormous blessing! Let us then cooperate with God in the miracle of the creation of human life and never abuse this great privilege.

*Reflection Questions:*

   *1. Do I know people who suffer from infertility? How do they deal with this cross?*

   *2. Do I see children as a gift or as a burden?*

   *3. What are other ways that we "force God's hand" in life? What are the results?*

# Stem Cell Research:
*Human life must be respected from the moment of conception!*

"A person's a person, no matter how small." This quote from <u>Horton Hears A Who</u>, a children's book by Dr. Seuss, emphasizes an important truth. Our dignity is not determined by how large or small we are - or our color or race or anything like that. Our dignity as persons comes from the fact that we are created in God's image - and that He sent His son, Jesus, to save all of us, no matter how small. With this in mind, we come now to the issue of stem cell research and the destruction of human embryos.

> "The Church is NOT against all stem cell research. Only embryonic stem cell research is immoral because of the destruction of the small human being."

Stem cells are basically "master" or undifferentiated cells that have the potential to develop into any type of cell in the human body - brain, blood, heart, etc. In other words, they are like blank slates; they have a potential that is not yet realized. Scientists believe that they can take these stem cells and cultivate them for therapeutic purposes. For example, if you have damaged heart tissue, stem cells could be grown into new heart tissue to help you heal. If you have damaged brain cells, stem cells could be grown and grafted onto your brain to help it heal. The potential for this new science is seemingly endless and very powerful indeed.

So, where do we find stem cells? Stem cells can be found in the human placenta, in umbilical cords, and in adult bone marrow. Some scientists believe, however, that even younger stem cells, which will be easier to manipulate in the laboratory, are needed. Thus, many have turned to human embryos - with "embryonic stem cells" - as their source. However, severe ethical and moral problems arise from the use of this kind of stem cell.

A human embryo is essentially a small human being - a grouping of cells that will eventually grow into a mature human person. Human life begins at conception. As Catholics, we believe that human life must be respected and protected from the very moment of conception. However, when embryonic stem cells are "harvested," the human embryo is killed. So, a tiny human, who has the same dignity as all of us, is harvested for his or her "spare parts."

Human embryos most frequently come from two sources. First, they are left over from the immoral practice of in-vitro fertilization. These embryos are frozen and remain in storage until implanted in their mother's womb - and thus are easy targets for this research. The second source is intentional in-vitro fertilization done specifically for "harvesting" purposes. Here, donor sperm and eggs are used in order to create a new human embryo from which stem cells are directly harvested.

It's easy to see why the Catholic Church is so vehemently opposed to embryonic stem cell research. It violates the very dignity of the human person by reducing human life to a spare parts bin.

Now, I realize that many people who are suffering from terrible diseases have said that they support embryonic stem cell research. However, as Christians, *we never can do evil to bring about good*. The end never justifies the means! A cure of an illness that is brought about by murder and harvesting of human parts will no doubt bring even greater illness and evil upon our culture.

Perhaps, more importantly, there is no evidence that embryonic stem cells actually work! There have been no cures from this research. However, using adult stem cells from other human sources such as an umbilical cord or a placenta has been very successful and has already brought about cures for many people. **The Church is NOT against all stem cell research!** Only *embryonic* stem cell research is immoral because of the destruction of the small human being.

"*A person's a person no matter how small.*" That's what Dr. Seuss said. Jesus said, "*Blessed are those who do not see and still believe.*" (John 20:29) Let us respect the dignity of all human persons - no matter how they look and no matter how small!

*Reflection Questions:*

  *1. Can we ever do evil to bring about good? Why or why not?*

  *2. Is the Catholic Church against scientific research? Is all scientific research good?*

  *3. What does the secular attitude towards human life mean for our future?*

# Homosexuality:
## *The sin lies in the action, NOT in being tempted.*

Throughout human history, there have been countless individuals who have developed some form of sexual attraction to a person of their same gender. Often, this is called same-sex attraction or homosexuality. Throughout the centuries and in different cultures, this attraction has taken different forms. Its cause is still largely unknown.

> "....homosexual activity is intrinsically evil and disordered. However, those individuals who suffer from same-sex attraction are not intrinsically evil."

Often, the realization of this attraction comes with a great deal of surprise for the individual and for his or her family. For many, it becomes a terrible trial, filled with much suffering. Culturally, there has been a great deal of misunderstanding regarding this issue. Those who suffer from this attraction sometimes have been treated with sinful discrimination and cruelty. Fortunately, as Catholics, our Faith enlightens and guides us in dealing with this difficult subject.

God's revelation to us, both from Sacred Scripture (the Bible) and Sacred Tradition (the living transmission of the message of the Gospel through the Church), is quite clear. The Bible contains numerous passages in both the Old Testament and New Testament in which homosexual activity is condemned as great depravity. The teachings of the Church, as guided by the Holy Spirit, constantly declare that homosexual acts (acts of sodomy) are disordered and intrinsically evil. Thus, the Judeo-Christian practice has been to condemn homosexual activity as gravely immoral.

Why is this the case? The reasons are many. First and foremost, homosexual acts are a perversion of the gift of sexuality. The beauty of heterosexual activity is that it can create new life. However, homosexual acts always are closed to new life - this would be a biological impossibility. Also, these acts do not proceed from a genuine affective and sexual need for complement, but rather out of lust and selfishness. Nothing good can come from these sexual acts - no natural union and no children. Thus, homosexual activity (or sodomy) is intrinsically selfish. It is little more than mutual self-gratification.

Now, we must always maintain the proper distinction between homosexual persons and homosexual acts. God and His Church always have taught that homosexual activity is intrinsically evil and disordered. However, those individuals who suffer from same-sex attraction are not intrinsically evil. In other words, the sin lies in the action, not in being tempted.

For example, one can be tempted to steal something, but this alone doesn't make a person a thief. Only if the person follows through with the action of stealing is he guilty of sin. We must never condemn someone who suffers from, or is tempted by, same-sex attraction. If a person does commit the sin of sodomy, we must hate the sin, but never the person.

Homosexual persons are called to chastity. By acknowledging their weaknesses (as all people are called to do), they learn to carry this heavy cross of abstaining from sexual activity. Through God's sure grace, all of us will come to live lives of holiness.

Today, there are numerous Catholic groups which promote an authentic path to holiness for people who suffer from same-sex attraction. One very fine group, founded by Father John Harvey, is called "Courage." In this nationwide network, those who suffer from same-sex attraction can receive help and support.

Recently, the homosexual lifestyle has been very evident in our popular culture. The plight of the homosexual person has been taken up by some as a cause to be defended. Many of our young people have been brainwashed by educators who support the homosexual agenda and who see any opposition to the "gay" lifestyle as discrimination.

Interestingly, the mere mention of this rather intimate subject would have been almost unheard of some 40 years ago – especially in a church bulletin! Today, however, there is much confusion over what the Church teaches on this subject and why. For the Christian, true liberty is freedom from sin. Sin is not freeing – it is enslaving.

Rather than being freed from oppression, homosexual persons are constantly bombarded by a culture that regards their inclinations and subsequent actions as perfectly normal. This is tragically wrong. Those who suffer from same-sex attraction, as well as their families, should be supported by all of us in living a Christian life. Let us pray for them.

*Reflection Questions:*

1. *Do I struggle with same-sex attraction? Have I ever met a person who struggles with same-sex attraction?*
2. *How have the sexual revolution and the breakdown in the family led to a rise in homosexual activity?*
3. *Do I pray for those who suffer from this temptation?*

# An Introduction to Same-Sex Marriage:
*Let's review basics.*

What is marriage? Often, we hear this question. With the divorce rate as high as 60 percent, and couples of all ages living together in sin, it is no wonder that the nature of marriage is questioned. One of the effects of this breakdown in marriage – and the general weakening of morality in our society – is the recent movement to legalize homosexual or same-sex marriage.

> "As Catholics, we have a moral obligation to oppose all attempts to legalize same-sex marriage. Such activity is contrary to our Faith and to the good of society."

As Christians, we believe that marriage is part of God's plan. We believe that it is to be a faithful, fruitful, exclusive and lifelong covenant between one man and one woman. Historically, marriage was legally recognized for the good of the spouses and for bringing children into the world. Legal recognition brought stability to the institution, as well as protection under the law.

Marriage is not merely a religious institution. Even from the point of natural law or reason, the union of one man and one woman is for the good of society. Men and women are created for each other both physically and emotionally – and from this union often comes new life. A homosexual relationship, on the other hand, never can be seen as equal in dignity to marriage – it is not based on any kind of physical complementarity and never can bring new life into the world.

Today, certain individuals say that marriage is a merely private relationship and that the state should recognize it regardless of its makeup. However, we all must understand that marriage also has public consequences. It is a widely held truth that a committed, stable and loving relationship between a man and a woman provides the best environment in which to raise children. Those children, themselves, grow up to be adult contributors to society – for better or for worse.

Many claim that to deny marriage to homosexual persons is to discriminate against them. At the heart of any form of discrimination is injustice – depriving a person of his or her due. However, in permitting same-sex marriage, the state would in fact be harming homosexual persons by justifying their lifestyle and by weakening the nature of marriage.

As Catholics, we have a moral obligation to oppose all attempts to legalize same-sex marriage. Such activity is contrary to our Faith and to the good of society. We should work equally hard to strengthen marriage (between a man and a woman), by encouraging better support structures and education. Finally, we should assist those who suffer from same-sex attraction, by sharing the message of the Gospel and telling of Jesus' mercy and compassion.

Let us all pray for a greater respect for marriage in our culture!

*Reflection Questions:*

1. *Why is homosexual marriage immoral?*
2. *How can I work to support those (heterosexual couples) who are married and struggling in their commitment?*
3. *Is opposition to same-sex marriage the same as discrimination? Why or why not?*

# Same-Sex Marriage – Part I:
*No way. Nohow. God has spoken.*

As Catholics, we must be in the world but not OF the world. We believe that we are called by Jesus to be his ambassadors, his missionaries in the world and in the culture. We are called to share our Faith and to defend this Faith when necessary. However, we are not to be of the world by giving in to its ways of lust, power and pride. Christians are not to be worldly, but rather simple travelers passing through this world on our way to the next. This, we must remember.

> "As Christians, we always have believed that homosexual sex or sodomy – is a grave sin condemned by God. The Bible is filled with references against this practice."

Today, our Western Civilization is in decline. Financially, militarily, culturally, academically and morally, we are decaying. There are many reasons for this decline, and certainly, history has shown that civilizations do rise and fall. However, because of the powerful influence which Europe and the United States have throughout the world, our struggles have quickly become the world's struggles. One of the many examples of this decay is the phenomenon of the legalization of so-called homosexual marriage. True, it is one issue among many, but it symbolizes well the struggles of our time and the difficulties which we, as Christians, will face in the future.

"Gay marriage" now is legal in several states in our country. There is every indication that it will continue to spread throughout our land. Even throughout the countries of Europe, it quickly is becoming codified in law as a fundamental human and legal right. Tragically and shamefully, most of the states in our country that have legalized the practice of gay marriage have a majority population that professes to be Catholic. In Europe, many of the countries that have legalized this practice had, up until recent times, a majority of residents who were Catholic. Indeed, it is Christian or former Christian countries around the world that are advancing this practice. Why is this happening?

Certainly, the rise of gay marriage is a symptom of a much larger cultural malaise, but the Church is not without blame. One major reason for this decline in morality and the rise of this practice is that there has been poor "catechesis" (or teaching) in passing along the Catholic Faith to new generations. Weak leadership from the clergy also has contributed to the problem.

However, there are many other reasons that arise from outside the Church. The breakdown in marriage throughout our country and the world has most certainly helped lead us to this point. With more than 50 percent of marriages ending in divorce, and no doubt many more unhappy marriages, other forms of marriage are being sought by young people. Hence, we see the rise of cohabitation before marriage or so-called "trial marriages." This trend was largely caused by the sexual revolution begun in the 1960s. Now, guided by this revolution, our culture has been pushed towards greater experimentation with alternative sexual practices and lifestyles.

The fuel of the sexual revolution remains the wide availability of birth control, which not only has led to legalized abortion, but also has caused the breakup of many marriages. Today, we face another consequence of sterilized or contracepted sexual activity, with the rise of the homosexual lifestyle and the push for gay marriage. After all, some may wonder, if heterosexual intercourse is intentionally closed to the gift of new life, how is this any different from homosexual intercourse which can never beget life?

As Catholics, we always have believed that homosexual sex - or sodomy - is a grave sin condemned by God. The Bible is filled with references against this practice, both in the New Testament and the Old Testament. The testimony of both God and the Church is clear on the sinfulness of this activity. Even the teachings of other major world religions are practically unanimous in their condemnation of this activity. In addition to this, natural human reason has determined through the ages that sodomy and its widespread acceptance are contrary to the good of society and, indeed, to the continuation of the species. Today, however, there seems to be a widespread questioning of these beliefs and teachings among Christians and non-Christians alike.

# Same-Sex Marriage - Part II:
*Don't let the pressure to be "nice" lead to acceptance!*

Why has the practice of homosexual marriage been advanced so successfully in our own time? Clearly, it is contrary to traditional and orthodox Christian teaching. Yet, the practice has gained the most ground in predominantly Christian countries. In addition to the many reasons I mentioned on previous pages, we must not discount the triumph of "feelings" over reason in this debate.

> "Thus, the tone of the debate revolves around name-calling, emotions and feelings - rather than around logic, biology, tradition or truth."

Ours is a popular culture based largely on emotion and not on rational thought. A 24-hour news cycle, political correctness, sensitivity training and the avoidance of giving offense seem to have eclipsed genuine Christian charity in our daily lives. For example, as Christians, we have been subtly trained by our culture to believe that giving offense to another person is the greatest of all sins. Not true! Charity always reveals the truth, in love, about a person and never is determined by the other person's feelings. However, popular morality today is based solely on feelings and so, as Christians, we find ourselves in a quandary. The definition of charity has been re-written behind our backs.

Those who actively advance the gay lifestyle and promote homosexual marriage know this. They realize that Christians generally do not know their faith very well. Perhaps those who advance this lifestyle were at one time Christians themselves, or still profess to practice the faith, and twist the teachings of the faith to fit their own agenda. Comparisons with the venerable and largely peaceful African-American civil rights movement often are used to legitimize this new movement and to confuse the issue further.

So, gay marriage is touted as a "right." It is about "families." It is about "inclusiveness" and "dignity." Who could possibly be against such things? Only bigots, perhaps - as well as fascists, hate mongers, religious zealots and homophobes - could oppose this, we are told. Thus, the tone of the debate revolves around name-calling, emotion and feelings - rather than around logic, biology, tradition, or truth. Activists believe that if they yell loudly enough, bring enough pressure to bear, and vilify the opposition, they will get their way. They are succeeding! Those who oppose them are seen as hateful and cruel human beings. Because Christians are supposed to be "nice," many cave in under cultural pressure and the world becomes darker.

What can we do to stop all of this? First of all, we must hold fast to our faith! We know what Jesus teaches about marriage and sexuality. We also know what He teaches about charity. Jesus was perfectly charitable but he never condoned sin. People left him, went away sad, disagreed with Him, and eventually crucified Him, but He loved them to the end. We must endeavor to do the same. As Christians, we certainly must love those who struggle with same-sex attraction. Any unjust discrimination against them is most certainly sinful. However, we may never condone the sin - and here, we must hold fast.

We will be called names. We will be hated. Families will be divided. Soon, they will haul us into court and we will be persecuted because of our faith. It sounds a lot like what Jesus said would happen, doesn't it? In the midst of this, we need to return to the practice of our faith. We must reverence and protect the Sacrament of Marriage while we rejoice at the gift of children. We simply must be different from the people we see on television; we must be different from our neighbors and even our friends. If we are true followers of Jesus Christ, now is the time to stand up for our faith. When we do this, when we live this faith of ours, despite the cost, our world will become brighter.

As the days of our lives pass, and we see this world as we know it passing away, we must not become too frustrated or upset. We have been this way before and the Christian faith has triumphed. Christ never will abandon us! So, we smile a bit at the foolishness of this world, we pray for those who suffer in it, and we look forward to the heavenly dawn.

*Reflection Questions:*

1. What is the difference between charity and "niceness?"
2. Why is homosexual activity immoral?
3. How have "feelings" displaced reason in this debate?

---

# Divorce:
*There are no winners; all are left wounded.*

February 7, 1992 was a difficult day for me and my family. On that day, my parents divorced. I really didn't see it coming and I certainly didn't understand why, at the time. As the years have gone by, I have come to understand more about my parents' decision and their marriage. My love for both of them has remained strong, although the pain of that moment has not disappeared. It remains a cross that I will carry for the rest of my life.

We need to speak a bit about divorce. Divorce is the process in which the indissoluble marriage bond validly entered into by a man and a woman is broken. Divorce is really a civil and secular concept; it has no equivalent within the Church.

> "(Even after divorce) the couple still is married sacramentally and remains so until death or until the marriage is declared invalid by an annulment."

It must be said, quite clearly, that divorce is **not** a good thing. Obviously, most people who fall in love and get married do not plan to split up. However, lack of respect or abuse sometimes exists in marriage – and this is a bitter tragedy. In divorce, there are no winners; all are left wounded. Indeed, as we read in the Bible, *"I hate divorce, says the Lord, the God of Israel."* (Malachi 2:16)

Today, the divorce rate has climbed above 50 percent. This rate remains pretty much the same for Christians and for non-believers. It seems that we must, once again, learn the reason for the sanctity of marriage and why our faith opposes divorce.

For all Christians, marriage is something sacred - something holy. It is a sacred and holy commitment - indeed it takes three to get married: one woman, one man and God. For Catholics, marriage is something more. It is a sacrament - a visible sign of an invisible spiritual reality. In the Sacrament of Marriage, we see personified in the husband and wife the spiritual unity of Christ and His bride, the Church. This is the reason why divorce always has been condemned in Christianity and why, in the Catholic Church, a person cannot simply divorce and marry again.

However, we all know that married life can be quite difficult. Sometimes, there is abuse within a marriage, sometimes infidelity, sometimes neglect. Husbands and wives sometimes do cruel things to each other and to their children. Nevertheless, these cruelties (which are rightly called sins), in and of themselves do not directly provide cause for divorce. For Christians, the sacramental bond of marriage is much stronger than any of these circumstances or sins.

Yet, sometimes a point is reached where a couple can no longer live together or their personal safety is imperiled. If a *civil* divorce is the only possible way of ensuring that certain legal rights are protected (protection from abuse or the care of children), then a *civil* divorce can be tolerated and as such is not necessarily immoral.

Notice, however, that the civil nature of divorce in no way alters the sacramental or spiritual permanence of the marriage. The couple still is married sacramentally and remains so until death or until the marriage is declared invalid by an annulment. They cannot marry again until the previous marriage is annulled. Often, it happens that one of the spouses has been unjustly abandoned through divorce. Individuals who have been abandoned by a spouse through divorce are certainly not at fault and are, in fact, innocent victims.

Divorce often has a very negative effect on children. It seems that having an intact family with one mother and one father is becoming a rarity. We are paying a heavy price for this in our society, today. Families that are no longer intact are severely hampered in providing positive examples for their children of what a family ought to be. Of course, constant arguing and abuse between spouses does not provide a positive example, either. Such can be the tragedy of selfishness and cruelty in marriage. However, a civil divorce only may be sought as a last resort for an impossible situation.

Those who are divorced sometimes feel alienated from Christ or His Church. This also is a tragedy. It is precisely at this moment when God's great mercy and forgiveness are needed the most! Those who are divorced often must reconcile themselves with God and the Church as part of their healing process. We all must remember that our God is the God of second chances and that any sin, no matter how great, can be forgiven.

If you or your children have suffered from a divorce, please feel free to speak to a priest. Let us pray for stronger marriages, greater respect among spouses, and an end to the breakdown of the family in our culture.

*Reflection Questions:*

1. *Why is divorce so common, today? What does it do to children?*

2. *Why does the Church teach that the Sacrament of Marriage is permanent?*

3. *How can marriages be strengthened so that divorce can be avoided?*

# The Annulment Process:
*It can heal wounds, help one return to spiritual health.*

In earlier pages, I spoke about divorce and its negative effects on families. However, as we all know, sometimes marriages do fail and divorce occurs. Along with the many pastoral programs that the Church has to offer people who are suffering from a divorce, the annulment process is a possibility which can bring healing and peace.

> "The Church...is simply stating that the sacrament never took place because something was missing."

I am certain that most of you have heard the word "annulment" before. However, I must warn you that, although the word is used often, very few people actually know what it means or what it entails. Some may say that an annulment is basically a Catholic divorce. Others might state that it really is a money-making scheme of the Church. Still others might say that an annulment makes children from a previous marriage illegitimate. All three of these statements are categorically false! Let us now learn more about annulments so that we can better understand the process.

Any sacrament, no matter which one of the seven you choose, has three parts: form, matter and intention. For example, in Baptism, the form is the words, "*I baptize you in the name of the Father, and of the Son and of the Holy Spirit.*" The matter is - you guessed it - water! The intention is provided by the parents and godparents of the child, or by the person to be baptized if he or she is old enough.

Now, if one of those three parts is missing, the Sacrament of Baptism would not occur - it would be *invalid*. For example, what if the priest poured motor oil over the baby's head instead of water? That would be an invalid sacrament; the Baptism would not have occurred because the matter was improper. Even though the baby was in Church, even though the priest was there, even though you have the pictures to prove it, water was not used and the sacrament never happened.

The same can be said for the Sacrament of Marriage. In marriage, there are three parts. The form of marriage for Catholics is marrying in front of a priest, deacon or bishop. The matter is effectively one man and one woman marrying. The intention is the ability of the couple to give full and proper consent at the time of the ceremony. Now, if one of these three parts is missing, the Sacrament of Marriage is invalid. An annulment deals with the third or last part - the faulty intention or an inability or unwillingness to give proper consent at the time of the marriage.

We use the word "annulment," but really, the Church is not annulling anything. The Church, which is the guardian and custodian of the sacraments, is simply stating that the sacrament never took place because something was missing. Thus, the person is free to marry again because his or her first marriage was sacramentally invalid.

How about an example? A man and a woman get married. They married in the Church, in front of the priest; and they have pictures to prove it. They had a big wedding cake and a huge reception; they even were married for 25 years and had four kids. However, their marriage was rocky; they never seemed to get along. Finally, when all the kids were off to college, they divorced. "*Why?*" everyone asked.

Looking back, we might be able to find the real reason why they got married in the first place. A few months before the wedding, the father of the bride told his daughter that unless she married this fellow, he would disinherit her and kick her out of the family. So, she went through with it - not because she wanted to, but because she was forced to marry. I hope you can see from this example that this marriage is, in fact, missing something. The free intention to marry is missing, so it is, in fact, an invalid marriage. After this marriage was investigated by the Church, an annulment would most likely be granted.

The annulment process is not a "Catholic divorce," as I hope you can see. If a sacrament never happened, then, of course, one can marry anew. No children are made illegitimate by any annulment, because a marriage is considered valid until proven otherwise. Besides, all of us are legitimate in the eyes of God!

The administrative cost of an annulment may be several hundred dollars. However, the fee is sometimes waived. Not all annulments are granted, but many are. I urge you to contact a priest if you would like to seek an annulment. The process takes about a year – or more – but it can bring you great healing in your life.

The bottom line is this. Those who are divorced are not exiled or kicked out of the Church. Following the example of Jesus the Good Shepherd, the Church wants to work with you to heal your wounds and bring you back to spiritual health.

*Reflection Questions:*

1. *Why are annulments not "Catholic divorces?"*
2. *Do you know someone whose previous marriage was annulled? How is he or she doing today?*
3. *Why does the Catholic Church have the right to grant annulments?*

# The "Just War" Theory:
*Here are five criteria to consider ...*

All of us are upset and angered when we hear about acts of terrorism around the world. Some terrorist attacks have affected our own country. We have become painfully aware that we are no longer immune. With our country's involvement in conflicts around the world, especially in wars in the Middle East, it's a good time to pause and reflect on the proper Christian response to issues of war and peace.

> "....governments have the right to a lawful self-defense, but only after all peaceful efforts have failed. Peace always is preferred."

As Christians, we first look to the example and teachings of Jesus – as recorded in the Bible and taught by His Church. When we look at the Scriptures, we see countless examples of war. However, throughout, we see an overwhelming longing for peace. One thinks of the beautiful passage from Isaiah speaking of the coming Messiah: *"They shall beat their swords into plowshares, and their spears* into pruning hooks; nation shall not lift up sword against nation, neither shall they learn war any more." (Isaiah 2:4)

War is seen as a negative thing – something to be avoided and only undertaken as a last resort. The Church teaches that as long as the danger of war persists, governments have the right to a lawful self-defense, but only after all peaceful efforts have failed. Peace always is preferred.

When we look at Jesus' challenging teaching of "turning the other cheek," it may seem at first that Christians are to be strict pacifists. However, we also must remember that there is a moral obligation to protect one's neighbor from harm: *"Love your neighbor as yourself."* (Luke 10:27) Legitimate defense, then, is not only a right but an obligation for those entrusted with caring for others. Thus, war can sometimes be justified in order to keep others from harm.

In the Fifth Century, St. Augustine, a great teacher of the Catholic Faith, outlined what later became known as "The Just War Theory." This theory, which eventually gained wide acceptance, holds that war sometimes is necessary, but never preferable. In this theory, there are five criteria which must be met for a war to be morally legitimate. They are as follows:

1. One must have a just cause (protection of the innocent, etc.).

2. One must have the right intention in seeking to restore justice and order (not for vengeance).

3. The use of force must be ordered by a competent and lawful authority (legitimate leader).

4. There must be a reasonable probability of success. (A war that cannot be won is not just.)

5. All peaceful means of resolving the conflict must be exhausted. (War must be a last resort.)

Today, of course, the nature of war is changing. With weapons of mass destruction – chemical, nuclear and biological – modern warfare presents a challenge to The Just War Theory. Add to this the appearance of terrorism, which the theory never envisioned.

Nevertheless, this theory is a good starting point for discussing whether a given conflict is moral or not. Certainly, the deliberate targeting of civilian populations is always reprehensible and immoral. Also, the widespread destruction from modern warfare is reason enough to weigh seriously the morality of any given conflict. However, sometimes war is permissible – but only as a last resort.

Today, there are varying opinions as to what our public policies should be regarding war and defense. Whether the wars in which we currently are involved are just or not is beyond the scope of this article. However, one thing is for certain. As believers in Jesus Christ and members of His Body, the Church, we should work towards and earnestly pray for peace in our world. Jesus is rightly called, "The Prince of Peace," and so we ask Him to use us as peacemakers in the world.

*Reflection Questions:*

1. It has been said that *"war is Hell."* What does this mean?
2. Can I give an example of a just war? Of an unjust war?
3. Have I ever spoken to a veteran about war? What did he or she say?

---

# Death and Dying:
*You'll never be an angel - but, consider one for your gravestone!*

Every October 31, we celebrate two special occasions. Most people know this day as Halloween. However, we Catholics also celebrate All Souls Day - a special time to pray for the souls of our loved ones who have died.

The prayers we say are very valuable. If the souls of our loved ones are in Purgatory, we pray that they might quickly be purged of their attachment to sin and so enter into eternal life in Heaven. Our Catholic funeral rites reflect this practice of praying for the dead, as well as celebrating the Faith we shared together on earth.

> "It is extremely presumptuous to assume that a loved one is *automatically* in Heaven."

Today, it is so sad that fewer and fewer Christians are actively practicing their faith. Every family seems to be affected. When these inactive Christians die or when their parents who were active in the Faith pass away, issues often arise which must be dealt with delicately, but truthfully. Let us look at a few of these issues and perhaps clear up a few misconceptions.

A Catholic funeral Mass is NOT a canonization service for sainthood. It is extremely presumptuous to assume that a loved one is *automatically* in Heaven. Yes, indeed, we hope for eternal life for our loved ones who have died, and we certainly pray for this. However, we do not presume to judge one way or the other - God is the judge of that. In her prayers for the dead, the Church reflects this understanding. In my homilies and in my demeanor, I try very hard to make funeral Masses indeed what they are - the perfect prayers for the ones who have died, and remembrances of their lives. We hope and pray for happiness in Heaven for our loved ones, but we do not presume.

When a loved one - either a child or an adult - dies, he or she DOES NOT become an angel. An angel is a separate being created by God to do His bidding. Angels are pure spirits and they are completely different creatures than human beings. Please consider this: Jesus Christ did not assume an angelic nature, but a human nature. Our Lord did not suffer and die to save the angels who had fallen, but us. What a blessing! When we die, our souls remain human souls - and, at the end of the world, our bodies will rise again and be reunited with our souls. We never will become angels.

When we die, we are not reincarnated. This is not a Christian belief; it is contrary to our human dignity and to the dignity of our souls. Our souls, which are immortal, remain human souls for all eternity. We do not become dogs. Or mosquitoes. Or wallabies. Or whatever. Our souls have been redeemed by Jesus Christ and do not need to become anything else to be saved.

If we consider ourselves Christians, we should have some kind of Christian symbol on our graves. What is the most important part of our lives? How will we want to be remembered? As football fans? For fishing? Hunting? Music or a band? All of these are nice and fun things, but what about Jesus? I have noticed that very few graves today even have a cross on the gravestone. Could we sneak in a cross, another religious image or a line from the Bible on our gravestones, in between all of the references to the fleeting hobbies of this world? Which is eternal?

A note to parents: Please make EXPLICIT instructions to your children or grandchildren as to how you would like your funeral arrangements to be handled. If you would like a Mass, you must tell them. The Church still prefers bodily burial over cremation. With cremation, there often is the risk of no burial at all. Children who have strayed from the Faith sometimes like to put Mom and Dad in an urn on the fireplace mantle and not have them buried. That way, they can "remember you." This is not Christian. If your children are not practicing the Faith or are no longer Catholic, please be most explicit with your instructions for your funeral. Consider assigning this task to someone you trust.

I realize that these are difficult issues to face. However, as Christians, we believe in eternal life. Let us witness this faith by being respectful toward the funeral rites of the Church.

*Reflection Questions:*

1. *Those who have strayed from the Faith typically have the oddest notions about funerals and death and dying. Why is this true?*
2. *Have I expressed to my loved ones my intentions for my funeral?*
3. *Death is the last absolute in our culture today. How does our popular culture deal with it?*

---

# End-of-Life Decisions – Part I:
*There's no "mercy" in "mercy killing."*

Recently, the Vatican issued a clarification for all Catholics regarding the necessity of providing nutrition and hydration for those in a persistent vegetative state. Pope Benedict has approved this statement and thus, we now have clear guidelines as to how we should deal with this emotionally trying issue.

One of the miracles of modern medicine is that we can live longer, overcoming a number of diseases and conditions that once proved fatal. Although this is truly marvelous and indeed a great gift to humanity, the frailty of our human condition does not disappear. For example, illnesses which previously never affected people who died in their 50s now are ravaging people in their 80s.

> "Rather than administering a lethal drug to kill the person outright, the practice of euthanasia now has gone underground and accomplishes its grim task in secret…"

One of today's challenges is knowing what to do when a person nears the end of his life and his illness renders him unconscious or – even more seriously – puts him into what is called a "persistent vegetative state." In this state, recovery is medically doubtful. Today, it is becoming all too common for individuals in such medical conditions to be deprived of nutrition and hydration and thus, in effect, starved or severely dehydrated. This is euthanasia or so-called "mercy killing" and it always is contrary to the Gospel. Rather than administering a lethal drug to kill the person outright, the practice of euthanasia now has gone underground and accomplishes its grim task in secret – by starvation and dehydration. It is murder under the guise of being merciful.

The teaching of our Catholic Faith is that nutrition and hydration are basic forms of care, and thus, are "ordinary" means that a person must receive regardless of his or her condition or expected outcome. Nutrition and hydration can be withdrawn from a seriously ill patient only when these elements cannot be assimilated by the body or are directly causing the patient significant physical discomfort.

Perhaps we might understand this better by asking ourselves if we would deny a starving person in a refugee camp food or water. We strive to care for those who are suffering and hungry. Someone who has had a serious illness that incapacitates him or her deserves the same treatment as everybody else. Yes, that individual's life may not appear to be as "productive" or his so-called "quality of life" might be impaired. However, watch out when people use these words! These are the words that often are used to advocate for euthanasia today.

Our human dignity remains, regardless of the situation in which we find ourselves. Intentionally removing nutrition or hydration from a person who is in a persistent vegetative state is murder.

# End-of-Life Decisions – Part II:
## *Don't let the Culture of Death invade your home!*

To illustrate the complexity of end-of-life issues, let's consider the following situation ...

*An elderly woman has a stroke which causes unconsciousness with severe complications. Her children and loved ones have differing opinions on what to do about her. Some say she should stay in the hospital until she gets better, or at least until things stabilize. Others say that Mom, "didn't want any tubes. She wanted to die naturally, not hooked up to some machine."*

*The son who has health care power of attorney decides to take his mother home and let her die naturally. Since the home hospice organization with whom the family contracted refuses to accept patients with an IV line, the mother is taken home to the son's house without provisions for nutrition and hydration. After a week and a half, she dies while still unconscious – of dehydration and starvation, simply because the stroke prevented her from eating or drinking. The family remains forever divided as to whether Mom was killed by the ones she trusted and loved.*

Although this story may seem far-fetched, this kind of scenario is quickly becoming common today.

> "When the moment comes for a decision to be made about a course of treatment, we need a loved one who knows our desires and our Faith to make the right decision for us."

So, what should we, as Catholics, do? First of all, we need to stand up against our culture that so often regards the seriously ill as burdens to be eliminated. We must not let the Culture of Death invade our homes and our families. If or when we are faced with a loved one who is dying, we must, in charity, provide him or her with the ordinary means of human comfort - which always include nutrition and hydration.

We all need to make it known to our loved ones that we demand that they give us these simple aspects of care if or when our life comes to this point. It is not enough to tell our loved ones, "*I don't want any tubes. I don't want to be hooked up to a machine,*" etc. Nobody wants these things! However, sometimes these tubes, these machines, when used for a short period of time, will save our lives.

Family members often find themselves in heart-wrenching situations in which decisions are made on whether a loved one lives or dies because of a document, signed at a lawyer's office, on some sunny day five years ago. Living wills are fine tools to provide for one's health care - but they are not perfect. When the moment comes for a decision to be made about a course of treatment, we need a loved one who knows our desires and our Faith to make the right decision for us. Many health care ethicists recommend having a *health care proxy* - or a person designated to make health care decisions for us - as the best means to assure moral decisions in this regard.

We don't like to think about these issues. However, the fact remains that each of us will die some day. Although we all desire to die in our sleep at age 100, this will probably not be the case for most of us. Talk to the ones you love and place someone you trust in charge of your emergency health care.

*Reflection Questions:*

1. Why must nutrition and hydration be provided for seriously ill people?
2. "Quality of life" is a code phrase for the Culture of Death. Why?
3. We live in a time of medical miracles. This has a darker side. What is it?

# Euthanasia:
*This is thinly disguised murder!*

There once was a mother who said to her son, "Pick up your tired old grandmother, put her in the rusty old wheelbarrow, and take her out to the woods to die." The son followed his mother's instructions, and took his grandmother out to the woods.

However, as he returned, the mother saw that her son had brought back the wheelbarrow. Enraged at him for returning with the rickety contraption, she screamed, "Why did you bring back that worthless, old thing? You should have left it in the woods with your grandmother." Her son replied, "I brought it back so that when you become sick and old, I can use it to take you out to the woods to die."

Putting an end to the lives of the handicapped, the sick, or the dying is called "euthanasia." This practice is morally unacceptable. In reality, it is thinly disguised murder. Mercy killing is just that – killing – and it is a serious sin.

> **"This (euthanasia) is a great evil – and the result of seeing life as a burden rather than as a gift."**

Those who practice euthanasia assume that they alone have a right of ownership over human life. Euthanasia requires that those doctors or officials in charge be called upon to make a choice – a subjective choice – as to who will live and who will die. A veritable smoke screen of reasons is wafted for these actions, whether it be the supposed pain of the patient, or his or her emotional well-being. Behind these actions, however, lies the truth of euthanasia, which almost always includes financial reasons and incentives to end life, and subjective opinions as to who will live and who will die.

In addition, there is a growing movement across our country today to allow sick or suffering individuals to take their own lives. Often, this is called "physician assisted suicide." It is represented by its proponents as a fundamental human right, even though this action is gravely contrary to both the natural and divine laws. Under this cloak of supposed freedom of determination, lie sadness and despair. Those who champion this "right" denigrate human life by seeing it as merely physical – where pain is the greatest of evils. The spiritual nature of a human being is not acknowledged. Suffering is meaningless and human life is expendable, they seem to contend.

What should we, as Christians, do in the face of this attack on human life? We must remember that life is a journey and that we never walk this way alone. Christ is our guide. During this journey will come suffering, some little and some great. However, we have the greatest of assurances that Jesus Christ has made suffering meaningful by His own suffering and death on the Cross. Therefore, as members of His Body, the Church, we unite our own sufferings with Christ's sufferings. Just as the sufferings of Christ made possible our salvation, so our own sufferings, united with His, bring us to salvation!

At the end of life, when there is often much loneliness and pain, we need others to assist us in living our faith. It is precisely here, at this crucial point, where those who support the evil of euthanasia or physician assisted suicide intervene and say, *"Your suffering means nothing; just end it all."* Rather than dying in hope, the individual is led into despair, hence placing his or her soul in danger. What a tragedy.

Now, discontinuing medical procedures that have become burdensome, dangerous, extraordinary, or disproportionate to the expected outcome, is not euthanasia - and hence is not sinful. Rather than intending death for oneself or another, here, the individual, the doctor or family member realizes that death is inevitable. However, there must always be a balance in favor of continuing nutrition and hydration of a sick person, if at all possible.

Like the young son who returns with the wheelbarrow, those who advocate and practice euthanasia aim to expand its practice to all times of life. Today, in countries such as the Netherlands, euthanasia not only is legal, it is being expanded to include other lives that are unwanted. This is a great evil - and the result of seeing life as a burden rather than as a gift. As Christians, we must vigorously oppose this practice and show our world that all life is a gift from God.

*Reflection Questions:*

1. *Have I ever been around a terminally ill person? How did I react?*
2. *Is there meaning in suffering? How does a Christian respond to this question?*
3. *What are the dangers of euthanasia in our society and in our culture?*

# Suicide:
*Is it still possible to go to Heaven?*

Thankfully, most of our mistakes in life are not permanent. We rely on this - it seems that no matter how bad something is at the moment, there soon will be another opportunity for things to improve. Paint usually washes out of clothes, broken items can be replaced, and Spring always follows Winter. We hope in these things - we know that bad days often turn into good days.

Sadly, some things in life are permanent. Suicide is one of them. It is a permanent solution to a temporary problem. It is a great tragedy and a cause of lingering sadness for many families.

> "The taking of one's own life is contrary to our human nature and dignity. If intentionally done, it also is a serious sin."

It should be obvious to most people that suicide is gravely wrong. The taking of one's own life is contrary to our human nature and dignity. If intentionally done, it also is a serious sin. It seems that many families have had some member, young or old, who has taken his or her own life. The pain still remains - even if it happened some 10, 20 or 50 years ago. Those who survive often are wounded by the memory. Questions remain. People want to know, "Why?"

Our Christian faith helps us with this issue. I'm often asked whether a loved one who takes his or her own life can go to Heaven. After all, murder is a mortal sin - and dying in the state of mortal sin condemns one to Hell. Also, killing one's own self presumably allows no time for repentance. So, the question remains - can my loved one be saved?

As Christians, we always have considered suicide to be a serious evil and always morally wrong. As recently as 100 years ago, those who had taken their own lives were not given Christian burial services, but rather buried in other ground - sometimes at the fork of a road. This symbolized not knowing where the person went after he or she died. Sometimes, crosses were erected at such places, leading to the common phrase, "coming to a crossroad."

In the past 50 years, science has begun to look more closely at issues of mental distress and illness. With the advance of these studies, we recognize that certain individuals do not have full control of themselves or their actions. In other words, more often than not, those who take their own lives are under such great emotional distress that perhaps they do not fully realize what they are doing. Hence, the seriousness of the sin might be reduced.

In my own pastoral experience with suicide, I've found that, most of the time, it is related to an emotional issue so strong that the person could not control himself. Today, the Church permits funerals for those who have taken their own lives, if it appears that they did so not fully realizing what they were doing. In the end, God will sort it out - He Who is very merciful and very just. We entrust all those who have died to the mercy of God - even those who have taken their own lives.

All of us are our brother's and sister's keeper. As adults, we must keep a watchful eye on our young people - especially those in their teens and twenties. Young people today are beset by a culture of death - a popular culture of movies, television and music that offers little hope and much despair.

As Christians, we must talk with our children and grandchildren about the perils of suicide and tell them that we are always there to help. Listen to your children – listen to your loved ones who are suffering – and reach out to help them. Remind them that tomorrow is another day – and that things will get better.

That's what our faith is all about – that is what Easter is all about! Let us pray for those families who have lost a loved one to suicide.

*Reflection Questions:*

1. *Why is suicide wrong?*

2. *What effects does suicide have on the family and the community?*

3. *How can we prevent this terrible tragedy?*

---

# Cremation:
*Is it okay to do this? Could my ashes be sprinkled in the lake?*

It's always interesting to watch popular trends. For example, at every wedding I have witnessed these past two years (almost 40!), the same processional song has been played: Pachelbel's Canon in D. Then, there are kitchen appliances – today, the rage is stainless steel, something that was popular 50 years ago! Even with cars today, chrome (fake chrome, mind you) is popular again, just as it was in the 1950s. Styles change, people change, and some things become popular. Then, for no particular reason, these trends seem to fade away.

> **"I would recommend against cremation, unless you are certain that the remains will be buried with dignity and respect."**

Today, there is a trend in our country regarding funerals – and this trend is called "cremation." I call it a trend because the practice of rendering a dead body to ashes by fire was almost unheard of in Western culture for the past 2,000 years. The primary reason for cremation's disappearance was the rise of Christianity. The funeral rites of Christianity closely followed the Jewish custom of bodily burial in the earth. For the Christian, bodily burial strongly symbolized and pointed towards the resurrection of the body. (We pray about this every weekend at the end of the Creed.) Because Jesus rose again from the dead, so shall we rise again – and bodily burial better symbolizes this part of our faith.

With this in mind, the Catholic Church until quite recently strictly prohibited cremation. It was thought that those who were cremated had explicitly, by their actions, denied our faith in the resurrection of the body. This prohibition was somewhat modified in the 1983 Code of Canon Law. This document states, *"The Church earnestly recommends that the pious custom of burying the bodies of the dead be observed; it does not, however, forbid cremation unless it has been chosen for reasons which are contrary to Christian teaching."* (Canon 1176)

This is further illustrated in the current Rite of Christian Funerals which states, *"Although cremation is now permitted by the Church, it does not enjoy the same value as burial of the body."* (p. 391, paragraph 413) So, to reiterate what we, as Catholics, believe, cremation is permitted by the Church as long as it does not involve a denial of the resurrection of the body. However, bodily burial still is preferred.

I realize that some of you may have difficulty with this. So, let us look at the spirit of this teaching. Those of you who were well trained in your Faith probably remember that one of the corporal works of mercy is "to bury the dead." Today, because of the increasing popularity of cremation, coupled with a lack of Christian understanding, relatives of the deceased often do not bury their loved one's cremated remains. The remains are kept on a fireplace mantel, put on a bedside table, scattered in the ocean or in a lake or woods, or even, (according to an advertisement I saw) compressed into a kind of "diamond" ring to be worn on one's finger! My friends, let's not fall into trends which are pagan!

Respect for the body of a deceased loved one is critical to our Faith – for this body will one day be glorified and rise again. Respect for the body of a dead loved one demands burial, so that his remains will be treated with dignity and left at peace. With bodily burial, the above abuses are not an issue. However, with cremation comes the potential for disrespect. Remember that respect is the spirit behind the Church's teaching.

Trends come and go. With the loss of a Christian culture in our country, there will be more trends facing us that are foreign to our Catholic traditions. I would recommend against cremation, unless you are certain that the remains will be buried with dignity and respect. Please pray over this.

*Reflection Questions:*

1. What was the most beautiful or moving funeral I ever attended?
2. Have I ever visited a cemetery? Do I pray for the dead? Why or why not?
3. At the end of time, how will our resurrected bodies look? Do we know?

# Capital Punishment - The Death Penalty:
*We must not short-circuit the process of repentance!*

About 100 years ago, there was a young Italian girl named Maria Goretti. She was innocent and pure and she loved to help her family on their farm. When she was 12, a hired hand named Alexandro took a liking to her. His attraction soon turned to lust, despite the fact that Maria rejected his overtures and sinful suggestions.

After numerous attempts to seduce her, Alexandro, in a fit of range, took a dagger and stabbed Maria multiple times. As she lay dying, she forgave her attacker and prayed for him. Soon, Alexandro was caught and convicted of murder. Although some people wanted him to die for his crime, he was sentenced to many years in prison.

> "....as Christians, we should work to protect all life, even those lives which we don't consider particularly loveable."

For the first 10 years, Alexandro was bitter. He hated Maria and what had happened because of her. However, Maria came to him in a dream one night and offered him forgiveness. She told him that she would pray for his conversion. Soon, Alexandro began to change. He started to pray. He received the Sacrament of Confession; he began to receive the Eucharist again.

The prison officials were so amazed at his transformation that he was released early. Alexandro immediately joined a religious order where he spent his time in prayer. The highlight of his life was one day in 1950, when the young girl he had killed some 50 years before was canonized a saint. Here, for the first time in Church history, a saint was canonized in the presence of her mother and her siblings - and while her murderer was still alive. Alexandro died a changed man, known for his humility and his holiness.

What a beautiful story! However, what if circumstances had been different? What if Alexandro had been executed for his crime? If he had, chances are he would never have had the time to repent for what he had done. Perhaps he never would have made it to Heaven. What a tragedy that would have been!

Capital punishment or the "death penalty" is a controversial subject today. When the crime is so great, and the desire for revenge so overwhelming, we must remember this story. Repentance sometimes takes time, but with it comes eternal life. We must never cut the process short!

In the Old Testament, there are more than 36 capital offenses - that is, crimes deserving of death. Truly, the morality of the time was "an eye for an eye, a tooth for a tooth." With the New Testament, however, came a fulfillment of the Old, and the teachings of Jesus Christ. Our Lord asked us to love our neighbor as ourself and forgive our enemies.

In the early Church, capital punishment was still a reality. Indeed, Jesus Himself was a victim of it, as well as many of the apostles and disciples. Despite these events, the early Church believed and upheld the right of the State to execute a criminal who was justly deemed a danger to society. The State was determined to be acting in self defense - much like a soldier in battle. Thus, capital punishment never was explicitly rejected by the Church - it always was acknowledged as a right of the government to keep order in society. This teaching has not changed.

In our own time, however, the Church's teaching on the death penalty has developed. Pope John Paul II stated that the death penalty should be rare and that it is often unnecessary. This teaching is reiterated in the Catechism of the Catholic Church. It is always preferable to protect the common good from a dangerous criminal by bloodless means, rather than capital punishment (CCC #2266).

In order to understand this complex issue properly, we must recognize that the Church still teaches that capital punishment is permissible. However, it must be rare and only used as a last resort. In our own country, there is no good reason for capital punishment because of our stable criminal justice system. The common good can be protected adequately without taking someone's life. Hence, capital punishment in our own country is unnecessary and immoral and we should pray for its end. We must remember that, as Catholics, we should work to protect all life, even those lives which we don't consider particularly loveable.

*Reflection Questions:*

1. *Have I ever wanted to take revenge on another person for what he or she did to me?*

2. *Is the death penalty about safety, justice or revenge?*

3. *If a loved one was murdered, would I want the death penalty for the criminal?*

# Morality in Elections:
*Truth is not measured by a majority vote.*

Each year, elections are held across our country at a local, state, and sometimes national level. Candidates vigorously campaign, with plans of how our communities and our nation can be bettered. Politics can be a noble activity when the common good of citizens is kept in mind and the protection of our life and liberty is its goal.

As we all know, politics in our country today is very polarized – perhaps as polarized as it has ever been. Often, polls show our population to be almost evenly split on a variety of issues that pertain to our way of life. As Catholics, how do we bring our Faith into this often controversial – and secular – arena?

> **"Sadly, many Catholic voters and politicians choose to gain the whole world of popularity and secular esteem, and thus risk losing their souls."**

Currently, Catholics make up about 25 percent of the United States population. We are the largest single religious group in our country. If history has shown us anything, it is that the Church must stand independent of the civil authorities. It often is tempting to want to marry the Church to politics or to use the Church for leverage or political gain. We must flee from this temptation.

However, it is true that the teachings of Our Lord Jesus Christ and the teachings of His Church often give us insights into the political issues of the day. When this happens, our Faith never can be set aside because of political preference or gain. Rather, our Faith must engage the issue at hand.

It is important to remember that politics, for all of its high-minded rhetoric, in the end simply desires to make this small piece of the world a better place. Our Catholic Faith is concerned with something much greater: the salvation of souls and eternal life in Heaven. Thus, those involved in politics who are believers in the Lord have two grave responsibilities. The first is respect for the will of their constituents, those who have elected them to office. The second is respect for the Will of Christ who is both our Merciful Savior and Our Just Judge. For those politicians of conscience, this can be an agonizing road to travel. Often, balance is elusive and pressure exercised by various groups can be enormously powerful. What are we, as Christians, to do?

First and foremost, we must remember the words of Christ, *"What profit it a man, if he were to gain the whole world yet lose his soul?"* (Mark 8:36) Many of today's political issues were unheard of just 50 years ago. Today, as voters, we face issues of life and death almost regularly. The dignity of the human person is under constant attack. This fundamental dignity is vastly more important than roadways or schools, national defense or agriculture. Without human life being protected absolutely in the law, not one of us is safe.

It should be obvious to all who strive to live their Faith that abortion, euthanasia, embryonic stem cell research, gay marriage and human cloning are non-negotiable issues for us as Catholics. The teaching of Christ and His Church on each of these issues is abundantly clear – all are intrinsically evil practices and must be opposed. Sadly, many Catholic voters and politicians choose to gain the whole world of popularity and secular esteem, and thus risk losing their souls.

Catholics involved in politics, either as voters or as politicians themselves, must never turn a blind eye towards Christ. Truth is not measured by a majority vote, nor faithfulness measured by popularity. Rather, we must vote according to our well-formed consciences, enlightened by Jesus Christ and the teachings of His Church. We must never be ashamed of Christ.

Whenever we vote, let us vote to better our community, our state and our country. Let us also remember, however, that Jesus is the Way, the Truth, and the Life, and any betterment can come only through Him.

*Reflection Questions:*

1. *What would you, as a Catholic, do if you were elected to political office? Would you allow your Faith to influence your decisions? Why or why not?*
2. *Why do some Catholic politicians abandon their Faith for political popularity?*
3. *Is it still possible to be a believing Christian and run for political office in our country? Why or why not?*

# The Internet:
*Beware – it can lead to sinful choices!*

Many times, we "date" ourselves by mentioning the kind of technology that was around when we grew up. For example, I never learned how to use a typewriter – mine was the first class in grade school to learn how to use computers. Even though I collect vinyl records as a hobby, most people my age and younger think that these objects are black Frisbees! The list can go on and on for all of us.

Perhaps one of the most amazing and useful developments of our time has been the invention and proliferation of the computer internet. This tool has opened up many new lines of communication, commerce and study. However, like anything else, the internet can be used for good purposes or for evil ones. Sadly, I now must address the darker side of this new technology.

> "Let us be prudent in how we use this technology and not forget that Heaven is our final goal."

One of the great strengths of the internet, with its accompanying e-mail and search engines, is the ability to access information quickly – and anonymously. Tragically, this very attribute sometimes can lead to sinful choices. Online services can connect old friends and help us to stay in contact with new ones. However, they also can serve to rekindle old passions or to develop new romances in a make-believe fantasy world.

Unfortunately, it is common today, among married couples, for infidelity to begin with online communication. In this fantasy world, a secret romance unknown to one's spouse often can lead to adultery. This, all too often, ends with the destruction of marriage and family life. Typically, the spouse runs away to be with the online lover only to discover that this individual is not as attractive in reality as online. However, the damage has been done and children often become the innocent victims of this kind of selfishness. Spouses should be honest with each other and have a common e-mail site in order to guard against this temptation. <u>Nothing is as tempting as a secret love affair online.</u>

Other options of the internet include online chat rooms and dating services. These dating services have moved into the mainstream, including several Catholic sites that I have recommended to people discerning marriage. However, one must be cautious here as well. There is no substitute for meeting face-to-face and getting to know a person in this way. Often, you become the person you want to be online – not necessarily the person you really are.

Aside from dating services, there are several social networking sites that cater to young adults and teens. Parents should monitor these sites closely. Many times, predators stalk innocent victims here. Your teen's safely is more important than his or her privacy. Parents, be aware!

Internet pornography is a multi-billion dollar industry that frequently targets men and victimizes women. It is incredibly addictive and extremely dangerous to the life of the soul. Vocations are destroyed by this instant display of sexual images which seep into one's mind and always leave emptiness behind. Wives should monitor the internet to make sure that their husbands have not fallen prey to this addiction. As Christians, we should love people for who they are, not for what they are. Pornography treats people as objects and it is always wrong.

Finally, the internet and e-mail are quite entertaining and informative. However, they also are very tempting diversions which waste time! This is time away from family, time away from work, time away from serving others, time away from prayer - wasted time! Use e-mail and other internet services as tools - not as replacements for a family or time spent with friends. Remember, once the computer is turned off, we have little to show for our time. Let's make sure that we spend our time on earth wisely.

The internet is the great invention of our era and we are fortunate to have it. Let's make sure that it remains a tool - not a replacement for the intimacy of friendship. Let us be prudent in how we use this technology and not forget that Heaven is our final goal.

*Reflection Questions:*

1. *List the amazing benefits of the internet.*
2. *List the dangers of this new technology.*
3. *How can I use the internet to grow closer to God?*

# Gambling:
## *Don't let the "bright lights" blind you to the risks!*

Every evening, when I drive down the highway, I am taken by the bright lights in the northern sky. No, this is not a beautiful manifestation of the Northern Lights phenomenon. Rather, it is the aura from the many gambling casinos present in our community!

The issue of casino gambling is a complex subject. Is it entertainment? Is it a blessing to our Native American communities? Is it a temptation to sin? Is it an injustice to those who are poor? These are just a few of the many questions raised. Perhaps, more importantly, beyond the politics and moneymaking, what does our Catholic Faith tell us about the issue of gambling?

> **"(Games of chance or wagers) become sinful when they deprive someone of what is necessary to provide for his or her needs and the needs of others."**

Although the Bible speaks only indirectly about gambling, the Lord's intentions are clear. In I Timothy 6: 8-10, we read: *"For if we have food and clothing, we shall be content with that. Those who want to be rich are falling into temptation and* into a trap and into many foolish and harmful desires, which plunge them into ruin and destruction. For the love of money is the root of all evils, and some people in their desire for it have strayed from the faith and have pierced themselves with many pains." (NAB)

In the Catechism, we read that games of chance or wagers are not, in and of themselves, contrary to justice or sinful. However, they become sinful when they deprive someone of what is necessary to provide for his or her needs and the needs of others. Also, we read that the passion for gambling can become an enslavement or addiction.

Until very recently, gambling, lotteries and other games of chance were regulated tightly, both legally and socially. Lotteries or raffles for charitable causes were seen as socially acceptable and even good for the building of the community and for having fun. Today, however, raffles and simple games of chance have given way to something much larger and more secular with the growth of an entire "culture of gambling." Cities such as Las Vegas owe their entire existence to gambling and its attendant lifestyle.

The issue now at hand is whether large, modern institutions such as casinos and state lotteries are morally acceptable. What purpose do they serve in society?

The gambling industry is intentionally and openly hedonistic; it is about being a winner, making lots of money, and having lots of fun in the process. On the surface, it sounds innocent enough. However, behind the slick media campaigns, you'll find a wake of many ruined marriages, addictions and bankruptcy. Certainly, nobody is forced to participate in gambling. However, casino gambling today attracts a disproportionate number of poor persons who hope that they might end their financial woes by "the big win." They rarely do. Gambling addiction, which affects the poor and the rich alike, has enslaved many lives and ruined many marriages. This is a high cost to pay for just "having fun."

A further complication for this issue is the fact that Native American tribes run many gambling casinos. It is true that the tribes often benefit greatly from the increased revenues from gaming. However, the end never can justify the means. Does the increased revenue from casino gambling truly help the tribes or the State? Is the increase in poverty and addiction to gambling too high a price to pay? Furthermore, is the Native American community, which so often has been treated unjustly, truly helped by such casinos? Is this just a quick and shallow fix for the deeper problems of injustice and a cycle of poverty? These are but a few of the questions that must be asked as we address the issue of gambling.

So, when is gambling wrong? Is it always wrong? Sometimes? Never? It would seem that small-scale gaming and lotteries can be fun and morally acceptable. However, the more these pastimes are institutionalized and secularized, the more dangerous they can become. When does a game turn into a sinful act of injustice towards others? As Christians, we must ask these questions. It seems that modern gambling is saying, *"What God has provided is not enough. We need more than God can provide. Being poor is bad and being rich is good."* What message does this send?

Let us all pray to discern God's Will on this issue.

*Reflection Questions:*

1. *It has been said that addiction to gambling is the fastest growing addiction, today. Why is this true?*

2. *The lives of those who have won millions of dollars at gambling have been documented. The clear majority go on to lose everything they won – and more. Why does this happen?*

3. *What do you think Jesus would tell us about gambling?*

# Section IV
## Remember the Golden Rule

# Racism:
*God doesn't care about skin color – and neither should we!*

When I was growing up in Milwaukee, Wisconsin, I attended Marquette University High School. It is a Catholic, Jesuit-run, all-male school in downtown Milwaukee. I had a fantastic experience there and highly recommend it. The academics were strong, the sports were excellent, and many of the friendships I made while there still exist today. However, it was on the trip to and from school every day, and in the friendships I made, that I learned the most valuable lesson.

> "Racism – or the idea that one group of people is somehow better than another group of people – is contrary to our Christian faith and…wrong."

My family lived in a western suburb of Milwaukee, a village filled with trees, sidewalks, big homes and clean yards. However, as I traveled to school each day, the scene outside my window changed. The houses grew smaller, the yards grew more cluttered, and soon, I was seeing real poverty outside the car window.

During my four years of high school, I met numerous young men who looked different from me and who came from very different backgrounds. However, as we got to know each other, the pigmentation of our skin, how our hair looked and where we lived suddenly didn't matter anymore. What mattered most was that we were friends and that God created us and loved us all. My experience in this racially-diverse high school setting, in an inner-city neighborhood, taught me many things about people. It also taught me a thing or two about the sin we call "racism."

Racism – or the idea that one group of people is somehow better than another group of people – is contrary to our Christian faith and always, always wrong. It's silly, really, to think, for example, that because my skin is light and your skin is dark, I am better than you are. Because I was born in one place and you were born in another, doesn't make either of us a better person. Our country has struggled with the issue of racism for hundreds of years and we continue to struggle with it. However, as Christians, we must realize and accept deep in our hearts the hard fact that God really doesn't care about skin color or our country of origin.

Oftentimes, we equate poverty with the color of a person's skin or the neighborhood in which the person was born. To refute a common prejudice, believe it or not, there are many successful and wealthy African American and Hispanic people in our country! There also are many, many poor white people who commit crimes! Yet, so often, we say, *"The neighborhood is changing … "* or *"Those people … "* What we really mean is, *"I don't like those people because they are different from me!"* All of us need to be careful not to fall into the trap of categorizing people and treating them differently because they don't look or act like us. Racism is always ignorant and it is always wrong.

Many Hispanics work, across our nation, in agricultural work AND a great variety of other jobs. A great number of these individuals are immigrants – legal or otherwise – who have come to this country to support their families. Most of them share our Catholic Faith and have the same dreams we have. We forget so quickly that the majority of our families were poor immigrants at one time. Many of our ancestors were treated badly by others who were already here.

Let us remember that, no matter what we look like or where we come from, God is our loving Father. Because of this, we have great dignity. There is no room for discrimination, bigotry, or racism in the Christian life.

*Reflection Questions:*

1. *Have I ever been a victim of discrimination or bigotry?*
2. *Does God really care about the color of our skin or our country of origin?*
3. *How can I work to end prejudice in my community?*

# Reaching Out To Your Struggling Neighbor:
*Even a small gesture can mean so much!*

We've all had the experience of hearing of a misfortune that has befallen a neighbor or relative. After feeling sympathy for his or her suffering, we wonder what we should do. Should we call or should we visit? Should we pretend that the situation doesn't exist? Should we simply stay away so that he or she can "have peace?" What should we say if we do say something? Will the words come out right, or will we do more harm than good? Most people wonder about these things when, for example, a neighbor has a life-threatening medical diagnosis, a co-worker has lost a loved one, or a family member has experienced a breakup in a relationship.

> "It is very important for all of us to remember that it is not so much <u>what</u> we say, but the act of <u>being</u> there for a person who is suffering, that really matters."

It is very important for all of us to remember that it is not so much <u>what</u> we say, but the act of <u>being</u> there for a person who is suffering, that really matters.

This is sometimes called "the ministry of presence" and it is very powerful! (Of course, we need to be sensitive about the words we use to console one who is struggling.) Perhaps a card with a nice note inside, or a visit to her home just to see how she is doing, will brighten her day. A phone call is very kind. Bringing food usually is appreciated.

What we need to avoid is the temptation to draw back from those who are suffering because we feel uncomfortable about what to say or do. If we pull away, the individual may find himself abandoned, at the very moment when he most needs friends! Then, the suffering can become so much worse.

As Christians, we believe that we all are Christ-bearers. Christ is present in us in a very beautiful and powerful way. This is why we must reach out to those who are suffering - because they need to see God through us! Do not be afraid to reach out. Even if it seems like a small gesture, it can make a world of difference to one who is experiencing so much darkness. Remember Our Lord's words, *"Whatsoever you did for the least of my brothers and sisters, you did for me."* (Matthew 25:40)

*Reflection Questions:*

1. *Why is it so important to reach out to those in need?*
2. *Why is it sometimes tempting to draw back from those who are suffering?*
3. *"Being is more important than doing." What does this mean in relation to caring for those who are suffering?*

# Miscarriage:
*The death of a child is an occasion of sadness - yet hope.*

Over the past few weeks, I have received sad news from a number of couples. Each couple had been so happy to learn that they were expecting a baby, but then had experienced a miscarriage.

I must say that I grieved with all of them. Children are such a gift. The death of a child, any child, through miscarriage remains a tragic mystery.

> **"We should not despair for the souls of children who die without Baptism, and this is precisely why the Church allows funeral Masses for them."**

Miscarriages often are treated as a taboo subject - something to be avoided.

When the issue arises, many of us are at a loss for words. However, as Christians and especially as Catholics, we can rely upon our Faith to help us understand this difficult issue.

A miscarriage is the death of a baby. It would be best for all of us to acknowledge this fact. It's not the loss of a *"mass of tissue"* or *"the body's way of getting rid of junk,"* as some would have us believe. It is the death of a child, our friend's or neighbor's child, and it always is an occasion of sadness.

I am certainly not a medical expert in this field. Yet, it is commonly held that miscarriages are more common today than in the past. Perhaps pollution is a factor. Maybe our diet, or the greater stress in our lives, plays a part. Most of the time, it can be presumed that something has gone wrong, physically, with the child. Whatever the reasons, a miscarriage often is a tragically sad event for the expectant parents.

The death of a child before birth raises many questions. Obviously, it was not possible to baptize the baby. So, some wonder about the state of his or her soul. The concept of "limbo" - a place of perfect natural happiness where children go if they die without baptism - remains a *theological opinion*, an opinion which was left out of the most recent <u>Catechism of the Catholic Church</u>.

Perhaps it would be better to entrust such children to the mercy of God. Indeed, we always must entrust all of our lives to God. It was Jesus Himself who said, *"Let the little children come to me ..."* (Matthew 19:14) We should not despair for the souls of children who die without Baptism, and this is precisely why the Church allows funeral Masses for them. We ought to remember that we are bound by God's Law, but God is NOT bound by His own law.

Often, we wonder what to say to those who have had a miscarriage. This can be difficult. What several women and men have told me is that the only thing more painful than the loss of their child was the careless and (unintentionally) cruel statement of another person. People say things such as, *"Don't be so sad, you're young, you'll have another."* Someone might say, *"It just wasn't meant to be."* Then there is the clincher, *"Thank goodness it wasn't born retarded! This is much better!"* I hope that you can see how these statements, although perhaps well-meaning, are shallow and cruel.

What we might say to couples is what we would say to anybody who has lost a loved one: *"I'm sorry. I will pray for you. Is there anything I can do?"* It is important to remember that those couples who are suffering after a miscarriage often blame themselves. Our words must be chosen with great care.

Couples who have lost an unborn baby often find much healing in talking about their experience with others. Most of the time, they will discover that many other people have dealt with the very same issue. Sometimes, parents choose to name the child whom they have lost through miscarriage. After prayerfully discerning whether it was a boy or a girl, they select a name. They also might ask the child to pray for them and their family. This often brings great healing. If there are discernible remains of a child who has died before birth, a funeral Mass or service is certainly possible.

In the end, miscarriages remain a mystery. We all realize that there are so many people in the world who have children but don't want them. Yet, there are so many people who greatly desire to have children and are unable to have them. This is a great hardship. As I often tell the couples grieving the loss of their child through miscarriage, when they see God face to face some day, their first question to Him can be about their child.

All life is precious. Let us reach out and care for those who grieve the loss of their children.

*Reflection Questions:*

1. *How would I console a parent who has had a miscarriage?*
2. *As Catholics, we believe that all life is precious. Our culture does not. How can we engage the culture to respect life more fully?*
3. *What happens to the soul of a child who dies before receiving Baptism?*

# Disagreements Between Friends or Family Members:
## When all else fails, apologize!

When a family or a group of friends has a falling out, it can cause great heartache. This may be due to a difference of opinion, a poor decision or life choice, or a lack of communication. I have found that, in most cases, it is a simple misunderstanding that causes most arguments or breakups. What can we, as Christians, do in such a situation?

> "I have found that, in most cases, it is a simple misunderstanding that causes most arguments or breakups."

First of all, let's review a few basics. A friendship is a living thing and, like all living things, it needs to be nourished. A true and lasting friendship cannot be done on the cheap or achieved quickly. It also is important to remember that although our Lord Jesus told us to <u>love</u> everybody, even our enemies, he did not tell us that we must <u>like</u> everybody all of the time. Sometimes, people say and do very nasty things, things which hurt us a great deal. We still are called to love such people, as difficult as this may be. However, sometimes it's okay not to like them very much. <u>Loving</u> is being able to pray for people and desire Heaven for them. <u>Liking</u> is being able to be friends. There is a difference.

When there is a disagreement, it is important to talk things out. Obviously, emotions are involved - but that's normal. Talking things out requires really listening to the other person. If the other person does not think that he or she has been heard, the disagreement will not go away. Sometimes, it's helpful to repeat back to the person what you hear him saying. For example, after you have heard the other person's complaints about you, you might say, *"What I hear you saying is that you are angry with me because I didn't come to your house for Christmas."* If you do this simple exercise, it helps you to understand the issue better and the other person can see that you really are listening. If a person is unwilling to speak with you, writing him or her a letter or sending a card might help. If even that is rejected, prayer is perhaps the one option on which to focus.

Sometimes, a disagreement has to do with an important issue, something related to morality, justice - or even our Catholic Faith. It is vital, in these issues, to stand up for what is right and good. If, by standing up for what is right, you are challenging the other person, perhaps your good example might lead to a change of heart. What we all need to avoid is going along with a friend or family member's sinful behavior because we don't want to make him angry. That would truly hurt him and harm us, as well.

As I mentioned, a simple misunderstanding often is at the heart of an argument in a family or among friends. What was communicated? Could it have been said better or differently, or at a better time? Is the other person stressed about something else in life - such as a job, marriage, children, or health? Most of the time, when people "fly off the handle" over a little thing, there is something much bigger behind the scenes. Also, when WE are at fault, we must be willing to admit that we made a mistake, said something stupid, or acted in a cruel or inappropriate way. Many times, in relationships, we need to apologize - even if a problem was only slightly our fault. Somebody needs to make the first move to apologize!

Friendships and family life are among our greatest blessings. Let us work at healing them so that we might all have peace.

*Reflection Questions:*

1. *One of life's biggest regrets is broken relationships. What does this mean?*
2. *How can we demonstrate to another that we really are listening?*
3. *Why is it so difficult to take a stand for what is right when our family or friends disagree with us?*

---

# When a Loved One Leaves The Church:
*Use love - not a stick - to coax him back!*

Many of us have family members who are not practicing their Catholic Faith. In fact, some of us have relatives who have actually left the Catholic Church. Sometimes, this is due to an argument with someone working in the parish, because of the priest, or because of circumstances surrounding a marriage. Usually, it involves a lack of proper understanding of what we believe - and why - as Catholics. In any event, it is a tragedy.

> "If people truly realized that our Church is the one founded by Jesus, then nobody would ever think of leaving!"

Catholics make up the largest religious denomination in our country today. Fallen-away Catholics (by number) make up the second largest group. Why has this happened? I think that this is primarily due to a lack of understanding of what the Catholic Church really is. If people truly realized that our Church is the one founded by Jesus, then nobody would ever think of leaving! Sadly, this is not the case today...

Certainly, when a loved one leaves the Church, there is a sadness on the part of those left behind and a desire to welcome the person back. However, this can be a challenge because of those very same family ties. It's difficult to minister to one's own. (Believe me, I've tried!) What we can do, though, is to pray to God and ask the Lord to send someone else to guide our family member back to the Church. This, I have found to be most comforting and helpful. Remember Our Lord's words, *"A prophet is not without honor except in his hometown and in his own household."* (Matthew 13:57) How true this is in family life!

We must be charitable to those who have left. Often, there is a strong anti-Catholicism that sets in among them and their words can hurt us. However, we must answer in a spirit of love, for it is only love that will bring back home those who have strayed. Never use your Faith as a stick, but always as an invitation.

A popular expression attributed to St. Francis says, *"Preach the Gospel at all times and when necessary use words."* In the end, God will sort things out. However, all of us are His representatives – we are the face of His Catholic Church. By seeing how we live, are others attracted to the Catholic Faith? This is a good question to ask ourselves!

*Reflection Questions:*

1. *Do I have relatives or friends who have stopped practicing their Catholic Faith?*
2. *What have I done to pray for them or to invite them back?*
3. *Why do you think people leave the Church?*

---

# On Answering The Difficult Questions of Children:
## *(OR, where is THIS in the parenting manual?)*

Children have a natural curiosity. Sometimes, they ask questions that make adults feel uncomfortable! We may feel this way because we don't know the answer to the question, *"Why is the sky blue?"* Other times, the question can be repetitive and annoying, *"Are we there yet?"* However, there also are questions that make us feel uncomfortable because they point out a problem in our lives or in the lives of our family members.

For example, a child might ask, *"Why don't we go to Church? My friend Anne does!...Why is Aunt Cindy living with that man – is he her husband?... Why is Cousin Dave's picture on TV, and why are his hands and feet tied together? Why is he wearing striped pajamas?...Why is Uncle Charlie staggering around after he drank that stuff?... Why is Uncle Bill living with another man – and why are they holding hands? Is he his friend?"* As adults, how do we answer these difficult moral questions that children so often ask?

> **"The questions always come at awkward times...(but) Christian parents have a solemn moral obligation to educate their children about right and wrong."**

The first thing that we, as adults, must realize is that children are unique human beings with immortal souls. They might be immature and unlearned, but many young people have a natural wisdom. Some call it innocence, others call it purity, but this gift must be protected and reverenced in any young child. This is why, for example, good parents naturally want to shield their children from the uglier side of life – from violence, vulgarity, cruelty, or lust. Of course, try as any parents might, their children will come into contact with people, situations or activities which the parents would have preferred to avoid. Then, the questions come!

How we answer children's questions depends upon the youngsters' age and maturity. Naturally, an explanation to a three-year-old will differ from that to a 10-year-old. Experienced parents often say that "less is more" when answering the question of a three-year-old!

When children become older, however, the challenge grows. For example, let's say that an aunt is living in sin with her boyfriend. A parent might first ask his 10-year-old child what she knows about marriage, just to start the conversation. Then, the parent might gently tell the child that what Aunt Cindy is doing offends God and that it is a sin. Right away, the parent must remind the child to pray for Aunt Cindy and to love and respect her, even though she is doing wrong.

Now, when a child grows into a teenager, the opportunity will present itself for a more in-depth conversation. For example, let's say that Uncle Bill is living a homosexual lifestyle. The teen will know this to be the case from family gatherings. So, what do parents tell their son? How can they cultivate respect for a member of the family while not giving the impression that they are turning a blind eye towards sin? Perhaps the parents might first ask the teen what we, as Catholics, believe about homosexual activity. Then, the parents should guide the teen into making the distinction between loving the person and hating the sin. Perhaps a discussion might take place about the sacredness of sex and the dignity of Christian marriage. Then, the family could pray for Uncle Bill.

All the while, respect must be shown to the relative or friend who is giving a poor moral example so that the child does not hate him or her or become afraid of the person. Of course, parents must evaluate each individual situation and the issue involved and take common-sense precautions if there is a risk of the child being harmed.

Granted, these situations usually are not this clear-cut. The questions always come at awkward times and some answers may not be worded in the best way! However, Catholic parents have a solemn moral obligation to educate their children about right and wrong. In appropriate ways, known only to them, they must educate their children about sin and point out its sad consequences. Even if this involves a member of the family, parents must do this so that their children do not fall into a similar error. Any situation, whether good or evil, can be turned into a learning experience! I urge all parents to be courageous in teaching the Faith to their children.

*Reflection Questions:*

1. *How would you explain the immoral activity of a family member to a child?*
2. *Why is giving a charitable and faith-filled answer to a question about morality so important to our young people?*
3. *"Do as I say, not as I do." Why doesn't this work in real life?*

# Section V

*The Commandments and Seven Virtues (plus one!)*

# The Ten Commandments:
*They're more than a list of what NOT to do! They're a "road map."*

In the following articles, I would like to address the most basic guideline for Christian living. The "Decalogue" - or, the Ten Commandments, as they are popularly known - remain the bedrock moral foundation for all Christians. Far from being cold and impersonal laws or simply a series of things NOT to do, the Ten Commandments, if understood properly and followed closely, will deepen our relationship with Jesus Christ.

> **"The first three commandments speak of our obligation to love God above all things. The following seven commandments teach us how we are to love our neighbor."**

In His noted conversation with the rich young man in Matthew's Gospel (19: 16-19), Jesus responded to the young man's quest for eternal life by telling him to, *"Keep the commandments."* Our Lord goes on to tell the young man that if he desires to be perfect, he should sell what he has, give to the poor and follow Him. In this conversation, we see our Christian relationship with the Decalogue of the Old Testament.

The Ten Commandments remain God's law for His people, yet they are fulfilled and take on greater meaning in Jesus Christ. By His teaching and earthly ministry, Our Lord helps us to understand the meaning behind the Ten Commandments. It was our Lord who most perfectly summed up the entire law of God by telling us to love God above all things and love our neighbor as ourselves. At their deepest level, the Ten Commandments speak about love!

As we read in the Word of God, in the Old Testament, the Ten Commandments were written by the finger of God and given to His people through Moses. Thus, they are directly and preeminently the Word of God! We find two listings of the Ten Commandments in the Bible. The first is found in the book of Exodus 20:1-17. The second is found in the book of Deuteronomy 5:6-22. Although identical in message, these two versions of the Ten Commandments have led to variations in their numbering. Catholics and Lutherans typically follow the version found in Deuteronomy, while other Christians follow the ordering found in Exodus.

The Decalogue can be broken down into two parts. The first three commandments speak of our obligation to love God above all things. The following seven commandments teach us how we are to love our neighbor. Taken together, the Ten Commandments are the primary road map for Christian living and provide the richest way to examine our consciences before God. Far from being a burden, the Decalogue teaches us how we are to love.

So, together, let's explore what a great gift the Ten Commandments are for our life in Christ!

*Reflection Questions:*

1. How are the Ten Commandments really all about love?
2. Can I list the Ten Commandments from memory? Can I memorize them?
3. Look up the two versions of the Ten Commandments in Exodus and Deuteronomy.

---

# The First Commandment:
## Are there other "gods" in your life?

First Commandment: *"I am the Lord your God; you shall not have strange gods before me."*

Most of us, when we hear the First Commandment, pat ourselves on the back and are relieved. I assume that most of us have not worshipped fire, the sun, the moon or various other pagan deities recently - and this is very good! Alas, the First Commandment goes a bit deeper than we might initially think.

> **"People worship wealth, power, sex, themselves, children, their country, even a spouse. As Jesus said, 'Where your treasure is, there will your heart be.'"**

Faith is a gift - it cannot be forced. We can propose the Faith, but we must never impose the Faith. However, with the gift of the Christian faith comes the responsibility of following Jesus Christ as our Lord and Savior. There never has been and there never will be another Savior except Jesus Christ. Anyone who is to be saved is saved through and in Jesus Christ. Because of this, we worship Jesus Christ, the Second Person of the Holy Trinity, with the Father and the Holy Spirit. Any other worship of a god or minor deity is sinful.

Tragically, we sometimes do worship other gods - perhaps without even realizing it. I'm not talking about the sun or fire or Krishna or Buddha, but rather material things or even human beings. People worship wealth, power, sex, themselves, children, their country, even a spouse. As Jesus said, "Where your treasure is, there will your heart be." (Luke 12:34) A certain balance is needed here. God's creations are for our benefit. They are good and beautiful, if treated properly. However, when possession or adoration of earthly things or people becomes the end-all of our existence, the basis of personal happiness and fulfillment, we are on the road to idolatry.

Detachment is the virtue by which we can be IN the world but not OF the world. A spirit of detachment from the material things of this world is necessary for us if we are to follow Christ more fully. Detachment means not holding on to things too tightly, not being overly excited when we obtain these things, and not being crushed when these things are taken away.

We also must be careful not to "worship" other people. Spouses, children, sports heroes, politicians, celebrities, church or religious figures, or others whom we respect, all are human beings and must not become our gods. People make mistakes – people are imperfect. Yet, if we are honest, we sometimes place other people ahead of our relationship with God. How many times have we fallen into serious sin because we wanted somebody to love us more, to think we were great, to be impressed? The First Commandment reminds us to put God first and not to put anything or anyone in His place!

Other offenses against the First Commandment include superstition, use of horoscopes or tarot cards, and any type of divination or sorcery. The New Age Movement, which is centered on the worship of self, is explicitly contrary to the First Commandment. The worship of images, in which worship is directed towards the object itself rather than towards God, is a form of idolatry that is against this commandment. In addition, any mixing of Christianity with another religion to produce a kind of hybrid religion obviously is contrary to this commandment. God wants us to worship Him and Him alone!

The First Commandment speaks about loving God. May we all keep this commandment more completely and love God more fervently!

*Reflection Questions:*

1. What are some of the "gods" of our modern world?
2. Why is it so easy to worship creatures and not the Creator?
3. How can I make sure that I put God first in my life?

# The Second Commandment:
## What do YOU say when you're upset?

Second Commandment: "You shall not take the name of the Lord your God in vain."

Most of us immediately think about cursing, when we hear this commandment.

We may think back to the "naughty" words we were not allowed to say when we were young - even though our parents might have said them. Does this commandment speak about using vulgar words, or is it just about including God's name in those vulgar things we say? Is it just about taking oaths? This commandment is a bit more complicated than we might originally have thought.

> **"People have gotten into a rut. When something doesn't go our way, it's common to drag God's name into it. It is a habit that people must break! Find another word!"**

For the Jews of the Old Testament, and even for many devout Jewish people today, the name of God is too holy to be spoken. They speak around it, they say "the Lord" or use other descriptive phrases, but they will not say the name of God, or "Yahweh." They abbreviate it by writing YHWH. This is as close as they will come. If God's name is spoken, it is seen as blasphemy.

Why is this? In the ancient world, when you knew a person's name, you had a certain control over that person. To reveal one's name was to humble oneself in the presence of another and to subject oneself to the person who now knew your name. Thus, names were seen as sacred and were used with reverence. Traces of this custom still can be seen in our own discomfort when someone makes fun of our name or mispronounces it. Names are powerful and, for this reason, the Holy Name of God is to be respected.

The Second Commandment speaks about using God's name in a frivolous, disrespectful or blasphemous way. This is commonly called cursing: *"Oh, my—!"* or *"——damn it!"* These are just a couple of the disrespectful expressions in which God's name is used. Imagine for a moment if someone took your name and used it that way: *"Oh, my John!"* or *"Mike damn it!"* Not too pleasant is it?

Then, why do we do this to God's name? The reason is that it's simply a bad habit - and commonly used in our culture, today. People have gotten into a rut. When something doesn't go our way, it's common to drag God's name into it. It is a habit that people must break! Find another word! God deserves better than this.

What about other vulgar words that refer to excrement or bodily functions? Is it a sin to use these words? Let's just say that when such language is used, the world becomes an uglier place. As previously mentioned, this is usually a bad habit. Try to choose words that are more uplifting, witty, and more precise. There's enough ugliness to go around; let's not add to it.

The Second Commandment also speaks about false oaths. Often, at trials or on other formal occasions, we take oaths that are based upon God being our witness. This remains a most solemn event in our culture. Perjury occurs when a person swears a false oath and does not tell the truth when asked. Punishable by civil law, perjury also is a serious sin against the Second Commandment.

God's name is holy! As Christians, we have the great privilege of calling God "Abba" - or Father. Jesus Christ is our brother. The Holy Spirit is our friend and guide. What intimacy we have with God! The love that we show towards God is reflected in how we keep His name holy.

*Reflection Questions:*

1. *It is truly silly and wrong to use God's name when we are upset. Why do we do it?*

2. *Has anyone ever made fun of your name? How did you feel about it?*

3. *Vulgar language is ugly and speaks about ugly things. Why do we use it?*

---

# The Third Commandment:
*You must go to Mass - AND take some time for relaxation.*

Third Commandment: *"Remember to keep holy the Lord's Day."*

Go to Mass on Sunday! This is what we usually think of when we hear the Third Commandment. Of course, worshipping God on Saturday evening or Sunday is a large part of this commandment for us, as Catholics. However, the principle goes much deeper and speaks to the very ordering of our lives.

As we read in the Book of Genesis, God created the world in six days. On the seventh day, He rested. God rested! So, why can't we? In our busy world today, with its many commitments, diversions and distractions, many of us are not finding time to rest. Built into the very law of God is that we are to dedicate one day of the week to Him. It is to be a day of rest, but also a day of prayer - a day quite simply to be a human being and not a machine. Sadly, we often forget this.

> **"To determine why it is a sin to miss Mass on the weekend, we simply ask ourselves, 'What is more important?'"**

For the Jews, the Sabbath was the last day of the week - Saturday. The Sabbath was to be a day of memorial for Israel's liberation from bondage in Egypt. The Jewish people today continue to take their day of rest on Saturday, and it remains a day of prayer and worship. Because Jesus Christ rose from the dead on Sunday, and because the Holy Spirit came upon the Church on the Sunday of Pentecost, the early Church began to celebrate the Lord's Day on the first day of the week: Sunday. This has remained the practice for most Christians.

As Catholics, we begin to fulfill the Third Commandment by going to Mass on the weekend. Unlike other Christian communities, we, as Catholics, are morally obliged to go to Mass every weekend. Why is this so? It is because we believe that Jesus Christ becomes really and truly present on the altar at every Mass. If we are able to receive Communion, we are nourished with His Body and Blood. Why would we ever want to miss such a miracle of God's love?

To determine why it is a sin to miss Mass on the weekend, we simply ask ourselves, *"What is more important?"* What are we putting in the place of Mass? Sometimes illness, weather, ignorance, or necessary work excuses us from this Sunday obligation. Laziness, a hangover, or a sports event does not! As Catholics, we begin the Lord's Day in the most beautiful way possible: by worshipping God.

Sunday also is to be a day of rest. If possible, make it a day for family and friends. Avoid shopping, because our shopping often makes it necessary for other people to work. Some individuals who provide needed community services, such as police, hospital employees and fire fighters, must work on Sundays. Also, those who provide for the necessary rest and care of others often need to work on Sundays. So do priests! Whatever our duties in life, we must try to make Sunday look different from the other days of the week. In this way, Sunday can become a day of prayer and relaxation that energizes our entire week.

As Catholics, we should mark out our day of rest and dedicate it to the things of God. Although increasingly challenging today, let us give glory to God on this, the day that He rested. Let us worship Him at Mass, and serve Him by loving and caring for others. Let us keep holy the Lord's Day!

*Reflection Questions:*

*1. Why did the early Church make Sunday – not Saturday – the day of rest?*

*2. Why is it increasingly difficult, today, to make Sunday a day of rest?*

*3. Do I go to Mass every Sunday? Why or why not?*

# The Fourth Commandment:
*As the song says, we're talking about r-e-s-p-e-c-t.*

Fourth Commandment: *"Honor your Father and your Mother."*

This commandment generally makes us think of how children should not "talk back" to their parents. However, it is much more far-reaching than it initially appears! Let's take a look...

> "Love of our parents, relatives, superiors and country often is not as easy as it seems, but the respect that we owe remains necessary."

God has willed that, after Him, we should honor our parents to whom we owe life itself – or the beginning of a new life through adoption. They are the ones who have handed on to us the knowledge of God. Flowing from this commandment, we also see that mutual respect is necessary for all members of a family. Parents must respect their children, individuals must strive to love and honor their grandparents and other relatives, and all of us are called to love and honor our neighbor as ourselves. Finally, from this commandment, flows the respect we all owe to legitimate authority – whether this be exercised by the Church or by the government.

Marriage is divinely intended for the good of the spouses and the procreation and education of children. The union of one man and one woman in marriage and their openness to the gift of new life constitute the basic Christian understanding of family life. For Believers, the family is a community of people who reflect the very nature of God Himself in the Holy Trinity. The family is rightly called the "Domestic Church," because it is the primary source for values of life and Faith.

While it is true that families come in all shapes and sizes, we must never forget that a family is knit together by chaste love and mutual understanding. A family is not to be based on lust nor mutual gain and exploitation. Because of selfishness and numerous other factors today, the family is seriously threatened. Since the family is the basic building block of society, its breakdown has had a profoundly negative effect on our culture. Governments and social leaders must work to strengthen marriages and protect families.

The Bible is filled with passages that speak of the duties of family members towards each other. Examples are found in Proverbs 6:20 and 13:1 as well as in Sirach 7:27 and 3:2-6. Respect for parents is based on the fact that they were the ones who cooperated with God to create or adopt new life – our life. Obedience towards parents is lived out through patience and respect for their rules and wishes. Sadly, sometimes, parents give poor examples to their children and are negligent in their duties towards their family. In this tragic situation, the children must persevere in prayer while respecting their parents, even though they may not be able to be completely obedient to their unjust demands.

Children have a serious responsibility to care for their aging parents. In the twilight years of life, when there can be much loneliness, fear and pain, an elder's burdens often are made lighter by children and relatives who care. Brothers, sisters and other relatives also have natural ties to each other and must show respect towards each other. Although disagreements often happen, those who are knit together by family ties must strive to live together in harmony. All people are joined together into the human family. Love of neighbor is part of being a Christian and fulfilling God's commandment of love.

Finally, we all belong to the "families" of civil society and the Church. In each case, there are certain laws and patterns of behavior that are expected in a well-ordered life. The exercise of authority in each case must be aimed at service to the other and not towards exploitation. Respect always must be shown to legitimate authority.

As we have seen, there are many subjects that are covered by one commandment! Love of our parents, relatives, superiors and country often is not as easy as it seems, but the respect that we owe remains necessary. In respecting our parents, relatives and superiors, we really are demonstrating love and respect for God who is the source of all authority and who governs the universe with His justice and love.

*Reflection Questions:*

1. *The Fourth Commandment covers more than just honoring parents. Give some examples.*
2. *It is easy to honor parents who are loving and kind. It is much more difficult to respect those who are cruel and selfish. How can we fulfill this commandment when our parents have failed us?*
3. *Jesus tells us to love others. He does not tell us that we must like them. How might this help us, in fulfilling the Fourth Commandment?*

# The Fifth Commandment:
*It covers abortion, euthanasia, stem cell research, and more!*

Fifth Commandment: *"You shall not kill."*

The Fifth Commandment is perhaps the easiest to understand – and seemingly, the easiest to fulfill. After all, most of us have not killed anyone lately! However, the Fifth Commandment is much deeper than it first appears.

The wording of this commandment can sometimes be confusing. *"You shall not kill."* What about the spider in the corner? What about the defense of our country? Does this include hunting? The wording might be more properly understood as, *"You shall not commit murder."* All human life is sacred from its natural beginning to its natural end. Because we all are made in the image and likeness of God, we have a dignity that is the highest of all created things. No one can claim the right to directly destroy an innocent human being.

> **"All human life is sacred from its natural beginning to its natural end...we all are made in the image and likeness of God...No one can claim the right to directly destroy an innocent human being."**

Murder of another person is perhaps the most abominable of crimes. It is a serious sin to take the life of another person. Direct and intentional homicide or indirectly bringing about another person's death by abuse, neglect or risk-taking, is always contrary to God's law.

The abortion of an unborn child is rightly called the crime of murder. Indeed, the Church attaches the penalty of automatic excommunication to those who perform, procure or cooperate in any abortion. This penalty is not a rejection of the person, but rather a medicinal punishment calling the sinner to repentance. God's mercy endures forever and is available to everyone! Catholics must do all in our power to pray and work towards an end to the murder known as abortion.

Euthanasia is the act of intentionally ending the life of a seriously ill or frail person. Any act or omission which intentionally causes death in order to eliminate suffering constitutes murder. It is gravely contrary to the law of God and the dignity of the human person. Euthanasia is not "death with dignity," but rather the action of the strong deciding that the weak are no longer productive and must be eliminated. Physician-assisted suicide is nothing more than suicide – the murder of one's own self. It remains a serious sin. Those who are suffering with serious illnesses or nearing the end of their lives must be aided by the community and given the medicine necessary to alleviate their pain without directly causing their death.

Embryonic stem cell research and human cloning, if they result in the death of the human embryo, also constitute murderous behavior. Under no circumstances can a human life, even at its earliest stages, be taken or harvested for the supposed benefit of others. Adult stem cell research is moral, and research in this field of science is highly recommended.

Then, there is the death penalty to consider. The Church does not exclude recourse to the death penalty, assuming that the guilty party's identity and responsibility have been fully determined, and that this is the only possible way to effectively defend human lives against the unjust aggressor. However, if non-lethal means are sufficient to defend and protect people's safety, these are to be employed instead. Today, in our Western society with its developed criminal justice system, the cases in which the execution of the offender is an absolute necessity are very rare, if practically nonexistent.

Self-defense, which results indirectly in the death of the aggressor, is not murder. In the case of law enforcement or those in the military, sometimes lethal force is necessary to protect oneself from harm. If nonlethal means are possible, these should always be employed. All citizens and governments are obliged to work for the avoidance of war. In war, there often are no winners – and many evils and injustices may occur. However, all nations have the right to provide for their own defense – with war being regarded as a last resort.

Let us all work for a greater respect for human life...from the moment of conception to natural death!

*Reflection Questions:*

   1. *"You shall not kill." How might the Fifth Commandment be more accurately interpreted?*

   2. *Other than murder, what are some actions that are contrary to this commandment?*

   3. *Is war or the exercise of capital punishment wrong – always and everywhere?*

# The Sixth Commandment:
*There's nothing very "adult" about "adultery."*

Sixth Commandment: *"You shall not commit adultery."*

One time when I was hearing confessions, a child who was about eight years old was telling me his or her sins. It was along the lines of: *"I disobeyed my parents. I stole a cookie from the cookie jar. I pulled my sister's hair, and I committed adultery."*

Somewhat alarmed, I asked the child what exactly was meant by "committing adultery." The youth responded, *"Oh, that means that I acted like an adult instead of being a kid..."* I was very much relieved!

> **"There is nothing more cruel than infidelity in marriage. Remember your commitment. Think of your children's future. Be aware of your own mortality."**

Reflecting on this humorous story, we realize that the child also was wrong in another regard. Those adults who commit adultery are in reality not acting like adults at all, but rather like immature fools. The sin of adultery is marital infidelity – it is being unfaithful in marriage. Adultery involves sexual relations between two individuals, at least one of whom is married to another person. Adultery is very widespread today in our culture. It destroys marriages, children's lives and our society in general. It is a very serious sin which risks eternal damnation.

Marriage is a sacred commitment between one man and one woman. Regardless of culture or religion, this sacred bond of marriage is to be permanent and inviolable. Between Christians, marriage has been raised by Christ the Lord to the dignity of a sacrament – a sacred sign that points to the invisible spiritual reality of the unity of Christ and His Church. Every marriage counts. In fact, marriage remains the essential building block of culture and society.

All Christians are called to chastity. Chastity is the successful integration of our own sexuality into our vocation in life. In other words, married people are called to chastity, religious who take vows are called to chastity, and single people also are called to chastity. We all live out this chastity in different ways. However, every offense against chastity has traditionally been understood by the Church to fall under the Sixth Commandment. (Other sins in this area often are seen as being covered by the Ninth Commandment.)

When a couple marries, they give themselves completely and totally to each other. They are no longer two, but one body. Cheating or unfaithfulness in marriage strikes at the heart of this most intimate of unions. Because of his or her own selfishness, the person who commits adultery causes serious injury to this union. The innocent spouse is left with the lifelong knowledge and the pain of being betrayed. Regrettably, the tragedy of divorce often follows.

As Christians, we are called to forgive and to love our persecutors. Although this seems practically impossible in the case of adultery, with God all things are possible – including forgiveness. If you or a loved one has fallen into the sin of adultery, do not despair! Please speak with a priest and he will direct you to various resources that are available to couples who are struggling. Your marriage can be saved, but both the victim of adultery and the perpetrator of the sin must desire forgiveness and mercy.

For those of you who are married, avoid this sin! There is nothing more cruel than infidelity in marriage. Remember your commitment. Think of your children's future. Be aware of your own mortality. If you remain faithful to your marriage in spite of temptation, you will be greatly rewarded.

*Reflection Questions:*
1. Why is adultery so common today?
2. Who is harmed by adultery?
3. "For any marriage to succeed, the couple must continually work on their relationship." What does this mean?

# The Seventh Commandment:
*It also applies to human dignity, animals – and the environment!*

Seventh Commandment: *"You shall not steal."*

This commandment seems pretty straightforward. Don't take what is not yours! Pretty basic – the stuff most of us learned in kindergarten. However, like all of the commandments, there is more here than first meets the eye...

The Seventh Commandment forbids the unjust taking or keeping of the goods of one's neighbor. It also forbids wronging him in any way with respect to his goods. The virtues of justice and charity are the two pillars which uphold the Seventh Commandment. Justice demands that each is given his due in life. Charity requires that we love others and treat them as brothers and sisters.

> **"The virtues of justice and charity are the two pillars which uphold the Seventh Commandment. Justice demands that each is given his due in life. Charity requires that we love others..."**

The resources of the earth have been given to all of us. They are for our benefit and enjoyment. However, the right of private property is subordinate to this "universal destination of goods" whereby God has blessed and entrusted all of us with the resources of our world. Governments exist to regulate the legitimate exercise of private ownership, while balancing it with the common good.

Theft involves a sin against the Seventh Commandment. Nevertheless, in the case of urgent necessity, the essential needs for survival which include food, water, shelter and clothing, can be taken even against the consent of the owner. Such an action would not be immoral because of this universal destination of goods.

Sins against the Seventh Commandment also may include the deliberate keeping of objects lost by others, business fraud, paying unjust wages, extortion of money, work which is intentionally done poorly, laziness on the job, tax evasion, unnecessary or irresponsible gambling, forgery of checks or invoices, cheating and excessive waste. All of these activities in one way or another constitute stealing from another person. Restitution, if possible, is required in making amends for the sin of theft. In justice, we always must pay back what we have taken unjustly from others.

The uncharitable treatment of other people also may be a form of stealing. Slavery is always morally reprehensible, because it presumes to treat another human being as an object which is used only for monetary gain. Animals can be used for human benefit - for food, clothing or labor. However, animals must be treated with dignity and never abused. It is contrary to our human dignity to cause animals to suffer or to die needlessly. Other created things, indeed the entire earth, must be treated with respect. Pollution and needless destruction of the environment are a type of theft from future generations who deserve an intact planet.

Everything we have is a gift from God. Sins against the Seventh Commandment really are sins of ingratitude for what we have been given in life. May we treat others with justice and charity, while together thanking God for the gift of life.

*Reflection Questions:*

1. "Everything we have is a gift." Reflect on this. What does it mean?
2. Have I ever stolen anything? How long was I happy with it?
3. Has anything ever been taken from me? How did I feel?

# The Eighth Commandment:
*You don't lie? What about boasting, rash judgment or gossip?*

Eighth Commandment: *"You shall not bear false witness against your neighbor."*

The Eighth Commandment is concerned with the truth. When we speak, we always must speak what is true. When we act, we always must act according to the truth. Offenses against the truth often are called lies - and they lead us away from God. However, this commandment forbids more than just lying...

Jesus Christ is the Way, the Truth, and the Life. He is the Truth incarnate. As His followers, we must endeavor to speak, to live and to act in this Truth which is God. When we are truthful, we witness to Christ. When we deny the truth, we follow the "father of lies" who is the Devil. Anything that is true or good - whether it be in science, mathematics, literature, politics, the arts, philosophy, science or in nature - reflects God. To the Christian, Truth is not something but somebody: Jesus Christ.

> **"Today, (with relativism dominating our Western culture) no truth is seen as absolute. Rather, all truths are variable, depending upon the culture, the time and the individual."**

The very foundation of our society, culture and civilization is the presumption that people are being truthful with each other. If we lived in a culture of lies, how could we even dare to leave our homes every day? Think about it. Would we worry that our home would tumble down? Would we always question whether the food we eat is poisoned, or whether our doctor has incorrectly treated us, or whether the brakes on our car are faulty? When lies abound, trust is lost. Very soon, we have anarchy. We are a society based on truthfulness, and this truthfulness must be protected.

To lie is to speak falsehood with the intention to deceive. Lying is the most direct offense against the truth because it implicitly denies the origin of all truth which is God. The seriousness of the sin of lying is measured by the type of truth it deforms, the circumstances, the intention behind the lie and the harm that it causes. Lying is morally wrong - except in very rare and very serious special circumstances.

There are many other variations on lying. Boasting, the act of claiming some attribute or accomplishment which does not exist (or should not, in all humility, be proclaimed), also is an offense against the Eighth Commandment. So are the following…Rash judgment is the rush to judgment of another person without sufficient evidence or reason. Detraction or gossip is the disclosure, without sufficient reason, of another's faults or failings to others. Calumny or slander is the intentional act of lying about another person, with the intention of harming his or her reputation. Every one of the above-mentioned offenses against truth requires reparation of some kind to make up for what we have done.

Today, the philosophy of relativism is a common offense against the Eighth Commandment. In this philosophy, which dominates our Western culture, no truth is seen as absolute. Rather, all truths are variable depending upon the culture, the time and the individual. Some things which are held as true in one time and place can be seen as falsehoods in another. Perhaps Pontius Pilate was the first relativist when he said to the condemned Christ, *"What is truth?"* (John 18:38) By denying the absolute truth about morality, nature and the essence of the human being, the philosophy of relativism denies Christ who is the Truth.

All of us must endeavor to be truthful in our lives, by what we say and by what we do. Every time we reflect the truth, Jesus Christ is proclaimed. Every time we fall back into a lie, Jesus Christ is denied. Let us not bear false witness.

*Reflection Questions:*

1. *Often, it is so easy to lie. Why is this?*
2. *What are some offenses against the Eighth Commandment – other than lying?*
3. *How does the philosophy of relativism negatively affect our culture today?*

# The Ninth Commandment:
*If it might involve lust, just don't do it!*

Ninth Commandment: *"You shall not covet your neighbor's wife (or husband)."*

Although the Ninth Commandment is closely linked with the Sixth Commandment, it stands alone as God's teaching to us about the dangers of lust. Covetousness – in this case, lust for another person – remains a dangerous temptation. Today, it seems that the temptation to yield to sexual permissiveness is present around every corner. From fashion to music, from television to magazines, the suggestiveness of our culture lures many to break the Ninth Commandment of God. The Lord who knows of what we are made and Who is very merciful, always calls us to a greater love – not one of base lust but of chaste love which reflects the very love of God Himself.

> *"Lust is the disordered desire for or inordinate enjoyment of sexual pleasure...In other words, sexual pleasure is sought for selfish reasons..."*

In order to more fully understand the Ninth Commandment, we must understand what lust is. Lust is the disordered desire for or inordinate enjoyment of sexual pleasure. Sexual pleasure is disordered when sought for itself, isolated from its procreative and unitive purposes. In other words, sexual pleasure is sought for selfish reasons and not with an openness to life or a desire to strengthen the bonds of marriage. Lust takes on many forms today. Some of these are:

1. Fornication, or **sexual intercourse before marriage** between unmarried persons, remains a serious sin. It cheapens the beauty of human sexuality

and is an injustice both to the children who come from such unions and to the dignity of marriage.

2. Couples **living together before marriage** are presumed to be committing the sin of fornication. The scandal of this situation greatly harms society and contributes to the breakdown of family life and the institution of marriage. It is a serious sin.

3. **Masturbation**, or intentional self-stimulation, also is a gravely disordered action. The sin of masturbation derives from the fact that it is an intrinsically selfish activity – sexual pleasure is sought only for personal pleasure without openness to life or union with one's spouse. Habit or immaturity can lessen the seriousness of this sin.

4. **Pornography** is the display of sexual activity to a third party for his or her enjoyment. The production, distribution and viewing of pornography is gravely sinful. It treats individuals, typically women, as objects rather than as people created and redeemed by God. It immerses all who are involved in the illusion of a fantasy world.

5. **Prostitution** is the exchange of sexual activity for payment of some kind. Injury is done to both participants in this social scourge. It always is gravely sinful to engage in prostitution because people are treated as mere objects of pleasure and then discarded.

6. **Homosexual activity** also is an offense against the Ninth Commandment. Sexual activity between individuals of the same gender is, by necessity, closed to life and physically incapable of producing a union of any kind. Such activity is intrinsically disordered. A distinction must be made between those who have same-sex attractions but who nevertheless strive to live chaste and holy lives and those who actively engage in homosexual activity. The sin exists in acting out on such lustful temptations and not in the temptation itself. Same-sex attraction is a heavy cross for many individuals.

7. The use of **artificial birth control** greatly contributes to the general lowering of morality and increase of illicit sexual practices outside of marriage. Contraception used within a marriage places a barrier between the couple and separates the unitive and procreative aspects of marriage. It is closed to God's gift of life.

8. **Rape, incest** and **sexual abuse** often are closely related, and are serious offenses against God's law. The forcing of sexual activity onto another person is an offense against his or her dignity and often does great physical, psychological and even spiritual harm. When a child or a young person is the victim of such activity, the offense cries out to Heaven.

All Christians are called to chastity. Our bodies are temples of the Holy Spirit - we all have been redeemed by God, and at a great price. Let us all strive to follow God more closely and to avoid giving in to the tragic temptations of lust.

*Reflection Questions:*
1. We live in a lust-filled age. In your opinion, why is this true?
2. What is chastity? Why is it important?
3. The Ninth Commandment can be a difficult commandment to follow. Why?

# The Tenth Commandment:
### Don't be left with "emptiness, junk and debt."

Tenth Commandment: *"You shall not covet your neighbor's goods."*

Everything we have is a gift from God. The beating of our hearts, the shining of the sun, the dividing of our cells, the working of our minds, our Faith in Him - everything is from God. Yet, so often, we are dissatisfied. We want more and more and more. The more we place our hopes and dreams in the material things of this world, the more empty we become. Sadly, this state of affairs is very much a part of our American consumerist culture today - buying on credit so that we can keep up with what everybody else has and believing that then, we will be happy. In the end, all we have is emptiness, junk and debt. It is very sad.

> **"The more we place our hopes and dreams in the material things of this world, the more empty we become."**

The Tenth Commandment follows the Ninth Commandment in addressing covetousness. In the Tenth Commandment, it is not lust of the flesh - but rather lust for material things - which is addressed. This commandment forbids greed, which is the desire to amass earthly goods without limit. It forbids avarice, which is the passion for riches and their accompanying power. It forbids envy, which is a sadness at the sight of another's goods. It also forbids one of the lowest reflections of our fallen humanity: vicarious pleasure. When another person struggles and fails, we sometimes take pleasure in his or her misfortune. This stems from an envious and greedy heart that desires to succeed - regardless of the cost.

We live in a capitalistic system in which goods are bought and sold. Capitalism is neither good nor bad - it can be used for good purposes just as easily as it can be used to do harm. Part of our economic system in this country is free enterprise – with its marketing to the general public. However, when this system strays from its Christian roots, then the market determines what is bought, sold, advertised and desired – not consciences formed in the mind and heart of Jesus Christ.

Such is fast becoming the reality today. If the polls are correct, most Americans have a great deal of debt and often are living in fear of their debts. Indeed, our entire country is in debt and has an ever-growing deficit which we are leaving to the next generation. To what end? Why do we tend to spend more than we have? Sadly, it is at least in part because of greed, avarice and envy.

As Christians who follow God's law and commandments, we rejoice in His many gifts to us. In justice, we can make use of the fruits of our labor. The money that we earn can justly be spent to provide for ourselves and others. However, we must be careful not to take on a consumerist attitude. We can possess goods – we can own many things. Yet, we must be very careful that the things we own do not own us! As Christians, we should live simply and provide adequately for ourselves and for those in our care. If we have money or other resources left over, after prudent reflection, we should give what we have to those in need.

Again, remember that everything we have is a gift from God. The Tenth Commandment reminds us of this. May we all be satisfied with the gifts He has given us and make better use of the blessings we have received.

*Reflection Questions:*

1. *Is it wrong to be rich? Why or why not?*
2. *Is it wrong to be poor? Why or why not?*
3. *All that we have could be taken away in a moment. Where should our "treasure" be?*

# Introduction to The Seven Virtues (plus one!):
*Does this sound a little dry? They can change your life!*

In the following articles, I will focus on the seven virtues. Frequently, we hear about the three Theological Virtues of **Faith, Hope** and **Charity**. However, we'll also take a look at the four Cardinal Virtues of **Prudence, Justice, Fortitude** and **Temperance**. Following, there's even a "bonus" virtue of Humility!

Together, these virtues add depth and richness to the "road map" for the Christian life set out by the Ten Commandments, guiding all people towards greater holiness. Certainly, there are many other virtues which could be listed, but the Church always has held up these seven as the overarching virtues to which all others are related.

> "Together, these virtues add depth and richness to the 'road map' for the Christian life... guiding all people towards greater holiness."

So, what exactly is a virtue? A virtue is a habitual and firm disposition to do good. It's kind of like a positive habit of doing what is right and good, although it runs much deeper. We all admire people who are virtuous - people who are kind, honest, gentle and chaste. As St. Paul said so beautifully about the virtuous life in his letter to the Philippians, *"Whatever is true, whatever is honorable, whatever is just, whatever is pure, whatever is lovely, whatever is gracious, if there is any excellence, if there is anything worthy of praise, think about these things."* (Philippians 4:8) As Christians, this is what we should do!

The three "Theological Virtues" are given this title because they are directly related to our relationship with Our Lord. They dispose Christians to live in a closer relationship with God. Our **faith** is in God. He is our **hope**. We are to love God above all things and our neighbor as ourselves (**charity**).

The other four virtues are called the "Cardinal Virtues" because all human virtues can be related to them. **Prudence** allows us to discern good from evil. **Justice** leads us to give others their due, to respect their rights, and to fulfill our promises and obligations. **Fortitude** is what is needed to persevere through the difficulties and temptations of life. **Temperance** is the virtue whereby balance in life is achieved, whether this is with food, drink, entertainment, or work.

Although the seven virtues might initially appear to be a rather dry subject, I hope to show their life-changing significance, in the following articles. If we become more aware of these virtues and strive to live them more completely, we will draw closer to Our Lord Jesus. That's what our Faith is all about!

*Reflection Questions:*

1. *List the three Theological Virtues.*

2. *List the four Cardinal Virtues*

3. *Why are the virtues important?*

# The Seven Virtues - Faith:
*It's a gift - which someone must CHOOSE to accept.*

Most of us have some idea of what the virtue of Faith is. We typically define it by using the word "believe." That's part of it, but it runs deeper than simply believing in something.

Faith is both a gift of God and a human act by which a believer accepts personal adherence to God. Faith is a free assent to the whole truth that God has revealed. As we read in the Bible, in Hebrews 11:1, *"Faith is the assurance of things hoped for, the conviction of things not seen."* Faith remains first and foremost a gift from God - a gift that invites our response.

> **"As we read in the Bible, in Hebrews 11:1,** '*Faith is the assurance of things hoped for, the conviction of things not seen.*' **Faith remains first and foremost a gift from God..."**

Most of us have been exposed to the way of the Lord Jesus from early childhood. Perhaps our family took us to Church, had us educated in the Catholic Faith and provided positive examples of a "lived Christian life" for us. From this fertile ground, the seed of our faith in God was planted and began to grow. However, in and through this process of growth, God was active. God gave us the gift of faith, typically through the instrument of our family and friends. After we had been given that great gift, it was then up to us to nourish and protect it - to pray, to learn and to live out our Christian lives.

Faith is certain. As <u>The Catechism of the Catholic Church</u> states, *"It is more certain than all human knowledge because it is founded on the very Word of God who cannot lie."* (CCC #101) Faith is more than simply believing in God - it is a deep-seated conviction of the reality of God and His Will for our lives. Faith is not something which can be imposed upon an individual or a population. Sadly, history is filled with examples of this. Rather, faith is proposed, not imposed. We can suggest, we can invite, we can beckon others to follow Christ, but we never can force them. It often is very subtle and mysterious, but faith remains a gift from God.

Faith in God never contradicts the use of human reason. There is no contradiction, for example, between faith and science, or faith and academic inquiry. There is fundamentally only one Truth in this world, and whether the study is mathematics, languages, science, or religion, all pursuits should lead to this one Truth which is God. It is one of the great tragedies of our modern world that faith often is portrayed as being in opposition to the use of reason.

Lastly, to obtain salvation, it is necessary to believe in Jesus Christ and in the

One who sent Him to save us. It's true that those who, through no fault of their own, do not know the Gospel of Christ or His Church, but who nevertheless seek God with a sincere heart, and, moved by grace, try to do His will as they know it through the dictates of their conscience also may achieve eternal salvation. However, salvation is more difficult without knowing the Lord Jesus. This reminds us once again of the importance of Christian missionaries who propose the Christian faith to a waiting world. Sadly, those of us who do believe in the Lord also can lose our faith. Those who knowingly and intentionally abandon their faith in Christ risk eternal damnation.

Faith usually stays with us. It becomes part of who we are and desire to become. As Christians, our faith defines our very being. How we live our lives should reflect this faith. Through the successes and struggles of life, our faith in God should remain. Let us protect and nourish this greatest of all gifts and once again place our faith in the Lord!

*Reflection Questions:*

1. *What is the virtue of Faith?*
2. *How can faith be gained and preserved?*
3. *How can faith be damaged or lost?*

# The Seven Virtues - Hope:
## *It's something needed by our modern world!*

In a spiritual sense, Hope, like Faith, is a virtue that we all know and understand. Yet, like Faith, it is very difficult to explain in words. The Catechism of the Catholic Church defines hope as the confident expectation of divine blessing and the beatific vision of God (CCC #1817). Put another way, hope is the confidence that, in the end, things will turn out for the best - that, with God's grace, we will get to Heaven. Thus, hope has eternal life as its ultimate goal.

> "....hope is the confidence that, in the end, things will turn out for the best - that, with God's grace, we will get to Heaven."

We live in an age which is badly lacking in hope. It was for this very reason that Pope Benedict XVI wrote his second encyclical (or teaching document) on the subject of hope. The title of the encyclical is "Spe Salvi" or "Saved in Hope," a reference to St. Paul's Letter to the Romans 8:24, *"In hope we were saved."*

The 20th century was an age of world wars, multiple Holocausts, and the threat of nuclear annihilation. Along with this came the rise of totalitarianism, as seen in Communism and Nazism, and the Atheism that was contained in both. The aftermath of all of this is the moral relativism of today in which absolute truth is denied.

Where is Christ in all of this? It is precisely in the Resurrection of Our Lord – in the Easter event – that our hope as Christians, indeed of the whole world, lies. Christ is risen! We have hope – we, too, will rise again! This hope that lies at the very center of our Christian faith must be presented anew to our waiting, modern world.

The opposite of hope is despair – the denial that we can be saved and that God will save us. Despair is the rejection of God's promise and the abandonment of hope for eternal life. It is, in a sense, giving up on God. Despair is one of the most frightening of sins because the individual believes that he or she is lost. The Devil is very near when a person falls into despair. The Lord, who never gives up on us, desires us to place our hope in Him. Remember, even if we do despair, His grace is still poured out upon us for our repentance. As Christians, we must avoid and fear the sin of despair. Daily and fervent prayer, frequent reception of the sacraments, and good friends who will support us in our Catholic Faith are necessary to combat this loss of hope.

Another sin against the virtue of Hope is presumption. There are two kinds of presumption. On the one hand, an individual might presume that he could save himself solely by his actions and good works, apart from the saving grace of God. Another type of presumption is the notion that God's mercy is automatic and does not require repentance on our part. Both forms of presumption are rampant today. The pagan New Age Movement of self-help, self-realization, and self-worship has at its core the idea that we can save ourselves, by ourselves, apart from God. This is utter foolishness. On the other hand, the popular notion of a loving God devoid of divine justice has led many Christians to reject the existence of Hell or the possibility of personal eternal damnation. Hope properly understood is not presumptuous. It rather is the confidence that God will give us the grace necessary to get to Heaven and that we must cooperate with this grace to get there.

Many of us struggle with the virtue of Hope. We can grow in hope, first of all, by having that daily conversation with the Lord we call prayer. In our prayer, our hope is replenished. We also can grow in hope by bravely carrying the cross of our sufferings. If we believe that for every Good Friday of life there will be an Easter Sunday, our hope will be secure. This is our Faith – this is our Hope, our

Lord Jesus Christ! May we place all of our hope in Him.

*Reflection Questions:*
1. What is the virtue of Hope?
2. How can it be sustained and nourished?
3. How can it be damaged and lost?

---

# The Seven Virtues – Charity:
*We use the word "love" a lot - but, do we <u>live</u> it?*

Charity is another word we use for love. It is the virtue by which we love God above all things for His own sake, and our neighbor as ourselves for the love of God.

Love is the highest and most wonderful, powerful, beautiful thing on earth. Love can transform lives, move mountains and save souls. Love is the overwhelming reason behind most works of art, music and other human endeavors. Love is the ultimate reason for our existence - for God is love!

> **"Love is not simply an emotion...We love others by giving them the gift of ourselves – in our service, in our sacrifice, in our lives!"**

As Christians, our faith reflects this belief. Indeed, the Holy Trinity - God Himself - is love within Himself. God the Father loves His Son, Jesus, and Jesus loves His Father. This divine love between the Father and the Son takes on a life of its own: the Holy Spirit. So God is love within Himself first, and then from this inexhaustible divine love, God loves us, His creation. So, all love, if it is authentic, should reflect the very source of all love which is God.

Lofty stuff, isn't it? Yet, love is a very common word in our language that all of us understand but find so very difficult to describe. St. Paul gives us a clue in his famous passage in the First Letter to the Corinthians in which he speaks of love as being patient, kind, not jealous, not pompous, not inflated, not rude, etc. However, our English language is especially hindered by using only one word – "love" – to describe everything from loving pizza to loving one's spouse, from loving our country to loving God. In addition, we know that the word love often can be misused and misunderstood today. So, what exactly is love?

Jesus shows us the way! Over and over again, He gives us His law of love. His new commandment is this: love one another! Love God above all things, love your neighbor as yourself. Yet, so often, we can put the love of worldly things ahead of our love for God. We sometimes can be so cruel to other people - the very people whom we should love as we love ourselves. Indeed, this teaching of our Lord is so simple and so beautiful, while at the same time so challenging.

We all know that there are many people in our lives who are difficult to love. Perhaps they have hurt us; perhaps we disagree with how they are living their lives; perhaps we just don't have anything in common. Nevertheless, even though we are not called by God to *like* everyone, we are challenged to *love* everyone. Love is something very different than liking. Love is the desiring of the greatest and highest good for the other person - which ultimately is eternal life in Heaven with God! With that in mind, hopefully, love becomes somewhat clearer.

Love is not simply an emotion. It is not "luv." Our popular culture wants us to think that it's Valentine's Day, or puppy dogs, or late-night programs on television that we ought not to be watching.

None of this is love - it is sentimentality at its best and lust at its worst. No, true love is the giving of oneself to the other. We love others by giving them the gift of ourselves - in our service, in our sacrifice, in our lives! The ultimate sign of love is Jesus Christ on the Cross. So, if we love God above all things and our neighbor as ourselves, we give of ourselves as Jesus did for all of us. That is one of the main reasons why the Cross is so very important for us as Christians - because it is THE sign of the love of God for us and for the entire world.

As St. Paul said, *"Faith, Hope, and Love abide, but the greatest of these is love."* (1 Corinthians 13:13) May we all endeavor to love more completely in our daily lives.

*Reflection Questions:*

1. What is the virtue of Love?
2. How can we grow in this virtue?
3. How could we lose this great gift?

# The Seven Virtues - Prudence:
*With the choices in today's world, this really comes in handy!*

Prudence is a word that many of us associate with a certain politician or a Beatles' song from the late '60s. Remember the expression, *"Wouldn't be prudent!*", attributed to President George H. W. Bush and satirized on "Saturday Night Live?" Perhaps you've heard the Beatles' song, "Dear Prudence," sung by John Lennon on the White Album from 1968. Also, there is the cruel remark, "*What a prude!*" - which is a twisting of this very beautiful virtue. Let's learn more about the <u>positive</u> meaning of this word...

> **"The virtue of Prudence involves thinking before doing, looking before leaping, and praying before acting."**

Prudence is the Cardinal Virtue that disposes a person to discern the good and choose the correct means to accomplish it. Prudence aids us in following Christ and in living out our daily lives as Christians. It is a vitally important virtue today, especially for young adults who have a dizzying number of moral choices required of them every step of the way. The virtue of Prudence involves thinking before doing, looking before leaping, and praying before acting. Many times, it is the very lack of prudence that gets us into the most trouble in our lives! If we had only listened to the Lord speaking to us through our consciences...

Perhaps some examples might help. I ask you, is it prudent for a married man to spend his entire vacation with the female secretary from his office? After all, they're just friends ... Forget it! This is not prudent - the temptation is too great! How about parents who say, *"Well, our teens are going to drink anyway, so we might as well let them have a party at our home with alcohol we provide. At least they won't get hurt..."* How foolish! This is not prudent - you are enabling your teens to sin! Let's consider one final example: Suppose a person has a gambling addiction. Should he or she go on vacation alone to Las Vegas? Alas, the person will most likely fall - this is not a very prudent decision!

Now, prudence is not about being afraid or timid. It is not about fear, but rather about wisdom and faith. Traditionally, prudence has been called "the charioteer of the virtues" because it guides us in proper use of all of the other virtues. Being a prudent person means thinking about God and His Will for our lives before we make decisions. It's about knowing ourselves and our limits. It's also about knowing when we've gone too far and when we need to turn back again and seek Our Loving Father's forgiveness.

Sadly, we so often deceive ourselves or are deceived by the evil one. We think, *"Well, I won't be affected. I'm strong enough! I won't be tempted. I can do it, etc., etc., etc..."* What a pity! So often, we're not prudent about the choices we make, and soon find ourselves in a sinful mess. Following Christ means staying close to Him! VERY CLOSE! I believe that this is prudence in a nutshell - staying close to Our Lord. If we do this, we will know our limits, while grasping His Will for us in our lives. So, if you are called "a prude," remember - in your life of faith, this actually is a great compliment! Well, sort of...So may we all be prudes for the Lord!

*Reflection Questions:*
1. What is the virtue of Prudence?
2. How can we cultivate this virtue?
3. How could we lose it?

---

# The Seven Virtues - Justice:
*Listen to the inner voice which tells you, "That's not fair!"*

We all remember a common complaint from our childhood: *"That's not fair!"* Whether the issue at hand was fair or not is lost in history, but we all remember making this comment. Even as adults, we often are keenly aware of decisions and practices that appear to us to be unequal or unjust.

This is the subject matter of the Cardinal Virtue of Justice. Justice is the virtue by which a firm and constant effort is made to give God and neighbor their due. Far more than simply being fair, a just person is one who endeavors to do the right thing in any given circumstance.

> **"Justice is the virtue by which a firm and constant effort is made to give God and neighbor their due. ... (doing) the right thing in any given circumstance."**

Giving God His due also is called the "virtue of religion." We can be just to God by living our faith and striving to give Him glory by our prayers and service. We must strive to give God the best that we have - the best of our lives and of our time, talent and treasure. So often, we do the exact opposite - we give the Lord the "dregs." We pray only when we need something and we go to church only when we must, for family functions. We witness our faith begrudgingly and with embarrassment. We keep our talents to ourselves and use them solely to make money and achieve earthly fame. We think not of Heaven, but only of earth. Remember, God deserves our best - He gave us everything we have!

We also are to practice the virtue of Justice in our interaction with other people. When we respect the rights of others, we contribute towards a peaceful society. *"Do unto others as you would have them do unto you,"* is the Golden Role as taught by Our Lord. It also is the basis for just behavior. From this, we see that any type of discrimination is unjust because it robs people of the respect due to them. Defrauding others is unjust because they have a right to their livelihood. Depriving a person of liberty because of his or her personal opinion on a given issue is another sin against justice.

As followers of the Lord Jesus, we must make it our goal to act justly in all circumstances. When "things are fair," the Kingdom of God becomes a greater reality in our daily lives.

*Reflection Questions:*

1. What is the virtue of Justice?
2. How can this virtue be maintained in our world?
3. What happens when it is lost?

# The Seven Virtues - Fortitude:
*You don't need to be a superhero to live your Faith.*

Strength! Courage! Perseverance! These words might sound like part of a recruitment ad for the military or a description of a superhero! However, they actually refer to the very real human virtue called Fortitude. Fortitude is the Cardinal Virtue that ensures firmness in difficulties and constancy in the pursuit of the good. In other words, fortitude is the virtue by which we live our Faith and persevere in it. It is a very important virtue for Catholics today.

> "Many of us silently persevere in our Faith. Day by day, sometimes hour by hour, we say 'Yes' to Our Lord. This is fortitude!"

Why are we sometimes so afraid to live our Catholic Faith? I suppose the Lord predicted this when He told us over and over again in the Scriptures, *"Be not afraid!"* Nevertheless, so often, we do have fear. The lure of sin, the temptations of the world, the struggle against our own weaknesses - all of these can cause us to be afraid. Add to this an uncertain world, a struggling economy and a decadent culture, and it is no wonder that Christians are frightened today. Yet, again and again, we hear the words of Our Lord, *"Be not afraid!"* He means it!

The virtue of Fortitude is God's gift to us. With it, we conquer our fears and boldly live our Faith. This is a virtue that often works in concert with the promptings of the Holy Spirit. Examples of fortitude are many: the courage to speak up on an issue even though people might disagree with us, the strength to care for one's family despite the sacrifice, the perseverance in avoiding temptation and the living of a moral life. All of these flow from the virtue of Fortitude.

The virtue of Fortitude can be both visible and invisible.

Certainly, the courage of the martyrs who gave their lives for the Faith inspires us. Other stirring examples include: making the difficult choice to avoid the near occasions of sin and persevering in the Faith while suffering from a serious illness.

However, there are countless numbers of people who live this virtue in a silent and equally beautiful way, every day. Consider the wife who perseveres in her marriage despite a lack of love from her husband. Then, too, there is the man who cares for an invalid wife for decades simply because she is his wife and he loves her. Don't forget the teenager who avoids drugs by not being part of the "in" crowd! Many of us silently persevere in our Faith. Day by day, sometimes hour by hour, we say *"Yes"* to Our Lord. This is fortitude!

We all need to pray for the virtue of Fortitude. It is, quite simply, the courage to say *"Yes!"* to God and *"No!"* to sin!

*Reflection Questions:*

1. What is the virtue of Fortitude?
2. How can we live this virtue?
3. What happens when we do not make use of it?

# The Seven Virtues - Temperance:
*Remember moderation?*

*"Everything in moderation."* This is good advice for all of us. It's true, too! This expression reflects the last of the Cardinal Virtues that we will cover in this series. It is the virtue of Temperance.

Temperance moderates the attraction of pleasures and provides balance in the use of created goods. In other words, it helps maintain equilibrium in our lives. Food is good. We all like food. However, we can eat too much! Drink is good. We all like to enjoy a cold beverage on a hot day. Yet, we can drink too much! Driving, spending, reading, working, exercising - just about everything in the created world - can be done too little or too much.

> "....there is nothing wrong with wanting to enjoy the goods of creation that have been given to us by God. However, everything has a purpose."

Moderation is the key. For example, let's take carrots. You may like to eat carrots. However, if this is your total diet, you will turn orange and die! Let's take another example: use of the internet. Most of us enjoy using this wonderful tool. Yet, it also can be a HUGE waste of time and sometimes even an occasion of sin. It's the same with hobbies or sports. These are fun and enjoyable - but also must be done in moderation. If all we do in life is play sports or work on our hobbies - and nothing else - our lives quickly become a total mess. Yes, there even are people who spend too much time doing "church things!" Everything must be in balance, depending upon our state and calling in life.

God created the world and, as we hear in Genesis, *"It was good!"* (Genesis 1:4-31) Thus, there is nothing wrong with wanting to enjoy the goods of creation that have been given to us by God. However, everything has a purpose. If this purpose is not followed or becomes twisted, the sin of a lack of temperance is committed.

Typically, temperance has been associated with the use - or misuse - of alcohol. Many adults can have one drink and be fine. Even the Bible speaks about the benefits of wine! However, typically, after three, four or five drinks, things start going wrong. Balance is lost - literally. You can't walk, think or drive properly. What was a good thing was used in an improper way, by drinking too much. Hence, there was a lack of temperance.

Sometimes, individuals suffer from addictions, which are psychological or physical attractions to a given substance or activity. Often, these addictions arise from an initial lack of temperance.

We live the virtue of Temperance by acknowledging God's great gifts to us in this world and by reverencing these gifts. We need to carry ourselves, the greatest of God's gifts, gently. All things in moderation. Balance. This is what we seek. We know when we don't have this. Let us pray for greater temperance in life!

*Reflection Questions:*

*1. What is the virtue of Temperance?*

*2. How can we grow in this virtue?*

*3. What happens when this virtue is lost?*

# Living in Humility:
*Our role model is a Baby born in a manger.*

We will conclude our discussion of the virtues with a reflection on the virtue of Humility. Once again, we find that Our Lord Jesus Christ is our perfect role model.

When we think about how Jesus came to this earth, we realize that He came in the most unusual of ways. After all, He's the Son of God. One would think that there would have been a great fanfare. Perhaps large crowds would have gathered to cheer Him on. However, our God came at a moment and in a place that was very quiet and peaceful. It was a very humble setting.

> "Jesus Christ, the Son of God, is truly very humble."

Think about it for a moment. If you could poll 100 mothers as to where they would most desire to give birth, a feed trough in an animal barn would not rank high on the list! Yet, that is what happened. On a cold and dark night, because there was no room at the inn, Mary and Joseph were allowed to use a stable. There, Jesus was born.

Jesus Christ, the Son of God, is truly very humble. He humbled Himself throughout His entire life. First of all, He was carried and born by one of his own creatures. The Lord of Lords and the King of the Universe chose to be contained within the womb of a human being. At His birth, He chose to come into the world like all of us - small and vulnerable.

It's a harsh world for a baby to enter - especially when He is subjected to the drafts and aromas of a stable. As Jesus grew, there were only a few people in attendance who knew His true identity. For 30 years, He lived a life of relative obscurity. Then, in His 30th year, He began to teach. He was misunderstood, He suffered and died. He did all of this in great humility because of His even greater love for all of us.

Humility is indeed a virtue; it is the opposite of pride. Jesus Christ showed us how to live in humility - by giving our lives in service to others. Let us prepare for His coming this Christmas by living lives of greater humility.

*Reflection Questions:*

*1. How is Our Lord Jesus Christ a model of humility?*

*2. How is humility the opposite of pride? Give examples.*

*3. How does Christmas demonstrate the humility of God?*

# Section VI
Prayer – The Faith Prayed

# The Sign of The Cross:
*It's a gesture that goes to the heart of Catholicism ...*

As Catholics, we have a simple gesture, a simple prayer that begins and ends every religious action. It is called the Sign of the Cross, so-named because one touches the forehead, chest, left shoulder and right shoulder, making a cross pattern. The Sign of the Cross is accompanied by its formula of blessing: *"In the name of the Father, and of the Son, and of the Holy Spirit."*

Our prayers usually begin and end with this sign, as do the Mass and the sacraments of Confession and Matrimony. The sacraments of Baptism, Confirmation, Anointing of the Sick and Holy Orders all include anointings with holy oil tracing the Sign of the Cross.

> **"....when we make the Sign of the Cross, we are publicly declaring that we are Catholics and that we live for and under the Cross of Christ."**

Indeed, during every Mass, right before the Gospel is read, we all pray silently, *"May the Lord be in my mind, on my lips, and in my heart,"* as we trace small crosses in these three locations. In so doing, all that we think, feel and do is blessed by the sign of Christ's Crucifixion and Resurrection.

Also, upon entering through the doors of a Church, we sign ourselves with Holy Water - making the Sign of the Cross. Thus, we call to mind that it was through Baptism that the doorway was opened to all of the other sacraments. There are so many other times and places in which the Sign of the Cross is present in our lives. It really is THE sign of being a Catholic.

This gesture is one of several actions that are called sacramentals. Sacramentals prepare us to receive the grace of the sacraments and dispose us to cooperate with these graces. They remind us and point towards the graces we have received through Baptism and the other sacraments.

Since the Sign of the Cross is such a vital and important gesture, we must be very careful not to make it in a thoughtless or in a haphazard way. After all, when we make the Sign of the Cross, we are publicly declaring that we are Catholics, and that we live for and under the Cross of Christ. When we sign ourselves with the Cross, we are reminded that our own crosses in life only make sense in the light of Christ's own Cross and that our prayers are answered only through Him.

So, next time you make the Sign of the Cross, remember what it signifies! It is a simple reminder of what it means to be a Catholic.

*Reflection Questions:*

1. *How do I make the Sign of the Cross? Do I do it too quickly?*
2. *Why am I sometimes ashamed to make the Sign of the Cross in public?*
3. *Why is the Sign of the Cross important and what does it say about me?*

# The Rosary:
*It won't be boring, if your heart is in the right place!*

Not long ago, I was asked to lead the Rosary at a funeral wake service. Once again, I was struck by the beauty of these prayers - and by the meaning they hold for so many people!

> "In the Rosary, we ask Mary to pray for us – just like we ask others to pray for us, in everyday life."

The word Rosary literally means "a string of roses." In the case of this devotion, the "roses" are our prayers offered to God. According to popular tradition, the Rosary was made known by St. Dominic in the 1200s as a method of prayer and devotion. However, the stringing together of beads and the saying of a prayer for each bead is believed to be a much older practice in Christianity. Indeed, similar practices can be found in other religions of the world. Many popes have strongly urged the praying of the Rosary. It is arguably the most popular and powerful of all devotions in the Church.

In the Rosary, we ask Mary to pray for us – just like we ask others to pray for us, in everyday life. Although the Rosary is a devotion honoring the Blessed Virgin Mary, it is strongly centered on Jesus Christ and the Gospels. In fact, the Rosary is one of the best tools to meditate on the Life of Christ. What is the Name at the center of every *"Hail Mary"* we pray? It is *"Jesus!"* Jesus remains at the center of the Rosary because all 20 of the "mysteries" – or subjects that are contemplated – directly or indirectly relate to Our Lord. What are these 20 mysteries? Let's take a look ...

**The Joyful Mysteries** have to do with the Birth of Christ and His early life. They are:

> *The Annunciation of the Angel Gabriel to Mary, The Visitation of Mary to Elizabeth, The Birth of our Lord – the Nativity, The Presentation of Our Lord in the Temple, and The Finding of Jesus in the Temple by Mary and Joseph.*

**The Sorrowful Mysteries** have to do with the Passion and Death of Jesus. They are:

*The Agony of Jesus in the Garden, The Scourging of Jesus at the Pillar, The Crowning of Jesus with Thorns, The Carrying of the Cross by Jesus, and The Crucifixion and Death of Our Lord.*

**The Glorious Mysteries** have to do with key elements in our life of Faith. They are:

*The Resurrection of Christ at Easter, The Ascension of Our Lord into Heaven, The Sending of the Holy Spirit at Pentecost, The Assumption of Mary into Heaven, and The Coronation of Mary as Queen of Heaven.*

**The Luminous Mysteries** are the newest mysteries of the Rosary, added by Pope John Paul II. Focusing on the Life and Ministry of Jesus, they are:

*The Baptism of Jesus in the Jordan, The Wedding Feast at Cana, The Proclamation by Jesus of the Coming of the Kingdom of God, The Transfiguration of Jesus on the Mountain, and The Institution of the Eucharist by Jesus at the Last Supper.*

Many people claim that they dislike the Rosary because it is repetitive, boring, or meaningless. Not so! Yes - many of the prayers are repeated, but if said with a heart fixed on Jesus, in a manner that is unrushed and focused on prayer, the Rosary is anything but boring and meaningless. Prayers uttered to God must be from the heart. The Rosary is a great help for entering into such prayer.

There are various pamphlets available that explain how to pray the Rosary. I urge those of you who have not prayed this devotion to try it. You might discover what so many people have already found: the power and beauty of this means of praying to God.

*Reflection Questions:*

1. *What are the mysteries of the Rosary? What do they represent?*

2. *Why do some people dislike the Rosary? How can we understand it better?*

3. *When was the last time I prayed the Rosary?*

# Praying for Others:
*Do this if someone asks – or even if he DOESN'T ask.*

It seems that, every day, someone asks me to pray for him or for his intention. I'm always honored to be asked and I earnestly try to pray for all of the requests that I receive. Praying for others is an important part of my role as a pastor. However, I am not the only one who can pray for others! As Christians, all of us are called to pray for others. Why do we do this?

First of all, praying for others is a great act of love. No gift can be greater than a prayer. We believe in the words of Jesus, who said, *"For everyone who asks receives, and he who seeks finds, and to him who knocks it will be opened."* (Matthew 7:8) We believe that God hears our prayers and that He will answer according to His Will. This is perhaps the most awe-inspiring part of Christianity: the great humility of God in promising to hear our prayers! Let's make use of His promise!

> **"….praying for others is a great act of love. No gift can be greater than a prayer…We believe that God hears our prayers and that He will answer according to His Will."**

All of us have particular intentions or needs for which we pray. We should ask others to help us, by praying with us for these needs. When we join our prayers together for a particular cause or intention, there is immense spiritual power. Certainly, God hears our prayers, no matter how many people pray or how few – it's not a question of achieving a "critical mass" of people praying so that God will hear! No, God hears our prayers always, but when many people earnestly and humbly pray for a given intention, Faith is increased and blessings abound.

What should we do when someone asks us to pray for him or her? Above all, don't forget! How terrible it is to forget the prayer intention of someone who asks us for this favor. Secondly, immediately pray for the person – that same day. Perhaps an "Our Father" or a "Hail Mary" might be a good starting point. Perhaps you might stop by Church and pray for the intention for a while. You also might simply take a quiet moment and bring the prayer intention – and your intentions – before the Lord. Sometimes, an act of fasting can be a most appropriate prayer. Giving up a meal, a dessert, a television program, or something else you enjoy, can be a powerful way of praying for others.

Whatever method you use, make sure that you pray when someone asks you. Next time you see him, tell him that you are praying for him. This simple reassurance can offer a powerful boost to another's perseverance through a difficult time. After a while, you might move on to another person's intention, but, from time to time, the Holy Spirit may prompt you to return to the original intention.

Let us pray for each other! Even if someone never asks, pray for her! The more that we pray, the more the Lord will bless us, the more our Faith will grow, and the closer we will become as a community.

*Reflection Questions:*
1. *Why is praying important?*
2. *Do I pray every day? Why or why not?*
3. *In prayer, it often is quality, not quantity, that counts. What does this mean?*

# The Bible - Where Do I Begin to Read?:
*(Start with the New Testament. It's about Jesus.)*

Over the past months, many people have asked me questions about the Bible and about how to begin to really study, read and pray over God's Word. Bible study is a wonderful means to come to understand God's message and to come to a deeper relationship with Jesus Christ.

However, the Bible is a large collection of books. Reading it cover to cover can be a daunting task. Many people have started at the beginning, with the Book of Genesis, but have given up soon thereafter. The words can be difficult to pronounce and the culture of Biblical times can be difficult to understand.

> "Read small amounts of the Bible - perhaps a chapter or two each day...it's quality - not quantity - that counts!"

We must not give up! It is vitally important that we all come to know and hear God's Word in the Scriptures. So the question many people ask is, *"Where do I begin?"* Here are some helpful hints for reading the Bible and coming to know God's Word:

1. Find or purchase a good Catholic Bible. The Catholic Bible has 73 books, but most Protestant Bibles have only 66 books. Examples of good Catholic Bibles are the Revised Standard Version - Catholic Edition (RSV-CE), The New American Bible (NAB), and the New Jerusalem Bible (NJB). Make sure that you find a Bible with many footnotes that will help you in reading God's Word.

2. Purchase a copy of the Catechism of the Catholic Church. This collection of Church teachings is based on the Bible. It will help you greatly when

you come across a passage in the Bible that is challenging or confusing. Remember, it was Christ's Catholic Church that assembled the Bible in the first place! So, our Church's commentary on the Sacred Scriptures is most important.

3. Begin with the New Testament. The New Testament speaks about Jesus Christ and will be an easy place to begin. Again, most people who try to read the Bible straight through don't make it. It is much easier to begin with what is most familiar. I recommend beginning with the Gospel of St. Luke, followed by the Acts of the Apostles. After this, you may begin to read some of the books of the Old Testament.

4. Read small amounts of the Bible - perhaps a chapter or two each day. Spend the rest of your time reflecting on God's Word and praying over it. Remember, in reading the Bible, it's quality - not quantity - that counts! Read slowly, so that you can digest God's Word more fully.

5. An alternative method of reading the Bible is to follow the readings for the Church year. Every day at Mass, there are three or four passages or readings from the Bible. This is an excellent way to read the Bible and it is a great preparation for Mass. After three years, you will have read most of the Bible! A good source for these readings is the monthly magazine, "Magnificat."

These are just a few helpful hints. Please remember that the Bible is God's Word - not just some decoration in our homes or a family heirloom. Please, open your Bible and read it. If you do, you will come to know Christ more deeply and your life will be forever changed.

*Reflection Questions:*

 1. *Why is reading the Bible important?*
 2. *Is every Bible exactly the same? How are they different and why does it matter which one we read?*
 3. *Do I have a Bible at home? Have I ever opened it to read it? Why or why not?*

# Adoration of The Blessed Sacrament:
#### Who could say "no" to being in the presence of Jesus?

Holy Hour. Adoration of the Blessed Sacrament. Eucharistic Adoration. These three phrases all speak about the same thing. They speak about the experience of being in the presence of the Lord Jesus. Catholic churches offer opportunities each month to come and pray in this special and most profound way. I would like to take this opportunity to explain this practice, so that if you are unfamiliar with it, you might come to know it better.

> "The consecrated Host is reverently displayed inside a small glass window of this golden receptacle, and then situated on the altar for all to see."

As Catholics, we believe that Jesus Christ is truly present in the Eucharist – Body, Blood, Soul and Divinity. He is not merely symbolically present, or present WITH the bread and wine. Rather, the bread and wine cease to be bread and wine and truly BECOME the Body and Blood of Our Lord. This is the miracle of the Eucharist! Thus, at every Mass, Christ becomes truly present among His people.

At the end of the Mass, what remains of the Precious Blood is consumed by the priest or the ministers, but the remaining, consecrated Hosts are placed in a holy and safe place called a "tabernacle." These consecrated Hosts (the Body of Christ under the form of bread) are reserved there in case of an emergency and also for prayer and adoration by the faithful. So, every time we enter into a Catholic Church, Christ is truly present. (Yes, it is true that God is present everywhere, but in the Eucharist, Christ is truly and substantially present in His Body and Blood.) What a great blessing we have been given!

Our Lord is present in Church at all times. However, there is a particularly beautiful practice called Eucharistic Adoration, which follows an ancient practice of the Church. In preparation for Adoration, the consecrated Host is taken from inside the tabernacle and placed in an ornate gold object, called a "monstrance." The consecrated Host is reverently displayed inside a small glass window of this golden receptacle, and then situated on the altar for all to see. In this way, we can enter into an even deeper relationship and exchange with Our Lord in the Eucharist. Usually, various prayers are said during this time of Adoration, and candles and incense are used.

This profound practice of Adoration would be meaningless and silly if Christ were not truly present in the Eucharist! However, Christians have believed for 2,000 years that Our Lord Jesus is present and wants to be with us.

Many people have been touched by spending time in front of our Eucharistic Lord in Adoration. Why don't you take this opportunity to visit a Church and bring your prayers and lives to Jesus? I promise, you will find the silence refreshing. It will give you time in your busy schedule to pray. Most importantly, I guarantee that this time in front of the Eucharist will draw you closer to Our Lord. After all, that's the very essence of our Faith!

*Reflection Questions:*
1. What is Eucharistic Adoration and why is it important?
2. In any friendship, the relationship is maintained by frequent contact. How do we accomplish this in our relationship with Jesus?
3. Silence can be distracting and even frightening. Why do we need it to pray?

---

# Fasting:
*It benefits more than the waistline. It has soul!*

On New Year's Day, it's common to make a resolution. More often than not, these resolutions have something to do with losing weight and eating less. This is all fine and good. However, I would like to tell you about a scriptural and religious practice of sacrifice that also could greatly help us. It's called "fasting" and it can be a very powerful way to pray.

> **"....we can 'fast' from many favorite things, other than food. Perhaps we might give up television, use of the internet or something else we really enjoy for a period of time..."**

Fasting is the refraining from food or drink as a penance for our sins or for prayer intentions for another person. This limiting of food or drink for a religious purpose is done in imitation of Jesus' fast in the desert for 40 days. Similarly, by giving up a meal during the day or eating more simply, we are offering up our sufferings for the good of another person or in reparation for our own sins. Fasting can be a very effective form of prayer if done with the right intention, in moderation, and with a humble heart.

Currently, there are only two days during the entire year when Catholics are generally obligated to fast: Ash Wednesday and Good Friday. However, there are many more occasions when we might give up a meal or a candy bar, soda, or coffee as a form of prayer. Perhaps we have a sick relative who needs our prayers. Maybe we want to avoid a particular sin which is troubling us. Perhaps we want to pray for a spouse. It could be that we just want to do something extra to make a difference in our world. By giving something up, we offer a sacrifice back to God and thus humble ourselves before Him.

Traditionally, "fasting" meant that a person would have only one meal per day, although this can be altered depending upon the circumstances. However, we also can "fast" from many favorite things, other than food. Perhaps we might give up television, use of the internet or something else we really enjoy for a period of time, for a given intention. This is a sacrificial prayer to God.

Why does fasting matter? First of all, the Bible is filled with examples of fasting. Jesus fasted and said that some things require both prayer and fasting to achieve. Examples of fasting are found throughout the Scriptures: Judges 20, Esther 4, Deuteronomy 10:12, Acts 13:2 and 14:23. The reason for fasting is based on our complete dependency on God. When we give something up and begin to realize the effects of our decision, we start to see things differently and perhaps more clearly. Fasting is sacrificial - we are giving something up to remind ourselves how much Jesus gave up to save us. When used as a prayer, fasting can be a very humble way to ask for God's mercy or intercession.

Fasting can be a big challenge - just try it! However, nothing seems to make us aware of our human frailty more quickly than doing without something we really want. The humility that this activity brings, as well as the accompanying sacrifice, can make a real difference in our lives.

Let us begin to fast more often - for ourselves and for our suffering world.

*Reflection Questions:*

1. *When was the last time I fasted? For what purpose?*
2. *Why is fasting so difficult?*
3. *Fasting can involve more than giving up food. Give some other examples.*

# Sacramentals and Devotions:
*These sacred signs and prayers help us prepare for Easter.*

Each year, as we enter into the holy season of Lent, it is a challenge to make the most of this time of fasting, almsgiving and prayer. Our lives are so fast-paced today that sometimes it's difficult to slow down and enter into the season. However, as Catholics, we have a rich history of Lenten sacramentals and devotions that can greatly assist us in making our Lenten season more meaningful!

> "Chief among all of the sacramentals are blessings...A 'devotion' is a particular prayer which strengthens...faith in God."

So, just what is a *"sacramental?"* The Catechism of the Catholic Church says that sacramentals are sacred signs which bear a certain resemblance to the sacraments, and by means of which spiritual effects are signified and obtained through the prayers of the Church. (CCC #1667) Sacramentals often point towards the sacraments; they are reminders of God's presence in our lives. Chief among all of the sacramentals are blessings.

Every year, we begin Lent with such a sacramental: the blessing of ashes and the placing of these ashes on our foreheads. This calls to mind our own mortality and the importance of repentance from our sins. Towards the end of Lent, we receive another sacramental - on Palm Sunday we are given a blessed palm as we remember how Christ was welcomed into Jerusalem. Many of us keep these palms in our homes, weaving them into crosses or other sacred shapes. As you can see, sacramentals play an important part in marking our journey through Lent.

A *"devotion"* is a particular prayer which strengthens our faith in God by focusing us on an aspect of His mercy and love. There are many devotions in the Church, but the devotion which is most often associated with Lent is the Stations of the Cross. The 14 stations recall the Passion, Death and Resurrection of our Lord Jesus Christ. Praying the stations can be a very moving experience when we place ourselves in the scene with Jesus and reflect upon what part we play. Sometimes, we are like Jesus being persecuted, sometimes we are like the bystander pressed into service, and sometimes we are the ones who do the scourging.

Another Lenten devotion is the reading of Sacred Scripture. The Bible is the Word of God and it is such a great gift to us! This Lent, open your Bible and read one of the four Gospels, one of St. Paul's letters, or perhaps a book in the Old Testament. Pray before and after reading the scriptures so that your heart truly can be opened to receive His Word. (Don't forget to have your Catechism nearby, in case you encounter a confusing passage.)

Yet another devotion that many have discovered is the praying of the Liturgy of the Hours. This official prayer of the Church, which includes Morning Prayer and Evening Prayer, offers a wonderful way to punctuate the day with devotion. Often, parishes have groups who gather to pray the Liturgy of the Hours during Lent, or perhaps you could start such a group. While praying these prayers, we are united with the universal Church, praising and thanking God for His goodness.

Besides sacramentals and devotions, a word must be said about worship. Eucharistic Adoration is a most powerful way to enter into the season of Lent. Visit one of the many Eucharistic Adoration chapels or attend one of the various holy hours that parishes provide. However, perhaps the greatest opportunity to enter into Lent is to worship the Lord at Mass. In addition to attending Sunday Mass, you might try attending during the week. Many people have been profoundly changed by this!

So, try taking advantage of some of these ideas during the season of Lent. Prepare to walk with the Lord on this journey. Your devotion, worship and sacramental blessings will help lead you to the joy of Easter!

*Reflection Questions:*

1. *What is a sacramental? Do you have any favorite sacramentals? Why?*

2. *What is a devotion? Do you have any favorite devotions? Why?*

3. *What will you do during Lent to truly prepare for Christ's Resurrection?*

---

# Images of Mary and The Saints:
## We DON'T worship them! They remind us of our "heroes."

If you were to look in your wallet or purse, you would probably see a number of cards, a driver's license, perhaps - and hopefully, some money, too. Another item that you might find would be photographs. Most of us carry around pictures of our loved ones to remind us of them. Whenever we get lonely, or want to be near them and remember them, we simply look at the pictures and we feel better. Pictures remind us that we are not alone.

> **"No Catholic worships saints, statues or images. To do so would be a great sin. We worship God alone!"**

In our Catholic Faith, we have a similar practice. In order to remember those who have gone before us, especially our "heroes" in the faith - the saints - Catholics adorn churches with images of those whose memory we cherish. These images (works of art, really), have taken on many different forms throughout history. Sometimes, statues were used, sometimes frescoes, sometimes paintings, other times icons.

These images have been used to help us remember our loved ones in the Faith who followed Christ closely and who now are in Heaven: the saints. It is interesting to note that the earliest example of Christian art is a primitive image of Mary. Images of Mary and the saints, as well as Our Lord, have always been a part of Christian life and worship.

Periodically, throughout Church history, religious images in churches have been criticized and even destroyed. It has been claimed that such images were in fact idolatrous and sinful. This reaction against liturgical images was especially strong in the 700s, and returned again in some strains of Protestantism in the 1500s.

Today, among certain groups of fundamentalist Protestants, there is a belief that Catholics worship statues and other images in their churches and thus are idolaters. This is not true. No Catholic worships saints, statues or other images. To do so would be a great sin. We worship God alone!

Lighting a candle next to a statue or kneeling in prayer next to an image of a saint is not at all worshipping the image - or the person it represents. *Rather, it is asking the given saint to pray for us to the Lord our God.* Even in our veneration of Mary, we always ask her to pray for us. We never pray to her! Indeed, we pray to God alone, but there is nothing wrong in asking a saint or one who has died to pray for us. After all, we ask people who are living to pray for us; death does not, in reality, separate us spiritually from each other. So, we ask the saints to pray for us and we admire images of them because they remind us that we are all called to be saints.

Ecumenically, as Catholics, we must be aware of the concern many Christians have that we sometimes pay too much attention to Mary and the saints - and not enough to Our Lord Jesus. We must always put Jesus Christ front and center in our lives. He alone is our Lord and Savior. However, the veneration of the saints and gazing upon images of them is not sinful, but rather a very human way in which we can remember them and follow their example. It's rather like a picture of your loved one in your purse or wallet!

*Reflection Questions:*

1. *Why do we have statues and other images of saints in our churches?*
2. *Do we see Mary and the saints as our spiritual friends? Why or why not?*
3. *We all need heroes to admire. How do the saints act as our spiritual heroes?*

# Making a Retreat:
*Try getting away from it all - to find God.*

What is a retreat? Many of you have asked me, and I really don't blame you for being a bit confused about the subject. The word "retreat" is one of those terms we so often use without stopping to explain what it means! Let's learn a bit more about it...

As Christians, "retreat" should make us think of a time away from our daily routine and responsibilities. In military language, a retreat is a turning away from battle. Sometimes, we, too, need to turn away for a period of time from the battle against sin and evil in our lives. This is what a retreat is all about. It is a time away, when we reconnect with God. In this change of routine, we may become better able to listen to His promptings in our lives.

> "In this reflective atmosphere, we are able to think about our lives and recommit ourselves to following Christ."

For the early Christians, retreats usually took place in the desert. By leaving the community and going out into the wilderness, people found that they could experience God in a more profound way. Over the ages, monasteries were built as places for Christians to go to step away from the activity of the world and recommit themselves to prayer. Today, retreat centers, as well as some monasteries, serve as places to find this "time away."

What happens on a retreat? First of all, we s-l-o-w down. This very action of slowing down and altering our daily routine may help us to better perceive God's movement in our lives. In this reflective atmosphere, we are able to think about our lives and recommit ourselves to following Christ.

There are many different kinds of retreats. Some have themes, such as retreats for women or for men. Some retreats are more formal and directed by a priest, religious brother, sister or layperson. Others are simply time away from everything, alone with God. Retreats typically last from one to 30 days. I typically recommend at least three to five days for a person to be able to step away from it all and reconnect with God. A 30-day Ignatian Retreat, based on the spiritual exercises of St. Ignatius of Loyola, is perhaps the most intense kind of retreat.

Despite their differences, retreats all focus on the same thing: reconnecting with God. I strongly urge everyone to try this experience. Just make the time and take advantage of one of the many opportunities available. You'll be glad you did. No time spent with the Lord is wasted!

*Reflection Questions:*

1. *What is a retreat?*

2. *Why is going on a retreat important?*

3. *When was the last time I went on a retreat? Are there retreat opportunities in my area?*

# Section VII
## *A Year of Faith*

# The Liturgical Year:
*(OR, there's nothing "ordinary" about Ordinary Time.)*

As we watch the seasons of the year change, we become more aware of the passage of time. Another year ends; a new one begins. As Catholics, we live our lives of Faith within the seasons of the Church's year.

The Church year begins with the start of Advent in late November or early December and concludes the following calendar year with the feast of Christ the King in late November. The four weeks of the season of Advent give way to the joyful season of Christmas. Then, usually in February or March, we enter into the penitential season of Lent. After the weeks of Lent have passed, we come to the Easter celebration and the weeks that follow and complete this glorious season. In the midst of all of this, we have feast days for various saints including the Blessed Virgin Mary. The colors of the decorations and vestments change from purple to red to white.

> "As Catholics, we live our lives of Faith within the seasons of the Church's year."

However, what about the rest of the year? What season comes in between all of these high points in the Church's year? This, my friends, is the season of green – Ordinary Time.

Ordinary Time. It sounds boring, doesn't it? Well, it shouldn't be. This is the time between the Christmas season and Lent, and also between Easter and Advent, where we spend most of the Church year. The color green has many meanings. Perhaps the simplest interpretation is that green is worn during a season of growth – spiritual growth in our lives of Faith.

During this season, which includes deepest Winter as well as the beauties of Summer and Fall, we strive to grow in our Faith. It's a reminder of "everything in moderation!" We can't do penance all of the time, just like we can't celebrate all of the time. Ordinary Time is about moderation – walking with Our Lord Jesus Christ as we live our daily lives. There is, in fact, nothing ordinary about it. It is, rather, a season in which our Faith should grow!

As we travel through the years of our lives and witness the passage of time with the seasons, let us remember that the seasons of the Church change with us. As time passes, we hope and trust that we are ever one day closer to our heavenly homeland.

*Reflection Questions:*

1. *What is Ordinary Time?*
2. *How long does Ordinary Time last?*
3. *How does the Church year mirror the seasons of our lives?*

---

# New Year's Resolutions:
*It's time to tackle that issue – you know the one!*

When I was young, my Mother assigned me various household chores. This was great fun. Actually, it wasn't fun until I discovered that I could quickly dispose of the dust and dirt I had swept – by putting it under the living room rug. The dust was still there, of course, but it was out of sight, out of mind. This worked well, until Mom discovered it – and I was in big trouble!

> **"Might I suggest that, next New Year, you make it a point to address the issues you may have swept under the rug these past few years?"**

Little did I know, at the time, that I was fulfilling the time-honored phrase of "sweeping it under the rug" – or side-stepping an issue because I didn't want to deal with it. We all do this in various ways, every day. However, those of us who have lived long enough to see the consequences of our actions, know that most issues are best addressed head on and immediately. If left to stew, they cause greater trouble at a later time.

Might I suggest that, next New Year, you make it a point to address the issues you may have swept under the rug these past few years? This might include family issues, financial issues, issues of work and prayer. Perhaps you've been meaning to have a "heart-to-heart" talk with a loved one about his drinking or smoking or another bad habit. Perhaps you need to exhibit some "tough love" with a child who is acting disrespectfully or living a life you know will end in tragedy. (You are the parent, remember?) Perhaps this is the year to get out of debt, or at least pay it down. Above all, it's time to start praying and going to Mass at least every weekend, don't you think?

Maybe it's also time to address an issue which has been bugging you about a co-worker, but you've been too afraid to begin. Perhaps you had a disagreement, and said something you regret. Perhaps you have noticed a dishonest practice and wish to speak to the co-worker involved before you contact a supervisor.

Until you resolve such an issue, it continues to bother you...and doesn't go away. No more sweeping under the rug - time to do something about it!

It often is very difficult to confront sensitive issues with others. What will they think? Will they tell someone else about us? Will they get angry and hurt us? Prayer comes first, before any such difficult discussion with another. It's also important to consider your personal safety and not tackle a volatile situation alone. Then, and only then, proceed. Choose your words carefully, in speaking to the other person, and remember that less often is more. Speak out of love, not out of anger. After you have cleared the air and cleaned "under the rug," you should feel better. Although there might be some lingering hard feelings, the situation often will begin to improve.

*Reflection Questions:*

1. *We all "sweep things under the rug." What issues do I need to address in my own life?*
2. *Why is it so difficult to speak honestly with other people about our concerns or differences?*
3. *"In all things, charity!" What is meant by this excellent advice?*

# The Feast of Mary, Mother of God:
*She is our heroine - a role model for the ages!*

On January 1, we celebrate New Year's Day - as well as the Feast of Mary, Mother of God. This feast day calls to mind one of the greatest events in human history - when God who created us chose to come among us to be our Savior, by being born like all of us.

> **"All of creation and human history were yearning for her 'Yes.' If she said yes, our Savior would be born for us. If she said no, all would be lost."**

Think about it! The Lord of Lords and the King of the Universe, who created everything out of nothing, chose to be contained in the womb of one of His own creatures. Mary is rightly called the Mother of God, and, because of this fact, she is venerated. Jesus is God. Mary is Jesus' Mother. Mary is the Mother of God.

Mary said "Yes" to God. However, what if she had said, "No!" We would certainly be in a big mess today! All of creation and human history were yearning for her "Yes." If she said yes, our Savior would be born for us. If she said no, all would be lost. Mary is important because she reversed the disobedience of Eve.

With Mary's obedience, our salvation became possible. This is why we respect her so much - her *"Yes"* is a powerful example for us!

As Catholics, we always have venerated Mary. We look to her as our heroine - THE example of living our Faith well. However, we never have worshipped Mary or treated her as a goddess. To do so would be to commit the horrible sin of idolatry. Some people today, who do not know what we believe, make this accusation - but it is untrue. Nonetheless, Mary is special. After all, the Angel Gabriel said to her, *"Blessed are you among women."* Mary, because of her faithfulness and because of God's grace, was able to be God's instrument in the world.

Are we letting God into our lives so that we, too, can be part of His plan? We look to the obedience of Mary, her faith, her trust, as we live our Christian lives. May we have that same faithfulness and love, so that we might bring Christ to others.

Mary, Mother of God, pray for us!

*Reflection Questions:*

1. *What does it mean that Mary is the Mother of God?*
2. *Do Catholics worship Mary?*
3. *Why is Mary important?*

# Mary as "Theotokos":
*A day to celebrate the wonder of God's birth to a human being.*

On January 1, we celebrate numerous occasions: the arrival of a new calendar year, the Octave or Eighth Day of Christmas, and last, but certainly not least, the great feast day of Mary, the Mother of God!

It seems simple enough to state that Mary is the Mother of God. Mary is Jesus' mother. Jesus is God. Therefore, Mary is the Mother of God. Perfectly clear! However, things are rarely as simple as they first appear. Throughout Church history, there have been several distortions and misunderstandings of this basic, yet profound truth.

> "The miracle is this: that God Himself chose to be born of one of His own creatures. What a humble God and Savior we have!"

Fifteen hundred years ago, there was a bishop named Nestorius who preached that Mary was more properly called the mother of Christ, not the Mother of God. He incorrectly held that Jesus was a human person with whom the Word of God had united Himself. In other words, he said that God simply took over an existing human body. Effectively, Nestorius said that there were two christs: the human Christ who was the son of Mary and a divine Christ who was the Son of God. Although Nestorius' teaching was condemned as heresy, it did great damage and spread great confusion among Christians at the time.

To combat this false teaching, Pope Celestine summoned an Ecumenical Council (like Vatican II) in A.D. 431, in order to clarify Catholic belief. There, the bishops of the Church solemnly declared that Mary should rightly be called the Mother of God. Through the action of the Holy Spirit, she had conceived and given birth to God. He assumed a human nature in her womb. In other words, since God had taken on a human nature in the womb of Mary, God had been born of Mary. Thus, Jesus Christ born of Mary is God, and Mary is properly called the Mother of God.

I realize that all of this is quite technical - that's why Jesus said that we must be like little children in order to inherit the kingdom of God! The miraculous truths of our Faith can be understood only if we humble ourselves before God. The miracle is this: God Himself chose to be born of one of His own creatures. What a humble God and Savior we have! He not only suffered and died for our sins in order to save us, but He was born like us, from one of us. Now, that is something to ponder ...

*Reflection Questions:*

1. How do I honor Mary in my daily life?
2. How do I, like Mary, bring Jesus to our waiting world?
3. How can we become more like little children and accept the many mysteries of our Catholic Faith?

# The Feast of the Epiphany:
*(OR, the secret meaning of "a partridge in a pear tree.")*

We begin our celebration of the Christmas season on December 25, the feast of the Nativity of Our Lord. This season actually includes five major feast days. They are: Christmas; The Feast of the Holy Family (the Sunday after Christmas); the Solemnity of Mary, The Mother of God (January 1); the feast of the Epiphany (the Sunday after January 1); and the Baptism of the Lord (the Sunday after Epiphany). These major feasts, along with several saints' feast days, make for quite a celebration!

Traditionally, the Feast of the Epiphany was celebrated on January 6. Still today, many Christians celebrate Christmas on this day. After all, it was at the first epiphany that the "Three Kings" came to discover Jesus and bring Him gifts. The phrase, "The Twelve Days of Christmas," refers to the period from Christmas Day (Dec. 25) to the Feast of the Epiphany (Jan. 6). The song with the same title comes from this – and dates back hundreds of years to England.

> "The song, 'The Twelve Days of Christmas,' was written as a kind of memory aid, in code, to help young Catholics learn about their Faith."

Perhaps you were not aware that, from the mid-1500s to the early 1800s, it was illegal to practice the Catholic Faith in England. Many Catholics gave their lives for the Faith during those 250 years of persecution. The song, "The Twelve Days of Christmas," was written as a kind of memory aid, in code, to help young Catholics learn about their Faith.

The words of the song, *"my true love gave to me,"* refer to God as the true love and *"me"* as every baptized person. Christ is represented as a partridge in a pear tree, in memory of His sadness over the fate of Jerusalem. The Bible quotes Him as saying, *"Jerusalem, Jerusalem! How often would I have sheltered you under my wings as a hen does her chicks, but you would not have it so..."* (Matthew 23:37) The other symbols in the song have the following meanings:

2 **Turtle doves:** the Old Testament and the New Testament

3 **French hens:** the three Theological Virtues of Faith, Hope and Charity

4 **Calling birds:** the four Gospels

5 **Golden rings:** the first five books of the Old Testament

6 **Geese-a-laying:** the six days of creation

7 **Swans-a-swimming:** the seven sacraments

8 **Maids-a-milking:** the eight Beatitudes

9 **Ladies Dancing:** the nine Fruits of the Holy Spirit

10 **Lords-a-leaping:** the Ten Commandments

11 **Pipers piping:** the eleven faithful Apostles

12 **Drummers drumming:** the twelve articles of the Apostles Creed

This is an interesting historical twist on a popular Christmas song! Remember this rich, Catholic context next time you hear the song!

*Reflection Questions:*
1. *Does the persecution of Christians still take place today?*
2. *Have I ever been ridiculed or hated because I am Catholic?*
3. *How can I help those who are attacked because of their faith in Jesus?*

---

# The Feast of St. Joseph:
## What if he had been a vindictive man?

Next March 19, on the feast day of St. Joseph, I invite you to reflect with me on the character of this man. Sadly, not much is known about him, but we do know that he played an important role in salvation history.

Scholars surmise that Joseph was older than Mary, and that he probably died well before Christ's crucifixion, since he was not mentioned in those narrations. We hear nothing about him in the Bible after Our Lord was found in the temple at age 12. However, what little we do know about St. Joseph provides us with a beautiful picture of this man who is a model for Christian fathers and, indeed, for all of us.

> **"The greatness of this man lies in the fact that he DID cooperate with God and that the Lord did great things through him."**

Joseph, as the Scriptures say, was *"a righteous man."* (Matthew 1:19) Despite the shocking revelation of Mary's pregnancy, he did not turn her into the authorities for punishment. Such punishment would have meant certain death for her. Joseph was merciful and decided to leave her quietly. Such was his intention when an angel came to him in a dream. Joseph listened to God's message through the angel. He took Mary as his wife and he protected her and the Christ Child through many difficulties.

When we look at this great saint, we see a gentle man. He was uninterested in revenge, or gossip, or the holding of a grudge. We see a man who listened to God and was open to doing His will. We see someone who trusted and had faith despite the circumstances of life. We see a man who loved his wife and who loved her Child. No wonder St. Joseph is the patron saint of Christian fathers! What a great model he is for all of us.

However, if we look a bit deeper, we are forced to ask the following questions... What if Joseph had been a vindictive man? What if he had jumped to conclusions, or not listened to the angel? What if he had done his own thing and not listened to God? If Joseph had not cooperated with God's grace and acted in the way he did, his life, our lives and the world as we know it might have been very different. The greatness of this man lies in the fact that he DID cooperate with God and that the Lord did great things through him.

Can we, as Christian men and women, have that same spirit of openness to doing God's Will? If we truly listen to God, we might be surprised what He can do through us. Like St. Joseph, may we always say *"Yes!"* to God.

St. Joseph, pray for us!

*Reflection Questions:*

1. *How was St. Joseph a "righteous" man?*

2. *How is he the model for all Christians, especially for Christian men?*

3. *What if St. Joseph had not listened to God? What would have happened to Mary and Jesus?*

# Lent - Prayer, Fasting and Almsgiving:
*Start planning how you can do something extra.*

The season of Lent is a 40-day journey of preparation for the great feast of Easter. Beginning with Ash Wednesday, we spend time, as Christians, reflecting on our life in Christ and looking forward to the joy of the Resurrection. Now, the three traditional disciplines of Lent are prayer, fasting and almsgiving. What exactly do we mean by this?

> "Christ gave us ALL, by dying for us on the Cross. Next Lent, what can we give back?"

**Prayer:** First of all, prayer is a conversation with God. Certainly, you should be praying every day, but during Lent you should redouble your efforts. There are many ways to accomplish this. If possible, perhaps you might go to daily Mass. Parishes also offer the Stations of the Cross - a moving and powerful Lenten devotion. Have you opened your Bible recently? Perhaps you might try to read the entire New Testament during Lent - much easier than the Old Testament!

Other ideas for prayer might include praying the Rosary every day or following some other devotion. Perhaps you might pray simply by taking an extra 15 minutes each morning or evening, in order to reflect on your life with Christ.

Whatever form you choose, prayer is a conversation with God which must be cultivated. Next Lent, take advantage of this opportunity!

**Fasting:** Fasting actually is another form of prayer and a very powerful one at that! What is fasting? Fasting is willingly giving up something that is good (Chocolate counts. Sorry, rutabagas and parsnips don't count!) and offering this as a sacrifice to God. Traditionally, fasting has been a sacrifice of food and drink, although you certainly can fast from other things.

Now, fasting can be difficult! Nothing causes us to pay attention and come face to face with our frail humanity like giving up food or water for a period of time. Physically, we notice it - we have cravings, and we become acutely aware. Yet, it is precisely in this act of fasting that we make room for God. Whether we give up food and drink, or whether we do without watching television, surfing the internet, or another activity that we enjoy, when we fast, we open ourselves to God. Then, the sacrifice of giving up this particular thing that we enjoy can be offered back to God. Try it; it works! Of course, fasting must be done in moderation and with good judgment, but there is no denying that this is a powerful prayer. So, what will you give up for Lent?

**Almsgiving:** The giving of alms to the poor is another traditional Lenten practice. Typically, almsgiving has involved donating money to those who are poor or suffering. Instead of money, you might give away excess clothing or other items to those in need. Perhaps you could volunteer time, as a way of almsgiving. Any way that you can reach out to those in need is a powerful means of identifying with Christ who is so present in the poor and the suffering.

During difficult economic times, almsgiving can be a challenge. It makes us sit up and take notice when we give, not from our excess, but from our needs and out of sacrifice! Christ gave us ALL, by dying for us on the Cross. Next Lent, what can we give back?

So, let's make next Lent a time of great prayer, fasting and almsgiving. Let's take this opportunity to focus on what is most important in life: our Faith in Jesus. Let us walk the way of the Cross with Him and look for the bright and glorious light of Easter morning!

*Reflection Questions:*

　1. *Why do we pray?*

　2. *Why do we fast?*

　3. *Why do we give alms?*

# The Season of Easter:
## It's actually 50 days of rejoicing!

The season of Easter is a time of rejoicing in our Risen Lord. This season includes a total of 50 days from **Easter Sunday** until **Pentecost Sunday**.

The first eight days of the Easter Season are called the **Octave of Easter** - from the Latin, meaning "eight." These eight days are treated as solemnities of the Lord and each is considered to be another Easter.

> "This is a glorious season...let us rejoice with the risen Christ."

The eighth day of the Octave of Easter is the Sunday after Easter Sunday. In the year 2000, this day was given the title of **Divine Mercy Sunday** by Pope John Paul II. On this day, we celebrate and rejoice in God's great gift of mercy. However, there is much more of the Easter season still to come!

According to the Acts of the Apostles (1:3), *"In the time after His sufferings, He showed them in many convincing ways that He was alive, appearing to them over the course of forty days and speaking to them about the reign of God."* Now, the number 40 is a holy number and refers to fullness or completeness. It is found in numerous places in the Scriptures. For example, there were the Israelites' 40 years in the desert, Noah's 40 days in the ark, and Jesus' 40 days of temptation in the desert. Thus, these 40 days represent the time when the risen Christ walked among His followers and completed His earthly ministry.

The Easter season commemorates these 40 days, beginning with Easter Sunday and continuing through to **Ascension Thursday**. Today, the Ascension often is celebrated on the Sunday following Ascension Thursday. On this day, we remember Christ ascending into Heaven, his mission on earth completed. Ten days after the **Ascension**, the Easter season ends with the celebration of **Pentecost**.

On the first Pentecost, the Holy Spirit descended upon the Apostles and Mary with great power. With this outpouring of the Holy Spirit, the Third Person of the Holy Trinity was given as a gift to the Church. Thus, the feast of Pentecost also is considered to be the birthday of the Church! After Pentecost, we return to **Ordinary Time**.

This is a glorious season. At this time of year, new life is springing from the ground and our hopes are lifted. Let us rejoice with the risen Christ, each time we live the Easter season.

*Reflection Questions:*

1. How is the Easter season different than the season of Lent?
2. In our part of the world, the Easter season of Resurrection and new life mirrors the changing of the seasons with the coming of Spring. How is this an added blessing?
3. How is Pentecost the birthday of the Church?

---

# The Celebration of Easter:
*Here are the answers to the three most important questions of life!*

Do you know the significance of Easter? There's much more to it than the chocolate bunnies and colored eggs that the popular culture likes to stress!

During this holy time, we celebrate Our Lord's suffering, death, and Resurrection - and the hope and joy that this brings. We also stop to ponder how our Faith in Christ provides us with the answers to the three most important questions of life. The Sacred Triduum of Holy Thursday, Good Friday and Easter Sunday provides us with a unique response to these questions:

> *"'Who is God?...Why do I suffer?... Why will I die?'...*Easter is our hope and our answer to life's questions."

The first question often is phrased: *"How do I become closer to God? How can I know God more fully?"* In short, *"Who is God?"* On Holy Thursday, we remember how Jesus gave us the gift of Himself - the Holy Eucharist. The Last Supper is commemorated on this day, which is, after all, the anniversary of the first Mass. It is precisely in the Sacrament of the Eucharist that we come into "Communion" with God. It is here that we receive the Body and Blood of Christ.

In receiving Communion, we draw into a greater closeness with God and come to know Him more fully. The Eucharist is Jesus' gift of Himself to His Church, to nourish us along the way. It is our means to know Him and to love Him more completely. How can we come any closer to God than by receiving His Body and Blood into ourselves?

The second question asks, *"Why do I suffer? Why do I have pain? Why do bad things happen to good people?"* The problem of evil, as it often is called, has always bothered humanity. Indeed, every major world religion attempts to answer this most vexing of questions. However, in Christianity, this question is answered most fully and completely. For Jesus Christ, the Son of God, comes and suffers with us and for us to redeem us. God loves us enough to suffer for us!

So, the answer to the question of why we suffer comes in the form of a Person. Jesus, in suffering on the Cross, makes suffering redemptive. He makes it something good! Thus, our suffering, our pain, only makes sense in the light of His Cross - where suffering takes on meaning and leads us to salvation.

The third question of humanity is this: *"Why will I die? I don't want to die – I want to live forever!"* It is a natural human reaction to recoil from death - it somehow strikes us as illogical and absurd. How can we die? Yet, all of us know that our life on earth will end and this troubles us. The answer to this final question of life is answered by Easter - the Resurrection of Our Lord! Yes, He dies to save us from our sins, but He also rises again to give us hope!

The Resurrection of Christ tells us that, even though we die, we are offered a future filled with hope. Death will not triumph over life. We, too, will rise again. This is the joy of Easter - that no matter what happens to us in this world, if we stay close to Jesus and are united with Him in His Church, our lives will have a happy ending. Death will not be the bitter end.

So, my friends, at Easter, we celebrate the most important day for us as Christians. Easter is our hope and our answer to life's questions. Jesus is the Way, the Truth and the Life. He is the answer. He is risen! Alleluia!

*Reflection Questions:*

*1. People have an innate longing for unity with God. Give some examples.*

*2. How does Jesus give us the answer to the mystery of human suffering?*

*3. Everybody loves a happy ending. How is Easter the ultimate happy ending?*

# The Hope of The Resurrection:
*Easter gives us the happiest of happy endings.*

We all love happy endings! Movies, stories, lives - we all want good to triumph over evil, the good guy to win, and what was thought of as lost to come back to life again. This is one of the deepest of human desires: for things to work out in the end. At Easter, we, as Christians, remember that God has given us the happiest of happy endings.

> *"....as Christians, we know that no matter what happens to us in this life, there will be a happy ending for us – if we stay connected with Jesus and allow Him to lead us ..."*

There could have been no greater evil in the world than the death of Jesus Christ, the Son of God. It looked for a moment as though evil had won out over good. However, Jesus' Resurrection, three days later, demonstrates to the world that God is stronger than sin and death. It shows that these two great evils that always have plagued humanity are conquered by Him. He saves us by paying back the ransom of death for our sins, and He rises again to give us hope.

In our lives, sometimes things go well and sometimes we suffer. All of us have experienced both of these realities, perhaps many times. However, as Christians, we know that no matter what happens to us in this life, there will be a happy ending for us – if we stay connected with Jesus and allow Him to lead us through this life. If He rose again, we will rise again. This is the hope of the world, and this is the gift that only Our Lord Jesus can give us.

On Easter Sunday, the most joyful of days, let us again thank God for the hope that the Resurrection of His Son, Jesus, has given us. Also, let us share our faith with others so that they too may have the hope and joy we share!

*Reflection Questions:*

1. *Easter is all about hope. What does this mean?*
2. *Why do we need a Savior?*
3. *What would it be like not to have the Hope of the Resurrection in our lives?*

---

# Divine Mercy Devotion:
*Remember that no sin is too great to be forgiven by God.*

All of us make mistakes in life and do things that we regret. We all rely on God's mercy, forgiveness and patience! Despite our many sins, God always gives us a second chance. All that is needed is sorrow for sin and the intention to do better. No sin is too great to be forgiven by God!

Each year, we celebrate Divine Mercy Sunday on the second Sunday of Easter, a day when we, as Catholics, call to mind the great patience, love and mercy that God has for each one of us. Although this concept of our Faith is quite ancient, the devotion to Divine Mercy is a more recent development. I would like to make you more aware of its power to transform lives.

> "....God is merciful, and He wants us to turn towards Him and repent of our sins."

The Divine Mercy devotion began in Poland. In the 1930s, Jesus revealed Himself to a holy nun named Sister Faustina Kowalska. In a series of private visitations, Jesus revealed to her the desires of His Heart and the ways in which He wants us to respond to His mercy. He promised special blessings to all who honor and proclaim His mercy.

Our Lord asked Sister Faustina to pray and work for the establishment of a Feast of Divine Mercy on the Second Sunday of Easter. On this day, the whole Church should call to mind God's great love and mercy. After years of investigation by the Church, the devotion that Sister Faustina advocated was formally approved in 1978. From that time on, the devotion spread quickly throughout the world. Sister Faustina was canonized a saint in 2000.

So, Divine Mercy Sunday is a powerful reminder that God always gives us a second chance. The message of this day is simple: God is merciful, and He wants us to turn towards Him and repent of our sins. This message is not new - indeed it has been proclaimed throughout salvation history. However, in our own time, Saint Faustina has become a "prophet of divine mercy." Through her, Christ is calling us again to repent of our sins and return to Him.

Divine Mercy devotion is not limited to this one Sunday of the year. As part of this devotion, special prayers such as the "Divine Mercy chaplet" may be recited at any time. Reception of the Eucharist and Sacrament of Confession also is recommended.

The Divine Mercy illustration depicts Jesus with rays of light coming forth from His heart. Under the image are the words, *"Jesus, I Trust in You!"* This is the whole message of Divine Mercy: trust in the mercy and love of God. Once again, no sin is too great to be forgiven!

*Reflection Questions:*

   1. *Have I ever asked God for mercy in my life? Does this idea frighten me? Why or why not?*

   2. *Do you think that our world and our culture need God's mercy, today? Give some examples.*

   3. *How is Divine Mercy Sunday related to Easter?*

# Corpus Christi – The Feast of the Eucharist:
*We celebrate the greatest gift we have been given ...*

Each year, the Catholic Church celebrates a grand occasion: Corpus Christi – the Feast of the Holy Eucharist. On this day, we celebrate the greatest gift we have been given – the gift of Jesus! When we receive Holy Communion, we receive the Body and Blood of Christ – not just symbolically or spiritually, but actually His Body, Blood, Soul and Divinity into ourselves. If Baptism is the door or gateway to the seven sacraments, then Holy Eucharist is the treasure inside – it is the heart of the Church.

> **"It is precisely in Holy Communion that we, as Catholics, come into this union or 'communion' with God."**

Throughout human history, people have yearned for union with the divine – togetherness with God. It is precisely in Holy Communion that we, as Catholics, come into this union or "communion" with God.

There is an old saying that, *"You are what you eat, from your head down to your feet."* When we receive Communion, two things happen to us. First, we receive what we already are by our Baptism: The Body of Christ. Secondly, we receive what we are to further become: The Body of Christ! Thus, through the Eucharist, the Church as the Body of Christ is built up into completion. Since Jesus and His Church are one, when we receive the Eucharist we are receiving Jesus and further becoming His Church at the same time. What a marvelous exchange!

As Catholics, we need to ask ourselves why we build such beautiful churches. Why do we dress appropriately for Church? Why do we genuflect upon entering and leaving the Church? Why do we fast for an hour before receiving Communion? Why do we abstain from receiving the Eucharist if we are guilty of a serious (mortal) sin? Why does the priest dress in fancy vestments and why are the chalices and other Communion vessels all made of silver and gold? Why does the priest take so long in cleaning the chalice after Mass? Why are we obligated to go to Mass every weekend? The answer to all of these questions comes back to our Catholic Faith in the Eucharist!

If the Eucharist were not truly Jesus Christ, but only a pleasant symbol of our fellowship, we would be wasting our time in regard to the preceding questions. However, if it truly is Jesus, then we would do this and more because of the miracle of the Eucharist.

I ask you to reflect on this greatest of gifts. Let us pay special attention to truly living our Faith - and building up the Body of Christ in our world!

*Reflection Questions:*

1. Why do we call the Eucharist, "Holy Communion?"
2. Do I sometimes take the Eucharist for granted? Why?
3. The Eucharist is at the heart of our Catholic Faith. What does this mean?

---

# The Assumption of Mary:
*It's as beautiful as a fairy tale - but REAL!*

Every August 15, we, as Catholics, celebrate the Solemnity of the Assumption of Mary. This feast day calls to mind one of the most unique aspects of our Catholic Faith: that the Blessed Virgin Mary, at the end of her earthly life, was assumed body and soul into Heaven. Let's learn more about this beautiful teaching...

If Jesus is God, and Mary is His Mother, then Mary is the Mother of God. With this awesome status comes a great dignity. One of the gifts that Jesus gave His Mother was her conception in the womb of St. Anne, without any stain of original sin. Subsequently, Mary had no actual, committed sin in her earthly life. It was necessary for her to be given such a gift because she needed to be a fitting mother for the Son of God. This belief is reflected in our Catholic dogma of the Immaculate Conception of Mary. It is important to remember that Jesus is the Savior of His Mother, but in a preventive manner - by keeping her from sin.

> "No remains ever have been claimed or found - simply because they are not there! She was assumed, body and soul, into Heaven where her body is glorified with her Son."

As St. Paul writes, *"the wages of sin is death."* (Romans 6:23) However, because Mary had no sin, the pain and decay of death would, logically, not affect her. Consequently, when her earthly life came to an end, God took her up or "assumed" Mary's body and soul into Heaven.

In our own time, 1950 to be exact, Pope Pius XII solemnly declared the Assumption of Mary to be a dogma of the Catholic Faith. Although this is a relatively recent declaration in Church history, Mary's Assumption into Heaven has been held as true by the Christian faithful for 2,000 years. It is part of our Faith, passed down orally and in written form through the Sacred Tradition of the

Church. Like the dogma of the Holy Trinity, it is not mentioned explicitly in the Bible, yet is has been constantly believed and held by the faithful. Although the Church has left it an open question as to whether Mary experienced biological death before being taken up to Heaven, we do believe that her body was not left behind to decay on earth. She was granted this dignity by her Son, Jesus.

Besides the constant testimony of the Church over the many centuries, we also have the following examples to support this aspect of our Catholic Faith ...

Throughout Church history, and especially in our own time, there have been many formal reports of Mary's appearance around the world. For example, we can believe that she has appeared at Lourdes in France, at Fatima in Portugal, and as Our Lady of Guadalupe in Mexico. In each and every approved apparition of Mary in the world, she has taken on the cultural appearance of a woman in the given area. Her appearance is only made possible if she has a glorified body – a body free from decay and made capable of moving from place to place and assuming a different appearance.

Also, never in the history of the Church, has anyone made a credible claim to have a part of her mortal body as a relic. Relics of saints are quite common throughout the world - the remains of holy men and women are venerated by the faithful as signs of God's grace and goodness to His people. This is not so for the greatest of all saints: the Blessed Virgin Mary! No remains ever have been claimed or found - simply because they are not there! She was assumed, body and soul, into Heaven where her body is glorified with her Son.

The Catholic Faith is an incarnational Faith - we rejoice in what God has done with his beautiful creation. That's why we honor Mary and adore her Son - she has been given the highest honor accorded to any human being. She said *"yes"* to God, and because of this we have our Savior, Jesus. She now rejoices with Him, glorified body and soul, in Heaven. Where she has gone, we hope to follow!

*Reflection Questions:*

1. *What is the Assumption of Mary?*
2. *Why do Catholics believe this about Mary?*
3. *What does Mary's Assumption tell us about our Catholic Faith?*

# Halloween/All Saints' Day:
*Whatever happened to the "hallow?"*

On October 31, it has become customary in the United States to celebrate Halloween. In fact, our Halloween is a combination of a number of festive days that originated in Europe and were mixed together in the New World. Of course, the word Halloween means "All Hallow's Eve" – the day before the great Catholic feast day of All Saints' Day on November 1. Whereas All Saints' Day is a celebration of holiness, Halloween recently appears to have taken on the opposite approach. Every year, many seem to think of this day as a celebration of death, violence and evil.

> *"Every year, many seem to think of this day as a celebration of death, violence and evil...Are they laughing at death or are they worshipping it?"*

Now, I am not saying that there is anything wrong with children dressing up in decent costumes and going door to door looking for candy. It is the stuff of family traditions and memories, and it is fun! However, it is alarming how the culture of Halloween has otherwise changed in recent times.

More and more, I see houses and yards decorated with images of dead bodies, tombstones, figures hanging from nooses in trees, and devilish scenes on the front lawns. I am not talking about decorating with cornstalks, pumpkins, scarecrows, or even "friendly ghosts," but rather with evil and scary things.

The question that comes to my mind is, "Why would somebody want to do this?" Certainly it is a fad, and like all fads, the use of one's intelligence is optional. Still, why do so many people feel compelled to decorate their homes with symbols of death, evil and violence? Are they laughing at death or are they worshipping it? Perhaps people don't even realize what they are doing. It seems to me that a person who decorates his or her house in this manner had better do some soul searching. He might ask himself, *"Why am I so fascinated with death? Why do I have figures of evil and violence in my front yard? How does this reflect my Christian faith which abhors violence, looks to the resurrection of the dead, and stands in opposition to the Devil?"*

Maybe those who feel compelled to decorate their houses in such a manner, or to wear devilish or violence-inspired costumes, just mindlessly follow the crowd. This is such a pity. I assume that those who glorify death at Halloween would never think to visit an actual cemetery and pray for those who have died. Do those individuals who spend hundreds of dollars decorating their houses each year, making them as evil-looking as possible, donate an equal amount to care for the innocent victims of evil and violence around the world?

My hunch, and this is just a hunch, is that there is a direct correlation between the violence, death and evil that are sometimes depicted around our homes or in our costumes at Halloween, and the presence of the Evil One in our souls. Think about it.

Reflection Questions:

1. Halloween is becoming more and more about death, violence and evil. Why?
2. How should Halloween point towards the next day, November 1, which is All Saints' Day?
3. When was the last time I visited a cemetery and prayed for the dead?

# Advent - Preparation for Christmas:
## As nature waits for Spring, we wait for Christ's coming.

Toward the end of each calendar year, we observe the season of Advent. It comes at a time, in our hemisphere at least, when the world of nature is going dormant, waiting for Spring. This time of Advent is a time of waiting - a time of preparation for Christ's coming at Christmas. It also is a time when we remember that Christ will come again.

Advent is meant to prepare us for Christmas, when Christ's first coming is remembered. It also is a season that directs our hearts and minds to Christ's second coming. Advent is thus a period of prayerful and joyful hope and expectation.

> **"(Advent) allows us to prepare spiritually for... Christmas. It also allows us to reflect on whether we are ready for Christ when He comes again."**

As early as the 300s, Catholics marked some period of time before Christmas as a time of preparation. The length and kinds of preparation varied from place to place. Four weeks were usually set aside - three with subdued purple decorations which symbolized the penitential spirit of the season, and one with rose-colored (not pink!) decorations which symbolized the joy of the season.

Today, these same colors are used, along with various scripture readings that highlight the meaning of this season. The Gospel features John the Baptist speaking of Our Lord's coming and of the necessity for repentance. The first reading features the Book of Isaiah, in which Our Lord's coming is prophesied. The Gloria is omitted during Mass and the Church is decorated simply. This is in keeping with the subdued nature of the season.

Advent is good for us. It allows us to prepare spiritually for the great feast of Christmas. It also allows us to reflect on whether we are ready for Christ when He comes again. This Advent, let us open our hearts and minds to Christ. Let us welcome Him into our lives again so that we might be changed.

*Reflection Questions:*

1. What does the word, "Advent," mean?
2. What are the two "comings" that we call to mind every Advent?
3. What are the two colors used in Advent? What do they mean?

---

# Advent - Season of Hope:
*The "rose" reminds us that the Lord is right beside us.*

Half way through the season of Advent, half way to the celebration of Christmas, you may get to see the priest wear PINK! Okay, it's officially known as "rose," NOT pink!

It is Catholic tradition for the priest to wear rose-colored vestments and for us to light a rose-colored candle on the Advent Wreath on "Gaudete" Sunday to symbolize hope. Purple - or violet - is the more typical color for the Advent season, representing penitence. However, for this one Sunday, the color rose indicates that, despite this time of preparation and penance, Christ already has come into the world and, thus, we have hope.

> **"Hope really is holding on to the Lord by the hand, despite the pitfalls and dangers of life, the frightening things that surround us."**

Hope is one of the three Theological Virtues - the other two being Faith and Charity (love). Hope seems to be in short supply today! Faith is believing in God. Charity is loving one's neighbor. However, hope is something more intangible. It is the sense that no matter what has happened, or is happening, in the end things will turn out okay. As the Catechism of the Catholic Church puts it, *"Hope is the theological virtue by which we desire and expect from God both eternal life and the grace we need to attain it."* (CCC #1817)

We all have had the experience of going through hard times. Difficulties at work, disagreements with spouses, illnesses and the like have sometimes made life ugly and discouraging. When life becomes dark and we turn in on ourselves, rather than reaching out to others, we often fail to see the Lord standing right beside us.

We've all heard it said, *"things will be better in the morning."* So often, they are! Hope really is holding on to the Lord by the hand, despite the pitfalls and dangers of life, the frightening things that surround us. Hope is not letting go.

The opposite of the Virtue of Hope is the sin of despair - which can make us lose hope in our salvation, in the forgiveness of our sins, and in God's great love for us. Often, when we have fallen into serious or "mortal" sin, hope is lost. For example, people willingly choose to enter into a seriously sinful situation (an invalid marriage, for example) and soon find themselves drifting away from the Faith. All sorts of excuses are given to justify their behavior, but life is lived with the crushing burden of guilt. Soon, despair begins to set in and the individual becomes lost.

So many times, I have spoken with people in such situations and they firmly believe that they cannot be saved by God; that they are unlovable and lost forever. This is the terrible effect of mortal sin: despair. Hope is the antidote.

During the Advent and Christmas season, we call to mind the reason for our hope as Christians. Jesus Christ is the reason for our hope - without Him, the world would truly be hope-less. If we keep our eyes fixed closely on the Lord and turn to Him when we have fallen, hope never will be lost. Let us continue to hold fast to Jesus and live in the hope He provides. Let us share this hope with others who are yearning for peace.

*Reflection Questions:*

1. *What is hope?*

2. *Why is it in such short supply today?*

3. *How does our Christian faith represent hope for the world?*

---

# Advent:
## *Are YOU ready for the Lord to come?*

Each year, we observe the liturgical season of Advent - a time of preparation for the coming of Christ at Christmas. What does the word, "Advent," mean? The Latin word, *"advenire,"* means *"to come to,"* *"to reach,"* or *"to arrive at."* Basically, the word advent means *"coming."* Indeed, this is what the season is all about.

> **"Advent is a time when we reflect on the Lord's coming into our lives and our own preparedness."**

As Christians, we recognize that Jesus came to us more than 2,000 years ago in the form of a baby, born in Bethlehem to the Virgin Mary. We also recognize that, for nine months prior to His birth, He was already in the world. He had been conceived by the Holy Spirit and carried in the womb of His Blessed Mother. Thus, even before His actual birth, the Savior was present in the world.

Christ also will come again. As we pray in both the Apostles' Creed and the Nicene Creed, the Lord *"will come again to judge the living and the dead."* As to the exact time when that will occur, *"we know not the day nor the hour."* (Matthew 25:13)

The best way to prepare for the Lord's second coming is to prepare ourselves for the end of our lives. When the moment of our death arrives, we will need to make a complete accounting of our lives - all secrets will be revealed, and we will answer for what we have done and for what we have failed to do. In anticipation of that day, we must make every effort to live our lives in such a manner that we are prepared.

Advent is a penitential season. Sometimes, we forget this, however, thinking only of Lent as a penitential season. Advent is a time when we reflect on the Lord's coming into our lives and our own preparedness. Violet vestments are worn, symbolizing this penitential season. The Gloria is omitted from the Sunday Mass, and churches are decorated in a simple manner. In this way, we prepare ourselves to celebrate the fact that the Lord has come, will come, and is in fact, coming.

Certainly, the Lord has entered into the world in numerous ways. He is present in the community, in the Sacred Scriptures, and in the sacraments - most especially in the Holy Eucharist. However, the season of Advent reminds us of three things. Not only has the Lord of Lords and King of Kings come into this world to save us, He also will come again at the end of the world <u>and</u> He personally will meet us at the end of our lives.

The Lord is coming! Be prepared!

*Reflection Questions:*

1. *What if I met Jesus today? What would I say to Him? What would He say to me?*

2. *How can I best spend the four weeks of Advent, preparing for the Lord's coming?*

3. *Am I ready to make an accounting of my life before God?*

# The Feast of the Immaculate Conception:
*Honoring Mary, the most perfect of all human beings.*

During Advent, in the midst of all of our spiritual preparations for the celebration of Christmas, there is a very special Holy Day. We relax our penitential disciplines of prayer, fasting and works of charity to celebrate the feast of the Immaculate Conception. Every December 8th, we remember the Blessed Virgin Mary and call to mind her part in salvation history.

> **"We do not worship Mary – to do so would be a serious sin. However, we do look to her as an example of what it means to be a disciple of Jesus."**

Often, Mary's Immaculate Conception is confused with Jesus' miraculous conception by the Holy Spirit in the womb of Mary. They are not the same thing! The "Immaculate Conception" refers to Mary herself being conceived without sin. We, as Catholics, believe that, *"From the first instant of Mary's conception, by a singular grace and privilege of Almighty God, and by virtue of the merits of Jesus Christ ... Mary was preserved immune from all stain of original sin."* (CCC #491)

In other words, Mary was conceived in a normal way by her parents, Saint Anne and Saint Joachim. However, by a special grace from God, she was kept free from the stain of original sin in order to be a most perfect mother of our Lord Jesus Christ.

As a human being, Mary would have been subject to the stain of original sin and consequent sin in her life. However, since she was chosen by God to give birth to His Son, Jesus, it was necessary that she be preserved from the stain of original sin so she might be the mother of the sinless Son of God. Put another way, Jesus looked just like his mother – He gained His humanity through her. This humanity had to be sinless because, as God, He has no sin. Thus, there could be no sin in either the Child or the Mother.

Now, Jesus is sinless because He is God. Mary was sinless because God preserved her from sin in a unique way that anticipated the redemptive work of her Son. Jesus was His mother's Savior, but in a way that preserved her from sin, rather than cleansing her from sin after she had fallen. In both ways, Jesus is our Savior, but in Mary's case, once again, He saved her by preserving her from sin.

On the feast of the Immaculate Conception, we recall the singular privilege by which God created the Blessed Virgin Mary to be the most perfect of all human beings, the Mother of God. Mary allowed herself to become the "handmaiden of the Lord" by agreeing to bear life in her womb, the life of our Savior. Her willingness to bear that life made our deliverance from sin and death possible. This is why we, as Catholics, venerate Mary and hold her up as an example. We do not worship Mary – to do so would be a serious sin. However, we do look to her as an example of what it means to be a disciple of Jesus.

Christians always have believed in Mary's Immaculate Conception. It was not always understood as fully and completely as we understand it today, however. When Pope Pius IX declared the Immaculate Conception to be a dogma of our Catholic Faith in 1854, it was merely a confirmation of what Christians had believed all along: that Mary had no sin. The Lord of Lords and King of the Universe – He who created every star and every speck of dust – chose to be contained completely and totally in the womb of a human being, the Virgin Mary. What a great dignity we have as human beings, that God chose one of us to be His Mother!

*Reflection Questions:*

1. *Do I ask Mary to pray for me? Why or why not?*
2. *Can I imagine what it must have been like to be Mary?*
3. *Why do we, as Catholics, respect and honor Mary?*

---

# Have A Merry Christmas:
## *(Notice, I didn't say, "Happy Holidays!")*

One of my favorite quotations is from St. Francis of Assisi, who said, *"Preach the Gospel at all times and when necessary use words."* How true! Certainly, our actions speak louder than our words. How we live as Christians is generally much more powerful than what we say. However, most of us use words to communicate. Words do mean something – they always convey a message.

An example of this is the often-repeated phrase, *"Happy Holidays,"* in place of the more established, *"Merry Christmas."* A small change, some might say – but I would counter that it is a step away from the true meaning of the season. Christmas is a Christian celebration of the birth of Christ. As Christians, we must strive to keep Christ in Christmas.

> **"....when we are unable to wish people, *'Merry Christmas,'* for fear of being politically incorrect, then something has gone terribly wrong."**

"Happy Holidays" is somehow thought to be more inclusive – encompassing all faiths that celebrate feast days at this time of the year. (Ironically, the word "holiday" is derived from the Catholic words, "holy day," although the meaning is somewhat lost today ... )

However, if we look at any general calendar, we see only one non-Christian feast at this time of year. That is the Jewish feast of Hanukkah, which is not even a major Jewish feast day. The High Holy Days of Judaism are Yom Kippur and Rosh Hashanah – both in Autumn. In fact, some Jews are insulted by the disproportionate attention given to Hanukkah!

To be sure, there are some other feasts that are celebrated during this time of the year. One of them is Kwanzaa, a modern-day African feast. Another is the Winter Solstice which often is celebrated by followers of New Age spirituality and has its origin in ancient Druidic spirituality. Both pale in comparison to the importance of Christmas to Christians.

Now, I am not saying that we should intentionally insult those who are non-Christians by wishing them *"Merry Christmas."* We must be both prudent and charitable. However, we also must avoid hiding our Christian faith simply because we don't want to offend people. Hiding our faith offends Christ! So whom do we want to offend, God or man? Choose wisely ...

Sadly, Christmas is a day that has become more and more secularized. However, when we are unable to wish people, *"Merry Christmas,"* for fear of being politically incorrect, then something has gone terribly wrong. Actions do speak louder than words, but when our actions involve hiding our Christian faith, everybody loses.

Next time someone wishes you, *"Happy Holidays,"* respond with a nice, loud and joy-filled, *"Merry Christmas!"*

*Reflection Questions:*

*1. What does our culture tell us about Christmas?*

*2. Can people tell, from how we speak, that we believe in Jesus?*

*3. How can I make sure that the religious meaning of Christmas is honored?*

# Section VIII
## The Similarities – and Differences – Between Catholicism and Other Religious Denominations

# Divisions Within the Christian Faith:
*This is NOT what Jesus intended!*

On the following pages, I would like to address the divisions within Christianity. In order to do this properly, I believe that we need to understand the many and varied churches and ecclesial communities that claim to accept Jesus Christ as their Savior.

So, I will attempt to explain the differences between the Catholic, Orthodox and Protestant denominations – with the goal of working towards unity. Unity within the Body of Christ is something for which we must pray every day. One of the main reasons why there is so much confusion and tragedy in our world today is that Christians are not united in actively living our faith. By knowing our differences, perhaps we may focus anew on our similarities – and thus, on unity.

> **"One of the…reasons why there is so much confusion and tragedy in our world today is that Christians are not united in actively living our faith."**

What did Our Lord say about unity in His flock? Jesus prayed, *"That they may all be one. As you, Father, are in me and I am in you, may they also be one in us … so that the world may know you have sent me."* (John 17: 21) Our Lord prayed for unity!

The current divisions among Christians, with thousands of different groups worshipping separately, fighting among themselves, and believing entirely different and contradictory things, cannot possibly be the Will of Our Savior. Many of you have experienced this disunity within your own families and communities.

As Catholics, we work towards Christian unity first and foremost by understanding what we believe and why – so that we are prepared to enter into a dialogue with other Christian believers. This work towards Christian unity is called "ecumenism." It is one of the most important tasks for us, as Catholics.

We believe that the Church Jesus Christ founded and gave to the world was, is, and remains the Catholic Church. As the Second Vatican Council so clearly taught, *"For it is through Christ's Catholic Church alone, which is the universal help toward salvation, that the fullness of the means of salvation can be obtained."* In another place, the Council teaches, *"The sole Church of Christ is that which our Savior, after his resurrection, entrusted to Peter's pastoral care, commissioning him and the other apostles to extend and rule it … This Church constituted and organized as a society in the present world, subsists in the Catholic Church, which is governed by the successor of St. Peter and by the bishops in communion with him."* Thus, we believe that Christ founded our Church. We believe this with good reason, for it is supported both by Sacred Scripture and by history. Another valid reason for this belief is the constant succession of popes going back to St. Peter. Certainly, there have been various rifts throughout the history of Christianity. However, in the early days, these remained small and mostly reconciled.

The two major sources of disunity in the Body of Christ date back to 1054 when the Eastern Orthodox Churches broke with the Western Catholic Church, and in 1517 when the objections of Martin Luther towards Catholicism led to the Protestant Reformation. These ruptures in the unity of Christ's Church did not occur without the presence of human sin – sometimes, on both sides. However, the fact remains that disunity among Christians is a great scandal to our world, and we all must work to repair the divisions.

So, as we begin our journey through the various Christian denominations, let us ask God to bless our world with Christians who are united and faithful to doing His Will. This prayer is most urgent today!

I would like to acknowledge the book, Separated Brethren, by William J. Whalen, published by "Our Sunday Visitor" in 2002[1]. For the following articles, I drew heavily from the facts and analyses of the various faiths contained in this book. I want to give full credit to this excellent source!

*Reflection Questions:*

1. *What are the three main divisions within Christianity?*
2. *Why do we need to understand our Catholic Faith well before we enter into serious dialogue with other Christians?*
3. *What is "ecumenism" and why is it important?*

# The Eastern Orthodox Church:
*We share most of the same beliefs!*

We will begin our journey through the various Christian and quasi-Christian movements with a visit to the Eastern Orthodox Church, the Christian body of believers closest to Catholicism. The Orthodox hold most of the same beliefs that we, as Catholics, do. The main difference between us remains the question of authority within the Church, including the role of the Pope.

---

[1] Whalen, William J., *Separated Brethren*, Our Sunday Visitor, 2002

Today, there are some 200 million Christians who are in the Orthodox church. Some are found in Western Europe and in the United States (about six million in our country). However, Orthodox Christians most commonly are found in Greece, Russia, Turkey and other eastern European and Middle Eastern countries. Eastern Orthodox Christians belong to 15 "autocephalous" - or independent - churches who elect their own bishops and govern themselves.

> **"The main difference between us remains the question of authority within the Church, including the role of the Pope."**

Orthodox Christianity has seven valid sacraments, a deep devotion to the Blessed Virgin Mary and the other saints, and a strong belief in the Holy Trinity. Although the primacy of the Pope over all of Christianity is rejected, the Orthodox accept his authority in a limited way as the Patriarch of the Western Church.

Practically speaking, the differences between Catholicism and Eastern Orthodoxy have to do with different manners of worship and the understanding of authority within the Church.

The Orthodox Mass is valid; unlike in Protestantism, Orthodox Holy Communion truly is the Body and Blood of Christ. However, the Mass has a very different structure than our own - it is longer, more ornate and more symbolic. Instead of statues or paintings which Catholics use to represent holy persons, the Eastern Orthodox use "icons" - or two-dimensional images covered with gold and symbols - to represent the saints.

The Orthodox object to the word *"filioque"* (the Holy Spirit who proceeds from the father **and the son**...) in the Nicene Creed, which they say was added by the Catholic Church. The Orthodox have a married priesthood, they use leavened bread for the Eucharist, they do not make use of indulgences, and do not profess the Marian dogmas of the Immaculate Conception and the Assumption. Perhaps the greatest difference between us remains the Orthodox rejection of the authority of the Pope over all of Christianity.

To recap some history, Christianity was united for its first 1,000 years. The Church was known as the Catholic Church and, despite the occasional sinfulness of some of its members, the Church held together as a unified whole. The early Church quickly grew throughout the Roman Empire, spanning large cultural divides. Soon, the Church was seen as having two parts, East and West, with different practices and ways of approaching theology distinguishing the two. There was unity in belief, just different ways of practicing the Faith.

As time passed, disagreements and sinful behavior on both sides began to affect the unity of the Church. These disagreements came to a head in 1054, when the two sides excommunicated each other and the East was separated from the West. The Western Church came to be known as the Roman Catholic Church and the Eastern Church came to be known as the Eastern Orthodox Church. The sack of Constantinople by the western crusaders in 1204 only served to further this divide. These mutual excommunications were lifted in 1965 by Pope Paul VI and the Orthodox Patriarch Athenagoras I. Today, there is great hope for reunion between our two churches.

Unfortunately, our two churches remain separated, despite our overwhelming similarities. Although Catholics permit Orthodox Christians to receive Communion in our Church, the Orthodox frown upon Catholics receiving Communion in their Church. With the growth of the Catholic Church in Eastern Europe and Russia, the Orthodox remain concerned about losing members to Catholicism. The rise of Eastern Rite Catholic Churches – churches that have adopted the Eastern manner of prayer and worship yet remain loyal to Rome – also has strained relations between us.

However, as the late Pope John Paul II said in 1988, *"Christianity has two lungs, it will never breathe easily until it uses both of them."* So, remember, among all Christians, Catholics and the Orthodox have the most in common. It is of the highest ecumenical priority to repair the damage our separation has caused and to work towards greater unity between us. Let us pray for this.

*Reflection Questions:*

1. *Who are the Orthodox Christians?*
2. *What do we have in common?*
3. *What are our differences?*

# Old Catholics and Polish National Catholics:
*Their main objection is to authority within the Church.*

Let's continue on our way through the various religious traditions by visiting two unique Christian churches. They are called the Old Catholics and the Polish National Catholics. These two churches can have valid sacraments and a valid priesthood. Unlike Protestants, they believe and hold many of the same doctrines and traditions as do Catholics. Their main objection surrounds the issue of authority within the Church.

The **Old Catholic Church** was formed in the late 1800s by various Catholics who protested against the dogma of Papal Infallibility. This teaching of the Catholic Faith holds that the Pope, as guided by the Holy Spirit, teaches infallibly and without error when he formally proclaims a Church teaching on an issue of faith or morals. This dogma is very narrow and precise and has been believed by Christians from the very beginning of the Church. However, some rejected its formal dogmatic definition in 1869 – and thus, the "Old" Catholics were born.

> "The Old Catholic Church was formed...(as a protest against) Papal Infallibility...(Polish immigrants found) most American bishops and priests to be of German or Irish descent."

Today, there are about 150,000 Old Catholics world-wide, mostly in Western Europe and the United States. Old Catholic priests and bishops highly value apostolic succession, which is the ordination by a bishop who can trace his own ordination back to the apostles. As Catholics, we are assured of this fact. However, since Old Catholics have broken away from the Catholic Church, they must go in search of a rogue bishop who will ordain their clergy so that apostolic succession can be maintained. Although it remains a bit hazy, at least some of the bishops and priests of the Old Catholic churches are validly ordained, and hence can celebrate the sacraments.

The Old Catholics instituted a number of changes from the Roman Catholic Faith. Fasting and the Sacrament of Penance were downplayed, and pastors of parishes were elected by the people. Priests were permitted to marry, and the Mass was said in the vernacular. Today, the Old Catholic churches are effected by internal strife and are beginning to die out.

The second group, the **Polish National Catholics**, are the only major group to break away from Catholicism that originated in the United States. For centuries, Poland has remained a strongly Catholic country. When many Poles emigrated to the United States in the late 1800s and early 1900s, they were surprised to find most American bishops and priests to be of German or Irish descent. These priests often did not understand Polish customs and traditions and the Polish immigrants quickly grew impatient. The issue of ownership of parishes and property also added fuel to the fire.

In 1895, in Chicago, some Poles gathered together to form the Polish National Church. Around the same time, in Scranton, Pennsylvania, a group of Polish Catholics wanted complete control over Church property and the ability to elect their own pastor. These two groups soon merged to form the Polish National Catholic Church.

Many of the *external* facets of Roman Catholicism, such as the rituals, are found in the Polish National Catholic Church. Their sacraments are mostly valid. Priests can marry in the Polish National Catholic Church, although it is not preferred. On moral issues, the Polish National Catholic Church is somewhat similar to the Roman Catholic Church, although there are differences in marriage law and in sexual morality. Today, as fewer people speak their native language and connection with the old country grows cold, the Polish National Catholic Church has ceased growing. Currently, they number only about 300,000.

Let us welcome both of these groups back to the Roman Catholic Church.

*Reflection Questions:*

*1. Where did the Old Catholic and Polish National Catholic churches originate?*

*2. What do we have in common?*

*3. What are our differences?*

---

# Protestant Communities - Part I:
### They have key differences with Catholics - yet, much in common!

As we continue our journey through the various Christian denominations, our next visit is to the Protestants. *"Protestant"* is a general name given to a person who believes in Jesus Christ and who has been baptized, but who does not profess the Catholic Faith in its entirety. Rather, he or she is a member of an ecclesial community whose roots are in the Reformation, begun in the Sixteenth Century.

> **"Catholics and Protestants both acknowledge the first sin of Adam and Eve...However, we differ on the consequences that flow from this first sin."**

Within the word, "Protestant," you will note another word - "protest." This protest, at least originally, was against the Catholic Church. However, it must be stated that we, as Catholics, have a great deal in common with our Protestant brothers and sisters. Protestants and Catholics all are Christians - we believe in Jesus Christ as our Lord and Savior; we believe in the Holy Trinity. We accept the authority of the Ten Commandments, and we often profess the same Nicene Creed. Catholics hold most forms of Protestant baptism to be valid and sacramental, and we celebrate many of the same religious feast days such as

Easter and Christmas. Both Catholics and Protestants realize the importance of reaching out to the poor and needy. Often, we cooperate in works of social justice.

Sadly, there also are differences between us. Generally speaking, the two major tenets of Protestantism are doctrines known as "Sola Fidei" and "Sola Scriptura." In English, these are best translated as "salvation by faith alone" and "the Bible alone is the sole rule of faith." Many of the practical differences between us stem from these two doctrines.

So, what exactly is Sola Fidei? Catholics and Protestants both acknowledge the first sin of Adam and Eve - often called the Fall of Man. However, we differ on the consequences that flow from this first sin. Catholic theology holds that humanity was weakened - our intellect, will and soul greatly wounded - by what we call "original sin." Protestant theology, following the lead of Martin Luther, holds that human nature was more totally and completely corrupted by the Fall.

Notice the difference in words: Catholics believe humanity was greatly weakened, Protestants generally believe humanity was totally corrupted. I do realize that this seems to be a rather small distinction, but it has had large consequences for our understanding of our relationship with Christ. Both Protestants and Catholics call the entering into right relationship with God and the forgiveness of our sins justification. This justification comes through Jesus Christ, Our Lord and Savior.

Now, Luther and the first Protestants believed that human nature was so completely corrupted by the Fall that, even after our justification in Christ, our past sins were just covered over. God, so to speak, chose to look the other way. As famously attributed to Luther, *"Humanity is a dung heap covered over by snow."* In other words, we still stink. Luther and others reasoned that our good works can merit nothing, since we still are corrupted - even after we are justified in Christ. Only faith can save us, and good works (feeding the hungry, caring for the sick, and even celebrating the sacraments) while good in and of themselves are of no avail to our salvation. Thus, we come to the term "sola fidei" - salvation by faith alone.

Catholics share the belief that we cannot save ourselves by our good works. In actuality, this is the heresy of "Pelagianism" which was condemned by the Church in the 300s. However, Catholics believe that after we are justified, we become new persons. We are transformed by God's grace, and are made pure and holy. Our sins are taken away, not simply covered over. Thus, our good works (charity, mercy, prayer) which necessarily stem from the gift of Faith we have received, can and do have some merit for eternal life.

In other words, we are saved only in and through Jesus Christ, but after we have accepted Him, the good that we do in His name has merit. As St.

Augustine famously said, *"In the crowning of our good works, God is really crowning his own gifts."* (St. Augustine, *On Grace and Free Will*, 20) Unfortunately from this difference has come much disunity between Catholics and Protestants in our beliefs and practices. We must pray for understanding, forgiveness and unity.

---

# Protestant Communities – Part II:
*Varying scripture interpretations led to various denominations.*

I would like to continue our discussion of the differences – and similarities – between Catholicism and Protestantism.

As you recall, there are two main doctrines of the Protestant tradition. The second doctrine is "Sola Scriptura" – or, "the Bible alone is the sole rule of faith."

After Luther and the other early Protestants broke from the Catholic Church, they suddenly found themselves in a position with little authority. If a disagreement arose between two Protestants, who or what could intervene and give guidance, since the authority of the Church had been rejected? Luther believed and taught that the supreme religious authority was to be found not in the Church which Christ founded, but in a book: the Holy Bible.

> **"What had seemingly been forgotten was that the Catholic Church had, in fact, pre-dated the completed Bible by some 300 years, and...assembled the completed Bible."**

At the time, Luther had witnessed unfaithfulness and abuse among some in authority within the Church, so he turned to the Bible for guidance. However, since the authority of the Church now was denied, Biblical interpretation was left solely to the individual believer. This led to a myriad of varying interpretations of scripture, which in turn has led to the thousands of different Protestant denominations we see today. With no authority to guide such interpretation, this was the inevitable outcome.

In addition, some seven books from the Old Testament were discarded by Luther. (Since the seven sacraments could not all be found explicitly in the Bible, most of them were abandoned, too.)

What had seemingly been forgotten was that the Catholic Church had, in fact, pre-dated the completed Bible by some 300 years, and that it was the Catholic Church, under the inspiration of the Holy Spirit, that had assembled the completed Bible. Certainly, the Old Testament was already in existence prior to Christ founding the Church, but the Divinely Inspired writings that comprise the New Testament had to be discerned, organized and accepted. The Catholic Church accomplished this great task.

Today, the average Protestant knows the Bible very well. This is a most wonderful thing - to know the Bible is to know Christ. It is His Word, and we, as Catholics, should read His Word more frequently. However, since the nature of Church authority is rejected by most Protestants, their private and personal interpretation of the Holy Scriptures can sometimes be mistaken. As Catholics, we believe that the Church is Christ's gift to the world and that this Church has an important role to play in guiding biblical interpretation as well as in other matters of Christian life.

Besides these two major doctrinal differences between Catholics and Protestants, there are a number of other wounds to our unity.

Most Protestants do not believe that the Church is divinely instituted with a visible structure, as Catholics do. Protestants believe that what we know as "church" is the fellowship of all believers in Jesus Christ and hence invisible.

Another difference between us revolves around how we worship. Protestant worship was initially patterned after the Catholic Mass, but it soon went its own way. Because the Sacrament of Holy Orders was rejected by the early Protestants, there was no possibility for a valid Eucharist.

Soon, there arose varying interpretations of what the Eucharist actually was. Lutherans held to the belief of consubstantiation - the Body and Blood of Christ and the bread and wine existing together at the same time. Presbyterians believed that communion was merely spiritual and symbolic. Methodists and Baptists saw the Eucharist as a simple memorial service. All of these differed from the Catholic understanding of the Eucharist as the Body and Blood of Christ, truly and really present. Devotion to the Blessed Virgin Mary also was eliminated by many of the reformers, as was the veneration of the communion of saints. Tragically, these are just some of the many differences between us.

Fortunately, in our own time, dialogue has begun between Catholics and many Protestants on how we can move towards greater unity. Our disunity is certainly a scandal to the world, and it is a barrier to the spreading of the Gospel. May we, as Catholics, along with our Protestant brothers and sisters, work and pray for a return of unity to Christ's Church. May we all be one!

*Reflection Questions:*

1. *What are the two main doctrines of Protestantism?*
2. *What do they mean?*

3. How do the Protestant and Catholic definitions of the word "church" vary?

---

# The Lutherans:
*Among Protestants, they have the most in common with Catholics.*

Let's begin our exploration of the various Protestant denominations by discussing the Lutherans. This is one of the most common Christian groups. Many of us have discovered that we have much in common with our Lutheran brothers and sisters. Let us visit their denomination now and see what we have in common and what still divides us...

> "....Luther had originally intended to reform the one Church that Christ had founded, and had not intended to break with the Catholic Church."

Lutheranism is one of the largest Protestant denominations, numbering 66 million adherents. In our own country, there are about 9.5 million people who consider themselves to be Lutheran. Of these, the majority belong to three bodies called synods These are: The Evangelical Lutheran Church in America (ELCA) with about 5.1 million members; The Lutheran Church - Missouri Synod (LCMS) which has some 2.5 million members; and the Wisconsin Evangelical Lutheran Synod (WELS) which has about 410,000 members. Those who practice the Lutheran religion are more common in the Midwest, with fewer Lutherans found in the Northeast and in the South.

The name *"Lutheran"* is associated with Father Martin Luther, a Catholic priest who is widely seen as having started the Protestant Reformation. In the early 1500s, much abuse and political intrigue had influenced some members of the Catholic Church. The clergy was poorly trained and many of the laity had strayed from living Christian lives. Reform was needed. Father Luther was acutely aware of the troubled situation, and in 1517, nailed his famed "95 Theses" on the door of the Catholic Church in Wittenberg, Germany.

Initially, many of Luther's positions were within the realm of Church teaching. However, he soon took more radical positions of challenging papal authority, changing Biblical translation and interpretation, and differing with the Church's understanding of the nature of salvation. He stood convicted of heresy and was excommunicated in 1520.

Meanwhile, some who agreed with his views and many others who felt oppressed by the political situation of the time, took matters into their own hands and began an outright rebellion. The Reformation was as much a political movement as it was a religious movement. By 1530, "The Augsburg Confession" appeared (this remains the most authoritative Lutheran document on teaching and doctrine).

Often, Martin Luther was carried along by the very revolution he had started. Sometimes, he was troubled by the direction the movement had taken. It could be said that Luther had originally intended to reform the one Church that Christ had founded, and had not intended to break with the Catholic Church. Sadly, this was not to be the case.

So, exactly what are the differences between Catholics and Lutherans? The first two differences between us involve the Protestant doctrines of "Salvation by Faith Alone" (we only need to have faith in Christ to be saved) and "The Bible Alone" (the Bible is the only norm of doctrine and life, the only true standard by which teachings and doctrines are to be judged). These two teachings of Luther himself, along with the Lutheran understanding of the nature of the Church and of Church authority, still divide us today.

Lutherans generally accept only two sacraments (Baptism and The Lord's Supper) and we differ greatly on the role of the saints and Mary the Mother of God. The Catholic dogma of Purgatory, with the accompanying understanding of indulgences, also is rejected by Lutherans. Divorce and remarriage is permitted in the Lutheran Church, and our understanding of the nature of the Eucharist is different. On moral and social issues, there is a great deal of difference between the individual Lutheran synods. The ELCA is generally much more liberal in outlook than the LCMS and WELS which are seen as more traditional and ultra-conservative, respectively.

That being said, among all Protestants, Lutherans are rightly seen as having the most in common with Catholics. We both believe in Jesus Christ as our Lord and Savior, we both believe in the Trinity and see the necessity of water baptism. Liturgically (the manner in which we gather together to pray), we have much in common – after all, the Lutheran service was derived from the Catholic Mass. Lutherans have a rich musical tradition from which Catholics often have benefited. Depending upon the particular synod, we may share many of the same moral and social views on life.

Perhaps the most optimistic step toward unity between us came in 1999, when the Lutheran World Federation and the Vatican signed an agreement on our views of justification and salvation. Indeed, we are growing closer together!

Let us pray for our Lutheran friends and share our Catholic Faith with them.

Reflection Questions:

1. What were Father Martin Luther's objections to the Catholic Church?

2. What do we have in common with Lutherans?

3. What are our differences?

---

# The Episcopalians:
*They are really two churches in one.*

In our journey through the various Christian denominations, we now come to the Episcopalians. They are known as "Anglicans" throughout the rest of the world.

Episcopalians – or Anglicans – trace their roots back to the Church of England, founded in 1529. Today, they number some 70 million world-wide. About 2.3 million members live in the United States, with the majority on the East Coast.

To recount a little history, King Henry VIII, a devout Catholic who had written numerous books defending the Faith against Martin Luther, desired a son so that he could have an heir to the throne. While already married to his brother's widow – Catherine of Aragon – he became enamored with Anne Boleyn.

> **"(King Henry VIII) wished to have his marriage to Catherine declared null by the Church. This, the Pope refused to do...Henry broke with the Catholic Church."**

Since Catherine was unable to provide him with a male heir to the throne, Henry wanted to divorce her and marry his mistress, Anne Boleyn. In order to do this, he wished to have his marriage to Catherine declared null by the Church. This, the Pope refused to do. So, in 1529, Henry broke with the Catholic Church.

By 1534, Henry declared himself to be the head of the Church of England. He immediately divorced Catherine and married Anne. Hundreds of bishops, priests and lay people who disagreed with his actions were murdered. They included his chancellor, St. Thomas More, and St. John Fisher, the only bishop in England to openly oppose him.

Despite this break with the authority of the Catholic Church, much of the structure of belief and practice within the Church of England remained the same as that of the Catholic Church, during Henry's lifetime. However, after his death in 1547, the Protestant Reformation from Continental Europe began to influence the Church of England. During the reign of Queen Elizabeth I, a persecution of Catholics began in England that would last for almost 300 years. Despite this fact, many of the Catholic beliefs and practices remained in the Church of England. By studying this history, we can see how the dual nature of the Episcopalian Church came about and why it still exists today. Because of their history, many Episcopalians see themselves as a bridge church, half way between Protestantism and Catholicism. Episcopalians divide into two groups, known popularly as "high" and "low" churches. Low Church is more Protestant in outlook while High Church appears quite similar to Catholicism.

The differences between the two encompass not only theology, but also worship. For example, High Church Episcopalians call their Sunday celebration a Mass and it looks very much like a formal Catholic Mass. Low Church Episcopalians align themselves with Protestant theology and practice. Today, the Low Church is dominant, especially in regards to moral and social issues, with the more conservative High Church strongly objecting. The tension is such today that unity among Episcopalians is in danger. A new Evangelical wing has emerged to try and bridge this gap, but it has, thus far, been unsuccessful.

For most of the 20th century, it seemed that the odds were very favorable for a reunification between Catholics and Episcopalians. Led by the Anglo-Catholic High Church, great progress was made towards unity. Indeed, the Archbishop of Canterbury and Pope Paul VI appeared together in public, and serious talks were underway. However, this was not to be.

With the ordination of women in the 1970s, and the more recent ordinations of openly homosexual bishops - as well as numerous other social and moral issues on which we differ - it appears, today, that unity is far from possible. Other key issues on which we differ include the invalidity of Anglican Holy Orders and the currently dominant Protestant theology of the Low Church.

Despite all of this, Episcopalians and Catholics do have much in common. We both believe in Jesus Christ as our Lord and Savior, we both believe in the Trinity and see the necessity of water baptism. Liturgically (the manner in which we gather together to pray), we also have much in common - remember, the Episcopalian service, sometimes called a Mass, was directly derived from the Catholic Mass. Episcopalians have a rich musical tradition from which Catholics often have benefited, and we share a respect for the Sacred Tradition of the Church and for the use of reason.

Due to the current unrest in their church, many Episcopalians are becoming Catholic - including some of their priests. Talks still are underway between our two churches to work towards unity.

Let us pray for our Episcopalian friends. Share our Catholic Faith with them, whenever you find the opportunity!

*Reflection Questions:*

1. Where did the Episcopalian – or Anglican – church originate?
2. What do we have in common?
3. What are our differences?

---

# The Methodists:
*They've been called the most "American" church.*

On our continuing journey through Christian denominations, we now visit the Methodists. How much do you know about this large Protestant denomination?

Today, there are about 29 million Methodists around the world. More than half of them live in the United States, with the rest in Europe and elsewhere. Until the 1850s, the Methodists were the most numerous Christian group in our country. Obviously, their roots still are strong here. The United Methodist Church is the most commonly found branch in our country, with some nine million members nationwide. Methodism often has been characterized as the most quintessentially "American" church.

> **"Methodism was started in 1738 by John Wesley. He was an Anglican priest who wanted to reform the Anglican – or Episcopalian – church."**

Methodism was started in 1738 by John Wesley. He was an Anglican priest who wanted to reform the Anglican – or Episcopalian – church. With his great zeal, Wesley desired to save souls and bring all to Christ. Defined doctrine or theology was never of primary interest to Wesley and his followers. Rather, their focus was on daily living of the Christian life and care for those in need.

In theology, however, Wesley differed greatly from Martin Luther's denial of the efficacy of good works. Wesley urged fasting, abstinence, daily prayer, devotions and frequent communion – all practices that seemed more similar to Catholicism than to Lutheranism. Wesley also rejected the doctrine of predestination to Heaven or Hell which John Calvin, a French lawyer who was a founder of the Presbyterian Church, taught. Wesley championed human free will, in making moral decisions and in issues of faith. Wesley himself was a tireless preacher who traveled throughout England preaching reform within Anglicanism. Early on, he and his followers began to be called "Methodists" because of their strict method of life and prayer.

The first Methodist preachers who came to America, in 1769, met with much success. Despite many Methodists' support of the British in the American Revolution, the faith still grew rapidly. This led to a formal break with the Anglican Church in 1784. The newly founded Methodist Church continued to grow in the United States. It splintered into many groups under the general name, "Methodist." However, in 1968, many of these groups came together again into what is now known as the United Methodist Church.

Today, Methodists are highly organized with numerous local and national outreach projects. Methodists have 100 colleges and 72 hospitals around the United States. In addition, they began Goodwill Industries.

Clearly, there are some differences between Catholics and Methodists. Although Wesley was positively influenced by the High Church Anglicans' view of Catholicism, he still was Protestant in outlook. Differences exist between us in the way we read and interpret the Bible, the nature of authority in Church, and the nature of the Eucharist. Communion is seen by Methodists as merely symbolic and a memorial, not as the Body and Blood of Christ. On some moral issues, such as abortion, Catholics and United Methodists also disagree.

Despite these numerous differences, Methodists and Catholics do have much in common. We both acknowledge Jesus Christ as our Lord and Savior and we both believe in the Holy Trinity. Like Lutherans and Episcopalians, we profess a common Creed. The importance of infant baptism and the value of doing good works are stressed by both. Methodists and Catholics have been in formal dialogue since 1970. Progress is slowly being made towards unity.

Let us pray for our Methodist friends and not hesitate to share our Catholic Faith with them!

*Reflection Questions:*

1. *Why were the Methodists founded?*
2. *What do we have in common with them?*
3. *What are our differences?*

# The Presbyterians:
*Their name comes from "presbyters" - or church leaders.*

As we proceed on our journey through the various Christian denominations, our next stop is with the Presbyterians. The Presbyterian religion is present throughout our country, with the greatest concentration of believers on the East Coast in the Mid-Atlantic States.

Currently, there are about four million Presbyterians in the United States, with the vast majority of these belonging to the Presbyterian Church (U.S.A.). Sixty colleges in our country are tied to the Presbyterian Church. The word "Presbyterian" comes from the form of governance which the individual congregations have adopted. Rather than appointing bishops, "presbyters" - or elders - are elected to guide the individual parishes.

> **"Father John Knox was a follower of John Calvin. He took what he learned from Calvin back to his native Scotland and established...Presbyterianism."**

Outside of the United States, this church is active in Switzerland, Scotland, Holland and France. Often called "the Reformed Church" in Europe and "the Presbyterian Church" in the United States, this denomination was begun by the French lawyer John Calvin around the year 1533. The beliefs of Calvin and the current practices and teachings of the Presbyterian Church vary widely. Nevertheless, most Presbyterians hold to the reformed tradition begun by him. To trace the roots of this church, we travel back to the beginning of the Protestant Reformation, when Father Ulrich Zwingli broke with the Catholic Church in Switzerland. Inspired by Father Martin Luther, Zwingli rejected Church authority and the importance of clerical celibacy. Soon, however, Luther and Zwingli differed on the nature of the Real Presence of Christ in the Eucharist. Luther believed and taught that Christ was present in the Eucharist while Zwingli taught that it was only a symbolic memorial service. This difference of opinion led to the split between the Lutheran and Reformed versions of Protestantism, a division which still exists today.

John Calvin was strongly influenced by Ulrich Zwingli and succeeded him in Switzerland as a religious leader. Calvin became a religious dictator, transforming the Swiss city of Geneva into a religious police state. Geneva became a haven for religious rebels from throughout Europe who were escaping either the Catholic Church or Lutheranism.

The city soon began exporting a new brand of Protestantism called the "Reformed" church. This form of Protestantism came to be called "Calvinism," incorporating the doctrine of "Predestination" with the standard Protestant teachings of Salvation by Faith Alone and The Bible Alone. This doctrine taught that God directly predestines some people to Heaven and others to Hell. Our fate is already determined; we just carry it out. Calvin's version of Christianity also was quite strict, prohibiting dancing, smoking and alcohol.

Father John Knox was a follower of John Calvin. He took what he learned from Calvin back to his native Scotland and established "The Reformed Faith" - soon to be called Presbyterianism - there. From Scotland and elsewhere in Europe, people emigrated to the United States in search of freedom and a new life. Presbyterians supported the cause of the American Revolution, and settled into the large American middle class where many remain today.

There are numerous differences between Catholics and Presbyterians. For example, we differ greatly on our understanding of the Eucharist. Presbyterians do not see baptism as necessary for salvation. Also, the nature of their church governance and authority differs greatly from ours. Although the doctrine of predestination has been rejected by most mainstream Presbyterians today, its effects still remain. We also disagree on important social issues such as homosexuality and abortion.

Catholics and Presbyterians do share some common beliefs. We have a common belief in Jesus Christ as Our Lord and Savior. We both believe in the Holy Trinity and acknowledge the Bible as the Word of God. We cooperate in good works to help the poor and needy, and recognize the importance of social justice.

We should continue to pray for and work toward greater unity with our Presbyterian brothers and sisters - and share our Catholic Faith with them.

*Reflection Questions:*

1. *Who were the major founders of the Presbyterian denomination?*
2. *What do we have in common?*
3. *What are our differences?*

# The Baptists:
*A "Born Again" experience is required for salvation.*

Next, on our travels through the world of Christian denominations, we arrive for a visit with the Baptists. Those who consider themselves "Baptist" comprise the largest group of Protestants in America. Indeed, after Catholics, Baptists are the most numerous Christian group in the United States. In the southeastern part of our country, they form the clear majority.

Unlike most other mainline Protestant communities, the Southern Baptist Convention (the largest group of Baptists), is growing quickly in size and influence throughout the world.

> **"All Baptists receive their name from their steadfast belief that infants cannot receive baptism. They have built upon Martin Luther's belief of 'salvation by faith alone.'"**

In all, there are some two dozen different groups that call themselves "Baptist." Since, as I mentioned, the Southern Baptist Convention (SBC) is the largest and most influential group, I will focus on them.

Southern Baptists originated in the South (as their name implies), but now they are found throughout our country - almost 16 million members strong. Current reports state that Southern Baptists are starting new churches every day. Their growth has been explosive.

All Baptists received their name from their steadfast belief that infants cannot receive baptism. They have built upon Martin Luther's belief of "salvation by faith alone." Since infants presumably do not have the use of reason, and hence cannot profess belief, baptism must be conferred upon adults only, this group believes. Baptism is not seen as a sacrament but rather as a symbolic action of being "born again." Immersion (complete submersion of the body in water) is the only form of baptism accepted by Baptists.

An equally important doctrine of this denomination involves a literal interpretation of the Bible. The words of the Bible are understood to be the literal Word of God, and must be followed explicitly.

The spiritual ancestors of modern-day Baptists were the Anabaptists. The Anabaptists were active at the time of the Protestant Reformation (1517) and called for the baptism of infants, autonomy for the local congregation, and biblical literalism. Their beliefs were highly criticized by both Catholics and Lutherans.

By the early 1600s, some of the beliefs of the Anabaptists had been adopted by a small group of Protestants. They called themselves "Baptists" and distinguished themselves from other Protestants by calling for the baptism of adult believers and not infants - and local autonomy for each congregation. Soon, this newly formed Baptist denomination traveled to the New World. In America, it spread quickly, especially among Southerners and former slaves.

Today, many Baptists, especially Southern Baptists, are seen as quite conservative and cautious in their interaction with other Christian churches. There is a strong emphasis on evangelization and aggressive missionary work. This has yielded many conversions to Christ throughout the world. With large congregations that give up to 10 percent of their income in tithes, the Southern Baptists can manage to give some 1.5 billion dollars per year to various programs. Baptists have been active in exploring new ways to use modern media such as television. Billy Graham and Jerry Falwell have ranked among the best known Baptist ministers.

So, what are the differences between Catholics and Baptists? For starters, Baptists do not consider Baptism and the Eucharist as sacraments. Both are called "ordinances" and seen merely as symbols. Baptism is not believed to be necessary for salvation. Rather, what is required is a "Born Again" experience in which a person comes to realize his or her faith in Christ and the assurance of salvation. Only then does baptism occur, they contend.

Baptists tend to believe that once a person is Born Again, he never can be lost – that his salvation, no matter what sin he later commits, never is undone. This often is referred to as, "Once saved, always saved." Catholics and most other Protestants disagree with this belief.

Another difference is that Baptist churches are autonomous – that is, they have no centralized authority such as a bishop. Thus, they lack the apostolic authority that Christ instituted. It also is troubling to note that Baptists have sent missionaries to mostly Catholic areas including Poland, Ireland and the territory of Puerto Rico in order to evangelize Catholics. In 2001, the Southern Baptist Convention ended 30 years of ecumenical dialogue with Catholics.

Despite these differences, Catholics and Baptists share a great deal in common. We both believe in Jesus Christ as our Lord and Savior, and we both believe in the Holy Trinity, the Bible as the Word of God, the existence of Heaven and Hell, the virgin birth and the Resurrection. Also, Catholics and Baptists have in common a missionary spirit to spread the Word of God to all nations, and we both see the great importance of evangelization to our modern world. On controversial moral issues, Catholics and Baptists are strong allies, united on issues of abortion, marriage and homosexuality.

So, let's remember to pray for our Baptist friends and include them in our own evangelization efforts to share the Catholic Faith.

*Reflection Questions:*
1. *What is the most unique aspect of the Baptist denomination?*
2. *What do we have in common?*
3. *What are our differences?*

# The United Church of Christ:
*Ever wonder who started Harvard and Yale?*

Let us continue our journey through the various Christian denominations. Our next destination is the United Church of Christ and its various individual churches. The United Church of Christ (UCC) was formed in 1957, from a merger of the Congregationalists and the Evangelical and Reformed Church.

Today, the United Church of Christ has about one million members. It is most prevalent in New England as well as in the Midwest. In some areas, the local Congregational Church retains its original name instead of the newer UCC label. The UCC prides itself on its progressive and liberal approach to theology. It is centralized in Cleveland, Ohio. The church takes its motto from John's Gospel: *"That they may all be one."* (John 17:21)

> "After much persecution in England, many of the new Congregationalists fled to the Netherlands. They had more difficulties there, and found a ... ship named the Mayflower."

The history of the United Church of Christ is steeped in the tradition of Colonial America. In the 1600s, there arose groups of English Christians who rejected any type of centralized control of individual congregations. They rejected bishops and proclaimed, *"No head, priest, prophet, or king save Christ."* Each individual congregation would remain independent and plot its own course. The name "Congregationalist" soon was associated with this group.

After much persecution in England, many of the new Congregationalists fled to the Netherlands. They had more difficulties there, and found a merchant ship named the Mayflower. In 1620, these Pilgrims set sail for the New World. By 1691, despite much hardship in America, Congregationalism had become the majority faith in the colonies. The Puritans, another breakaway group from the Church of England, eventually united with the Congregationalists.

The growth of this denomination slowed in the early 1800s, because of a number of disputes amongst its members over the existence of the Holy Trinity. Also, as the nation expanded west, there was less of a willingness to expand the church's influence into the frontier. The Congregationalists boast of starting many of our nation's finest colleges including Harvard, Yale, Dartmouth, Amherst, Smith and Oberlin. Education always has been a priority for ministers and laity alike.

As mentioned previously, the Evangelical and Reformed Church also helped to form the modern-day UCC. This church was made up of Germans who had not accepted Lutheranism but rather the reformed theology of John Calvin. Settling in Pennsylvania, members of this church gradually became more progressive in theology, boasting several well-known, liberal Protestant theologians including Niebuhr and Tillich.

Differences between the United Church of Christ and the Catholic Church include disagreements over authority in the Church, how to interpret the Bible, the nature and person of Jesus, the Eucharist, the understanding of the Trinity, and a whole host of moral and ethical issues such as abortion and homosexual marriage.

However, we both believe that Jesus Christ is our Savior. We both see the need for outreach to the poor and vulnerable. Catholics and UCC members often cooperate in acts of social justice, despite our many differences. Both Catholics and UCC members stress the importance of baptism, including the baptism of infants.

As we share our Catholic Faith with our Protestant brothers and sisters, let's not forget those in the United Church of Christ.

*Reflection Questions:*

*1. Recount the early American history associated with the United Church of Christ.*

*2. What do we have in common?*

*3. What are our differences?*

# The Quakers:
*Final religious authority rests in the individual.*

After learning about various Christian denominations, our journey continues with the Quakers. Often called, "The Society of Friends," the Quakers have positively influenced our country from its very beginning.

The majority of Quakers reside on the East Coast, in the mid-Atlantic states. Today, there are some 200,000 Quakers in the United States. Despite their small numbers, the Quakers are very involved in social justice and peace work. They are strict pacifists, refusing military service.

> "....George Fox founded the Quakers in 1649...One time, in front of a judge and jury, he exclaimed, *'The time has come for even judges to quake and tremble before the Lord.'*"

Quakers often consider themselves to have a different form of Christianity. The Lutherans rejected the Pope, the visible Church, and five of the seven sacraments. Calvin and the Congregationalists did away with all bishops and a centralized church government. The Quakers went beyond all of this and rejected all of the sacraments, every ritual, and even pastoral ministers.

Quakers do not hold that the Bible is the sole rule of faith, nor do they believe in justification by faith alone, as Luther taught. Rather, Quakers contend that the final religious authority rests in the individual. Quakers believe in something called the "Inner Light" which they perceive to be the movement of the Holy Spirit within the individual. Because of this belief, Quakers have a mystical approach to theology.

It is generally held that George Fox founded the Quakers in 1649. Fox was reacting against abuses he saw in the Protestant churches of the time, and he quickly gained followers. Often, Fox was persecuted because of his different views. One time, in front of a judge and jury, he exclaimed, *"The time has come for even judges to quake and tremble before the Lord."* The name stuck.

"Quakers" assumed a very strict outlook on life, with no entertainment, no acknowledgment of privilege or rank, and a simple dress code (See the Quaker Oats box...). Worship services were silent gatherings in plain meeting houses. Only when a person was moved by the Holy Spirit, did he or she speak. The rest of the time, silence was maintained. Women were treated as equals to men in religious matters – a rarity at the time – and decisions were made not by majority vote, but by consensus.

Quakers came to America in 1681, led by William Penn. The son of a British admiral, Penn was a convert to Quakerism and did much to spread his new denomination in the huge landholdings owned by his father. Pennsylvania is named after him. The city that he designed is called Philadelphia – the "City of Brotherly Love."

In this young colony in the New World, all religions were accepted, including Catholicism. Penn helped draft fair and equitable treaties with Native Americans and established programs to help the poor and needy. Because of these and other factors, Quakerism was the dominant religion in America by the early 1700s. However, this dominance declined around the time of the American Revolution. The Quakers' refusal to enter into armed conflict with the British or the Native Americans, as well as the strictness of their beliefs, led to a decline in numbers. Despite their small following today, Quakers are almost universally admired as people of deep religious integrity.

Catholics and Quakers do have differences in our Christian beliefs. We have a very different understanding of the sacraments, authority in the Church, and worship. Most seriously, Quakers reject baptism of any kind - thus separating themselves from mainstream Christianity.

Interestingly, Catholics and Quakers do have some things in common. We both acknowledge Jesus Christ as our Lord and Savior. We both disagree with Martin Luther and other Protestants who hold that the Bible is the sole rule of faith and that we are saved by faith alone. Quakers have a deep and mystical kind of spirituality which we, as Catholics, appreciate. Also, Quakers are very involved in acts of promoting social justice and equality - something which Catholics value.

Let's pray for our brother and sister Christians of the Quaker Faith. Let's share our Catholic Faith with them.

*Reflection Questions:*

   *1. How do Quakers see themselves as different from other Christian groups?*

   *2. What do we, as Catholics, have in common with them?*

   *3. What are our differences?*

# The Mennonites/The Amish:
## Traditional dress, behavior and family life are the norm.

In another interesting stop on our journey through the various Christian denominations, we now visit the Mennonites and the Amish. They are two small - but strong - families of Christians. Since their behavior and social practices are different than the current norm, they often stand out and are ridiculed. However, they are our brother and sister Christians and it is important for us to respect them and learn more about them.

The Mennonites and their more strict cousins, the Amish, originated in Western Europe. Both denominations moved to the United States early in our history and, today, they are most commonly found here. There are roughly 480,000 adults who belong to the Mennonite denomination. Of these, 80,000 form the breakaway and stricter Amish denomination. Most communities of Mennonites and Amish are in rural Pennsylvania; however, some are found in the Midwestern states.

> "Before and during the rise of Protestantism in the 1500s, a number of more radical groups called for the return of what they perceived to be primitive Christianity."

Those of the Mennonite and Amish traditions almost universally are involved with farming and agriculture. Both communities are quite strict in the living of the Christian life. Traditional dress, behavior, family life and use of modern equipment and technology are strongly regulated.

Mennonites and the Amish wish to construct a voluntary church made up only of saints. Hence, strict discipline is administered to those who vary from the accepted practice or way of life. Shunning and excommunication still are practiced in these communities. Members are strongly discouraged from marrying outside of their group.

The Amish have a motto: *"The old is the best and the new is of the devil."* They enforce strict rules that outlaw mirrors, high heels, silk clothing, bright colors, photographs, electricity, telephones, central heating, cars and computers. They often speak their own language called Pennsylvania Dutch. Education past grade school is rare and children, once baptized in their teens, are expected to stay and marry within the group. Anyone who disobeys these rules may be excommunicated and shunned. Both the Mennonites and Amish promote large families. Because of this, their numbers are growing despite the rigors of their religion.

Let's review a little history. Before and during the rise of Protestantism in the 1500s, a number of more radical groups called for the return of what they perceived to be primitive Christianity. They were called Anabaptists because they taught that baptism was only to be given to adults and not to children. The Anabaptists also rejected the structure of the Church and called for a more informal brotherhood of Christians without office or distinction.

This group was persecuted throughout Europe until a former Catholic priest, Father Menno Simons, gathered many of the Anabaptists together and became their leader. From this, the former Anabaptists took a new name – the "Mennonites," after their leader.

In 1693, the Swiss bishop Jacob Amman traveled to various Mennonite communities and challenged them to a stricter adherence to their beliefs. From this revival came the "Amish," again named after their leader. Today, the Mennonites and the Amish are almost universally respected for their excellence in farming along with their honesty, simple living and hard work.

Certainly, there are differences between the Catholic Faith and the Mennonite and Amish beliefs. Perhaps most seriously, we differ on the issues of infant baptism and the importance of structure and authority of the Church. Catholics differ with Mennonites and the Amish in many of our interpretations of the Bible and in our understanding of the Eucharist. Regarding social issues, Catholics believe in actively taking the Gospel to the world rather than withdrawing from the world.

However, there are a few similarities in Catholic, Mennonite and Amish traditions. We all believe in Jesus Christ as our Lord and Savior and we acknowledge the existence of the Trinity. Also, we recognize the importance of the family and that large families are always a blessing and never a burden.

When we meet our brother and sister Christians who are Mennonites or Amish, let us greet them warmly and show them the love of Christ.

Reflection Questions:

1. Where did the Mennonite and Amish denominations originate?

2. What do we have in common with them?

3. What are our differences?

# Seventh Day Adventists:
*They believe that Saturday is the Lord's Day.*

Our journey through the various Christian denominations would not be complete without including the Seventh Day Adventists. This is one of the fastest growing Christian groups.

Worldwide, the Seventh Day Adventists have 10 million followers, with about one million living in the United States. Their fast growth is due to many factors, but chiefly, the generosity of their members. Adventists are by far the most generous of all Christians in their support of the church - they tithe 10 percent or more of their family income to their church and towards its missionary activities. (By comparison, Catholics are generally at the bottom of the list of Christians who support their churches financially - coming in at around one percent or less!)

"....Seventh Day Adventism began in the early 19th century, amid Protestant groups attempting to predict the Second Coming of Christ."

Seventh Day Adventists take their name from their belief that Saturday is actually The Lord's Day or Sabbath. Sunday worship is in error and is the mark of the beast or Satan, they contend. Because the Catholic Church historically changed the date of the Sabbath from Saturday to Sunday, the Catholic Church is seen as the tool of the Devil.

Adventists believe that human beings do not have souls, rather that they are souls. They believe that, at death, we go neither to Heaven nor Hell. Instead, we enter into a state of deep sleep until the Second Coming of Christ when all believers will rise again. After this Second Coming of Christ, believers will reign with God for 1,000 years. At the close of these 1,000 years, the wicked and unbelievers will be raised from the dead and annihilated by fire.

By comparison, Catholics believe that human beings have souls which are judged after our death, and we go to Heaven, Hell or Purgatory. We believe that the second coming of Christ will eventually arrive, and that He then will judge the living and the dead. Our souls will be reunited with our bodies and we will go to eternal life in the kingdom of God or eternal damnation in Hell.

Seventh Day Adventists live lives of sober discipline. They do not smoke, drink, or for the most part, eat pork or other meat. Their strict observance of the Saturday Sabbath mirrors that of Orthodox Jews. Adventists run the largest Protestant school system in the world, with more than one million students attending. Adventist hospitals care for millions of people, as well. Their church is rapidly expanding.

To review some history, Seventh Day Adventism began in the early 19th century, amid Protestant groups attempting to predict the Second Coming of Christ. William Miller led the American version of this quest. He boldly announced that the end of the world would come in 1843. The year came and went without incident, so he recalculated the date to be October 22, 1844. Alas, the great day did not come - again - and Miller was rejected by most of his followers. Some held on, however, and reorganized around the self-declared prophetess Ellen White. Seventh Day Adventists adopted their name in 1860, centered on their battle cry against the Sabbath being celebrated on Sunday.

Unfortunately, Catholics and Seventh Day Adventists have many differences. We differ in our understanding of the human soul, the second coming of Christ, and on the doctrines of Heaven, Hell and Purgatory. We strongly disagree with the Adventist contention that Sunday worship is wrong. Catholics and other Christians celebrate the day of rest on Sunday because that is the day on which our Lord Jesus Christ rose from the dead.

Adventists interpret the Bible in a fundamentalist and literalistic way, which differs from Catholic teaching. Also, Catholics reject the Adventists' understanding of the Eucharist as a mere symbol. Catholics strongly object to our Church being called Satan's organization - and ourselves being labeled as tools of the Devil!

Despite our many and strong differences, it can be said that we share some common ground with the Adventists. We both believe that Jesus Christ is the Savior of the world. Both Catholics and Seventh Day Adventists see the importance of missionary activity throughout the world. We both see the great need for hospital ministry to care for the poor and the sick. We both place great emphasis on education.

As Catholics, let us remain strong in our Faith and pray for our brothers and sisters of the Seventh Day Adventist denomination. Let us invite them to become part of the Church that Jesus Christ founded.

*Reflection Questions:*

1. *What is the unique aspect of the Seventh Day Adventist denomination?*

2. *What do we have in common with them?*

3. *What are our differences?*

# Pentecostals and Evangelicals:
*Once called "holy rollers," now they're more mainstream.*

On our walk through the various Christian denominations, now we come to a group generally called the Pentecostals. Within this group are numerous churches and organizations that have as their common bond the belief that the gifts given to the early Church on the day of Pentecost have returned to Christians today. Chief among these gifts is speaking in tongues. Let us visit this fast-growing group of Christians and learn more about them.

> "The modern Church should possess all the gifts of the first Pentecost, and every Christian should expect...a second baptism that should lead to...speaking in tongues."

Those who claim to be Pentecostal Christians number in the tens of millions, worldwide. Pentecostals are found mostly in the United States, but they are becoming more common in Central and South America.

Pentecostal belief is best summarized as this: "The modern Church should possess all the gifts of the first Pentecost, and every Christian should expect something called a second baptism that should lead to the experience of speaking in tongues." Although it's sometimes difficult to discern whether an individual indeed has this gift, Catholics also believe that speaking in tongues can be a legitimate manifestation of prayer. Speaking in tongues or *"glossolalia"* was a common experience in the early Church. St. Paul speaks about it in Scripture (I Corinthians 12: 4-10, 28). Such a spiritual gift, however, always must be affirmed by the Church.

Specifically, Pentecostal churches include: The Assemblies of God (2.5 million members); The Church of God in Christ (COGIC) – a predominantly African-American denomination (5.5 million members); The Foursquare Gospel Church (238,000 members); and the Unitarian Pentecostal Church (300,000 members); along with many smaller or independent communities.

Typically, a Pentecostal church is an auditorium with a pulpit. Often, there will be a choir and many musical instruments. Pentecostals are considered to be Biblical fundamentalists, who interpret the Bible literally. Most Pentecostals believe in the Trinity, Original Sin, the Divinity of Christ and His Resurrection. Unitarian Pentecostals, however, do not accept the Trinity, and believe that Jesus is God who takes on the role of Father, Son or Holy Spirit. Thus, they baptize in the name of Jesus only, and not in the name of the Father, Son and Holy Spirit. This belief places them outside mainstream Christianity.

Pentecostals observe a strict code of morality borrowed from Puritanism. Smoking, drinking and dancing are frowned upon while a frugal life spent with family, friends, and in prayer, is highly praised. Pentecostals tithe much of their money to their church, which supports large and aggressive missionary activity throughout the world. This generosity allows for the fast growth of their church. Televangelists such as Jim Bakker and Jimmy Swaggert were Pentecostal pastors.

Let's review some history. From the beginning of the Pentecostal movement in the early 1900s until today, this church has experienced rapid growth. It has developed from store-front churches in the inner cities of America to expansive "mega-churches" in the wealthy suburbs. Pentecostals, who were once derided as being "holy rollers," are becoming more mainstream.

The Pentecostal revival in the early 1900s spread to other Protestant churches in 1960 and to Catholicism in 1967. Pentecostals claim that the modern revival of speaking in tongues first was experienced on January 1, 1901, by a Miss Agnes Ozman in Topeka, Kansas. The movement spread to Los Angeles and settled on Azusa Street. This became the headquarters for the early Pentecostal movement. From there, this movement spread throughout the country and the world.

Regrettably, there are differences between Catholics and Pentecostals. Pentecostals generally view Catholicism as a corrupt and superstitious religion on the fringes of Christianity. Catholics differ from Pentecostals in that we do not interpret the Bible in a literalistic way. The insistence on a second baptism in the spirit and the strict requirement of speaking in tongues are foreign concepts to our Catholic Faith. Indeed, speaking in tongues is a legitimate spiritual gift, but, as St. Paul says, *"There are many gifts, but the same spirit."* (1 Corinthians 12:4)

Catholics and most Pentecostals do share a belief in the Trinity, and in the Divinity of Jesus Christ. We agree on the importance of God's Word in the Bible, and we agree that there are spiritual and supernatural gifts, including speaking in tongues. We both place great importance on missionary activity and on a sober, simple lifestyle.

Despite our differences, let us share our Catholic Faith with those who are Pentecostal and invite them to experience the fullness of God's grace in the sacraments.

*Reflection Questions:*

1. *What is the main focus of the Pentecostal tradition?*
2. *What do we have in common?*
3. *What are our differences?*

# Nazarenes, Moravians and Salvationists:
*They're smaller - yet very devoted - groups.*

The next stop on our tour of Christian denominations is with three distinct Protestant denominations which are grouped together here, simply because of their relative size. They are: the Church of the Nazarene, the Moravians and the Salvationists. Let us briefly visit each of these Christian groups.

> "Let us share our Catholic Faith with these dedicated Christians, so that one day, we 'All May Be One' in Christ."

**The Church of the Nazarene:** This denomination is based on the teachings of John Wesley, who was the chief founder of Methodism. Wesley taught a doctrine called "Holiness" or the "Theology of the Holy Ghost." In this doctrine, a Christian could instantaneously receive a blessing from God which would free the person from all further sinful temptation or desire. Although this doctrine has since been dropped by modern-day Methodists, it still survives in the Church of the Nazarene and in several smaller churches such as the Free Methodists.

The Church of the Nazarene claims 627,000 members and is similar to the Methodist Church in structure. It was founded in 1908 in Texas. The church has a strong moral code, prohibiting lotteries, the circus, and offensive songs. Members of the Church of the Nazarene are very generous in supporting their local congregations. This enables large and dedicated missionary activity throughout the world.

**The Moravians:** The founding of this group actually predates Martin Luther's break with the Catholic Church in 1517. The founders of the Moravian Church were inspired by John Huss who was burned at the stake as a heretic in 1415. Huss appealed to the authority of the Bible alone, apart from the Church; he also rejected Purgatory and the intercession of the saints.

By 1457, many of Huss' followers had formed a group which would eventually become the Moravian Church. Centered in Germany, this group almost died out in the Seventeenth Century, but regained strength and numbers in the Eighteenth Century. By this time, Moravians began to send missionaries to America and other countries throughout the world. Indeed, Moravian missionary activity is very impressive, for such a small church.

Today's worldwide population of Moravians is 500,000, with 56,000 in the United States – mostly in North Carolina and Pennsylvania. Moravians have a rich liturgical tradition, with beautiful celebrations of Easter and Christmas.

**The Salvationists:** Commonly known as The Salvation Army, this Christian church is focused primarily on helping those in need. The Salvation Army is a Protestant church – not simply a charitable organization. It is structured in military fashion and can roughly be compared with a religious order.

The Salvation Army was founded by William Booth in 1878. Booth was a Methodist minister who cared for the poorest of the poor in the slums of London. Since those in his care often felt unwelcomed by other churches, he decided to start his own church. Booth assumed the title of "General" and dedicated his life to serving those in need. Honored throughout his lifetime, he died at age 84 after giving all of his money to the poor.

Clergy in the Salvation Army have some customs similar to the military – they receive training, have ranks, and wear military-like uniforms. Church governance is along the lines of a military command. Men and women play identical roles in the church. Initially, the Salvation Army combated liquor, tobacco and vice, and this effort continues today. The group also cares for those addicted to drugs and especially those who are afflicted by poverty.

Today, the Salvation Army has 471,000 members in the United States alone.

Theologically, members of the Salvation Army reject Baptism and the Eucharist, but otherwise are similar to Methodists in beliefs.

As Catholics, we find many things in common with these three Christian groups. Sadly, we have differences which keep us apart. Let us share our Catholic Faith with these dedicated Christians, so that one day, we "All May Be One" in Christ.

*Reflection Questions:*

1. *What is the unique aspect of the Church of the Nazarene?*
2. *What is the unique aspect of the Moravian Church?*
3. *What is the unique aspect of the Salvationists?*

*On the Edge of Christianity:*

# Unitarian Universalists:
*They're best described as "humanists."*

We continue on our travels through the various Christian denominations by visiting several groups which are on the very fringes of Christianity. Our first stop is with the Unitarian Universalists. This small but active group is found mostly in urban areas and near universities.

The Unitarian Universalists - or Unitarians, for short - have about 155,000 adherents. Despite its small size, this group has had a profound effect on American intellectual life. Many prominent politicians and professors have followed the Unitarian way. Unitarians are best described as "humanists." They value spiritual freedom, the use of reason, tolerance, diversity and service to others. They reject creeds, sacraments and religious laws of conduct - instead, placing emphasis on the autonomy of the human person in relationship to God.

> **"(Unitarians) value spiritual freedom, the use of reason, tolerance, diversity and service to others. They reject creeds, sacraments and religious laws..."**

Jesus is considered to be just one of many religious teachers, an equal alongside Buddha, Mohammed and Confucius. One may be a Unitarian and follow any particular denomination; however, one is to be open to the validity of other points of view. Where one member may believe that Jesus is God, another may deny the very existence of God.

Unitarians reject the Trinity - hence the name, Unitarian. They stress the unity of God and reject the concept of three divine persons. Christ is just another manifestation of God. A merger with the Universalists added the belief that all souls eventually will be reconciled with God and that there will be universal salvation.

Unitarian Universalists were one of the first religious organizations to oppose human slavery. They were the first to accept women as ministers. Unitarians usually support issues of civil rights, easier divorce, the right to an abortion, the widespread use of birth control, environmentalism, a strict separation between Church and State, and the validity of any heterosexual or homosexual relationship. Unitarians usually oppose censorship, capital punishment and war. Personal responsibility and ethical living are highly respected, while being judgmental is condemned. In short, Unitarianism provides a church home for the liberal outlook on life.

Now, let's trace the history of this church. Unitarians appeared on the scene in the early 1500s, around the time of Martin Luther's break from the Catholic

Church. A man by the name of Michael Servetus challenged the view of the Trinity and was condemned as a heretic by both Catholics and early Protestants. The denomination took hold in the 1600s in Transylvania, a part of modern-day Romania. The first Unitarian service in England was held in 1774. From there, the church traveled to the New World in the late 1700s where it took hold in New England and blended together with Congregationalism.

The Universalists had their start in America in 1770, led by John Murray, a former Methodist. His taught a doctrine of universal salvation, contending that none were damned to Hell. Universalism formally organized in 1866 and merged with the Unitarians in 1961. Today, the Christian background to both traditions has been eclipsed, for the most part, by secular humanism.

It is obvious that there are numerous differences between Catholics and Unitarian Universalists. Indeed, with their rejection of the Trinity and the absolute divinity of Jesus Christ, it becomes difficult to see Unitarians as Christians at all. Our differences also include understandings of the sacraments, the Word of God, and Christ as the universal Savior of the world - to name a few issues.

However, Catholics do have some social goals in common with Unitarians. We both assist the poor and the oppressed and we have a somewhat similar respect for freedom and conscience. The average Unitarian is searching earnestly for the truth which we believe we have found in Jesus Christ and in His Church.

Let us share our Catholic Faith with those who are Unitarian Universalists and invite them to meet Jesus.

*Reflection Questions:*

1. *What is unique about the Unitarian Universalist tradition?*
2. *What do we have in common?*
3. *What are our differences?*

# Christian Scientists:
## Sickness and death are "illusions."

The next stop on our journey through the various religious denominations is with the Christian Scientists. This group is quickly declining in membership - to about 125,000 followers, today. However, their beliefs are so unique among

American churches that they merit study.

> "Sickness and death are caused by something called Malicious Animal Magnetism (MAM) which is basically a kind of hexing or voodoo..."

Christian Science was started by Mary Baker Eddy around 1866. The basic teaching of the denomination is that sickness and death are illusions, and that suffering is not real. Matter, evil, sickness and death all are illusions and not created by God. They are, instead, errors of the mind. Sickness and death are caused by something called Malicious Animal Magnetism (MAM) which is basically a kind of hexing or voodoo of the mind. If these errors are discovered and removed, suffering and death soon will disappear.

The purpose of life is to discover these errors of the mind by following the religion of Christian Science. Once accomplished, this will lead to health, happiness and immortality. Eddy published a book entitled, <u>Science and Health with the Key to the Scriptures</u>, in 1875, and revised it often throughout her life. This book remains mandatory reading for all Christian Scientists and is the main source of teachings for the denomination.

Those who follow Christian Science take no medicine and see virtually no doctors since all sickness is an illusion. However, they do visit obstetricians and dentists. Vaccinations and fluoridation of the water supply are rejected. Since all matter is unreal, the group has no sacraments, does not baptize its members, and has no funeral rites since members do not really "die." The group has assumed a general aura and language of being Christian, yet they reject every major Christian dogma: the divinity of Christ, the Trinity, sacraments, and Heaven and Hell. Because of this, it becomes difficult to see Christian Scientists as being authentically Christian.

One of the group's newspapers, "The Christian Science Monitor," keeps the group's name in the news with its excellent reporting and world-wide coverage. The church is predominantly female, usually upper class, and often is involved in politics. Despite all of this, the basic tenet of the group - that all suffering and death is an illusion - is difficult for most people to accept.

The history of Christian Science is forever united with its foundress, Mary Baker Eddy. As a young girl, she often was bedridden with illness. Six months after she married, at age 22, her husband died of yellow fever. Eddy struggled to find meaning in suffering and formed her own views and answers by combining spiritualism (the conjuring of the dead) and various native religions. Her second marriage ended in divorce. Her third husband died soon after their marriage. Eddy maintained that her third husband died of "arsenic spiritually administered."

In Boston, Eddy founded the First Church of Christ Scientist and Massachusetts Metaphysical College where she taught her religion. She ordained herself head of the church and wished to be called "Mother" or "Leader." The church in Boston soon was called The Mother Church and remains an historical landmark in that city. Towards the end of her life, Eddy took personal control of all authority and wealth in the church. After suffering a long illness, Mary Baker Eddy died in 1910 of pneumonia.

It would seem obvious that Catholics have a great many differences with Christian Scientists. The group's rejection of most Christian doctrines and their refusal to accept the reality of human suffering make a mockery of the Cross and of our salvation in Christ.

Although difficult to discern, we, as Catholics, do have some things in common with Christian Scientists. We both acknowledge the spiritual aspect of illness and we, along with most modern medical practitioners, agree that the soul of a person is very much involved in the healing process.

Let us pray for our brothers and sisters who are Christian Scientists and help them to accept and embrace the cross of suffering in their lives as we all look to the hope of Christ's Resurrection.

*Reflection Questions:*

1. *Who was the founder of Christian Science and what did she teach?*
2. *What do we have in common with this group?*
3. *What are our differences?*

# Mormons - Part I:
*All of us are "potential gods."*

Now, we come to the Mormons, as our journey continues through the various religious denominations. The proper name for this group is, "The Church of Jesus Christ of Latter-day Saints." This is one of the largest, most influential, and fastest-growing religions in our country.

Worldwide, there are more than 11 million Mormons, with five million in the United States alone. Utah still is the center of the Mormon Church, with 75 percent of the state's population claiming membership. A large percentage of Mormons are highly educated. Many are involved in politics or serve in the military. Brigham Young University, a Mormon college, is the largest religious educational institution in the nation. Large-scale missionary activity is sustained by strict tithing, in which Mormons are expected to give 10 percent or more of their annual income to the support of their church.

> "As Brigham Young, an important leader of Mormonism, once said, *'What God once was, we now are...'*"

Mormons believe that their church is the continuation of the church that Christ founded. They contend that all other Christian churches, fundamentally, are in error. It is basic to Mormon belief that all of us are potential gods. As Brigham Young, an important leader of Mormonism, once said, "*What God once was, we now are; what God is now, we shall become.*" In order to become a god, it is important to reach the highest level of Heaven. Mormons believe in a kind of graded Heaven, where there are three ranks of kingdoms: celestial, terrestrial and telestial. Only those in the celestial kingdom of Heaven can become gods. Hence, Mormons engage in baptism of the dead which enables the dead to attain a higher place in Heaven. To this end, Mormons specialize in genealogies so that every person who ever has lived might have the chance to be baptized and perhaps become a god.

Family life is highly praised in Mormonism and large families with many children are seen as the ideal. If a marriage between a Mormon couple is "sealed for time and eternity" in a Mormon temple, the couple can experience after death what is called celestial marriage. In this relationship, a couple for all eternity bears children and these children then will worship them as gods of their own planet or world. It follows that celibacy is looked upon as an inferior state of life.

Mormons are initiated into their religion in a ritual called "endowment" in which they don long white garments (similar to long underwear) which they wear for the rest of their lives. Young Mormon men are required to spend two years in missionary work – often in their own country – to spread the doctrine of Mormonism. Usually dressed conservatively, in black pants, white shirts and black ties, these missionaries often attract followers by their preaching of strong family values, clean living, love of country, and the strong community offered by the Mormon Church.

# Mormons – Part II:
*They believe that angels told Joseph Smith he was to rebuild the true church.*

The history of the Mormon Church is quite interesting. Its founder was Joseph Smith (1805-1844). According to Mormon tradition, Smith was visited, early in his life, by angels who informed him of the error of all other churches and of how he was chosen to rebuild the one true church. One angel led him to dig up a box of golden plates written in "Reformed Egyptian." The angel gave Smith magic glasses called the Urim and Thummim which helped him to read this ancient "language."

> "Mormons claim that Christ visited the New World and set up His Church here. This history was revealed only when Smith discovered the golden plates..."

Smith claimed that God had made him both prophet and apostle. Fulfilling this role, he wrote a number of books; the chief of which is called, <u>The Book of Mormon</u>. This book contains the supposed history of North America at a time when the lost tribes of Israel came here to settle. Mormons claim that Christ visited the New World and set up His Church here. This history was revealed only when Smith discovered the golden plates in the ground, in 1820.

The early Mormon Church moved west from New York, first to Ohio, then to Missouri. Smith was accused by the government of immorality, counterfeiting and treason. He was to be tried in court, but, in 1844, a mob of 200 people accosted him and he was shot and killed. Shortly after Smith's death, Brigham Young took over leadership of the church and led it west to the Utah Territory.

In 1853, the Mormon Church began to advocate polygamy – or having multiple wives. Despite teachings in <u>The Book of Mormon</u> condemning this practice, polygamy became the norm until 1890 when the church "suspended" the practice under pressure from the U.S. government.

Although the Mormon Temple and tabernacle are located in Salt Lake City, today's Mormon Church has spread throughout the world, with much of its phenomenal growth taking place after World War II.

It is obvious that there are numerous differences between Catholicism and Mormonism. Indeed, with Mormonism's belief in many gods, and a view of Christ as a god among those gods, it is difficult to find common ground. Even though the words "Jesus," "Church" and "Saint" are used in their name, Mormons are not Christians and should be seen instead as another religion.

On a social level, Catholics and Mormons have a surprising amount in common. Family life and the gift of children are highly prized in both religions, as are patriotism, hard work and missionary activity. Indeed, Mormon missionaries show great courage and zeal as they attempt to share their beliefs with the world.

Let us respond with love to our Mormon brothers and sisters, and share the Truth, Who is Jesus Christ, with them.

*Reflection Questions:*

1. Who founded the Mormon religion?
2. Is Mormonism Christian? Why or why not?
3. What do we have in common with Mormons? What are our differences?

# Jehovah's Witnesses – Part I:
## "Only 144,000 people – born before 1935" will enter Heaven.

On our journey through the various religions, our next stop is with the Jehovah's Witnesses (JWs). The JWs are a rapidly growing group which specializes in door-to-door evangelization and preparation for the end of the world. They count many former Catholics among their membership.

> "The JWs are a rapidly growing group which specializes in door-to-door evangelization and preparation for the end of the world."

The Jehovah's Witnesses have six million adherents worldwide, with more than one million living in the United States. Owing to their widespread evangelization efforts, the JWs have grown five percent, yearly, since World War II. Meetings take place in "Kingdom Halls," not churches. A new Kingdom Hall is built when a given membership exceeds 200. All members are required to be active in the organization. All are strongly urged to contribute large portions of their annual income to the organization. Most are required to take part in door-to-door preaching. The headquarters for the church is in Brooklyn, New York, with a large publishing house located nearby.

The Jehovah's Witnesses' beliefs come from three main sources...

First, from Fundamentalist Protestantism, they adopted the rejection of the Catholic Church, and the centrality of the Bible with its literal interpretation. The JWs' Bible is called <u>The New World Translation</u> and it is quite unlike any other Bible, Catholic or Protestant. Indeed, it has been retranslated and rewritten to fit particular beliefs. The Catholic Church is seen by JWs as Satan's organization and the greatest deceiver in the world.

Secondly, from Adventism, they gain their expectation of the coming of the end of the world. Like Advents, JWs believe that human beings do not have souls, but rather *are* souls. Hell is not seen as eternal but rather temporary, with the wicked being annihilated at the end of the world. According to the JWs, Jesus Christ came to earth in 1914, but remained invisible.

Very soon, the battle between Jesus Christ and the Devil will take place, they contend. After this battle, the Devil will be defeated and cast into the abyss. True believers who survive will repopulate the earth for 1,000 years. In 2914, Satan again will come and be defeated at the end of the world. The wicked who have died will be annihilated but those who were righteous will live on earth in peace forever. However, only 144,000 people ever will enter Heaven, and they must have been born before 1935. Those born afterwards only can hope for an earthly paradise.

Thirdly, from the ancient heresy of Arianism, JWs glean their belief that Jesus Christ is not God, but merely the most perfect creature. They believe that Christ was actually Michael the Archangel and, after he died, he became "an exalted being." This belief places them outside of Christianity.

# Jehovah's Witnesses – Part II:
*They have success recruiting those ignorant of Christianity.*

Let's continue our discussion of Jehovah's Witnesses.

This group requires total commitment from its members. After completing a course on the Bible, salesmanship and speech-making, a new member is sent out to share the faith door to door.

Witnesses have a strict moral code that must be followed. They do not participate in civic organizations, vote in elections, salute the flag, or serve in the military. All governments, like churches, are seen as part of Satan's organization. Social justice and formal education are not stressed in this religion, since the end of the world is near. Blood transfusions ordinarily are rejected because the Old Testament rejects the eating of blood. However, racial diversity and respect have long been advocated by the JWs.

> "They do not (join) civic organizations, vote in elections, salute the flag or serve in the military. All governments...(are) part of Satan's organization."

This group publishes two magazines, called "Awake!" and "The Watchtower." JWs find the most success in evangelizing individuals who are ignorant of Christianity and who are looking for a supportive and loving community. People are offered instant support and strong moral guidelines and thus, are given meaning for their lives. Indeed, JWs stress family values and moral living which makes them very attractive to potential converts. However, if one leaves the JWs, he or she is immediately shunned and cut off.

To review some history, the Jehovah's Witnesses were founded by Charles Russell in 1872. Russell had been involved in various money-making schemes such as a "Cancer Cure," "Miracle Wheat" and "Fantastic Cotton Seed." His wife divorced him, charging infidelity and cruelty. Russell became distressed at the thought of Hell, and invented his own doctrine of a temporary hell with no everlasting punishment. He toured the country spreading his teachings until his death in 1916.

Russell was succeeded by Joseph "Judge" Rutherford who added scripture and "end-of-the-world" views to the beliefs. In 1931, the group adopted the name, "Jehovah's Witnesses." The word "Jehovah" comes from a poor German translation of YHWH or the name for God in the Old Testament. In English, this is more properly translated as Yahweh. Rutherford coined the slogan, "Millions now living will never die," but, alas, this was not to include him. He died in 1942. After attempting many times to predict the end of the world – in 1914, 1918, 1925, 1941 and 1975 – the group now claims only that "it is coming soon."

Regrettably, Catholics and Jehovah's Witnesses have very little in common. The JWs' denial of Christ's divinity, the Trinity, and all of the sacraments, soundly places them outside of Christianity. Thus, the Jehovah's Witnesses should not be thought of as Christians but rather as another religion altogether.

It should be noted that Catholics and Jehovah's Witnesses do have a few ideas in common. We both believe in the importance of community, and in sharing our beliefs. Catholics and JWs both place an emphasis on evangelization. We both look for Christ to come again.

Despite our differences, let us, as Catholics, share our Faith with the Jehovah's Witnesses. Let us always treat them with charity and kindness so that they can see and meet Jesus Christ in us.

Reflection Questions:

1. What are the core beliefs of the Jehovah's Witnesses?
2. What do we have in common?
3. What are our differences?

# Christian Unity:
*All Christians do NOT believe the same thing - yet.*

In the preceding articles, we have been looking at the various Christian and quasi-Christian denominations. I hope that you have enjoyed reading these articles as much as I have enjoyed writing them. I have learned a great deal about the many groups and I would like to share a few of these insights with you.

First, it is important to remember just how much numerous Christian religious traditions have in common. There still are many serious issues that divide us, but I was struck by how many similar beliefs we do have. This is important to remember since many of our friends, neighbors and members of our families are of various other Christian denominations.

> "With the rise of militant Islam and secular humanism throughout the world, believers in Christ must solve our differences and unite around the Lord."

Secondly, I was reminded of just how ignorant it is to say, *"It doesn't matter what you believe. We all believe the same thing."* If there is one concept that these articles should have made clear, it is the refutation of this way of thinking. We do not believe the same thing! To say that we do is insulting to our Faith and to the beliefs of the other person. Relativism has no place in religion, or in anything else, for that matter.

Thirdly, I was reminded of just how important the unity of Christianity now is. With the rise of militant Islam and secular humanism throughout the world, believers in Christ must solve our differences and unite around the Lord. If we want joy and peace to come to this sorrowful world of ours, we must preach the Good News of Jesus Christ together. This is most urgent.

One last thought... I would like to once again acknowledge the book, <u>Separated Brethren</u>, by William J. Whalen, published by Our Sunday Visitor in 2002[2]. For the preceding articles, I drew heavily from the facts and analyses of the various denominations contained in this book. I want to give full credit to this excellent source!

Let us pray, in the words of Our Lord Jesus Christ, *"That All May Be One."* (John 17:21)

*Reflection Questions:*

  1. *How can I work for greater Christian unity?*

  2. *How can I better explain my Catholic Faith to others?*

  3. *Can you imagine what we could accomplish if all Christians were united?*

2Whalen, William J., *Separated Brethren*, Our Sunday Visitor, 2002

*Religious Movements:*

# "Moonies" and Scientologists:
*They differ in their beliefs - but both are non-Christian.*

On our journey through the multitude of faiths, we arrive at two very different groups which are clearly not Christian. Their names are the Unification Church - commonly known as the "Moonies" - and the Church of Scientology. Both are small, but growing, groups.

Members of the **Unification Church**, popularly called **"Moonies,"** are led by the Reverend Sun Myung Moon. An estimated 10,000 Americans are involved with this church and are very committed to spreading its teachings. The Rev. Moon is a millionaire from Korea. Moon claims that, at age 16, he was visited by Jesus who asked him to start the church. Moon also claims that Christ visited him again in 1972 and ordered him to go to America to gain converts here.

> "Moon and his Unification Church teach that there are 'Three Adams' in world history...Scientology endeavors to remove...(unpleasant past experiences from the mind) by a process called auditing."

Moon and his Unification Church teach that there are "Three Adams" in world history. The first was Adam who married Eve and who was driven from the Garden of Eden. The second Adam was Jesus, whom the Moonies believe was a perfect human being, but not God. Jesus was supposed to get married and have children, but before He could find someone to marry, the Jews had Him crucified. Once again, God's plan was thwarted. The third Adam was born in Korea between 1917 and 1930, was married in 1960, and now lives in America. This third and final Adam will form the perfect human family and bring about the coming of God's kingdom. (These qualifications seem to point directly to Moon himself.)

There are no sacraments in the Unification Church except for marriage, which is seen as vitally important towards building the perfect human family. Moonie weddings often include hundreds or even thousands of couples in large stadiums. Moon claims that his Unification Church eventually will draw together all Christians. Because they reject the divinity of Christ, the Moonies clearly are not Christians.

Next, we move on to the **Church of Scientology**. This relatively new religion was started in 1950 by L. Ron Hubbard (1911-1986), a science fiction writer. In that year, he published a book called <u>Dianetics</u>. Four years later, he started the Church of Scientology, based on the book's teachings.

According to Hubbard, there are two parts of the human mind: the analytic and the reactive. The analytic is the rational part of the mind and is infallible.

The reactive part of the mind is the storehouse for all that is unpleasant, hurtful and painful from the past. These past experiences are called "engrams." Scientology endeavors to remove these unpleasant engrams from the reactive mind by a process called auditing.

The new convert to Scientology is called a "pre-clear." The person confesses all past life experiences to a Scientologist auditor and, by so doing, rids himself of engrams. This process involves holding two metal cans attached to something called an E-meter (E is for engram, one presumes...) and the auditor asks the pre-clear a series of questions until a "clear" status is achieved. Auditing sessions are expensive – the introductory price is around $15, but achieving a completely "clear" status and the supposed peace of mind that comes with it can cost thousands.

It is estimated that there are 30,000 Scientologists in America. This religion makes a special effort to recruit high-profile converts to the faith, especially movie stars. Tom Cruise, a former Catholic, is the most visible adherent to this faith. Scientology is not a Christian faith by any means and should not be seen as such. Salvation comes from Jesus Christ and not by spending money to become "clear."

We have just visited two faiths which are very different from our own. Let us share our faith in Jesus Christ, the Way, the Truth and the Life, with those who are so desperately searching for Him.

*Reflection Questions:*

1. *What is the Unification Church and what does it teach?*
2. *What is Scientology and what does it teach?*
3. *How can we share our Catholic Faith with members of both groups?*

# The New Age Movement – Part I:
*Shamans? Witchcraft? Magic? Beware!*

In the following articles, I will examine various movements or philosophies that are in direct opposition to Christianity and our Catholic Faith. The teachings of these movements often infiltrate our culture. From this culture, they may enter into our homes. It is of utmost importance for us, as believers in Christ, to know about these false teachings and to protect ourselves from their errors.

The first of these movements and philosophies that is in direct opposition to our Christian faith is the New Age Movement (NAM)[3]. This movement is, in reality, a rough confederation of pagan beliefs, various Eastern religions and Western individualism.

> "The NAM often is presented in a Christian light, even though it is pagan in origin. In reality, the NAM is a kind of new or neo-paganism."

The New Age Movement can include worship of gods and goddesses; and the use of shamans; witchcraft; tarot cards; astrology; magic and aromatherapy. Other common elements are mantras; horoscopes; yoga; Zen; self-empowerment; ESP; pyramids and vortex-finding. NAM also incorporates Feng Shui; personal aura- or energy-finding; crystals; pentagrams; sacred wolves; sacred stones; labyrinths and channeling. You'll even find Wicca; Reiki; reincarnation; Celtic music and much more.

Often, Christian symbols such as the cross, Church music such as Gregorian Chant, and spiritual beings such as angels are embraced by members of the NAM and redefined according to their own understanding. This can lead to confusion among Christians who are not well-grounded in their faith.

The New Age Movement sometimes has influenced other movements, including feminism; environmentalism; the counter-culture of the 1960s; the self-help and self-healing movements; and the peace movements. The New Age Movement has targeted Christianity and has strongly attached itself to some forms of liberal Protestantism. Indeed, the New Age Movement has been embraced by numerous Catholic religious orders of women and is actively promoted by some Catholic parishes!

The NAM often is presented in a Christian light, even though it is pagan in origin. In reality, the NAM is a kind of new or neo-paganism. As our culture turns away from Christ and its Christian roots, in some ways it is returning to its pagan roots of nature worship and self-centeredness.

Although difficult to characterize, the New Age Movement has four major beliefs...

The first belief is Unity. This belief holds that "all is one." Following this to its logical conclusion, it is the belief that everything is God. Nature; the cosmos; the spiritual world; human beings; you and I all are one. We all are divine, we all are God. This kind of pantheism is borrowed from Eastern religions such as Taoism and Hinduism, and often is combined with radical environmentalism.

---

[3] Burnham, Jim, *Beginning Apologetics Volume 4* (Farmington, San Juan: San Juan Catholic Seminars, 1999)

The second belief of the NAM is that of Pure Spirit. Only spiritual things are real; everything else is an illusion. The body is seen as a prison that entraps the soul or spirit. Only by various rituals, magic or other activity, can the spirit be set free. This belief is from the Eastern religion of Buddhism and from the pagan heresy of Dualism.

The third belief of the New Age Movement is in The Self. The NAM is concerned first and foremost with the self. The self is perfect and sin is only ignorance of the self's perfection. Since all are one, the self is the perfect representation of the divine. Those involved in the NAM often gravitate towards individualistic activities to bolster their own private spirituality. In reality, it is the worship of the self. This belief of the NAM comes from our Western culture of radical individualism.

The final major tenet of the NAM is its notion of Salvation. Salvation is, they contend, enlightenment whereby one comes to realize that all is one and all is spirit. Enlightenment through a kind of secret or hidden knowledge is part of this belief. Salvation also relies upon the individual discovering that the divine is within and that the individual is, in fact, God.

# The New Age Movement - Part II:
*Christianity is ending? The "Age of Aquarius" is coming?*

Continuing our discussion of the New Age Movement (or NAM), let's examine eight of 15 other common beliefs of followers. This will allow us to better understand this movement and see how it differs from Christianity.

> "...the Age of Aquarius (will be) a time of justice, peace and harmony...This is where they get the term, 'new age' – the New Age of Aquarius."

***Age of Aquarius:*** According to astrology, we currently are living in the age of Pisces. This symbol is associated with Christianity. However, this age is about to end and be replaced by the Age of Aquarius which will be a time of justice, peace and harmony. Christianity is ending, according to the NAM. This is where they get the term, "new age" – the New Age of Aquarius.

***Angels:*** The recent popularity of angels in our culture is directly related to the New Age Movement. For the most part, this popularity has nothing to do with Christianity. Indeed, angels are part of Christian belief. However, the NAM takes angels in another direction. Angels for those in the NAM are spiritual guides that are nothing more than energies that lead us to discovering ourselves.

***Channeling:*** Psychics or mediums claim to act as channelers of information from other beings who may be dead, or alive. This is nothing more that conjuring or spiritism – a séance.

***Christ:*** For the NAM, Jesus Christ is but one incarnation of an idea or energy that has been contained in Buddha, Mohammed, Confucius and others. The "Cosmic Christ" also is known as "christic" energy, but has nothing to do with Our Lord Jesus. It is rather an energy inside ourselves which individuals need to fully comprehend, for salvation.

***Crystals:*** These are believed to vibrate at significant frequencies and are useful for personal transformation. They are used as lucky charms and in various NAM therapies.

***Enneagram:*** This is a diagram composed of a circle with nine points on its circumference. The points are connected within the circle by a triangle and a hexangle. Originally used for pagan divination, this diagram now is used by some to determine "psychological personality."

***Feng Shui:*** This is an occult Chinese practice of finding the energy present in a room. Each room must be arranged in such a way as to maximize its energy and to prevent harmful imbalances.

***Karma:*** This is from the Hindu religion and is believed to be the universal law of cause and effect. A good act causes a good effect for the person doing the action. A bad act has a corresponding effect. For the NAM movement, karma has nothing to do with salvation but rather with maintaining the balance of the moral universe.

# The New Age Movement – Part III:
*It's helping to popularize "Wicca" - a revival of medieval witchcraft.*

Now, let's further our study of NAM (or the New Age Movement) by looking at seven more beliefs which are held by followers:

***New Age Music:*** The music of the NAM often is marketed as a tool for achieving harmony with oneself and with the world. Much of the popularity of Celtic music today is owed to the NAM which finds it to have great spiritual power. The resurgence of Gregorian Chant also is related to the NAM adopting this Catholic musical form and using it for meditation.

> "In encountering any of these activities or beliefs, Christians must be extremely cautious. These activities **will not** bring a person closer to Jesus Christ."

*Positive Thinking:* This is the conviction that people can change physical reality or external circumstances by having a positive mental attitude. Positive thinkers are promised health and wholeness, with wealth and even immortality. The NAM has embraced this practice.

*Reincarnation:* This NAM belief is borrowed from Hinduism and other Eastern religions. It is the belief that the soul continues to be reborn into another being until it reaches perfection. For the NAM, it is not sin which necessitates such rebirth but rather the pursuit of spiritual awareness.

*Shamanism:* This NAM practice is a communication with the spirits of nature or the spirits of the dead, through ritualized possession performed by a shaman. The shaman is an individual who serves as a medium for the ritual.

*Wholeness:* The word "wholeness" often is used in the New Age Movement. Humanity is seen as fitting into the universe as part of a single living organism, a harmonious network of dynamic relationships. When one understands one's place in nature and in the cosmos, one finds wholeness and peace.

*Wicca:* This is an Old English term for witches or witchcraft. Wicca was reinvented in England in 1939 and is seen by its followers as a revival of medieval witchcraft. Called "the Craft," it is growing rapidly in the United States where it often has been blended with women's spirituality. The NAM movement is involved in popularizing Wicca, with the rise in popularity of Halloween, novels for young girls which feature witches, and television shows about witches.

*Yoga:* This is a series of physical movements, drawn from Hinduism, which aims for unity with the divine. This has been popularized by the NAM and used as a gateway to further involvement in the Movement.

In encountering any of these activities or beliefs, Christians must be extremely cautious. These activities **will not** bring a person closer to Jesus Christ!

# The New Age Movement - Part IV:
### Be wary of practices disguised as our Faith that just don't feel right!

To summarize, the New Age Movement is, in reality, a complete rejection of Christianity. The Trinity is rejected because all is seen as one. The dual nature of

Jesus Christ as both God and Man is rejected because everything <u>and</u> everyone is God. Creation by a loving God is rejected because the world is equivalent to God. The salvific meaning of the Cross and the Resurrection of Christ is denied because we, in fact, save ourselves.

> **"The New Age Movement, fundamentally, is the ancient heresy of Gnosticism. (It) tempted many of the early Christians and has plagued the Church from time to time ever since."**

In the New Age Movement, individuals don't need to repent of their sins because they already are perfect. The sacraments are rejected because everything material is an illusion. The authority of the Bible and the Church are denied because all authority rests in the self. Finally, there are no such things as Heaven, Hell, Purgatory or judgment, because all is God.

The New Age Movement has arisen so quickly and has been so widely embraced by our popular culture for many reasons. The New Age Movement, fundamentally, is the ancient heresy of Gnosticism. This false teaching tempted many of the early Christians and has plagued the Church from time to time ever since. Gnosticism teaches that the spirit is the only reality, that material things are either evil or an illusion, and that salvation means being enlightened or gaining some secretly held knowledge.

Christianity teaches just the opposite: that there are spiritual and material worlds, and that both are created to be good. Salvation is open to all, and all are God's children.

The rapid growth of NAM has been made possible, at least in part, because individual Christians often fail to convincingly live and communicate our faith to the modern world. Those involved in the New Age Movement almost always are wounded people who are looking for answers. Perhaps a tragedy or a serious illness has occurred and, instead of finding Christ in the faces of a welcoming Christian community, a person who is hurting finds apathy and ignorance. Often, an individual then turns to "self-help" solutions and becomes convinced that the answers to life's suffering can be discovered by buying a book with a glossy cover at a major bookstore. Another reason for the NAM's success is that the very ideals it worships are the ideals of today's culture. These are: freedom, self-reliance and individualism. An astounding growth in communications, and greater cultural interaction, have added fuel to the fire.

It is important for every Christian to remain vigilant against this threat to our faith. Catholics must be wary of anything that comes wearing the disguise of our Faith, yet just doesn't seem right or makes us feel uncomfortable. Follow your well-formed conscience! Anything that is not centered in Jesus Christ, that does not preach Jesus Christ, which is not based on God's Word in the Bible and the teachings of His Church, must be avoided. As St. Paul says in his letter to the Galatians 1: 8-9, *"Even if we or an angel from heaven, should preach to you a gospel other than the one you have received, let that one be accursed."*

Reflection Questions:
1. What has led to the fast growth of the New Age Movement?
2. Have you ever encountered a person who was involved with NAM?
3. Why is it important for us to know our Christian faith well?

# Atheism – Part I:
*"God doesn't exist" – or, people just live as though that's the case.*

Most of the people we meet on a daily basis profess a belief in God. Many of the people we know were baptized at one time and might still claim to be Christians. Indeed, in poll after poll across our country, most Americans claim to believe in God. In response to these polls, we might question just what people mean by "God." Also, if baptized, do they live a life even remotely resembling that which a Christian is called to live? Nevertheless, most people claim to believe in some spiritual power higher than themselves.

> **"....there is an assault against religious belief in general and Christianity in particular. This attack often is led by secular and humanistic forces...( promoting 'tolerance')."**

Today, however, there is an assault against religious belief in general and Christianity in particular. This attack often is led by secular and humanistic forces in our society under the guise of promoting "tolerance." Increasingly, behind this drive against religion in the public square, we find the 500-year-old philosophy of Atheism, that fervent belief that there is no God, no divinity, no spiritual soul and no afterlife. As Christians, and especially as Catholics, we need to understand this current rise of Atheism in our culture and be prepared to answer its claims against our Faith.

Atheism is the denial in theory and/or in practice that God exists. There are two types of Atheism today. One is active and philosophically based in declaring that God does not exist. A second is a kind of practical hedonism or secular humanism whereby individuals live their lives as if God did not exist. Both are on the rise in our culture.

Atheism, as a kind of philosophy, was practically unheard of until about 500 years ago. Indeed, early Christian teachers dismissed the Atheistic belief in the non-existence of God as nonsensical and illogical. This was clearly demonstrated by the fact that every known culture and people worshipped some kind of divine entity – whether this was the sun; fire; Zeus; Buddha; Krishna; the Tao; Allah; or God Our Loving Father and His Son, Jesus Christ. So, why was this universal belief suddenly being questioned?

The philosophy of **Idealism** was one of the foundations of modern Atheism. This philosophy, credited to Rene Descartes, became dominant in the 1600s. It espouses a radical separation between the mind and the external world. For Idealists, the mind is exalted and ideas are primary. Human reason is seen as the highest good. Information gained through our senses about the external world is seen as faulty and untrustworthy. Thus, the motto of Idealism is, "I think, therefore I am."

With the rise of Idealism, the religious understanding of an absolute God – Who was beyond human understanding yet Who revealed Himself to us in the world – began to be questioned. After all, perhaps God is not external to ourselves but in reality a projection of the mind's imagination, some suggested. Perhaps, when we worship God, we really are worshipping ourselves. Hence, there is no God, and human intellectual progress is the highest good, they suggest. This philosophy of Idealism is the fundamental foundation of today's secular culture – and of modern Atheism.

# Atheism – Part II:
## Other philosophies have promoted its rise.

As we continue our study of Atheism, we should examine several other philosophies which have helped to promote its rise.

First, let's take a look at **Deism**. Deism is a quasi-religion that was made popular by the English philosopher, Edward Herbert. Deism is the belief in a "Supreme Being." In Deism, God is compared to a watchmaker, who constructs the universe, winds it up, and lets it play out according to its own laws. God is not actively involved in His creation, nor does He show concern for it. He is merely the maker who started the whole thing going.

> "In the religious arena, Utilitarianism ignores God because He is deemed useless to modern society. Modern Atheism was fostered by this neglect."

Deism began in the 1600s. In the following century, it became the religion of the Age of Enlightenment. Since the Enlightenment was concerned with questioning traditional religious beliefs and stressing the primacy of reason and science, Deism fit nicely within its world view. After all, the universe had to come from somewhere, so why not state that God created the universe and then "walked away?"

Deism was the philosophy of choice in the founding of our country. Many of our early leaders were Deists. When the word "God" was used in early American life, it did not necessarily refer to the Judeo-Christian definition of the word - but more to a Deistic definition.

Today, Deism is found primarily in Free Masonry. Philosophically speaking, once God began to be seen as distant, uninvolved and cold, it was very easy to reject Him completely and state that He never existed. Deism thus helped lead to modern Atheism.

Another philosophy that contributed to modern Atheism was **Pantheism**. Pantheism is the belief that God is everywhere. In general, Pantheism claims that God and creation are one and the same. God is not separate and distinct from the world, rather He IS the world. Elements of Pantheism can be found in various Eastern religions, especially in Hinduism. Philosophers of the 1600s, including Spinoza, advocated Pantheism. Furthering this line of thought, if all was God, and God was the world and not distinct in any way from it, why would a person want to waste time believing in Him? Instead, one should focus on the world alone. Thus, Pantheism helped give rise to modern Atheism.

Then, there is the influence of **Fideism** to consider. This is a philosophy derived from Protestantism which states that it is impossible, using human reason alone, to know anything about God because of our depraved and sinful human nature. Only a blind faith - or faith alone - will allow us to know anything about God. This teaching, advocated by the Protestant philosophers Kant and Kierkegaard, was based upon Martin Luther's erroneous teaching of salvation by faith alone. Taking this to its logical philosophical conclusion, intellectuals of the Enlightenment who valued the use of human reason saw Christianity as superstitious and irrational. Many became Atheists.

Other philosophies, of the 20th century, also have helped propel Atheism to its recent prominence. One example is **Utilitarianism**. This is the philosophy of acquiring information or acting on something only if it is useful and practical. It is one of the dominant philosophies in modern America. Related to Empiricism and Pragmatism, this philosophy focuses mainly on political matters. In the religious arena, Utilitarianism ignores God because He is deemed useless to modern society. Modern Atheism was fostered by this neglect.

# Atheism – Part III:
## *Since Atheism's roots were in Europe, Christianity was challenged.*

There are still more philosophies which have helped to encourage the Atheistic revolution..

Let's take a look at **Materialism**, for example. Materialists claim that unless a thing can be perceived by the five senses, it does not exist. Modern Communism is based on this philosophy and is Atheistic because of it. Materialism claims that if we cannot see, hear, touch, taste, or smell God, He must not exist.

> "....it is possible to believe in God through the use of reason alone. This is a powerful tool by which we can assist those who have fallen into Atheism."

Another philosophy is **Rationalism**. This school of thought claims that the only truth we can know for certain is truth gained through the use of human reason. The existence of God, other spiritual beings, the human soul, and all other supernatural entities, is contrary to human reason and to our understanding of things – and thus, is not real. Hence, Atheism is embraced and God does not exist.

Atheism also has been supported by the philosophy of **Scientism**. In this philosophy, the only truth that is knowable is that which is gained by the scientific method of research and exploration. If something cannot be proven scientifically, it is not true. Since God's existence cannot be empirically proven in this way, He does not exist.

Finally, modern Atheism is built upon the philosophy of **Evolutionism**. In this philosophy, the claim is made that the evolutionary process fully and completely explains the existence of life and its variety on earth. Quite simply, since life "creates" itself, there is no need for a Creator, and hence God does not exist.

As we can see, these philosophies had a profound effect on challenging belief in God. Since most of these philosophies came from Europe, it was Christianity that was most seriously challenged. Since these philosophies often were held by the elite or the highly educated, they eventually paved the way for the Atheism of our secular culture today. As Christian believers, how can we respond to these Atheistic claims?

First of all, as Catholics, we believe that there is no contradiction between Faith and reason. Both strive toward the truth and there is, by definition, only one Truth. Any religious or scientific pursuit must logically end up at the one and infinite Truth which is God. A uniquely Catholic belief is that human beings can come to know God through the use of human reason alone. Certainly, this knowledge is quite impoverished without the fullness of God's Revelation in Jesus Christ. Nevertheless, it is possible to believe in God through the use of reason alone. This is a powerful tool by which we can assist those who have fallen into Atheism.

# Atheism – Part IV:
*Try this approach to prove God's existence to them!*

In refuting Atheism, there is a powerful way to prove God's existence. It centers on the simple need for a "First Cause." We know that we can't get something from nothing. If we go back and back and back, we eventually need to admit that someone or something created the stuff of the universe. Even if we hold to the so-called "Big Bang Theory," the material must have come from somewhere.

From this First Cause line of thinking, we reason that it is an uncreated being who created the universe. This being must be spiritual because it is outside of the created universe. In addition, it must be infinite because it created something out of nothing. It is not a long jump to assume that this First Cause is loving. Why else would it have created in the first place? This First Cause then becomes what we philosophically call "God."

> "In my experience, most vehement Atheists hold to their beliefs because of an instance of suffering or evil in their lives by which they have been deeply wounded."

Another way of proving the existence of God is by examining the need for an "Intelligent Designer." The universe is an ordered place that runs according to a set of rules. This is an obvious fact. So, who made these rules? If, for example, one saw a ham sandwich sitting in the middle of the woods, one would presume that someone made the sandwich. It didn't just happen. There must have been an Intelligence behind the scenes, intentionally making the sandwich. When we take this principle from a ham sandwich to the level of intricacy of the human body, or the beauty of the cosmos, we see that the inherent order of things did not just happen by chance. If it is not by chance, then it must have an Intelligent Designer. This designer is called God.

Of course, these examples of Christian philosophical belief in the existence of God must be supplemented by Divine Revelation: the Word of God in the Bible and the Sacred Tradition of the Church. Faith in God is a gift and religion should never be forcefully taught. However, it is reasonable - quite reasonable - to believe in God. This is why most cultures of the world, for all of human history, have believed.

Why is there such widespread Atheism today? Apart from the philosophical backgrounds of Idealism and Materialism which most certainly have influenced modern thought, why does a person choose not to believe? Upbringing certainly has a role to play, as well as a secular education and indoctrination. However, most individuals who are devoted Atheists go beyond the normal apathy of our culture. They are committed. They write books, they teach in colleges, they file lawsuits, and often, they are vehement in their belief that God does not exist.

What fires this zeal? Most likely, it is hurt. In my experience, most vehement Atheists hold to their beliefs because of an instance of suffering or evil in their lives by which they have been deeply wounded. This could have been the death of a loved one, a serious illness or disability, a rejection by their peers, or a life of loneliness that led to despair. Militant Atheism often becomes a kind of retaliation against God - a kind of getting back at the Lord for not keeping them or their loved ones from harm.

To these individuals, we, as Christians, must witness the love of Christ. We must show them, in the midst of their pain and sorrow, the value and meaning of the Cross and the joy of the Resurrection.

# Agnosticism:
*They may "hedge their bets" about God.*

Atheists are not the only ones who reject God. There also are Agnostics. The latter are not involved in an active denial of God's existence, but rather a kind of practical Atheism whereby individuals live as if God does not exist or simply is not important. This kind of Atheism has affected a multitude of Christians today who are living their lives, basically, as baptized pagans. Yes, they were introduced to Christ, but, for a number of reasons, they have chosen to live a life of sin and rejection of God's teachings.

> "....the Agnostics claim that one cannot know anything about the existence of God, and hence, they are unsure about His existence."

We must pray for these individuals, for their practical Atheism has done more to foster the rise of militant Atheism than any other philosophy. Why believe in God when those who are supposed to believe in Him really are unsure? Such hypocrisy is a serious problem.

Today, many people are Agnostics. Often, this is a more polite form of Atheism. The Agnostics claim that one cannot know anything about the existence of God, and hence, they are unsure about His existence. This may be lived out as indifferentism.

Agnosticism often is the philosophy of choice of one who hedges his bets about God, while still not wanting to deny His existence – "just in case." Agnosticism is fundamentally a kind of spiritual laziness which, in many ways, is more serious than outright philosophical Atheism. At least the Atheist it talking about God – the Agnostic simply doesn't care.

In conclusion, over the past few articles, we have been investigating Atheism and Agnosticism, their causes, and some responses to their claims. Much of this material I derived from a booklet called, "Beginning Apologetics," published by San Juan Catholic Seminars. I do hope that these articles have proven to be helpful.

Belief in God's existence, although naturally logical and seemingly necessary, has fallen into question today. It is our responsibility, as Christian believers, to stand up and proclaim in the public square that God does exist, that we do believe in Him, and that He is knowable. Furthermore, as Christians, we have the antidote to the poison of Atheistic humanism which is so plaguing our culture today. The truth of Jesus Christ, Who so clearly shows us the love of God, is the answer to the despair of Atheism and Agnosticism.

Let us hasten to live our faith actively and boldly in our world so that others may come to know Christ through us.

*Reflection Questions:*

 *1. Atheism and Agnosticism are on the rise today. Why is this true?*

 *2. What response do we, as Christians and as Catholics, have to Atheism?*

 *3. "Ideas have consequences." What does this famous quote mean?*

*Other Religions:*

# Introduction to World Religions:
*Most have some elements of truth.*

Let's move along now to the study of other religions of the world. I admit that my writings represent an outsider's view of other religious traditions; however, I will strive to be as objective as possible. I strongly contend that the more we learn about various world religions, the more we can perceive the hand of God at work among all who believe.

> "The Church considers all goodness and truth found in these religions as a preparation for the Gospel of Christ and given by Him who enlightens all peoples."

Before we visit other religions of the world, it is important to remember that, as Catholics, we are Christians. The word "catholic" has been in use for as long as the word "christian" has been used. In the early Church, they were used interchangeably. Certainly, today, there are other Christians who are not specifically Catholic in their beliefs. However, it would be incorrect to say that a Lutheran or a Methodist or a Baptist is part of another religion. This is untrue. Because we all acknowledge that Jesus Christ is our Lord and God, we all are part of the same religion: Christianity. As we soon will learn, there are many other traditions in the world that are altogether different from ours and which are properly called different religions.

It also is important to call to mind the teaching of our Catholic Faith regarding other religions. There are elements of truth to be found in most world religions. First among these are the Jewish people, who are recipients of Divine Revelation and who remain God's chosen people. It is important to remember that the entire Old Testament, the Word of God, was given to the Jewish people and that Jesus and many members of the early Church were born into this Jewish religion.

After the Jews, Christians find some elements in common with Muslims. The Islamic religion professes to hold the faith of Abraham and, together with us, they adore the one merciful God who will be our judge on the last day. Along with the Jews, Muslims and Christians make up the three great monotheistic religions. The Church considers all goodness and truth found in these religions as a preparation for the Gospel of Christ and given by Him who enlightens all peoples.

Finally, before we embark upon this study of world religions, it is important to remember the teaching of our Catholic Faith regarding the future salvation of those who do not believe in Jesus. As the Second Vatican Council teaches,

"Those who through no fault of their own, do not know the Gospel of Christ or His Church, but who nevertheless seek God with a sincere heart, and moved by grace, try in their actions to do His will as they know it through the dictates of their conscience – those too may achieve eternal salvation."

Let us now learn more about the religions of the world and endeavor to share the peace of Christ with all who do not yet know Him.

Reflection Questions:

1. Have I ever met a person who practiced a religion other than Christianity?
2. Most of human history is the story of man's search for the divine. What do the many religions of the world tell us about our humanity and about the existence of God?
3. "It is a poverty not to know Jesus Christ." What does this mean?

# Judaism – Part I:
*Despite positive contributions, they've endured discrimination.*

As we begin our journey through other world religions, our first visit is to the religion of the Jews: Judaism. Of all of the world religions, the Jewish faith is the closest to Christianity. Indeed, our entire Old Testament is comprised of what are known as the Hebrew Scriptures, the holy books of the Jewish people. The Jews remain God's "Chosen People" and, as such, deserve special respect from us, as Christians. Let us now visit "our eldest brothers and sisters of the faith" and learn more about our Jewish roots...

> "....the Jewish tradition can be traced to Abraham... He was the first to believe that God was one, loving, merciful and just. This was a radical idea at the time..."

Judaism is the oldest of the three great monotheistic religions. Both Christianity and Islam are, to a greater or lesser extent, related to Judaism. Today, there are about 14 million Jews throughout the world. An estimated 47 percent of the world's Jewish population lives in North America. There are roughly 5.5 million adherents in the United States.

The Jewish people have contributed greatly to Western Culture. The arts; education; research; politics; media; entertainment; and commerce all have greatly benefited from the Jewish people's efforts. Sadly, despite these positive contributions to society and culture, the Jews often have been subjected to discrimination and violence. Within the past century, six million Jews were killed by the Nazi government. Anti-Semitism - the hatred of Jews - remains a terrible stain on our civilization.

Today, Judaism also is struggling from within. A great number of Jews living in the United States do not practice their religion. Because of very low birth rates and intermarriage with non-Jews, there is a concern about their future.

Looking back in history, the Jewish tradition can be traced to Abraham, a nomad who traveled through the Middle East and settled in the land of Canaan (the area we now know as Israel). He was the first to believe that God was one, loving, merciful and just. This was a radical idea at the time - for all other religions had numerous gods or deities. Often, these gods were cruel or manipulative, and greatly feared by the people. Christians, along with Muslims, believe that Abraham received a true revelation from God - since he was the first to hold to this radical notion of one, loving, merciful God.

The Jews, although a tiny group in comparison to other nations in the Middle East, exerted considerable influence on their neighbors. Even when they were exiled, persecuted, or killed in large numbers, the Jewish people held fast to their beliefs and preserved their culture.

Today, there are numerous forms of Judaism - and various groups within these forms. In the United States, the three main forms of Judaism are: Reformed, Orthodox and Conservative.

Reformed Jews are the most progressive in outlook. The reform movement began in Germany in the early 1800s as a way of updating religious practices and integrating these into modern life. The laws of the Jewish religion were transformed into a code of ethics, the liturgical language of Hebrew used at Synagogue services was changed into the vernacular (language of the people), men and women were allowed to sit together at services, dietary laws were not strictly enforced, etc. Rather than a personal Messiah, the Reformed speak of the coming of a Messianic age with justice for all.

Orthodox Jews believe that they follow the fullness of the Jewish creed. They strictly follow the ancient traditions and all of the laws of Moses, as found in the Hebrew Scriptures. Within Orthodoxy, there are the Hasidic and Hasidim branches that have mystical attributes and various pious traditions. Orthodox Jews, although fewer in number than the other branches of the religion, have a very strong influence on their religion worldwide.

The Conservative movement, concerned with the liberal attitude of the Reformed, tried to establish a middle ground between the Reformed and the Orthodox. Dietary laws and many traditions of Judaism were maintained, but mixed seating in synagogues and some use of the vernacular language in services were permitted.

The Reformed and Conservative branches of Judaism have about 600 synagogues each in the United States.

# Judaism - Part II:
## *We believe the Messiah is Jesus. Jews still await the Messiah.*

As we continue our exploration of Judaism, let us consider the Jewish creed. It is a noble one: *"Hear O Israel, the Lord our God, the Lord is One."*

We also should know about the "Torah," which is read and prayed over by devout Jews. The Torah is a collection of the first five books of the Old Testament. These are: Genesis, Exodus, Leviticus, Numbers and Deuteronomy. Devout Jews also study the "Talmud," which is a commentary on the Torah made by various rabbis.

> **"....the Passover or 'Seder' meal eaten on Friday night is an occasion of great prayer and unity for all devout Jews, and is the very foundation for our Catholic Mass."**

Most Jews strictly observe the Sabbath which begins at sundown on Friday evening and ends at sundown on Saturday. Orthodox Jews will do no work, cooking, writing, or even use appliances or cars, on the Sabbath.

Another part of Judaism is circumcision of the infant male child, eight days after birth. A Jewish male celebrates his "bar mitzvah" - a rite of becoming a full member of the local congregation - at age 13. A newer tradition of a "bas mitzvah" has been introduced for Jewish girls of 12 years of age.

Jewish feast days and religious holidays are many. The High Holy Days take place in the autumn of the year - Rosh Hashanah is the Jewish New Year and Yom Kippur is the Day of Atonement. These days are observed by most Jews, even if they do not ordinarily practice their religion - they are equivalent in importance to Christmas and Easter for Christians. Hanukkah, usually observed in December, is in fact a relatively minor feast day.

The traditional Jewish man prays while wearing a shawl called a "tallis" over his shoulders and a skull cap called a "yarmulka." "Phylacteries," small black leather boxes containing the scrolls of the law, sometimes are attached to the forehead and left arm during prayer.

Perhaps the most widely known of Jewish practices is the observance of various "kosher" dietary laws. The observance of these laws reminds the Jew of the covenant God made with His chosen people. Kosher laws forbid the eating of pork or any other food deemed to be unclean. Milk and meat are not mixed at the same meal and animals must be slaughtered in a ritual way for them to be considered kosher, or edible.

Jews generally believe in the afterlife, but vary in their understanding of it. Judaism generally does not include teaching about an eternal punishment. Jews worship at synagogues and prayers are lead by a rabbi (religious teacher). The worship service consists of prayer, the singing of a psalm, a sermon and readings from the Torah. However, the family is the main unit of prayer, worship and instruction. Indeed, the Passover or "Seder" meal eaten on Friday night is an occasion of great prayer and unity for all devout Jews, and is the very foundation for our Catholic Mass. Jews await the coming of the Messiah whom they believe will bring them hope, love and peace.

Sadly, there are differences between Catholics and Jews. The greatest differences center on the acceptance of Jesus as the Messiah and the nature of the Trinity. All Christians believe that Jesus is the long-expected Messiah who came to save us. The Jews counter that, because He claimed to be God's Divine Son, Jesus could not possibly be the Messiah. The real Messiah, they say, would always confirm their belief in only one God. Additionally, there are numerous smaller differences between our two traditions that separate us.

Both Jews and Christians accept that the Old Testament (or Hebrew Scripture) is the inspired Word of God. We both hold to the Ten Commandments and we both await the coming (or second coming) of the Messiah. Jews and Christians both place a strong emphasis on family and tradition. Orthodox Jews and Catholics have many of the same social and moral views, and we both oppose our increasingly secular culture.

Let us work and pray for greater respect and love between our two traditions, so that one day we might worship the One True God of Abraham together in harmony.

*Reflection Questions:*

1. *"The Jews are our eldest brothers and sisters in the faith." What does this mean?*
2. *What is "kosher" and why does it matter to devout Jews?*
3. *The Jewish people have steadfastly held to their beliefs through centuries of persecution and hatred. What example does this give us, as Christians?*

# Islam – Part I:
*Soon, there may be more Muslims than Christians.*

On our journey through the world's religions, now let us visit Islam. Islam, Judaism and Christianity are the three major monotheistic religions of the world. All three profess belief in one, infinite God. The religion of Islam is prominent in the news today, so it is important to learn more about this religion and its adherents.

> "The beginning of the religion of Islam is dependent upon one person, a man named Mohammed, who was born around 570 A.D."

Islam is one of the world's largest religions and it is rapidly growing. Today, there are more than one billion followers around the world. The word "Islam" is roughly translated to *"the peace that comes from submitting to the Will of God."* Followers of Islam are called Muslims and their religion is the dominant religion in the Middle East, North Africa, Pakistan and Indonesia. Islam is spreading to Western Europe and North America, through immigration. There are about the same number of Muslims in the world as there are Catholics. However, due to a high birth rate, Muslims soon may outnumber all Christians combined.

Let's consider the history of this religion. Muslims trace their roots back to Ishmael, who was the son of Abraham by his maidservant Hagar. After Abraham and his wife, Sarah, had their own son, named Isaac, Sarah demanded that Hagar and Ishmael be banished. According to Islam, they settled in Mecca and thus formed the community that would eventually see the first Muslims.

The beginning of the religion of Islam is dependent upon one person, a man named Mohammed, who was born around 570 A.D. Mohammed was born in the city of Mecca, which is in modern-day Saudi Arabia. He was a shepherd and a camel driver who married a wealthy widow. Mecca, a center of trade, also was known throughout the area for a large religious shrine called the "Kaaba." Being at the crossroads of a trade route, Mohammed no doubt came into contact with many religions. Since Mecca was at the outer frontier of the disintegrating Roman Empire, Mohammed probably was exposed to altered forms of Christianity and Judaism. It is entirely possible that he took elements of these forms of Christianity and Judaism and molded them into the new religion of Islam.

Mohammed claimed that the angel Gabriel appeared to him over a 20-year span and had him write down the words that would eventually become the Koran – the Muslim holy book. Mohammed eventually was forced to flee from

Mecca with his few followers and he settled in Medina in 622. After winning many converts to the religion there, he assembled an army and led his forces to attack Mecca in 630. After subduing the city, Mohammed destroyed the many idols and established a religious state. After his death in 632, his followers spread the religion of Islam throughout the Middle East and to North Africa. Through the "Jihad" or Holy War, the Muslims went as far as Spain, Portugal, and parts of France, before they were defeated in battle in 732.

Despite this setback, Islamic culture flourished in the Ninth, Tenth and Eleventh centuries and brilliant scholarship invented Algebra, pioneered the medical sciences, and advanced the arts. Muslim scholars rightfully are credited with rescuing from oblivion most of the philosophy of ancient Greece. This medieval rise of Islamic culture eventually was checked by various divisions within the religion. After numerous struggles - both internal and external - throughout recent centuries, Islam appears to be enjoying a new resurgence.

# Islam - Part II:
*Both Sunnis and Shiites worship Allah.*

To understand Islam better, we must learn of its two main branches.

The "Sunni" branch believes that the first four caliphs - Mohammed's successors - rightfully took his place as the leaders of Muslims. They recognize the heirs of the four caliphs as legitimate religious leaders and recognize and follow religious tradition. "Shiites," in contrast, believe that only the heirs of the fourth caliph, Ali, are the legitimate successors of Mohammed - and they tend to be more mystical in their theology. Sunni Muslims make up approximately 90 percent of the Muslim world, with Shiites and various other sects comprising the remaining 10 percent. Most Shiites are found in Iran, Iraq and Lebanon.

> **"Muslims believe that their religion is the fulfillment of Judaism and Christianity and that the latter two faiths are missing important parts of God's true revelation."**

Muslims believe that there is only one God whom they call Allah, and that Mohammed is his prophet. Although Mohammed is highly respected by Muslims, he is not regarded as a divine figure. The Koran is the holy book of Islam and its words contain the main teachings of the religion. The Koran contains 114 chapters and is about 80 percent of the size of the Christian New Testament. The Koran is read by most Muslims in a literal way, and they believe that it is the true word of God. To Muslims, the Koran is a continuation of the Old and New Testaments, bringing these teachings to fulfillment.

Muslims believe that their religion is the fulfillment of Judaism and Christianity and that the latter two religious traditions are missing important parts of God's true revelation. They believe that where Judaism's error was in worshipping the law and Christianity's error was in worshipping the prophet Jesus Christ, Islam is true because it worships God alone. Mohammed saw himself not as a founder of a new religion, but rather as the last in a long line of God's prophets - from Abraham, to Moses, to Jesus, and finally to Mohammed himself.

The foundation of the religion of Islam can be seen in its five pillars or precepts. These are:

1. There is no God but Allah, and Mohammed is his prophet.

2. Pray five times daily while facing Mecca.

3. Give alms to the poor.

4. Fast during the daylight hours of the holy month of Ramadan.

5. Make a pilgrimage to Mecca, at least once during one's lifetime.

Realistically, there are numerous differences between Christianity and Islam. Most important is the status and role of Jesus Christ - whom we believe to be the Son of God and the Savior of all mankind and whom Muslims regard only as a prophet. While Muslims do have religious leaders, often called "imams," there is no hierarchy or centralized leadership as there is in the Catholic Church. Because there is no main teaching authority, it is difficult to enter into religious dialogue. Many Muslims are not willing to separate religion from politics, and thus, strongly desire a kind of religious state.

In addition, the religion of Islam is not "incarnational" - God remains distant. Christianity, on the contrary, believes that God became man in Jesus Christ to save us from our sins and that we are all privileged to call God, "Abba," or Father. Beyond this major difference, lie our varying beliefs regarding the Bible as the infallible Word of God, the nature of marriage, the treatment of women, sacraments, and many other issues.

However, there are some similarities between our two religions. Both Muslims and Christians worship God - Who is one, merciful and almighty, the Creator of Heaven and earth, who has revealed Himself to mankind. Although they do not believe Him to be divine, Muslims respect Jesus as a great prophet. They also greatly respect His mother, Mary. Indeed, Mary is mentioned 34 times in the Koran! Both Muslims and Catholics have a strong love of philosophy and we both see that there is no contradiction between belief and reason.

Together, let us fight the evils of our secular culture and pray that we might know and do God's Will.

Reflection Questions:
1. Who started the religion of Islam? What is the holy book of Islam called?
2. What are the two main divisions within Islam?
3. What are the similarities between Christianity and Islam? The differences?

---

# The Bahai Religious Tradition:
*Their goal is unity for all humanity.*

On our continuing journey through the various world religions, our next stop is the Bahai religious tradition. This relatively new group is attracting members and growing throughout the world. One of its centers is near Chicago, Illinois.

Today, there are more than five million adherents to the Bahai religious tradition in almost 200 countries around the world. The writings of Bahaullah, the founder of this religion, guide the life of a Bahai follower. The purpose of the Bahai religion is to know and worship the divine, and to carry forward an ever-advancing civilization with unity among all peoples and cultures. The Bahai religious tradition has no formal clergy. Prayer meetings are planned by the local community and decisions are made by majority vote and democratic principles. All cultures and peoples are welcomed in this religion.

> "The Bahai religion was founded in Persia (modern-day Iran) by Bahaullah in the mid-1800s. He claimed to be a prophet who would usher in an age of peace for all peoples."

The Bahai religious tradition was founded in Persia (modern-day Iran) by Bahaullah in the mid-1800s. He claimed to be a prophet who would usher in an age of peace for all peoples. Although he was persecuted because of his beliefs and eventually exiled, after his death in 1892 his new religion continued to grow. Today, the center of the Bahai religious tradition is in the Holy Land in the city of Haifa, Israel. Bahai houses of worship can be found in Wilmette, Illinois, as well as in Australia, Germany, Uganda, Panama and India.

At the center of the Bahai religious tradition is the goal of unity for all humanity. This, they believe to be the will of God. They also believe that this unity eventually will culminate in one world government and civilization. To achieve this goal, Bahai teachings stress the fostering of character development, nourishing the spiritual qualities of a person, developing the unique talents of an individual, fostering equality between men and women, and establishing universal education. The Bahai religious tradition requires a period of fasting every year. Marriage is highly praised – and is to be permanent. Alcohol and drugs are prohibited. Daily prayer is required.

Those of the Bahai religious tradition often concentrate on interfaith or multicultural activities, encourage gender equality and offer classes on comparative religion. Acts of charity and social justice also are strongly encouraged.

The Bahai religious tradition professes that God has intervened in history a number of times and that different messengers or prophets of the divine have been sent. These have included: Moses, Jesus Christ, Mohammed, Buddha and Krishna, among others. Members believe that each of these great religious leaders has given some important teaching to the world. In our own age, the Bahai religious tradition holds that God has spoken again through their prophet Bahaullah and made His desire known for the unity of the human family.

It is obvious that there are numerous differences between the Bahai religious tradition and Christianity. First of all, Christians believe that Jesus Christ is the Son of God, the Savior of the World – not simply one prophet among many. We reject the idea that His teachings are equal to those of other religious figures in history. Jesus Christ is not merely a prophet come down from Heaven; He is God. In addition, we believe that Jesus saved us from our sins by dying on the Cross, rose again to give us hope, and gave us the Church as His Body in the world.

Catholicism and the Bahai religious tradition share the goals of striving towards greater understanding among peoples, a greater respect for the dignity of women, and a strengthening of marriage. We also share a love for education, and we strive for world peace.

Despite our differences, let us all pray that we might have peace in our world and that we might do the Will of God in our daily lives.

*Reflection Questions:*

1. *Who founded the Bahai religious tradition?*
2. *What are the main teachings of this tradition?*
3. *What do we have in common? What are our differences?*

# Buddhism – Part I:
*They neither accept nor reject the existence of God.*

As we continue our journey through the world's religions, let us stop to visit the Buddhists. Buddhism, once predominantly a religion of the East, now is gradually gaining followers in the West. Oftentimes, it is compared to Christianity – and the Buddha is seen by some as a kind of alternative Christ.

Today, there are roughly 350 million adherents to Buddhism, with about one million living in the United States. Although Buddhism began in India, it eventually spread to Sri Lanka, China, Burma, Thailand, Japan, Korea, Tibet, Indonesia, Southeast Asia. and beyond.

> "The main goal of Buddhism is to provide a way to escape suffering. Although this effort to escape suffering may take many lifetimes to achieve, its final goal is called 'Nirvana'…"

There are two main schools or paths followed by Buddhists. The first is called "Mahayana" Buddhism. The second is called "Hinayana" or "Theravada" Buddhism. Mahayana Buddhists invite all to their faith and hold that each person, regardless of his or her background, is part of the network of life. Zen Buddhism, a mystical form of the Mahayana path, is quite popular in the West. Theravada Buddhists believe that wisdom is the goal of life's search and that each person must follow this path alone. Monastic discipline and strict asceticism are required. Mahayana Buddhism is by far the more popular of the two paths! While considered by many to be a religion, Buddhism neither accepts nor rejects the existence of God.

To review some history, Buddhism is closely associated with one man, Siddhartha Gautama, who was born around 560 B.C. in India. He was born into a wealthy family with many privileges and opportunities. While in his 20s, he began to observe human suffering for the first time. This troubled him so deeply that he completely withdrew from the world. He left his riches, his wife, his son, and his birth parents, and began a search for truth and the meaning of existence. At first, he tried self-mortification. When this didn't work, he turned towards meditation. In a profound moment, while sitting under a tree at night, he achieved a spiritual awakening. For the remaining 40 years of his life, the Buddha – the name means "Enlightened One" – preached and taught his new beliefs.

The main goal of Buddhism is to provide a way to escape suffering. Although this effort to escape suffering may take many lifetimes to achieve, its final goal is called "Nirvana" – the extinction of all desire. Pilgrims who desire to set out on the path of Buddhist belief first must listen to Buddha's teachings, and follow certain rules.

The Four Noble Truths are the main starting points for Buddhist belief. They are: a) Human life is filled with pain and misery; b) The cause of this misery is the desire to act selfishly; c) Overcoming this selfish desire will bring one at last to Nirvana; and d) All of this can be attained by following the Eight-Fold Path. This Eight-Fold Path includes right understanding; right aspiration; right speech; right conduct; right livelihood; right effort; right mindfulness; and finally, right concentration – leading to Nirvana.

Buddhists believe that enlightenment can be achieved only by walking the Eight-Fold Path. All reality is in a constant state of flux. Buddhists believe that human beings are only temporary arrangements of body and consciousness. They do not admit that human beings have a soul – according to the Western concept of the soul. Attaining the state of Nirvana is equivalent to being with the divine, although Buddhists do not accept any personal relationship with God.

# Buddhism – Part II:
*This religious tradition is not "interchangeable" with Christianity!*

Buddhism and Christianity have several major differences.

First of all, Jesus said that He is the Way, the Truth and the Life. The Buddha merely claimed that he knew the way to the divine. Eternal life for the Christian is an absolute and eternal existence. Nirvana for the Buddhist is to cease to exist.

In addition, suffering for the Christian has meaning – in the redemptive sufferings of Jesus Christ on the Cross. Suffering for the Buddhist is to be avoided and negated. Christians claim we have immortal souls; Buddhists claim that we do not.

> "Although there is some surface similarity between the Beatitudes as taught by Jesus Christ and aspects of Buddhist teaching, the underlying principles of the two religions differ greatly."

We also have varying beliefs on charity. Since Buddhists claim that human reality is illusory, there is no reason to perform acts of charity or social justice. Any act of charity that is accomplished is to help oneself gain Nirvana – and to cease to exist. On the other hand, Christians perform acts of charity towards our neighbor because, in him, we see Christ.

While it has become somewhat common to claim similarities or even interchangeability between Buddhist and Christian theology, this remains a mistaken notion. Although there is some surface similarity between the Beatitudes as taught by Jesus Christ and aspects of Buddhist teaching, the underlying principles of the two religions differ greatly. For the Christian, Jesus Christ is God and our life is eternal. For the Buddhist, Buddha points the way towards Nirvana and the end of existence.

Some Christians have begun to embrace certain Buddhist practices, or even the total Buddhist religion. Buddhism has become popular in the United States for a number of reasons, chiefly because this religion primarily centers on the self – thus mirroring our contemporary culture. Other drawing cards for young adults of today include the religion's radical individualism, a relativistic understanding of human nature and the existence of the truth, the search for meaning in the midst of suffering, and the allure of Eastern thought common in the New Age Movement. Those Christians who are lacking in a personal relationship with Christ and His Church often fall away from the practice of their faith and turn towards a variation of Buddhism.

Even though our two religions have many and varied differences, we have some aspects in common. Both Buddhists and Catholics have a structured, vocational religious life which includes monks and nuns. We both strive for peace and harmony among all peoples, and we both reject the use of force in religious conversion. We both strive for holiness and to come to know the Truth.

Let us pray for our Buddhist brothers and sisters that they might come to know Jesus, who is the Way, the Truth and the Life.

*Reflection Questions:*

*1. How is Buddhism different from Christianity?*

*2. What do we have in common?*

*3. Why are so many people attracted to Buddhism, today, in our country?*

# Taoism and Confucianism:
*They profoundly influence the Asian way of life.*

Next on our tour of world religions, we stop to visit the two Asian religions of Taoism and Confucianism. Although these religions are not as widely known in the West, they have profoundly influenced the Asian way of life. Through travel and commerce, more Westerners are coming into contact with these religions. The two religious traditions are becoming somewhat popular in our culture as alternatives to Christianity.

The ancient religious tradition of **Taoism** began around the Fifth or Sixth century B.C. in China. It was founded by a semi-historical figure named Lao Tzu or "The Old Master." This faith is deeply philosophical and contains many seemingly contradictory teachings. One example is: *"Be bent and you will remain straight, be empty and you will remain full."*

> **"Through travel and commerce, more Westerners are coming into contact with these religions. The two religious traditions are becoming somewhat popular in our culture as alternatives to Christianity."**

The word Tao means "The Way." The Tao is a living reality often called the One, the Eternal, the Unmoving, and the Unchanging. Taoism is closely tied to nature, holding that all of the world, including the human race, is tied to the Tao. This Tao is a kind of life force that runs through everything. (The nature of the Tao is very similar to "The Force" made popular by the "Star Wars" movies.)

Virtuous living in this religious tradition involves abandoning all efforts and allowing oneself to be carried along through life, like a leaf in a stream. Perfect behavior is allowing one's actions to be surrendered and thus united with the Tao, thus fulfilling the Taoist teaching, *"By non-action, everything can be done."*

Taoism is the opposite of religions with strict doctrinal teachings. It rejects moral absolutes – and good and evil as both unknowable. All values are relative and blend into each other; there are no objective standards. Taoist philosophy is best symbolized by the yin-yang wheel seen in some Asian flags and artwork. Eternal life or salvation in Taoism is to achieve ultimate union with the Tao.

Taoism as a religious tradition rejects violence and embraces the beauty of nature. Taoism shares these aspects with Christianity. However, beyond this, the two religions differ greatly. Taoists recognize no personal God, no objective moral law and no moral authority. The divine remains hidden, unknowable and unapproachable in Taoism. Because of its rejection of absolutes and its embrace of nature, Taoism is quite popular among those in Western society who accept the relativistic philosophy of New Age spirituality.

The religious traditions of **Confucianism** originated in China and remain closely related to Chinese culture. "Confucius" or Kung Fu-Tzu often is called, "The First Teacher." He was that and more. He was a teacher of ethics and of a morality that still is followed by millions of people today. So influential was this man, Confucius is said to have authored Chinese culture.

Confucius was born around 550 B.C. As a young child, he enjoyed studying. Soon, he himself became a teacher. He wanted to serve in public office, so that he could teach his philosophy of life. Even when he was older, he traveled throughout China, offering advice to leaders about effective and just governmental practices. Throughout his life, Confucius attracted a loyal following. After his death, these disciples came to see him as "The Great Teacher."

Through the centuries, Confucianism has been seen either as a religion or as a code of ethics. Although not strictly worshipped as a god, Confucius is highly venerated. Perhaps this religious tradition can be seen as a philosophical guidebook to life – an ethical code that guides almost a billion people today.

*Reflection Questions:*

*1. What is Taoism? What do we have in common and what are our differences?*

*2. Who was Confucius and what did he teach?*

*3. Eastern religions are becoming more popular in the West today. Why?*

# Hinduism – Part I:
*They believe in a supreme god who created other gods.*

As we continue our journey through the various religions of the world, we come to the ancient tradition of Hinduism. Although closely associated with India, this religion also has had effects on other denominations and practices around the world. Today, the nation of India is perhaps the most richly religious country on earth. Indeed, the entire Indian subcontinent has long been a fertile ground for religions of all kinds.

The religion of Hinduism is quite complex and contains many facets and shades of belief. It maintains a deep reverence for the oneness of the divine, while at the same time worshipping a plethora of gods. This religious traditions is the world's oldest; it can be traced back 3,000 years or more. Today, there are some 750 million people, mostly in India, who consider themselves to be Hindu. The Hindu holy books include the "Bhagavad-Gita," and many other works.

**"They hold to the immortality of the soul, but they believe that this soul is reborn many times over in various creatures."**

Hindus believe in a supreme god who created the universe. This god created many other gods (highly advanced spiritual beings) to be his helpers. Hindus worship this supreme god under many names, depending upon the area of India in which they live. For some, it is "Brahma the Creator," for others it is "Vishnu the Preserver," for still others it is "Shiva the Destroyer." The many gods of Hinduism often are depicted as having elephant heads, many arms, or dancing the cosmic dance of life. A Hindu would say that he or she worships a supreme god, but that there are many other divine entities in the universe.. In Hinduism, the divine is both inside oneself and a transcendent mystery.

For the Hindu, salvation is to experience one's innermost soul, called the "Atman." At the moment of this revelation, one recognizes that this innermost soul participates in the godhead, called "Brahman." All peoples everywhere are striving and searching for this moment of revelation. Some actively search it out by religious practice, others initially reject it. Hinduism teaches that, as we all search for infinite being, infinite awareness, and infinite joy, we eventually discover them by searching within ourselves. This search for the inner awareness of the divine often takes place over many lifetimes.

Hindus believe in reincarnation. They hold to the immortality of the soul, but they believe that this soul is reborn many times over in various creatures. Throughout this process of reincarnation, the person has experiences of life, learns lessons, and evolves spiritually upwards or downwards. Eventually, the person will graduate from physical birth into the eternal bliss of Nirvana where rebirth is no longer necessary and the soul is at peace.

# Hinduism – Part II:
*All the world's a stage!*

Hinduism sees the world as a gigantic stage on which the drama of the human soul is played out. Some souls draw closer to Nirvana. Others regress. Each person and the effects of his or her moral choices in life are ruled by something called "karma," which means "action."

> "The law of karma puts the human person at the center of responsibility for everything he or she does or experiences. Put simply, people *'get what they deserve'*..."

Karma is the law of moral cause and effect. Every action affects a person either positively or negatively. An act of kindness is good karma; it always reflects positively back to its origin. Selfishness or theft is bad karma; the person is pushed farther away from eventual Nirvana. Because Hindus understand the effects of karma, they generally do not hate or resent people who do them harm. They believe that, in such a case, the other person is only giving back the effects of the causes they themselves set in motion at some earlier time. The law of karma puts the human person at the center of responsibility for everything he or she does or experiences. Put simply, people "get what they deserve" and "what goes around, comes around."

Another aspect of Hinduism is the role of "Yoga." Devout Hindus practice this form of religious discipline. The word yoga means "yoke." It is a type of spiritual training. There are four different kinds of yoga that reflect different temperaments of the person: knowledge, love, work and meditation. All forms of yoga strive for detachment from the self and the achievement of freedom from worldly distractions. The popular physical exercise of yoga derives from certain aspects of this Hindu practice.

Obviously, Hinduism and Christianity have many differences. Although Hindu scholars strongly attest to their worship of only one supreme god – in practice, Hindus worship many gods. For the Hindu, the divine is within oneself and is not incarnate in human history. Works of charity are carried out only to help oneself gain good karma and often do not take into account the dignity of the human person.

The Hindu belief in reincarnation often resigns a person to his or her fate. Someone may be unloved and ignored because it is perceived that his problems are his own fault. *Ex. This life will pass, the next life might be better...* A bitter caste system still imprisons many in Indian society who are seen as having bad karma and being deserving of their poverty. The effects of Mother Teresa of Calcutta and others, in countering this mentality with Christian charity, are widely recognized.

Christians and Hindus do share a great love of the divine, with all of its mystery and beauty. Catholics and Hindus share a respect for meditation, the mystical side of the human soul and its spiritual life. Interestingly, both Christians and Hindus strongly reject abortion as the killing of an innocent human being. Any Christian who has visited India returns with a profound sense of the love for the divine that is present there.

Let us continue to pray for understanding and unity between our two traditions as we strive to worship the true God.

*Reflection Questions:*

*1. How old is the Hindu religion? Where did it begin?*

*2. What do we have in common? What are our differences?*

*3. What is "karma?"*

---

# Conclusion - World Religions:
### We all believe "there must be something more."

In the previous articles, we have explored the major religions of the world. On our journey through Judaism, Islam, Bahai, Buddhism, Taoism, Confucianism and Hinduism, we have discovered new information and ideas.

Whenever we learn about the different peoples of the world, and their different customs and religions, we begin to discover that we have some characteristics in common with each other. We all have basic needs, hopes and dreams. Although our religions have major differences in practice and possession of truth, it is interesting to note that most people believe in some spiritual entity or God.

**"What is consistent among people of many religions is the innate part of our humanity that longs to worship, know and love our creator."**

Although religion often is a force for great good in our world, it also has been used as an excuse for violence, cruelty or discrimination. Religious belief always must be tempered by the fact that we are talking about the divine or God - there is a certain mystery to the spiritual and we do not know all of the answers. If we did, we would be God!

What is consistent among people of many religions is the innate part of our humanity that longs to worship, know and love our creator. People of all religions long for some form of peace. In addition, we share a notion that this world, for all its beauty and pain, is not all there is. There must be something more. This, it seems, is the basic nature of religion.

As Christians, our faith is unique. It is the only one that affirms that the divine - or God - assumed our human nature. It is the only one which reveres a God Who walked, lived and suffered with us. It is the only faith that gives meaning to the mystery of human suffering, shows us what love truly looks like, and gives us the hope of the Resurrection. In short, it is the only faith in which

God is Love. As Christians, we are enormously blessed to have had this revealed to us.

It is our sacred obligation to share our faith in Jesus Christ, a faith of hope and love, with our waiting world.

*Reflection Questions:*

    1. *What do all world religions have in common?*

    2. *How is Christianity unique among all world religions?*

    3. *"Atheism is unnatural." Reflect on this – what does it mean?*

# Section IX
## *Other Information You Need To Know*

# The Mystery of Priestly Activities/ A Day In The Life of A Priest:
*(Hint: I don't just sit there, with my hands folded!)*

From time to time, people ask me what I do all day long. After all, most Catholics only see their priest on Saturday evening or Sunday morning. What a priest does the REST of the week can be a mystery to many people. Let me assure you that I keep busy! Perhaps this article might shed a bit of light on the subject.

My days usually begin at 6 a.m. and I'm in bed by 11 p.m. During the course of a given day, I come in contact with many people and issues. Sometimes, the matters are quite serious and, other times, rather trivial. Each day is radically different from the next, so it's difficult to relate what an "average" day might be like.

> "Each day, I say Mass...I take time for prayer...phone calls...e-mails...pastoral issues...appointments...funerals ...weddings...meetings...shut-ins...confessions."

I'll start with what is common to each day. Each day, I say Mass. Sometimes, it's with people present at a normally scheduled parish Mass. From time to time, especially on my day of rest, I will say Mass by myself. Each day, I take time for prayer. This includes The Liturgy of the Hours and a Rosary I pray for the intentions of my parishioners. Every day, I receive an average of five to 10 phone calls. I typically receive 10 to 15 e-mails a day, and lots and lots of mail. Most of it is junk.

Monday is the day I typically take for rest. I leave the area so that I won't be tempted to start working again! I usually go to visit family or friends. Tuesdays, Wednesdays and Thursdays are the busiest weekdays. Fridays usually are slower. Weekends are, of course, quite busy with Masses, confessions and perhaps a wedding or funeral.

Each day, I address multiple pastoral issues. For example, I might take a few hours to write a bulletin article, or spend some time preparing my homily for the weekend. Almost every day, I have appointments with people who are having difficulties in their daily lives, such as problems at home. Often, these appointments have to do with marriage and family issues. Almost every day, I speak with our two parish secretaries about the inner workings of our parishes, financial issues, etc.

Then, every other week, I meet with our parish staff and we speak about scheduling parish events. We also discuss important pastoral issues facing the people of our parishes. Every month, I meet with the Pastoral Council, the Finance Council and the Worship Committee, where I gain much-needed advice from our parish leaders.

From time to time, there are extraordinary events in our parishes that involve me as a priest. Funerals, which usually are unexpected, take time and preparation. Weddings and Baptisms also are special sacramental events. I meet with people who are interested in becoming Catholic or who just have questions about the Faith. Fairly often, I attend meetings at the Diocesan offices to learn how to more effectively shepherd our parishes or to serve as an advisor to the Bishop.

I spend time almost every week visiting shut-ins or others who are unable to come to Church. Hospital visits are part of this. I also hear confessions at a regularly scheduled time or by appointment. I often am called upon in our parishes to mediate disputes and misunderstandings between individuals or groups. I call this "putting out fires" and, although it is extremely draining for me, it is part of my job as your spiritual Father.

So, you see, priests address multiple issues each day. Sometimes, these issues are placed together in stark contrast. For example, on a given day, I might visit an elderly person in a nursing home, then go and meet with a family who is grieving the loss of a child, then return to the parish and consult with a contractor about new gutters, and then sit down and try to write a homily! Sometimes, I am amazed, after a day is done, at the many and varied experiences I have had. It does make for an exciting life!

As you can imagine, my schedule is quite busy. However, I always have time for my parishioners – and I'm guessing that most priests would say the same thing. Please make an appointment with a priest, and time will be found to talk. I enjoy being here at my parishes and being part of my parishioners' lives.

Let us all continue to grow in faith together!

*Reflection Questions:*
1. *What does a priest do all day?*
2. *Does a priest work only on Sundays?*
3. *Have you prayed for your priest recently? Why or why not?*

# On Being Busy:
*Busy priests still want to help you!*

Recently, many people have said to me, "Oh, Father, you are so busy. I don't want to bother you by asking you for something…" The first part of this statement is true! I am very, very busy. So are many of you! The second part of this statement concerns me, though – and thus, I would like to speak with you about it.

Most of us are busy. However, it would be wrong of me to think of my busyness as any more pressing than yours. Most of us lead very full lives; our culture seems to dictate this. Whether this is healthy or not is another subject. Nevertheless, as a priest, I do have a lot to do. Many meetings, visits and emergencies fill the days of parish priests. Yet, YOU, our parishioners, always are important to us!

> **"If you have a problem, a question, or just want to talk about something on your mind, please feel free to contact a priest."**

Please, please, please, never think that we are too busy for you. If you have a problem, a question, or just want to talk about something on your mind, please feel free to contact a priest. You are not a burden.

Now, we do need to prioritize things. So, if you want to talk about oil prices in Saudi Arabia, we might have a few more important things to tackle first. However, if you or a loved one is having a rough time of it, we need to know. In short, we are busy being YOUR Spiritual Fathers – that's why we're busy! Please do not hesitate to contact us if a spiritual need arises.

The flip side of this is equally important. We cannot read your minds. If you don't tell us that you or a loved one needs to see us, we never will know. You need to contact us! Most of us check our voicemail and e-mail frequently. It does no good to complain that, *"Father doesn't know I'm here,"* if you don't let us know you need help! When you contact us, you might be surprised at how quickly we can see you.

So, all of us are busy. However, priests never are too busy for true spiritual needs. Thank you for respecting our time, but please keep us busy serving you!

*Reflection Questions:*

1. *Parish priests are very busy, today. Why do you think this is the case?*
2. *Why are some people afraid to ask for help from their parish?*
3. *Do I keep priests in my prayers?*

# What Do People Want in a Catholic Parish? Part I:
*(Hint: It's not rambling homilies, a "warehouse" building and off-key music.)*

What do people want in a Catholic parish? This is a very good question, and I believe an important one for all of us to consider. Perhaps we might ask ourselves the following questions: *"Why do people come to my parish? Why do I go? Why are these other people Catholic? Why am I Catholic?"*

> "Sadly, it seems that parish life which is not deeply rooted in the Eucharist will leave people feeling hungry."

Today, Catholics are the single largest religious group in our country. Roughly one in every four Americans considers himself or herself a Catholic. The second largest "religious group" in our country includes fallen-away Catholics. These are Catholics who, for a variety of reasons, no longer practice their Faith or no longer consider themselves Catholic. What a tragedy! What can be done to invite those who have drifted away to return? I strongly believe that a solution to this problem exists in the local Catholic parish.

When individuals are asked why they left the Catholic Church, they typically say the same thing: *"I wasn't being fed at my parish"* or words to this effect. This, of course, is very ironic because the very Bread of Life - the Eucharist - is found only in Catholic parishes! Presumably, those who are going to Mass are able to receive Communion and yet, despite this fact, they still feel as though they are not being fed. What is the reason for this subjective, yet real, feeling of emptiness? What can parishes do to help?

Sadly, it seems that parish life which is not deeply rooted in the Eucharist will leave people feeling hungry. Although the Eucharist is the greatest of gifts that we have as Catholics, people rightly expect that they will be nourished in a number of ways when they go to Church. Here are just a few of the things that they might expect...

One of the most important things that people are looking for in their parish is a solid, Christ-centered, relevant homily. Even though the priest's homily lasts only about 10 to 12 minutes, it may be the only source for many people to have the Faith explained to them during the entire week. Homilies are very significant and people are attracted or driven away by them. To be sure, priests have varying gifts in this regard. However, every parishioner deserves to have an original, well-organized, relevant sermon that teaches the Truth. Is the homily the most important part of the Mass? Certainly not! Is it the most memorable part? Typically yes, and that's why it's so important. If a priest's homilies are not heartfelt and "real," people may leave the parish.

Another aspect of parish life that is vitally important is the appearance of the Church itself. Is the Church decorated beautifully? Does it look like the house of God, or does it look like a basement storeroom? Does the Church building remind us that we are in God's house, or does it make us think that we are in a warehouse?

Music at Mass also is vitally important. We all have our favorite kinds of Church music. Some of us like the music to be "middle-of-the-road," others prefer more modern renditions, still others yearn for the hymns to be in Latin. Yet, we all know what it's like when the music is out of tune, too high-pitched, too fast, too slow, or presented in an unprofessional manner.

So, people are attracted to a parish that has meaningful homilies, beautiful decorations and uplifting, reverent music. If any one of these factors is missing, they may flee to another Church – or simply stop attending altogether.

# What Do People Want in a Catholic Parish? Part II:
*It's a basic formula of strong teaching, love and caring.*

A strong Catholic parish also must be welcoming. By this, I mean that its people must be warm and kind. From the priest to the usher, from the sacristan to the catechist, a parish must welcome newcomers and make them feel part of the family, in order for it to grow.

Many of us have been part of a particular parish for a long time. Others have joined a parish more recently. However, we're all attracted by a welcoming atmosphere in which people say *"hello"* and are honestly interested in each others' well-being. It seems so simple, yet people are drawn to love and caring. If the priest or parishioners are unfriendly and cold, people will leave.

> "....I believe that the most important requirement for a healthy parish is that the fullness of the Truth is taught and lived..."

A strong parish also must have an excellent program of religious education for people of all ages. From youth to teens, from young adults to senior citizens, we all need to grow in knowledge and love of Our Lord Jesus Christ. When education only focuses on young people and not on everyone else, parishes struggle. People are hungry, today! They want to know their Faith! They want to meet Christ! Bible studies, classes on the Catechism, programs to strengthen marriages, and various Faith-sharing groups all are vital to a parish's success. In short, people should meet Jesus Christ their Savior in a healthy parish - by learning more about Him. If this opportunity is not offered to people, many will leave.

Small Christian communities are a vital part of any strong parish. From the Knights of Columbus to Catholic women's groups, from a gathering for young mothers to a program for teens, any strong parish is constructed from the building blocks of these small communities. Especially in larger parishes where a person might only feel like a number, small Faith-sharing groups are absolutely essential to the health of the entire parish. Far from being cliques, these small groups welcome new members and support the larger parish in its mission. If a parish is solely about the weekend Mass and provides nothing else for the building up of the community, the parish will die and its people will leave.

Finally, I believe that the most important requirement for a healthy parish is that the fullness of the Truth is taught and lived there. Jesus Christ must be preached! The full and complete teachings of His Catholic Church must be presented. If the priest and the people are ashamed of Christ, or if they disagree and create an antagonistic environment, the parish will wither and die. We must not be afraid of preaching the Gospel - even if it is counter-cultural. We must not be ashamed of presenting what our Catholic Faith teaches - even if it might not be very popular. People might initially be shocked, but they always will be attracted by the Truth! Any parish which does not uphold the truths of our Catholic Faith is a dead parish and its people will leave.

So, how are you doing? May God continue to bless your parish family.

*Reflection Questions:*

1. *What makes a parish strong and vibrant?*
2. *What makes a parish weak - or kills its spirit?*
3. *What can I do to make my parish stronger?*

# Becoming a Member of a Parish:
*There are several good reasons. (Money isn't one!)*

When I visit with priest friends from around my diocese and around our country, one of the first questions I'm asked is, *"How large are your parishes?"* I usually say that there are four rural parishes clustered together that include about 700 families. The word "family" in this context means family unit or household. This might include one person – or many people – in a given household. This is the standard manner in which parish size is calculated throughout our country.

> **"I strongly urge you to register as a member of your parish if you haven't done so already!"**

My parishes, like most rural parishes, are rather small compared with city churches. Some urban parishes might have 3,000 or more families. That's a lot of people! The challenge for bookkeeping in any parish is to accurately calculate who belongs to a given parish. This is a difficult task fraught with potential confusion. What exactly do we mean by "belonging" to a parish? What do we mean by an "active" parishioner? Also, when, if ever, does a person cease to be on the list of parishioners?

First of all, a person does not need to "become a member" of a parish to be considered a Catholic. In fact, parish membership is an American invention. In most other countries, especially where the population is almost exclusively Catholic, there is really no need to "join" a parish. It's just assumed that everybody in the area is Catholic. However, in our nation, with its many different forms of Christianity and other religions, it is important to know exactly who is a Catholic and who is not. This is very helpful for bookkeeping, as well as for pastoral care and future parish planning.

You see, by having an accurate list of parishioners, we can better communicate with all of you. Secondly, we know how much material we need to order for the offices as well as what size financial budget we need to prepare. Thirdly, we are assessed a yearly fee by the Diocese for the running of the diocesan offices – according to how many family units we have. There are certainly many other reasons why we need to keep up-to-date lists on membership in our parishes.

However, like most plans, things are not as clear-cut as they first might seem. Today, people of my generation do not seem to be as interested in or aware of the need to register in a parish. This, coupled with the question of when young people cease to be part of their parental family and need to register on their own, makes the process confusing. (We recommend that when a young person turns 18, he or she should register in the parish.) Also, people move out of the area without telling the parish staff that they are leaving, thus affecting the parish census even more. Sadly, there also are those who are registered yet never come to church and do not contribute to the support of the parish.

It must be said most clearly that any person who is unable to support the parish financially still is considered a member! Money has nothing to do with it. Also, there are individuals who are not able to come to Mass on the weekends because of illness or infirmity.

So, you now know why it makes good sense to fill out that registration form. I strongly urge you to register as a member of your parish, if you haven't done so already! It will be a great assistance!

*Reflection Questions:*
1. *Why is parish membership important?*
2. *Does membership in a parish involve certain responsibilities?*
3. *Why do some cultures or countries not have formal parish membership?*

# Financially Supporting Your Parish:
*Tough times call for creative measures.*

Every day, in Catholic parish offices, the mail comes rolling in. Lots of it is junk mail – just like in your homes. Other pieces of mail are bills or official letters from the Diocese. However, we also receive a third kind of mail: contributions from our parishioners far and wide who greatly desire to support our parishes.

It always is moving for me to see a letter from an elderly parishioner who may be on a fixed income but who, nevertheless, supports his parish. Sometimes, we receive surprising gifts from anonymous sources, or from parishioners who wish to give back something extra to God.

> "Money is one means – and only one means – by which individuals can support their Church. Volunteering time, praying...can be...excellent..."

Most of us use those little envelopes which come in the mail – or are picked up at the Church – to financially support our parish. Some of us contribute each week, some of us semi-monthly, others of us once a month, still others yearly. Every month, I write out a $50 check to each of my four parishes. It's a lot of checks, but it's my way of supporting the parishes which I love and to which I belong. Regardless of the way in which people choose to contribute, all contributions are most appreciated and greatly help our parishes to grow and to stay strong.

Most parishes have finance councils and even trustees who meet regularly to discuss financial matters affecting the parishes. They explore how we can best be good stewards of our people's generosity.

Each week, in most parish bulletins, we see an accounting of what was given the previous week. As I'm sure you have seen, the collections vary from week to week. I do realize that some of us are under financial stress, today. Because of age, job cuts, illnesses, or other reasons, many of us are doing the best we can in supporting our parishes. I commend the generosity of all who make these sacrifices!

Might I make a suggestion for the rest of us, though? Could we all examine how much we give every week and perhaps increase it? After all, for how long have we been giving $10 each week? For 20 years? Alas, we all know that $10 doesn't purchase what it once did. Perhaps now is the time to raise this to $15 or even $20. Sometimes, we get into a rut of giving a certain amount and forget that times change and so do expenses.

Please reflect on how much you are giving to your parish. Financial support for parishes also comes through gifts from wills. Do you have a will? If you do, is your parish or some other charitable organization included? This is so important. All of our parishes have been richly blessed by gifts from deceased members of our communities. Sadly, an individual cannot always rely on his or her children or grandchildren to know that he or she wished to support the Church. If you feel so called, please explicitly remember your parish in your will.

Lastly, I do realize that some of us are unable to financially support our parishes at this time. Please know that your financial situation, which no doubt is a cause of some suffering, does NOT separate you in any way from your parish. Money is one means - and only one means - by which individuals can support their Church! Volunteering time, praying, even bringing food or flowers for an event, can be an excellent way to help your parish.

The bottom line is this: we all need to support our parishes which we deeply love and which are, in many ways, the symbol of our Faith. Let us reflect on this fact and give as generously as we can.

*Reflection Questions:*

1. *Why is it important to support my parish financially?*
2. *If I am unable to help financially, how else can I assist my parish family?*
3. *Some Christians give as much as 10 percent of their income to their church. How much do I give?*

---

# Visiting Other Catholic Churches:
## See the sights. Smell the smells. Pray well.

Okay, I admit it! I enjoy looking at churches. One of the things I like to do when I have some free time or when I'm traveling is to stop in at various Catholic churches and pray. I know you might think, *"Well, that's nice Father, but you're a priest – that's what you do for fun."* However, I think it goes deeper than that. Christians always have gone on pilgrimages – journeys to a holy place or a shrine. Visiting Our Lord in the Blessed Sacrament in numerous Catholic Churches is a way of making a pilgrimage – a journey of Faith and prayer.

> "....when we visit other parishes, we see that our Church is much bigger than our local parish."

You can learn a lot about different communities by visiting their churches. You can see what is important to them, what they hold dear. You can read their bulletins, see what hymns they sing, and perhaps meet new people. Many times, churches still are unlocked during the day, or there is someone looking out from across the street who has a key.

You will see many different styles of churches – some quite old and some quite new, some traditional and some modern. You will see beautiful stained glass windows, statues, altars and organs. You will see clean, streamlined structures, and smell church smells of incense, candle wax and wood polish which have remained virtually unchanged throughout the ages. You will learn how other Catholics live and pray, and perhaps you might gain an idea or two to use in your own parish!

The key to all of this is that when we visit other parishes, we see that our Church is much bigger than our local parish. Put another way, when we visit other Catholic parishes, we see how our brothers and sisters in the Faith live and pray. Indeed, when we visit the Lord in the tabernacle in each of these parishes just to say, *"Hello,"* we are praying exceedingly well! If you're not in a hurry to go somewhere, stop at parishes along the way. Follow the signs. Ask for directions. You'll be glad you did!

*Reflection Questions:*
1. *Have I ever stopped and visited a Church that was not my own? Was it a good experience? Did I pray?*
2. *Have I ever gone on a pilgrimage?*
3. *Do I miss things in life when I'm always in a hurry to get somewhere? Do I miss God?*

# Religious Education Challenges - Part I:
## *Where are the parents?*

Education in the Faith is one of the highest priorities for my parishes. Our Faith Formation programs include religious education classes for kindergarten through high school students, preparation classes for the sacraments, and RCIA (Rite of Christian Initiation for Adults) instruction for those who wish to become Catholics.

Education in the Faith always must be a high priority for any parish, but today, it is especially critical because we can no longer rely on our culture to support the Christian way of life. Our Faith is the one thing that will guide us through this world and lead us to eternal life.

> **"It appears that an increasing number of parents want their children to be educated in the Faith, yet neglect to practice the Faith themselves."**

However, we face a number of challenges. One of these challenges affects the religious education of our young people. It appears that an increasing number of parents want their children to be educated in the Faith, yet neglect to practice the Faith themselves. This problem seems to be fairly widespread, affecting both rural and urban parishes as well as other Christian faiths. Whatever the reason for this disconnect, it is troubling and a solution needs to be found QUICKLY.

Every Wednesday, a number of parents, grandparents and relatives bring the children in their care - or arrange for them to come - to the religious education programs in my parishes. It is increasingly common for grandparents or other older relatives to heroically assume the task of educating children in the Faith. For whatever reason, the parents of these children are unwilling or unable to provide for this education. What a blessing that there are grandparents, relatives, or friends who extend the great effort of educating these young people in the Faith!

Yet, why do so many parents avoid this responsibility? Let me give you an example - a painful one. Every year in my parishes, we celebrate the Sacrament of First Holy Communion. It is a big moment in the lives of the parishes and in the lives of our young people. We teach the children who are receiving this precious sacrament that it is necessary to go to Mass every weekend - and that to intentionally miss Mass is a serious sin. However, even on this joyous occasion, it makes me sad to realize that, more and more, the parents of these young children do not actively practice the Faith. By this, I mean that the majority seemingly never come to Mass with their children, take an active part in parish life, or take an active part in their children's religious education. When parents do not strive to live their Faith, their children are given a very poor example. Why is this happening?

# Religious Education Challenges - Part II:
## Have the courage to do what is right for your child.

I suspect that there are numerous reasons why some parents DO bring their children to religious education classes. Perhaps it is to fulfill the promises they made before God at the child's Baptism. Perhaps the parents might earnestly desire to share their Faith with their son or daughter and pass on the family tradition of Faith. Still other parents might bring their child to religious education because they feel guilty about not practicing the Faith themselves and want somehow to make amends to God. No doubt, there are other reasons as well.

> "If parents do not provide an example of a lived and active Faith to their children, much of what we do in religious education classes is in vain."

However, the fact remains that the majority - the majority of the children who come to us for education in the Faith - never are seen with their families at Mass or at any other parish function. This is harmful to our parishes, but also tragically harmful to the children themselves. Don't parents realize that they are placing their child's soul at risk by not educating him or her about God?

I think I can imagine the challenges facing families today. Families are pulled in every direction, it seems, by endless activities and programs. Broken families and blended families are increasingly becoming the norm, and many families are of a mixed Christian faith. Often, both parents work, yet the family still is struggling financially. Family life is under attack today and the stress must be enormous. However, there must be priorities and God must come first! If we do not put God first in the lives of our children, we are stealing from them what they rightly deserve: to come to know Our Lord Jesus.

The bottom line is this: parents are the primary religious educators of their children. Yes, this is true! Our parishes are entrusted with our young people for a little over an hour each week. We plant the seed of Faith, but we rely on the family to water it and help it grow. If parents do not provide an example of a lived and active Faith to their children, much of what we do in religious education classes is in vain.

To those parents who strive to be an example of lived Faith to your children, who pray as a family, who come to Mass every weekend, who are actively engaged in your children's religious education - I highly commend you for your efforts.

To those parents who have not upheld your promises to God, made at the Baptism of your child, I challenge you to be a better example of Faith. Please come back to Church - do not be embarrassed or afraid. We miss your presence in our community of Faith. Ask God to give you the courage and strength to do what you know is right for your child. You will not regret it, and your family will be richly blessed by your efforts. Please introduce your child to Jesus.

*Reflection Questions:*

*1. How can our Catholic Faith best be passed on to the next generation?*

*2. Why do some families succeed in passing on the Faith, while others fail?*

*3. How have I shared my Faith with my family today?*

# Religious Education - Attending Mass:
### "Walking the walk" is the best example for children.

*(The following is a letter that was sent to all parents of children in our parish Religious Education program.)*

Dear Parents,

It's hard to believe that Summer is almost done and Fall is right around the corner! Your children are getting ready to go back to school and our parishes are gearing up for a new year of Religious Education. There are many, many people in our parishes who are working hard and dedicating much time, energy and love to providing the best education in the Faith for our young people. I am very pleased that you have decided to send your child to our parish Religious Education program.

Some years ago, there was a memorable and beautiful day for your family. It was the day your child was baptized, the day your son or daughter was welcomed into the Church. Remember that, on that happy day, there were a number of things you promised the Lord you would do for your child. Chief among these promises was your commitment to bring your child up in the Catholic Faith. I am sure that one of the reasons you are sending your child to Religious Education classes is that you deeply desire to fulfill this commitment.

The most powerful way in which you can hand on your Catholic Faith to your children is by authentically living this Faith. Your good example as parents is the most effective means to make this happen! It seems that all of us must be reminded from time to time about how important it is for us, as Catholics, to go to Mass. Our gathering together and celebrating the Eucharist is at the very center of who we are as a Church. So, to successfully educate your children in the Faith, it is vitally important for you as parents to bring your children to Mass every weekend. Put another way, going to Mass every weekend is required for your children to come to know the Lord and to grow in the Faith.

I do realize that many of you have been very faithful to this commitment. Good for you! I also know that others have struggled in fulfilling this obligation to the Lord. I would like to challenge all of you to renew your commitment to going to Mass every weekend.

Sometimes, we are good at making excuses. Perhaps, some might incorrectly believe that their religious "obligation" is met simply by sending their children to Religious Education classes. Others might think that coming to Church doesn't relate to their daily lives or fit into their busy schedules. Still others might feel alienated from the Church because of a hurtful experience or a misunderstanding. Despite these sentiments, the fact remains that the most important part of religious education for all of us is experiencing Christ's presence in the Holy Eucharist at Mass. This is best accomplished by coming as a family to a weekend Mass at your parish.

By going to Mass on weekends and sending your children to Religious Education classes, you truly will be fulfilling the promises you made to God on the day of your child's Baptism. For the good of your child's soul and for the success of his or her education in the Catholic Faith, I ask you to please fulfill this important obligation.

> In Christ,
> Father John Girotti

*Reflection Questions:*

1. In most parishes, the vast majority of children in religious education programs and in Catholic schools do not go to Mass on weekends. Why do you think this occurs?
2. What can be done to educate families about the importance of the Eucharist?
3. "Parents are the primary religious educators of their children." What does this mean?

---

# Catholic Colleges and Universities:
*Beware, some are "Catholic" in name only!*

What's in a name? It's a question worth asking, because things are not always as they seem. Take for example an organization or group that calls itself "Catholic." Okay – we can presume that, by its very name, it shares our common Faith in Jesus Christ. We assume that it is in union with the same Church that Jesus founded some 2,000 years ago. Such is the presumption. However, today, it is not always the reality.

> "....many Catholic colleges and universities have lowered their Catholic standards...for greater funding...enrollment and worldly prestige."

I would like to speak with you about "Catholic" colleges and universities. The Catholic Church originated the concept of a university; the earliest universities in Europe were all started by our Church. Catholicism always has supported the search for what is true and good – and this should be the mission of a university. Since there is no inherent contradiction between our Faith and human reason, education in any subject should naturally lead a person closer to God – Who is Truth Himself. This is why our Church continues to support institutions of higher learning.

However, during the past 40 years, a rather interesting phenomenon has occurred in the Catholic college and university system. There has been a general drift away from our Catholic identity. In its place, a secular or even anti-religious mentality has taken hold.

There are numerous reasons for this. Many college and university leaders have decided to water down our Faith in order to be seen as more "modern" or more "serious" contenders in the academic world. Bowing to the pressure of our secular culture, many Catholic colleges and universities have lowered their Catholic standards in exchange for greater funding, student enrollment and worldly prestige. Teachers have been hired who do not support Catholicism or uphold the basic teachings of our Church. What is taught is often an atheistic secularism, rather than the Gospel. Consequently, many souls are led astray and grave scandal occurs.

Why does this concern us? First of all, these Catholic colleges are educating people for the future. If these individuals are not properly educated in our Faith in Jesus Christ - He Who is the Way, the Truth and the Life - then we are unwittingly participating in the "dechristianization" of our culture. Secondly, many Catholic parents send their sons and daughters to Catholic colleges and universities, believing that, at such schools, their children's Faith will be supported and nurtured. Sadly, this is often not the case.

In 1990, Pope John Paul II issued an official teaching of the Church called "Ex Corde Ecclesiae." The purpose of this document was to secure a strong Catholic identity within colleges and universities of the Church. It called upon bishops to take an active role in supporting these universities and insisted that the institutions remain Catholic. Those individuals who teach theology at Catholic schools need to receive a "mandatum" or official permission to teach from the local bishop.

Unfortunately, most Catholics colleges have not listened to the Pope. Today, some 20 years later, there are only a handful of Catholic colleges in our country that are in compliance with the Pope's request. The vast majority have steadily refused, claiming "academic freedom." What a tragedy!

Is a "Catholic college" that is ashamed of Jesus Christ and the Gospel really Catholic? It seems to me that the time has come to ask this question. There is no contradiction between the Truth that is Jesus Christ and the academic freedom of learning. I urge you to research any Catholic institution of higher learning before you send your children or grandchildren or support it with donations. Things are not always as they seem.

Let us continue to pray for greater faithfulness within our Church.

*Reflection Questions:*

1. Can we expect that the Catholic Faith will be taught and upheld in institutions supported by the Church? Why or why not?
2. Do you think that the sin of pride has affected some institutions of higher learning in the Church today? If so, how?
3. An authentic study in any academic field will lead a person closer to Christ. What does this mean?

# A Special Thank You To My Parishioners...

My Dear Brothers and Sisters in Christ,

Each year, I like to take the opportunity to thank you for your goodness and kind gestures towards me. This past year, like the years before it, has been a time of rich blessings for me as a priest. Every year that passes, I fall more deeply in love with you and our parishes.

I would like to thank you, first and foremost, for your love and support for me and my priesthood. It seems that when the days get long and frustration sets in, one of you always says or does something to lift my spirits. Thank you, also, for your faithfulness to Our Lord Jesus Christ. There is genuine holiness among us here in our parishes - we are surrounded by many saints. Thank you for your good example to me, demonstrating what it means to live the Christian life.

Thank you, also, for your patience! As we grow closer together as a parish family, we all must give and take a little. Like any family, we need to be patient and understanding with each other - and you truly have been. Thank you, too, for your patience with me as I strive to lead us in the footsteps of Jesus.

There are so many other things that come to my mind that I appreciate about our parishes. Sadly, I can't list them all! I appreciate the many people who volunteer and go the extra mile in our parishes and who truly help to make my job easier. From those who clean the altar linens, to those who cook and serve for funeral meals; from those who assemble the newsletter to those who arrange our churches for the seasons - your efforts are appreciated.

Thank you for the big, beautiful house I call my home and for all of the food and treats with which you fill it. Sometimes I need a few more fruits and vegetables than treats, but thank you anyway for your love and support!

Thank you to all who have invited me into your homes for a meal and who have cared for me in numerous other ways. I thank you also for your kind words, gestures and gifts that make me feel loved and appreciated. They always seem to come when I need them the most.

I would like to thank all of those who work and clean inside and outside of our churches and other facilities - your dedicated effort gives glory to God! I am deeply thankful for all of those who impart the Faith to our young people and our adults - those who teach and coordinate our Faith Formation programs. A great big thank you to our parish secretaries who work very hard to keep our parishes together. I thank our parish musicians who have been willing to travel and make all of our Masses so beautiful. I also wish to thank our deacons for their kind assistance at Mass and in the other varying ministries of our parishes.

In each new year together, let us all thank the good Lord for the gifts of life, our Faith, and our parishes!

May God bless you!

✠ Fr. John Girotti

*Reflection Questions:*

1. *When was the last time I said, "thank you," to my loved ones?*
2. *Why do we so often take things for granted?*
3. *"Every day is a blessing from God." Reflect on this.*

# Conclusion

Isn't our Catholic Faith wonderful? There is a depth here where the seed of Faith truly can grow. And grow it has - for 2,000 years, Catholics have brought the Good News of Jesus Christ to the ends of the earth. Now, it is your turn to do the same! I urge you to share the Faith with others. There is a great need today to learn why we believe what we believe as Catholics and to take this great gift of Faith to a waiting and hungry world. It is a poverty not to know Jesus Christ!

So, let us work together to spread the Good News. I urge you to become more involved in your local parish. Teach religious education classes to our young people. Get involved in sharing our Catholic Faith with adults, as well. Volunteer your time in the various ministries and activities of your parish. If you are interested in joining the Catholic Church, know that many of these programs are open to you, too! Let us go forth to evangelize our secular culture with the Good News of Jesus Christ.

If these many articles have assisted you in knowing and loving your Catholic Faith and falling more deeply in love with Jesus Christ, I am truly thankful. If you are not a Catholic, but have felt drawn to the Faith, I hope that this material has helped to welcome you to our Church! May God bless you!

✠   **Fr. John Girotti**